BIBLE VERSION SECRETS

EXPOSED

Over 400 Blockbuster, Editorial Memes You
Can Use to Demonstrate the Shocking Truth
About Modern Bible Versions:
 • THEIR ERRORS • DEFICIENCIES AND
 • DEFECTIVE DOCTRINES

Jack McElroy

© 2020 Jack McElroy

Bible Version Secrets Exposed

Over 400 Blockbuster Editorial Memes You Can Use to Demonstrate the Shocking Truth About Modern Bible Versions: Their Errors, Deficiencies and Defective Doctrines

See the non-exclusive license on the following page.

ISBN: 978-0-9622191-7-7 PB
ISBN: 978-0-9622191-8-4 Digital

McElroy Publishing

27-33 Fredonian Street
Shirley, MA 01464
978-425-4055
978-425-6116

Here is your Non-exclusive License to copy and reproduce *Bible Version Secrets Exposed* files digitally or in print

Here is your complimentary link to securely download all the digital files:

https://tinyurl.com/y6boqssa

Then they that feared the LORD spake often one to another: and the LORD hearkened, and heard *it*, and a book of remembrance was written before him for them that feared the LORD, and that thought upon his name. (Malachi 3:16)

Copy Editing by Kathleen Deselle; kd64@myfairpoint.net

Other Works by the Author

Books authored or co-authored by Jack McElroy

How I Lost My Fear of Death and How You Can Too
This easy to read, 158-page soul winning tool is really a feature length evangelistic tract. Thousands distributed in the USA, India and Korea. Available: Chick Publications or Amazon.

WHICH BIBLE WOULD JESUS USE? The Bible Version Controversy Explained and Resolved.
Proving why the Lord himself would choose only the King James Bible if he came to your church tonight. Available from Chick Publications or Amazon

Can You Trust Just One Bible?
Co-Authored with David W. Daniels. Answers to the Most Common Anti-KJV Accusations. Available from Chick Publications.

Adoniram Judson's Soul Winning Secrets Revealed—An Inspiring Look at the Tools Used by "Jesus Christ's Man" in Burma Co-Authored with April Tin Tin Aye. Available from Amazon.

Building His Father's Business—One Soul at a Time
The true story of a modern-day Apostle Paul, G.S. Nair, the Missionary-Entrepreneur of India. Available from Amazon.

Other Titles from McElroy Publishing

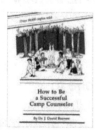

File Number and Title	Page

Preface

Do You Think the Devil Tinkers with the Text and Translation of Scripture?

****

I **do.** But most Christians would find this question uncomfortable because deep down inside, they know it suggests that some Bible versions are, shall we say, *tainted*. **And NO ONE wants to believe that THEIR Bible has been corrupted. Yet the truth is...**

We all know the Devil tampers with God's word. He has from the beginning. Why stop now?

The serpent said to Eve, "Yea, hath God said, Ye shall not eat of every tree of the garden?" (Genesis 3.1).

The Devil is subtle, clever and the best con artist in creation.

He actually got someone else (Eve) to corrupt God's words just by having a conversation with her. Notice her response...

> We may eat of the fruit of the trees of the garden: but of the fruit of the tree which is in the midst of the garden, God hath said, Ye shall not eat of it, neither shall ye touch it, lest ye die. Genesis 3.2–3

That's not what God said. It's true that the Devil lied but he got Eve to alter the text. How?

❶ <u>Omission</u>: Eve omitted the words "every' ("every tree") and "freely' ("freely eat").

❷ <u>Addition</u>: Eve added the words "neither shall ye touch it".

❸ <u>Substitution</u>: Eve substituted the words "lest ye die" for "thou shalt surely die".

She was duped. The Devil tricked her into corrupting God's word. And I think he tricks the creators of modern Bible versions also.

Bible Version Secrets Exposed lays bare the subtleties of the Devil (by omission, addition and subtraction) and proves (with over 400 editorial memes) that the deceiver of the brethren is still at work corrupting the Lord's words by means of multiple modern Bible versions.

Introduction

How This Book of Memes Will Help Make Your Case for the King James Bible

Dear Reader,

Memes are virally transmitted images embellished with text. They're a worldwide social phenomenon traveling from person to person quickly through social media.

I use them and encourage you to use them too.

Here's why …

1. They are visual storytellers effectively communicating deeply held beliefs, opinions, feelings, or experiences.
2. They are like graphic sound bites that are quickly and easily digested.
3. They are proven and effective. Savvy marketers use them to build their following and brand.

I use them all the time to influence others on the importance of the King James Bible, and so can you.

Here's how …

As a purchaser of the book (whether in print or digitally), you automatically receive a license to reproduce any and all the memes.

You can reprint and freely share them. Any way and anywhere you want.

Use them:

- In church bulletins.

- In slide presentations.
- In videos.
- For inspiration for articles you write.
- For proofs and demonstration of your beliefs about the Lord's book.
- As a launching pad or outline for your lessons on Bible versions.
- To create your own eBook on Bible versions.
- To share on Facebook, Instagram, Pinterest, and other social media platforms to start a conversation or answer common objections.

They'll save you time, effort, and agita (heartburn).

Why am I doing this?

Because I have a cause and purpose ...

My Cause is simple:

To promote the pure words of God as they appear on the pages of the King James Bible.

My Purpose is twofold:

1. To build up your faith in the words of God as they appear on the pages of the King James Bible. And ...
2. To supply those "on the fence" with information that will help them in their quest for the truth. I have absolutely no desire to try and convince somebody entrenched on the other side of the fence. It's not worth my time, theirs, or yours.

There are many on the other side of this issue, but no matter ...

I believe that the Lord's words to English-speaking people are found on the pages of the King James Bible.

All other Bible versions are nothing more than that—versions—and some are pretty lousy ones at that.

Introduction

My first book on the subject was *WHICH BIBLE WOULD JESUS USE? The Bible Version Controversy Explained and Resolved.*

In it, I lay the groundwork and philosophy for the fact that there must be a real, tangible Bible that contains all of God's words and only his words.

And that book has to be the standard for determining what God says.

I make the argument that the book in the English language has to be the King James Bible.

We all may disagree as to what the words mean, but first of all, we have to know what the Lord says. And to do that, we need a book.

Moreover, I proved that if the Lord Jesus Christ visited your church tonight, he would surely use the King James Bible to the exclusion of all the others because they are deficient both doctrinally and theologically.

If you haven't read it, the book is worthy of your consideration.

Here are some unsolicited comments from regular Christians (who I have gotten to know from Facebook) about the book:

Dan O'Dell "I have read this book through several times. Many chapters, many times. I have been blessed every time. A MUST READ for any child of God who really wants to know the basic truth regarding the inspiration of our old time tested and proven King James Bible."

Kevin Robert Airrington "... many great books on the subject ... but this one is my favorite. I have read it many times and I keep it handy as a reference tool.
I have often said that early on in my exploration of God's

Word ... if I had read this one first, I would have saved a lot of money."

Ed Watson "It's a great book, about the best I've read on the subject, and I've read many. Every Bible school teacher and seminary professor should read it, for that matter every Christian should read this book. It's not written like a text book, it's a very easy, page turner. Highly recommended."
Mari Goosen "After my search for the truth my daughter bought me your book as a birthday present. And I can only recommend your book to each and every person on earth. I love your book and your fb page and thanks for teaching us the truth."

Here's why I wrote that book and this one too ...

Our church leaders recommend we use a variety of "conservative translations." But multiple-choice standards don't work in business, and neither do they work when it comes to determining what God says or which Bible is God's Bible.

In fact, a close examination of the those modern "conservative translations" shows ...

Multiple versions are a curse, not a blessing.

From one version to another we see differences in names of people, ages, animals, plants, years, numbers, and so on, and yet Christians are taught that they must accept these contradictions without question.

Anybody who's ever attended a Bible study where multiple versions are used already knows that sometimes the versions say and mean different things.

And we all have seen how multi-version Bible studies leave God's children doubting and confused about what our Lord says.

Introduction

Yet the experts swear to us that the variations DON'T affect doctrine.

That is clearly not the case because if it were true, then there never would be a "King James only controversy" to begin with.

No matter what they say, you know for a fact that modern versions definitely and detrimentally affect doctrine.

Plus, you've seen and heard professional Christians (who should know better) hype modern versions that demote the Lord Jesus Christ and promote attacks on the King James Bible.

They even present their "preferred" version, which they don't hesitate to correct with "the original Greek." And to top it all off, they make fun of you and call you names for believing the King James Bible.

Bible Version Secrets Exposed is your secret weapon to combat this disturbing trend …

There are 401 one-page memes and 13 multi page memes in this book:

- Some are simple and straight forward faith builders meant to encourage KJB believers and plain enough for a kid to understand.
- Some memes hammer away at the foundational theories of modern textual criticism and defective translations (as compared to the KJB) of modern English versions.
- Some address complicated and complex textual issues so you can prove to the doubters that your position is not uninformed.
- Some address sensitive translational choices.

- Some address controversial theological issues and interpretations of Scripture that have their genesis in textual variants and/or translation choices.
- Some address the history of the biblical text.

More importantly, here's how the memes will help you make your case for the King James Bible …

They'll help you offensively and defensively. The book is broken into two parts

On offense: There are 256 memes that specifically reference particular Bible versions—
their errors, deficiencies, and defective doctrines.

78 NIV memes
75 ESV memes
58 NKJV memes
12 NASB memes
7 HCSB/CSB memes
9 NLT memes
8 NET memes
9 The Message and Other Lesser-Known Versions memes

Included among these are …

The best defense is a good offense.

- 10 memes with a Christmas theme—including one where the NET Bible nixes Isaiah's virgin birth prophecy.
- 7 memes that cover the crucifixion and Easter—including why *Easter* is not a KJB translation error.
- 4 memes that cover supposed KJB errors of translation— including why *kill* isn't a KJB error that should have been translated as *murder*.
- 12 memes showing how modern versions contain contradictions—including how the same verse in the NIV

says David killed Goliath whereas the ESV says Elhanan killed Goliath.

- 7 memes showing confusion where one version contains a particular verse and others do not—including one where the NASB has a verse that's omitted from the ESV.
- 6 memes where the versions say opposite things— including one where NKJV says *not increased* and the KJB says *increased.*
- 9 memes covering science errors and issues.
- 23 memes showing historical errors and issues.
- 2 memes covering geography errors in the ESV.
- 1 meme showing a legal error in the NASB.
- 53 memes covering doctrinal issues and errors—including where the ESV says *obey* instead of *believe* in John 3:36.
- 14 changes in the NIV from the ©1984 edition to the ©2011 edition—including one where Phoebe went from being a *servant* in 1984 to a *deacon* in 2011. And another where the character of the Lord Jesus Christ is sickeningly changed from *compassionate* to *indignant.*

On defense: Defensive memes quickly address common objections you get so often. There are 157 memes you can use defensibly:

- 27 demonstrate the Superiority of the King James Bible.
- 18 cover Original Languages and Translation.
- 10 discuss Inspiration and Preservation.
- 59 discuss Critics, Textual Critics, and Commentary.
- 12 answer the oft-repeated questions of Where Was the Bible Before 1611? and Which Edition Is Authentic?
- 16 present Multi-version Confusion—thereby demonstrating that God can't be like our leaders in recommending many versions because he is NOT the author of confusion.
- 14 cover Personal Statements and Comments from the Author.

And the book's organization will help you plan your strategy.

You'll find all 414 memes (401 single and 13 multi-page) organized by topic with a brief introduction to each section.

Within the first section, the memes are presented in the order they appear in the books of the Bible, making it easy to thumb through and find particular verses or quickly compare how the verses are handled across the various translations.

Spoiler alert: no translation is equal to the KJB.

The great part about using the memes is that they preach for you.

A picture is worth a thousand words. Plus, photo posts account for 93 percent of the most engaging posts on Facebook and they get more likes and comments than text-based posts.[1]

The memes have powerful headlines that will grab the attention of your readers and make them interested enough to read what you want them to read. They can help you "stand out" from the crowd.

Now you can turn the tables on your adversaries. You can post your opinion in the form of a meme and let it speak for you.

If there are comments, it's your choice whether or not to answer.

Moreover, since you didn't create the memes, you can easily post, comment, and walk away from them if you want.

The best part is that almost all of them are contained on one sheet of paper.

They work for me, and they'll work for you too.

---

1. https://www.businessinsider.com/photos-are-93-of-the-most-engaging-facebook-posts-2013-7

Introduction

But why should you listen to me?

First of all, I've done my homework.

I've been researching the Bible version issue for nearly 30 years.

I've studied the history of the Bible, textual criticism, and translation theory. I've read books and articles by KJV-only and anti-KJV-only folks; Textus Receptus (TR) defenders; and Majority Text, Critical Text, and modern version supporters.

I have invested countless hours examining, comparing, and considering the differences between the 1611 King James Bible, its subsequent reprints, and modern versions.

I'm familiar with the arguments on all sides of the issue—from KJV only to TR only to Majority Text Preferred to Critical Text Preferred—as well as the strengths and weaknesses of each position, including my own.

Although I've read through the Bible 20 times, taught it to all age groups from preschoolers to adults, and served for years as a deacon at a Baptist church, I never went to Bible college or seminary. And

I am not a pastor or theologian.

This benefits you, dear reader, because you're getting a unique and informed slant on the issue, not someone else's repackaged teachings.

I'm a former Roman Catholic who went to a Catholic grammar school and Jesuit high school. I was saved when I was 28 years old. I know personally the sickening despair and hopelessness of living in darkness, and I know the life-giving light of the Lord Jesus Christ.

Moreover …

I am a businessman.

I'm a 69-year-old entrepreneur with over 45 years of "in the trenches" business experience. I've been a CEO, manufacturer, distributor, publisher, and sales executive. I was even a roofing and siding contractor right after college.

I held Federal Communications Commission licenses to provide cellular telephone service in the Poughkeepsie, New York, and Minneapolis, Minnesota, markets. I was a limited partner in a cellular telephone system that served part of the Los Angeles market.

I've had two cases argued before the US Court of Appeals [McElroy Electronics Corp. v. FCC, 301 U.S.App.D.C. 81, 990 F.2d 1351 (1993) and McElroy Electronics Corp. v. FCC, 318 U.S.App.D.C. 174, 86 F.3d 248 (1996)].

It's one thing to sue the United States government; it's another thing to win. We won both cases.

If you're interested, you can learn more of my background at: www.jackmcelroy.com.

And finally, here's my position on translators, critics and social media posts:

1. I'm not personally against any <u>born</u>-<u>again</u> translator of any modern version. We are brethren.

   I think they have the best of intentions and truly feel they are doing God's work.
   - I just don't agree with them that "the Bible" needs to be translated into English again for the umpteenth time.

     And, with the introduction of competing texts that began in the 19th century, it seems to me that the whole thing breeds confusion among God's people.

   - Since I'm a believer, supporter and promoter of the King James Bible, **their products are in competition**

with mine. Hence, I produce the memes.

2. I'm not personally against any <u>born-again</u> believer who criticizes my work. We are brethren.

Some do it with good intention, which I appreciate. As a result, I have either modified or scrapped some of my memes. Sometimes, their comments have prompted me to make stronger arguments.

Others do it as a mockery, which I try to discern and ignore.

The Bible version issue is personal and controversial.

Unfortunately, sometimes the brethren on both sides get very emotional and say things they wouldn't (or shouldn't) ordinarily.

The memes contain my opinions and tell a visual story of what I have learned since I first became aware that there was such a thing as a Bible version controversy over 30 years ago.

I try to make them interesting and entertaining. Some folks find them offensive while others appreciate their insight and wit, but that's the nature of making an opinion public and defending it.

So, go ahead and use them to promote your own opinions, ministry, and work.

Your brother in Christ,

Jack

Fall 2019

P.S. I'm not sponsored by any organization, church, or denomination. The opinions expressed are my own and I don't ask for donations. This is a self-funded business and ministry.

Part One:
Knowledge and Understanding

Verses Compared, Contrasted and Summarized

He that is first in his own cause *seemeth* just;
but his neighbour cometh and searcheth him. Prov. 18:17

Here are 256 memes that specifically reference particular Bible versions—their errors, deficiencies, and defective doctrines.

78 NIV memes
75 ESV memes
58 NKJV memes
12 NASB memes
7 HCSB/CSB memes

9 NLT memes
8 NET memes
9 The Message and Other Lesser-Known Versions memes

Included among these are …

- 10 memes with a Christmas theme—including one where the NET Bible nixes Isaiah's virgin birth prophecy.
- 7 memes that cover the crucifixion and Easter—including why *Easter* is not a KJB translation error.
- 4 memes that cover supposed KJB errors of translation— including why *kill* isn't a KJB error that should have been translated as *murder*.
- 12 memes showing how modern versions contain contradictions—including how the same verse in the NIV says David killed Goliath whereas the ESV says Elhanan killed Goliath.
- 7 memes showing confusion where one version contains a particular verse and others do not—including one where the NASB has a verse that's omitted from the ESV.
- 6 memes where the versions say opposite things—including one where NKJV says *not increased* and the KJB says *increased*.
- 9 memes covering science errors and issues.
- 23 memes showing historical errors and issues.
- 2 memes covering geography errors in the ESV.
- 1 meme showing a legal error in the NASB.
- 53 memes covering doctrinal issues and errors—including where the ESV says *obey* instead of *believe* in John 3:36.
- 14 changes in the NIV from the ©1984 edition to the ©2011 edition—including one where Phoebe went from being a *servant* in 1984 to a *deacon* in 2011. And another where the character of the Lord Jesus Christ is sickeningly changed from *compassionate* to *indignant*.

The New International Version—
A Gender-Neutral, Inaccurate Version

Introduction

****

The NIV was a game changer. It was the darling of evangelicals since the NT first came on the scene in 1973. The complete Bible was introduced in 1978, then revised in 1984 and 2011.

They liked it for its readability. However, this readability "asset" was offset by a liability.

Problem #1: Accuracy versus readability

The NIV sacrifices accuracy for the sake of readability because of the nature of its translation. The problem is that although the Bible is meant to be read, it's also meant to be STUDIED.

Bible researcher Michael D. Marlowe, B.S. English Literature, M.A. Pittsburgh Theological Seminary, who is theologically conservative, Reformed, and not King James Only, says:

> There was some criticism of the NIV from conservatives who objected to the non-literal method of the translation in general. The moderate use of the so-called *dynamic equivalence* method of translation in the version involved a trade-off in which accuracy was sometimes sacrificed for the sake of readability.

> As Daniel Wallace of Dallas Theological Seminary observed, "Readability seems to have been a higher priority than anything else" in the making of the NIV.[1]

What's the big deal, you ask? Problem #1 led to ...

---

1. http://www.bible-researcher.com/niv.html

Problem #2: Political correctness

The readability gambit opens the door to all kinds of mischief. The main one that caught the attention of evangelicals is …

Political correctness in the form of gender neutrality. And as you'll see by some of the quotes, another is "patriarchy." Which is another term bandied about by today's social justice warriors.

Marlowe continues ...

The Inclusive Language Edition, 1996

> The appearance of this edition of the NIV in Great Britain provoked indignation among conservatives who were using the NIV … A statement in the Preface that the translators believed "it was often appropriate **to mute the patriarchalism** of the culture of the biblical writers through gender-inclusive language when this could be done without compromising the message of the Spirit" (p. vii) was hard to reconcile with conservative views of the Bible's verbal inspiration. **The whole affair raised suspicions of liberal tendencies in the International Bible Society.**[2]

GENDER NEUTRAL
RESTROOM

They were scared of liberal tendencies. Liberal tendencies in a Bible translation?

Who's doing that? What's their agenda? I thought translations were done by good, godly folks who had no agenda. But lets' dig deeper …

> … but when its plans for replacing the current NIV in America with the **"inclusive language"** revision became known in 1997, strong opposition arose among evangelical leaders. The pressure to abandon their planned revision was such that four of the men who were responsible for it

2. http://www.bible-researcher.com/nivi-preface.html

went so far as to sign a document (the Colorado Springs Guidelines) positively stating that they had dropped all intention of producing or publishing any such version.[3]

On the same day the International Bible Society also issued a statement in which it promised that it would continue to publish the NIV unchanged. But soon afterwards the IBS apparently re-evaluated the situation, and proceeded with the revision **as if its officers had never signed the Colorado Springs Guidelines.**[4]

Embarrassed and under heavy pressure from conservative groups, the IBS in 1997 announced that the "inclusive language" edition would not be published in America under the name, "New International Version," and that it would in the future continue to publish the NIV of 1984 unchanged.[5]

Ahh, promises, promises. But as time went on, they just had to fit the changing culture, so they published …

Today's New International Version (TNIV) © 2005

The version features the usual gender-neutral alterations: "brothers and sisters" is put instead of "brothers" (but the reader is not informed of the change in a footnote, as in the NRSV); the generic masculine use of "man," "he," "his," etc., is eliminated, usually by recasting the sentences with plural forms. In one respect, however, the TNIV breaks new ground by employing plural pronouns in a singular sense: Singular nouns (e.g. "someone") are followed by plural pronouns ("they" instead of "he"), so that the pronouns actually disagree in number with their antecedents. This solecism, **which feminist language reformers have lately sought to legitimize**, is common enough in casual speech; but the TNIV does not otherwise

---

3. http://www.bible-researcher.com/tniv.html
4. Ibid.
5. http://www.bible-researcher.com/niv.html

employ such colloquialisms, and it is very strange and somewhat confusing to see it in the midst of prose which otherwise adheres to the rules of English grammar.[6]

And finally, they came out with…

The 2011 Revision

An examination of the text reveals that this new edition of the NIV is actually a minor revision of the TNIV (see above).[7]

The explanation offered for the "updates" is also misleading in that it does not mention the real political and financial considerations that have caused the NIV committee to make three revisions within the past fifteen years. The considerations that set in motion this series of revisions are, however, indicated in a document that set forth a new "Policy on Gender-Inclusive Language" adopted by the committee in 1992. The document contains these paragraphs:[8]

Authors of Biblical books, even while writing Scripture inspired by the Holy Spirit, **unconsciously reflected in many ways,** the particular cultures in which they wrote. Hence in the manner in which they articulate the Word of God, they sometimes offend modern sensibilities. **At such times, translators can and may use non-offending renderings** so as not to hinder the message of the Spirit.[9]

D. **The patriarchalism** (like other social patterns) of the ancient cultures in which the Biblical books were composed is pervasively reflected in forms of expression that appear, in the modern context, to deny the common human dignity of all hearers and readers. For these forms, alternative modes of expression can and may be used,

---

6. http://www.bible-researcher.com/tniv.html
7. http://www.bible-researcher.com/niv.html
8. http://www.bible-researcher.com/niv.2011.html
9. http://www.bible-researcher.com/nivi-guidelines.html

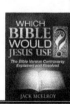

How Many Daughters Did Lot Have?

****

King James Bible Genesis 19:14
And Lot went out, and spake unto his **sons in law**, <u>**which married**</u> his daughters, and said, Up, get you out of this place...

New International Version Gen 19:14
So Lot went out and spoke to his **sons-in-law**, <u>who were pledged to marry</u> his daughters. He said, "Hurry and get out of this place..."

❶ <u>**The KJV's Lot**</u> had at least four daughters. At least two who were married and not living with them (Lot **went out** to warn them) and two others living with them (**"which are here"** vs. 15) who were "virgins:

Behold now, I have two daughters **which have not known man**; Gen. 19:8

❷ <u>**The NIV's Lot**</u> had only two daughters.

❸ The NIV folks will argue that Lot's two daughters were only "betrothed" and therefore still virgins living at home.

❹ But this argument breaks down when their husbands are called "sons-in-law" which is a LEGAL DESIGNATION for the husband of one's daughter, **NOT a fiancé.**

❺ A "son-in-law" is NOT a "son-in-law" **legally** (or biblically) <u>UNTIL</u> the children are married— **a truth you don't get from the NIV.**

If the NIV can't be trusted about Lot's kids, how can you trust it for anything else?

Available from

Learn more, get the book: WHICH BIBLE WOULD JESUS USE? The Bible Version Controversy Explained and Resolved By Jack McElroy www.JackMcElroy.com

NIV Turns Isaac's Blessing into A Curse

****

King James Bible Genesis 27:39	New International Version Gen. 27:39
And Isaac his father answered and said unto him, Behold, thy dwelling **shall be the fatness of the earth, and of the dew of heaven from above;**	His father Isaac answered him, "Your dwelling **will be away from the earth's richness, away from the dew of heaven above.**

❶ **Any reader of the King James Bible** realizes that although Esau was a jerk, **his father blessed him anyway**.

❷ **Any reader of the NIV** would believe that not only was Esau a jerk, **but also his father's blessing was no better than a curse**.

❸ **The truth is preserved on the pages of the King James Bible.** Verse 38 says:

> "And Esau said unto his father, Hast thou but one **blessing**, my father? **bless me**, even me also, O my father. And Esau lifted up his voice, and wept."

❹ **Like the loving and merciful father he was, Isaac was entreated by Esau's tears, granted his petition, and blessed him anyway.**

What the NIV corrupts, the KJB makes plain.

Available from

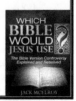

Learn more, get the book: WHICH BIBLE WOULD JESUS USE?
The Bible Version Controversy Explained and Resolved
By Jack McElroy www.jackmcelroy.com

NIV's Laban Used Divination

✱✱

King James Bible Genesis 30:27	New International Version Gen. 30:27
And Laban said unto him, I pray thee, if I have found favour in thine eyes, tarry: for I have learned **by experience** that the LORD hath blessed me for thy sake.	But Laban said to him, "If I have found favor in your eyes, please stay. I have learned **by divination** that the LORD has blessed me because of you."

<u>Any reader of the NIV</u> would believe that Laban practiced the occult art of <u>divination</u>.

<u>Any reader of the KJB</u> would know that Laban had seen many examples of the Lord's blessing on Jacob. He didn't need divination. He knew it by <u>experience</u>.

Why would the NIV introduce this occult practice into Laban's testimony?

Once again, the NIV falls short of the glory of God.

Available from

Learn more, get the book: WHICH BIBLE WOULD JESUS USE? The Bible Version Controversy Explained and Resolved By Jack McElroy
www.JackMcElroy.com

NIV Hides God's Name

* *

The King James Bible Exodus 6:3
And I appeared unto Abraham, unto Isaac, and unto Jacob, by the name of God Almighty, but **by my name JEHOVAH** was I not known to them.

New International Version Exodus 6:3
I appeared to Abraham, to Isaac and to Jacob as God Almighty, but by my name the **LORD** I did not make myself known to them.

Quick Search Results
From Biblegateway.com...

Showing results from <u>your default version</u>:

| New International Version ▾ | Change |

Keyword search results
0 Results
Sorry. No results found for **"JEHOVAH"** in Keyword Search.

How many people do you have a personal relationship with and you don't know their name?

You can search the NIV from cover to cover and NEVER ONCE find God's name, Jehovah. <u>Even</u> <u>pets</u> <u>have</u> <u>names</u>.

What kind of Bible eliminates God's Name?

Available from

Learn more, get the book: WHICH BIBLE WOULD JESUS USE?
The Bible Version Controversy Explained and Resolved By
Jack McElroy www.JackMcElroy.com

NIV Obscures Devil Worship

* *

King James Bible Leviticus 17:7
And they shall no more offer their sacrifices
unto <u>devils</u>, after whom they have gone a whoring...

New International Version Lev. 17:7
They must no longer offer any of their sacrifices to
the <u>goat idols</u> to whom they prostitute themselves...

❶ The NIV merely tells you that the children of Israel sacrificed to idols.

❷ The KJB reveals that those idols were actually inhabited by devils.

❸ *Demon Experiences in Many Lands* is a compilation of demonic experiences on the mission field. Mr. N. Daniel, founder of the Laymen's Evangelical Fellowship, was interviewed in the book. Mr. Daniel says **devils can inhabit inanimate objects:**

> "Sometimes there are idols. **Behind these idols are evil spirits.** Sometimes a portion of the wall is marked out for pictures to be worshiped. These pictures must be scraped off, the wall must be whitewashed and the man of God must pray. When God takes us to such homes, they are permanently relieved of all those troubles."[1]

What the NIV fails to teach, the KJB makes plain.

Available from

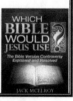

Learn more, get the book: WHICH BIBLE WOULD JESUS USE? The Bible Version Controversy Explained and Resolved By Jack McElroy www.JackMcElroy.com

1. *Demon Experiences in Many Lands* ©1960 Moody Press, p. 23.

Massive NIV Blunder Makes Our Lord Look Bad

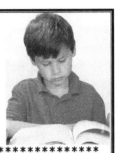

****

What if you showed an NIV user that if their Bible was printed before 2011 it contained a huge mistake that even a <u>fifth grader</u> could find? It's in 2 Samuel 21:19...

About 400 million old NIVs (©1978–2011) say:	All the new NIVs (©2011–Today) say:
In another battle with the Philistines at Gob, **Elhanan** ... killed ____ _____ ___ Goliath...	In another battle with the Philistines at Gob, **Elhanan...** **Killed <u>the brother of</u> Goliath**...

From 1978–2011, an NIV user is taught that Elhanan killed Goliath. From 2011–today, they're taught that David killed Goliath.
   Question: How did they get it wrong in the first place?

Maybe this won't matter to your friend, but it does matter to the Lord Jesus Christ. Because words in the Bible represent his integrity. 400 million NIVs out there are in error.

The KJB's been saying David killed Goliath from the get-go. Which Bible would Jesus use if the Lord Jesus Christ came to your church?

The one he's been using for over 400 years—the King James Bible.

Available from

NIV's God Contradicts Himself

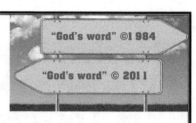

"God's word" ©1984

"God's word" © 2011

****

King James Bible 2 Samuel 21:19	©1984 New International Version 2 Sam. 21:19
And there was again a battle in Gob with the Philistines, where **Elhanan** the son of Jaareoregim, a Bethlehemite, **slew _the brother of_ Goliath** the Gittite, the staff of whose spear was like a weaver's beam.	In another battle with the Philistines at Gob, **Elhanan** son of Jaare-Oregim the Bethlehemite **killed ___ _____ __ Goliath** the Gittite, who had a spear with a shaft like a weaver's rod.

For over 400 years, the KJB has taught that David Killed Goliath and Elhanan killed Goliath's brother. As you see above, the ©1984 NIV says that Elhanan killed Goliath; which is NOT true.

But lo and behold; look what the NIV did in 2011...

> In another battle with the Philistines at Gob, Elhanan son of Jair the Bethlehemite killed **the brother of** Goliath the Gittite, who had a spear with a shaft like a weaver's rod. NIV ©2011

It's nice to see "the NIV" finally caught up to the 400-year-old standard English Bible. BUT there's a problem...

With over 400 million NIVs in print,[1] how many are still out there with the error? And worse...

What else is wrong with it?

Available from

Learn more, get the book: WHICH BIBLE WOULD JESUS USE? The Bible Version Controversy Explained and Resolved By Jack McElroy www.jackmcelroy.com

1. https://www.amazon.com/Thinline-Bible-Large-Print-Leather/dp/1444702483

NIV Misses Cross-Reference Invents Bogus Text

****

King James Version Job 1:21	New International Version Job 1:21
... Naked came I out of my mother's womb, and naked **shall I return thither**...	...Naked I came from my mother's womb, and naked **I will depart**...

❶ Kenneth Barker, Executive Director of the International Bible Society's NIV Translation Center said:

> "**First, the Hebrew text is not clear**...The suggestion that: 'thither,' or there, 'refers to Mother Earth as man's origin and goal finds no support in Scripture...'"[1]

❷ **Dr. Barker couldn't be more confused.**

You'll surely return to **"the earth"**, just NOT **"the earth"** of your mother's womb. Like they say, "***earth* to *earth*, ashes to ashes, *dust* to *dust*.**"

You see, Psalm 139:15 <u>ALSO</u> defines your mother's womb as "the earth":

> My substance was not hid from thee, when I was made in secret, ***and* curiously wrought in the lowest parts of the earth.** KJB

> My frame was not hidden from you when I was made in the secret place, **when I was woven together in the depths of the earth.** NIV

❸ Because they didn't compare scripture with scripture even **in <u>their</u> <u>own</u> <u>Bible</u>**, they misunderstood the Hebrew text and **<u>ADDED</u>** the bogus **<u>and</u> <u>meaningless</u>** words "**I will depart.**"

Had they just believed the KJB, they would never have made such an egregious error.

Available from

1.   Kenneth Barker, *Accuracy Defined and Illustrated: An NIV Translator Answers Your Questions*, p.17

NIV Reduces Scripture to Myth

****

King James Bible Job 26:12	**New International Version Job 26:12**
He divideth the sea with his power, and by his understanding **he smiteth through the proud.**	By his power he churned up the sea; by his wisdom **he cut Rahab to pieces.**

The Hebrew word is rah-hav (#7293). The KJB translates it as proud (2x), strength (1x), **and Rahab (3x) BUT not here.**

It's a choice for all translators. But what's odd is what **Kenneth L. Barker, one of the original translators of the NIV said about WHY they chose this translation...**

"**Rahab is a name for a Canaanite sea monster** and is sometimes symbolic of Egypt. Of course, Job's use of that **mythological term** in no way suggests that he believed in the actual existence of such a creature. Rather, the term points polemically to God's supremacy as the only God—the all-powerful One, who can conquer all alleged pagan gods and creatures such as Rahab."[1]

It's hard enough to convince unbelievers that the scripture is true without introducing a fairy tale into the text.

Why the NIV chose to go this route is very troubling.

Once again, the NIV falls short of the glory of God.

Available from

Learn more, get the book: WHICH BIBLE WOULD JESUS USE? The Bible Version Controversy Explained and Resolved By Jack McElroy www.JackMcElroy.com

1. http://www.cerm.info/bible_studies/Exegetical/NIV_AccuracyDefined.pdf, p. 18

NIV's God Is A Head Case

****

King James Bible Psalms 7:11	New International Version Ps. 7:11
God **judgeth** the righteous, and God is **angry** _with the wicked_ every day.	God **is a righteous judge**, a God who displays his **wrath** _____ ___ _____ every day.

❶ **Even the New Living Translation gets this one right:**
God is an honest judge. He is **angry with the wicked** every day. NLT Ps. 7:11

❷ **The NIV's God is unhinged.** He's freaking out and displaying his wrath every day with no focus.

❸ The KJB's God's anger (not wrath) is reasoned and focused on "the wicked" every day. His wrath will come later if they don't repent.

❹ Plus, the NIV reader is simply told in this passage that God is a righteous judge (no kidding) and NOT that God JUDGES the RIGHTEOUS, which he certainly does:
·For we must all appear before the judgment seat of Christ…" 2 Cor. 5:10 KJB

The NIV introduces you to a very strange God indeed.

Available from

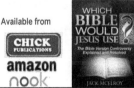

NIV Cheat on Psalm 12:5–7

****

King James Bible Psalm 12: 5–7
[5]For the oppression of the poor, for the sighing of the needy, now will I arise, saith the LORD; I will set *him* in safety *from him that* puffeth at him. [6]The words of the LORD *are* pure words: *as* silver tried in a furnace of earth, purified seven times. [7]Thou shalt **keep <u>them</u>**, O LORD, thou shalt **preserve them from this generation** for ever.

2011 New International Version Ps. 12: 5–7
"Because the poor are plundered and the needy groan, I will now arise," says the LORD. "I will protect them from those who malign them." And the words of the LORD are flawless, like silver purified in a crucible, like gold refined seven times.

You, LORD, **will keep <u>the</u> <u>needy</u> safe and will protect us forever <u>from the wicked</u>,**

The debate about Psalm 12 has persisted for centuries. Does it refer to God's preservation of his words or the poor or both?

The argument is based on grammar (gender) and context and **there are SCHOLARLY proponents <u>ON BOTH SIDES</u>, unlike what they'd have you believe.**

For example, Bible teacher Doug Kutilek says:
> "to continue to apply these verses to any doctrine of Bible preservation is to handle the Word of God deceitfully and dishonestly."[1]

Commentator Adam Clarke says:
> "Instead of the pronoun **them** in these clauses, several MSS., with the *Septuagint*, the *Vulgate*, and the *Arabic*, have **us**."[2]

Photo: Santeri Viinamäki (CC BY-SA 4.0 (https://creativecommons.org/licenses/by-sa/4.0)), from Wikimedia Commons

Like Mr. Kutilek, the staff of the NIV **so desperately wanted** the verse to **not refer to "words"** but to "the needy (or poor, KJB)" that they **(1)** went to the Greek Septuagint and some Hebrew manuscripts to get the reading "us" instead of "them." Then **(2)** they interpreted the word "generation" to be **"<u>the wicked</u>"** to make the passage fit their own doctrine.

The NIV staff thereby cheats you out of the opportunity to decide for yourself. **This is very disturbing.**

If the Lord can't be trusted to KEEP HIS WORDS <u>FIRST</u>, then how can you trust him to keep the poor?

Available from

WHICH **BIBLE** WOULD JESUS USE
The Bible Version Controversy Explained and Resolved

Learn more, get the book: WHICH BIBLE WOULD JESUS USE? The Bible Version Controversy Explained and Resolved By Jack McElroy www.JackMcElroy.com

1. http://www.kjvonly.org/doug/kutilek_why_psalm.htm. 2. https://tinyurl.com/y9pdufne

NIV Obscures Purpose of the Law

Thou shalt not

Thou shalt not

Thou shalt not

****

King James Bible Psalm 19:7	New International Version Psalm 19:7
The law of the LORD *is* perfect, **converting** the soul: the testimony of the LORD *is* sure, making wise the simple.	The law of the LORD is perfect, **refreshing** the soul. The statutes of the LORD are trustworthy, making wise the simple.

❶ The law may "refresh" the soul of a believer but more importantly, it CONVERTS the soul— a truth hidden here by the NIV.

❷ Every soul winner knows how to use the law to turn souls from sin and the world to God and holiness.

❸ The scripture of truth says:

"… for by the law *is* the knowledge of sin." Rom. 3:20 KJB

Wherefore the law was our schoolmaster *to bring us* unto Christ, that we might be justified by faith. Gal. 3:24 KJB

The NIV; missing the mark... once again.

Available from

Learn more, get the book: WHICH BIBLE WOULD JESUS USE? The Bible Version Controversy Explained and Resolved By Jack McElroy www.jackmcelroy.com

51

NIV Sells Doctrine of Original Sin

****

King James Bible Psalm 51:5	New International Version Ps. 51:5
Behold, I was **shapen in iniquity**; and in sin did my mother conceive me.	Surely I was **sinful at birth**, sinful **from the time** my mother conceived me.

❶ The KJB's David never said he was a sinner at birth.

❷ The verse is about King David and his mother: **No one else.**

❸ The event is the **conception** of David: Not his **birth**.

❹ KJB text clearly says **his mother** was "in sin" when she got pregnant. "**In sin** did **my MOTHER conceive** me."

❺ The NIV's David says he was "sinful at birth."

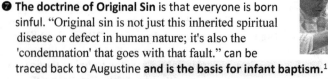

❻ The Scripture says, "…for the imagination of man's heart *is* evil **from his youth**;" Genesis 8:21 Notice; it is NOT **from his birth**. How can an infant be "sinful," having never sinned?

Augustine (354–430)

❼ The doctrine of Original Sin is that everyone is born sinful. "Original sin is not just this inherited spiritual disease or defect in human nature; it's also the 'condemnation' that goes with that fault." can be traced back to Augustine **and is the basis for infant baptism.**[1]

The doctrine of Original Sin is subtly introduced by the wording of the NIV.

Available from

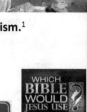

1. http://www.bbc.co.uk/religion/religions/christianity/beliefs/originalsin_1.shtml

Look What the NIV Does to Psalm 138:2

* *

King James Bible Psalm 138:2
I will worship toward thy holy temple, and praise thy name for thy lovingkindness and for thy truth: **for thou hast magnified thy word above all thy name.**

New International Version Psalm 138:2
I will bow down toward your holy temple and will praise your name for your unfailing love and your faithfulness, **for you have so exalted your solemn decree that it surpasses your fame.**

<u>Granted</u>, you have to make changes so as not to violate another version's copyright. And ...

<u>Granted</u>, you need to make a name for yourself and see your name included with other translator luminaries. And ...

<u>Granted</u>, shaking things up a bit will get you noticed. And ...

<u>Granted</u>, the NIV uses the newly invented "Dynamic Equivalence" translation technique. **BUT ...**

The Bible is no ordinary publication. It's God's word.

When will the madness end?

Available from

Learn more, get the book: WHICH BIBLE WOULD JESUS USE? The Bible Version Controversy Explained and Resolved By Jack McElroy www.JackMcElroy.com

3 Ways the NIV Defaces Psalm 138:2

****

King James Bible Psalm 138:2	New International Version Ps. 138:2
I will worship toward thy holy temple, and praise thy name for thy lovingkindness and for <u>thy truth</u>: for thou hast magnified <u>thy word</u> above all <u>thy name</u>.	I will bow down toward your holy temple and will praise your name for your unfailing love and your <u>faithfulness</u>, for you have so exalted your <u>solemn decree</u> that it surpasses your <u>fame</u>.

❶ <u>**Thy TRUTH**</u>: faithfulness is **not** the same as TRUTH. His **WORD** is <u>**TRUTH**</u>. And Jesus is **the** <u>**TRUTH**</u>.

❷ <u>**Thy WORD**</u>: God exalting some "solemn decree" is **not even close** to magnifying <u>**his** WORD</u>.

❸ <u>**Thy NAME**</u>: A "decree" surpassing God's "fame" is nothing but empty rhetoric. <u>**His** NAME</u> is above every name (Phil. 2:9). People say things like "my word is my bond." **Never is that truer than with your Lord.**

The NIV's presentation of Psalm 138:2 is a deplorable embarrassment.

Learn more, get the book: WHICH BIBLE WOULD JESUS USE? The Bible Version Controversy Explained and Resolved By Jack McElroy
www.jackmcelroy.com

Available from

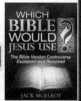

NIV Deprives You of God's Direction

****

King James Bible Proverbs 3:6	New International Version Prov.3:6
In all thy ways acknowledge him, and	in all your ways submit to him, and
he shall <u>direct</u> thy paths.	**he will <u>make your paths straight</u>.**

❶ The NIV folks think God "will make your path straight" (i.e. smooth and level) that "he will <u>remove obstacles</u>" and bring you "<u>straight</u> to his appointed goal."[1]

❷ Nothing could be further from the truth. When has your path ever been "straight"? Your pilgrim's progress down the path is full of all kinds of obstacles.

❸ Sometimes the Lord uses obstacles to <u>DIRECT</u> your path.

CHRISTIAN OVERKOMING APOLLYON

The NIV misdirects your pilgrim way.

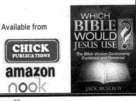
---

1. Kenneth L. Barker, *Accuracy defined and illustrated: An NIV translator answers your questions, p. 23*

NIV Proven
Scientifically Wrong

****

King James Bible Proverbs 6:6
Go to the ant, thou sluggard;
consider (her) ways, and be wise;

New International Version Pr. 6:6
Go to the ant, you sluggard;
consider (its) ways and be wise!

The NIV has lost lots of evangelical support because of their use of inclusive language. Being gender-sensitive is one way to be inoffensive. **BUT...**

Queen (female)

Shouldn't they be more concerned about offending the Lord and making him look silly?

Male

According to researchers at Ohio State University:

"A typical ant colony includes one queen and, in the case of harvester ants,
hundreds or thousands of sterile female workers
(**worker ants are always female** and, with a few exceptions, sterile. Soldier ants are larger versions of workers.)....
Male ants, which come from unfertilized eggs, **typically serve one purpose: to mate with a queen**. Males are usually in short supply, and a queen produces male eggs only when it's time to make more colonies."[1]

Worker (female)

How do you think the Lord feels about having his word translated so that it's not only unscientific but also untrue?

Available from

Ant illustration: https://askabiologist.asu.edu/explore/ant-anatomy https://askabiologist.asu.edu/explore/ant-anatomy

. 1. https://news.osu.edu/news/2005/01/11/harvant/

Should You be a Lifeguard or a Soul Winner?

****

King James Bible Proverbs 11:30	New International Version Prov. 11:30
The fruit of the righteous *is* a tree of life; and **he that winneth souls *is* wise.**	The fruit of the righteous is a tree of life, **and the one who is wise saves lives.**

Radio personality & Evangelist Tim Berends[1]

Saving lives is laudable. Lifeguards do it all the time, and it's a great choice when choosing a summer job.

BUT, Proverbs 11:30 in the NIV says NOTHING about winning souls.

Being a soul winner pays eternal dividends and is pleasing in the Lord's sight. **The King James Bible** clearly focuses on that truth.

It's the Bible soul winners have been using for over 400 years.

Available from

 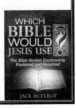

Learn more, get the book: WHICH BIBLE WOULD JESUS USE? The Bible Version Controversy Explained and Resolved By Jack McElroy www.JackMcElroy.com

1.   https://www.youtube.com/channel/UCnasTh-XMKd2MIcfGyIF1ag/videos

What's the Risk?

****

King James Bible Proverbs 7:27	New International Version Prov. 7:27
Her house *is* **the way to <u>hell</u>**, going down to the chambers of death.	Her house is **a highway to the <u>grave</u>**, leading down to the chambers of death.

Commandments are nothing but suggestions unless there is an enforceable penalty involved.

Both Bibles are admonishing a young man to stay away from a "strange" (KJB) or "adulterous" (NIV) woman because there will be consequences. BUT ...

The risk stated here by the NIV is the grave— not so bad. Young men are sometimes fatalistic. "We'll all die someday. No big deal. Maybe the pleasure of sin for a season is worth the risk."

The risk stated here by the KJB is hell— something to be seriously feared.

Dying's a risk and **the grave** is sure for all of us. **Hell** is an unimaginable terror and an unrecoverable disaster. **There's a big difference between the two**.

The truth about hell just isn't culturally or biblically, (as seen here in the NIV) acceptable today.

Available from

Learn more, get the book: WHICH BIBLE WOULD JESUS USE? The Bible Version Controversy Explained and Resolved By Jack McElroy www.JackMcElroy.com

NIV Fail in Proverbs 20

****

King James Bible Proverbs 20:1	**New International Version Prov. 20:1**
Wine *is* a mocker, **strong drink** *is* raging: and whosoever is deceived thereby is not wise.	Wine is a mocker and **beer** a brawler; whoever is led astray by them is not wise.

❶ The admonition of Prov. 20 in the NIV is **ONLY** about beer and wine. They're sold in some states at grocery stores.

❷ "On average, the ABV [Alcohol by Volume] for beer is 4.5 percent; for wine, 11.6 percent; and for liquor, 37 percent..."[1]

❸ **Not all Beer is alcoholic.**

❹ Hard liquor is more controlled in some states because of the greater alcohol content. You can only get it at a "packie" (i.e., a liquor store, aka package store).

❺ The admonition in the KJB is about **wine and strong drink.**

For an up-to-date Bible, the NIV is woefully behind the times.

Available from

Learn more, get the book: WHICH BIBLE WOULD JESUS USE? The Bible Version Controversy Explained and Resolved By Jack McElroy www.JackMcElroy.com

1 https://www.livescience.com/32735-how-much-alcohol-is-in-my-drink.html

59

NIV Attacks Certainty of God's Words

****

King James Bible Proverbs 22:21

That I might make thee **know** the **certainty** of the **words** of **truth**; that thou mightest answer **the words of truth** to them that send unto thee?

New International Version Prov. 22:21

teaching you to be **honest** **and to** **speak** **the truth,** so that you bring back truthful reports to those you serve?

Being "honest" and speaking "the truth" so you can "bring back" some kind of truthful report is **NOT EVEN REMOTELY CLOSE** to the Lord making you to "KNOW the CERTAINTY of the WORDS OF TRUTH" so that you can answer sincere seekers with "the words of truth."

The NIV is one of the most unreliable, corrupt, deceitful and God insulting versions ever hyped as a real Bible.

Would the Lord Jesus Christ ever use the NIV? Not a chance.

Available from

Learn more, get the book: WHICH BIBLE WOULD JESUS USE? The Bible Version Controversy Explained and Resolved By Jack McElroy www.jackmcelroy.com

NIV Makes Your Lord a Liar

****

King James Bible Isaiah 38:8
Behold, I will bring again the shadow of the degrees, which is gone down in the sun dial of Ahaz, ten degrees backward. **So the sun returned ten degrees**, by which degrees it was gone down.

New International Version Is. 38:8
I will make the shadow cast by the sun go back the ten steps it has gone down on the stairway of Ahaz.'" So the **sunlight went back the ten steps** it had gone down.

According to the King James Bible **"the sun"** returned 10° by which degrees it was gone down. Clearly, **"the sun" reversed its course**.

Evidently, the NIV folks believed the Nebular Hypothesis (the most widely accepted model to explain the formation and evolution of the Solar System) and **didn't believe the sun actually retraced its steps,** so they conformed the words to **THEIR BELIEF** and said that it was only **"the sunlight"** that went back.

Isn't this just another way of making God a liar?

Available from

Learn more, get the book: WHICH BIBLE WOULD JESUS USE? The Bible Version Controversy Explained and Resolved By Jack McElroy
www.JackMcElroy.com

CHICK
PUBLICATIONS

amazon
nook

WHICH **BIBLE WOULD JESUS USE**
The Bible Version Controversy Explained and Resolved

JACK MCELROY

Photo: By liz west (Sundial) [CC BY 2.0 (http://creativecommons.org/licenses/by/2.0)], via Wikimedia Commons

61

NIV Messes Up Isaiah 53

★★★★★★★★★★★★★★★★★★★★★★★★★★★★★★

King James Bible Isaiah 53:11	New International Version Isaiah 53:11
He shall see of the <u>travail</u> of <u>his soul</u>, *and* shall be satisfied: by his knowledge shall my righteous servant justify many; for he shall bear their iniquities.	After he has suffered, **he will see the <u>light</u> of <u>life</u>** and **be satisfied**; by his knowledge my righteous servant will justify many, and he will bear their iniquities.

<u>**God the Father**</u> says he saw **the travail** of the Lord Jesus Christ's soul and was satisfied as accurately reported in the King James Bible.

<u>**Good thing.**</u> It was through our Lord's pain, suffering, and shed blood (travail of his soul) that he made atonement for our sins.

<u>**The NIV says NOTHING**</u> about the Father being satisfied with the travail of our Lord's soul.

The NIV: Examined and found wanting ... again

Available from

CHICK PUBLICATIONS

amazon

nook

WHICH BIBLE WOULD JESUS USE?
The Bible Version Controversy Explained and Resolved

JACK MCELROY

Learn more, get the book: WHICH BIBLE WOULD JESUS USE? The Bible Version Controversy Explained and Resolved By Jack McElroy www.JackMcElroy.com

NIV Gets Worse, Now Peddles Works Righteousness

****

King James Bible Habakkuk 2:4

Behold, his soul *which* is lifted up is not upright in him: **but the just shall live <u>by his faith</u>**.

2011 **New International Version Hab. 2:4**
"See, the enemy is puffed up; his desires are not upright— but the righteous person will live **by his <u>faithfulness—</u>**

Faith or Faithfulness?
Quite a difference in <u>DOCTRINE,</u> don't you think?

❶ **It WAS "faith" in ALL editions of the NIV until 2011. That's when they changed it.**

See, he is puffed up; his desires are not upright—but the righteous will live **<u>by his faith</u>.** NIV 1973, 1978, 1984, 1995

❷ **In so doing they killed their own cross-references:**

For in the gospel the righteousness of God is revealed—a righteousness that is by faith from first to last, **just as it is written**: "The righteous will live **by <u>faith</u>**." NIV Romans 1:17

Although masquerading as a real Bible in the past, the NIV gets progressively WORSE as time goes on.

Available from

Learn more, get the book: WHICH BIBLE WOULD JESUS USE? The Bible Version Controversy Explained and Resolved By Jack McElroy www.JackMcElroy.com

WHICH
BIBLE
WOULD
JESUS USE

The Bible Version Controversy Explained and Resolved

JACK McELROY

NIV: God No Longer Hates Divorce

****

Malachi 2:16 King James Bible	Malachi 2:16 New International Version © 2011
For the LORD, the God of Israel, saith that <u>he hateth putting away</u> ...	"<u>The man who hates</u> and divorces his wife," says the LORD, the God of Israel ...

❶ The God of the NIV can't be the same as the God of the King James Bible because each God SAYS and MEANS different things.

❷ The KJB's God HATES divorce and SAYS so. The NIV's God doesn't say a word about his feelings on divorce.

❸ But wait!
The God of the <u>NIV CHANGED HIS MIND</u>; 16 years earlier, he used to agree with the God of the KJB

"I hate divorce" says the LORD God of Israel...

Mal. 2:16 NIV © 1995

With nonsense like this, it's no wonder there aren't any NIV Onlyists.

Available from

Learn more, get the book: WHICH BIBLE WOULD JESUS USE? The Bible Version Controversy Explained and Resolved By Jack McElroy
www.JackMcElroy.com

NIV's Jesus...
An Angry Sinner

****

King James Bible Matthew 5:22	New International Version Matthew 5:22
But I say unto you, That whosoever is **angry** with his brother **without a cause** shall be in danger of the judgment:	But I tell you that anyone who is **angry** with a brother or sister _____ __ _____ will be subject to judgment…

The NIV FORBIDS ANGER against a brother—**period**.

The KJB FORBIDS ANGER against a brother— **"without a cause."**

Here's the problem...

IF the NIV's statement in Matthew 5:22 that anger against a brother is sinful, then the Lord broke his own command here:

> He looked around at them **in anger** and, deeply distressed at their stubborn hearts, said to the man, "Stretch out your hand." He stretched it out, and his hand was completely restored.
> NIV Mark 3:5

This means the NIV:

1. Contradicts itself and

2. Makes the Lord Jesus Christ a sinner in doing so.

How can the Lord approve of the NIV when it presents him breaking his own commandment?

Available from

WHICH
BIBLE
WOULD
JESUS USE
The Bible Version Controversy
Explained and Resolved

JACK MCELROY

NIV Strips Your King of His Kingdom

****

King James Bible Matthew 6:13
And lead us not into temptation, but deliver us from evil: **For thine is the kingdom, and the power, and the glory, for ever. Amen.**

New International Version Mat. 6:13
And lead us not into temptation, but deliver us from the evil one.' ___ ___ __ ___ _____ __ __ ___ ____ ___ ___ ___ ____

❶ 14 very important words identify the owner of the kingdom in the King James Bible.

❷ The NIV says NOTHING about who owns the kingdom.

❸ Not surprisingly, the NIV matches nicely with the Roman Catholic Douay-Rheims Bible:

And lead us not into temptation. But deliver us from evil. ___ ____ __ ___
_____ __ ___ ___ ___ ___
____ **Amen.** Douay-Rheims Bible Matthew 6:13

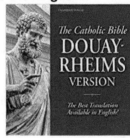

The Catholic Bible
DOUAY-RHEIMS
VERSION

The Best Translation Available in English!

The NIV...examined and found shamefully wanting.

Learn more, get the book: WHICH BIBLE WOULD JESUS USE? The Bible Version Controversy Explained and Resolved By Jack McElroy
www.JackMcElroy.com

Available from

amazon

nook

WHICH **BIBLE WOULD** JESUS USE
The Bible Version Controversy Explained and Resolved
JACK MCELROY

NIV Goes Common Core Math

Holy Bible
New International Version

****

See if you can find verse 21 in this scan of Matthew 17 in this NIV Children's Edition Bible...

The Transfiguration

17 After six days Jesus took with him Peter, James and John the brother of James, and led them up a high mountain by themselves. ²There he was transfigured before them. His face shone like the sun, and his clothes became as white as the light. ³Just then there appeared before them Moses and Elijah, talking with Jesus.

⁴Peter said to Jesus, "Lord, it is good for us to be here. If you wish, I will put up three shelters—one for you, one for Moses and one for Elijah."

⁵While he was still speaking, a bright stay with you? How long shall I put up with you? Bring the boy here to me."

¹⁸Jesus rebuked the demon, and it came out of the boy, and he was healed from that moment.

¹⁹Then the disciples came to Jesus in private and asked, "Why couldn't we drive it out?"

²⁰He replied, "Because you have so little faith. I tell you the truth, if you have faith as small as a mustard seed, you can say to this mountain, 'Move from here to there' and it will move. Nothing will be impossible for you.ᶜ'"

²²When they came together in Galilee, he said to them, "The Son of Man is

ᵃ19 Or *have been* ᵇ25 The Greek word means either *life* or *soul*; also in verse 26. ᶜ20 Some manuscripts *you.* ²¹*But this kind does not go out except by prayer and fasting.*

Above: Scan of a section of Matthew 17 out of The NIV Worship Bible © 1988 by the Zondervan Corporation

They went from verse 20 straight to verse 22 without leaving a space. Verse 21 is in a footnote, not in the text. If verse 21 shouldn't be in the Bible, why not renumber the verses? They can't. They're chicken.
Too big a risk of being called out as a FRAUD. Besides...

What kind of Bible tries to trick a kid?

Learn more, get the book: WHICH BIBLE WOULD JESUS USE? The Bible Version Controversy Explained and Resolved By Jack McElroy www.JackMcElroy.com

NIV Rubs Out
Matthew 18:11

****

King James Bible Mat. 18:11	New International Version Mat. 18:11
For the Son of man is come to save that which was lost.	_____ _____

Pretty important verse, don't you think?

It describes your Saviour's love for you.

Why is it missing?

Because the NIV staff bought the lame excuse that the words of

Our Saviour's Mission is Search and Rescue!

Mat. 18:11 were "very likely"[1] added by some **unknown** scribe, at some **unknown** time, in some **unknown** place; as if God wasn't watching over the transmission of his pure words. **Nonsense ...**

The Lord has presented Mt. 18:11 in billions of King James Bibles for over 400 years and in many others before that.

Do you really think your Saviour would ever use a Bible that leaves out his reason for dying for you in Matthew 18:11?

Available from

Learn more, get the book: WHICH BIBLE WOULD JESUS USE? The Bible Version Controversy Explained and Resolved By Jack McElroy www.JackMcElroy.com

Illustration: Mrs. Paul (Kay) Friederichsen, God's Way Made Easy, p. 126.

1. See: Philip W. Comfort, *New Testament Text and Translation Commentary*, pages 52-53.

NIV Crucifixion Omission

Ουτος εστιν Ιησους ο βασιλευς των Ιουδαιων.
THIS IS JESUS THE KING OF THE JEWS
[Matthew 27:37]

Ο βασιλευς των Ιουδαιων.
THE KING OF THE JEWS
[Mark 15:26]

Ουτος εστιν ο βασιλευς των Ιουδαιων.
THIS IS THE KING OF THE JEWS
[Luke 23:38]

Ιησους ο Ναζωραιος ο βασιλευς των Ιουδαιων.
JESUS THE NAZARENE THE KING OF THE JEWS
[John 19:19]

****

King James Bible Matthew 27:42
He saved others; himself he cannot save.
(If)he be the King of Israel, let him now come down from the cross, and we will believe him.

New International Version Mat. 27:42
"He saved others," they said, "but he can't save himself!
()He's the king of Israel! Let him come down now from the cross, and we will believe in him.

❶ **Leaders would NEVER outright SAY Jesus is the king of Israel. They were already on record as saying:**
Then said the chief priests of the Jews to Pilate, **Write not, The King of the Jews**; but that he said, I am King of the Jews. John 19:21 (but Pilate wrote it anyway)

❷ **They had already claimed Caesar as their King:**
Pilate saith unto them, Shall I crucify your King? The chief priests answered, **We have no king but Caesar**. John 19:15

❸ **Pilate stuffed it in their faces because he knew Jesus was innocent and that for envy they had delivered him up.**

In typical fashion, the NIV cuts the true text short and makes an erroneous report.

Available from

Learn more, get the book: WHICH BIBLE WOULD JESUS USE? The Bible Version Controversy Explained and Resolved By Jack McElroy
www.JackMcElroy.com

CHICK PUBLICATIONS

amazon

nook

Image: http://www.whatabeginning.com/SUPER/SUPER_S.htm

70

Which Mark Tells the Whole Truth?

****

King James Bible Mark 1:2	New International Version Mark 1:2
As it is **written in the prophets**, Behold, I send my messenger before thy face, which shall prepare thy way before thee.	As it is **written in Isaiah the prophet**, "I will send my messenger ahead of you, who will prepare your way"—

The Mark of the NIV is different from the Mark of the KJB because they say different things. How did this happen?

❶ The NIV folks KNOW for SURE that the cross-reference for Mark 1:2 is referring to **both** Malachi and Isaiah (the prophets) and NOT Isaiah alone (the prophet). But that matters not because...

Even though the know this, they were taught that "Isaiah the prophet" is "original".

❷ **BUT if that's true** then Mark's "Original Autograph" has an error of omission. The NIV's Mark should buy Errors and Omissions Insurance.

E & O INSURANCE

Textual Critic Philip Comfort says:

> "**Whatever his source**, Mark attributed the text to Isaiah only. **It may be that he was more familiar with Isaiah,** or that he thought Isaiah's name was the one which is readers most often associated with prophecies about the Messiah."[1]

❸ <u>What a pathetic explanation.</u> This means that the NIV'S Mark... Was so unfamiliar with what the prophets said (even under the direction of the Spirit of God) that he just blew the citation **OR** He purposely blew it for his "reader's" sakes. Wow. Anyway...

The KJB's Mark testimony is true, errorless and historically accurate.

If they willingly choose error here, what other errors have they chosen?

Available from

1.   Philip W. Comfort, *New Testament Text and Translation Commentary*, page 93.

NIV Jesus Goes Bad

****

King James Bible Mark 1:41	New International Version Mark 1:41 (©2011)
And Jesus, moved with **compassion**, put forth his hand, and touched him, and saith unto him, I will; be thou clean.	Jesus was **indignant**. He reached out his hand and touched the man. "I am willing," he said. "Be clean!" 

~ ~ ~ ~ ~ ~ ~ ~ ~ ~ ~ ~ ~ ~ ~ ~ ~ ~

Indignant: Showing **anger** or **annoyance** at what is perceived as unfair treatment.

Synonyms: Resentful, cross, mad, annoyed, offended, irritated.

Context: A leper kneels down and begs Jesus to heal him.

~ ~ ~ ~ ~ ~ ~ ~ ~ ~ ~ ~ ~ ~ ~ ~ ~ ~ ~ ~

Clearly, the compassionate Jesus of the King James Bible **IS NOT THE SAME** as the indignant Jesus of the NIV.

Which Bible tells the TRUTH?

Available from

Learn more, get the book: WHICH BIBLE WOULD JESUS USE? The Bible Version Controversy Explained and Resolved By Jack McElroy
www.JackMcElroy.com

WHICH **BIBLE WOULD** JESUS USE
The Bible Version Controversy Explained and Resolved
JACK MCELROY

NIV Greatly Insults Your Saviour

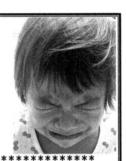

****

**King James Bible
Mark 1:41**

And Jesus, moved with <u>compassion</u>, put forth his hand, and touched him, and saith unto him, I will; be thou clean.

**New International Version Mark 1:41
(©2011)**

Jesus was <u>**indignant**</u>. He reached out his hand and touched the man. "I am willing," he said. "Be clean!"

How could they change your gracious and kind Lord from someone who was **moved with compassion** into a creep who was "put out" because someone needed help?

~ ~

Here's the same verse in the <u>1984 edition</u> of the NIV:

Filled with <u>compassion</u>, Jesus reached out his hand and touched the man. "I am willing," he said. "Be clean!" **New International Version (©1984).**

In 1984, the NIV editors said Jesus was "filled with compassion." **27 years later, he became indignant!**

Does this make you sick or angry?

Available from

NIV Stifles The Lord

****

The TV character Archie Bunker was famous for telling his wife Edith, "Will you Stifle yourself?" when he thought her comments were extraneous. He just wanted her to shut up.

See how the NIV stifles the Lord's 3-fold warning in Mark chapter 9...

King James Bible Mark 9:44 Where their worm dieth not, and the fire is not quenched.	**New International Version Mark 9:44** ___ ___ ___ ___ ___ ___ ___ ___ ___ ___.
King James Bible Mark 9:46 Where their worm dieth not, and the fire is not quenched.	**New International Version Mark 9:46** ___ ___ ___ ___ ___ ___ ___ ___.
King James Bible Mark 9:48 Where <u>their</u> <u>worm</u> dieth not, and the fire is not quenched.	**New International Version Mark 9:48** where '"<u>the worms</u> that eat them do not die, and the fire is not quenched.'

The NIV creators were taught that the Lord never gave a <u>3-fold warning</u> about "their worm" and "unquenchable fire" in Mark 9. Text critic Philip Comfort's lame excuse (**without ANY proof**) is that the verses were "added as a sort of prophetic refrain that makes for good oral reading."[1] **Sure thing. Proving, once again that...**

The NIV is nothing more than another cheap knockoff.

Available from

Learn more, get the book: WHICH BIBLE WOULD JESUS USE? The Bible Version Controversy Explained and Resolved By Jack McElroy www.JackMcElroy.com

1. Philip W. Comfort, *New Testament Text and Translation Commentary*, page 133.

NIV Misreports Historical Event

What Did Jesus Say to The Rich Young Ruler?

✱✱✱

King James Version Mark 10:21	New International Version Mark 10:21
Then Jesus beholding him loved him, and said unto him, One thing thou lackest: go thy way…and come, **take up the cross**, and follow me.	Jesus looked at him and loved him. "One thing you lack," he said. "Go…Then come, _____ ___ ___ _____ follow me."

Why is it missing in the NIV? Because the "experts" claim that the phrase "take up the cross" was added by some unknown "scribes" at some unknown time in some unknown place.

<u>Proof?</u> There is none. Just scholarly idle speculation to fit their 19th century conspiracy narrative. But one thing is clear…

<u>The Jesus of the KJB</u> told him to "take up the cross" in Mk. 10:21.

<u>The Jesus of the NIV</u> didn't.

The Jesus of the KJB and the Jesus of the NIV can't be the same because they say different things in Mk. 10:21.

Available from

Learn more, get the book: WHICH BIBLE WOULD JESUS USE? The Bible Version Controversy Explained and Resolved By Jack McElroy
www.JackMcElroy.com

NIV Misses Divine Intervention

****

King James Bible Luke 1:3
It seemed good to me also, having had **perfect understanding** of all things from the very first, to write unto thee in order...

New International Version Luke 1:3
With this in mind, since I myself have **carefully investigated** everything from the beginning, I too decided to write an orderly account for you...,

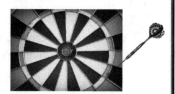

❶ **Careful investigation** can be done by anyone.

❷ **Perfect understanding** is given by God.

The NIV misses the mark ... again.

Available from

Learn more, get the book: WHICH BIBLE WOULD JESUS USE? The Bible Version Controversy Explained and Resolved By Jack McElroy
www.JackMcElroy.com

CHICK PUBLICATIONS

amazon

nook

WHICH **BIBLE WOULD JESUS USE**
The Bible Version Controversy Explained and Resolved
JACK MCELROY

NIV's Odd Choice to Present as "God's Word"

****

King James Bible Luke 1:37	New International Version (©2011) Lk. 1:37
For with God nothing shall be impossible.	For no word from God will ever fail.

While it's true that "no word from God will ever fail," the Lord is more emphatic here, revealing that with God NOTHING shall be IMPOSSIBLE. **By itself, this verse (in the KJB) is a reason to pray; especially when the deck is stacked against you.**

Though they'll argue that such a translation is possible, this is also a textual variant and NOT necessarily a translation choice. And a lousy one at that. But, that didn't stop the NIV folks from adopting it. They need to be different. **BUT look what happens …**

Even its modern version cousins **AND the old NIV** read like the KJB.

NIV (© 1984)	For nothing is impossible with God.
ESV	For nothing will be impossible with God.
NASB	For nothing will be impossible with God.
HCSB	For nothing will be impossible with God.
NET Bible	For nothing will be impossible with God.
Young's Literal	because nothing shall be impossible with God.

Did God change his mind, or is the NIV getting progressively worse?

Available from

Learn more, get the book: WHICH BIBLE
WOULD JESUS USE? The Bible Version Controversy Explained
and Resolved By Jack McElroy www.JackMcElroy.com

NIV Presents a Forgetful Saviour

Don't forget

****

King James Bible Luke 4:4	New International Version Lk. 4:4
And Jesus answered him, saying, It is written, That man shall not live by bread alone, **but by every word of God.**	Jesus answered, "It is written: 'Man does not live on bread alone.' ___ ___ ___ ___ ___

Here's the Old Testament verse the Lord was referencing:

> And he humbled thee, and suffered thee to hunger, and fed thee with manna, which thou knewest not, neither did thy fathers know; that he might make thee know that man doth not live by bread only, **but by every *word* that proceedeth out of the mouth of the LORD doth man live.** Deuteronomy 8:3

❶ The Lord quoted Deuteronomy 8:3 in his own style (which he can quote any way he wants.)

❷ The NIV staff was taught that the Lord NEVER wanted the phrase "but by every word of God" in Luke 4:4; in spite of the fact that over 99.5% of all known Greek manuscripts include it.

The NIV cuts your Saviour off midsentence, thereby omitting that you live by "every word of God."

Available from

Learn more, get the book: WHICH BIBLE WOULD JESUS USE? The Bible Version Controversy Explained and Resolved By Jack McElroy www.JackMcElroy.com

78

NIV Greatly Dishonors Your Loving Saviour

****

King James Bible Luke 4:18
The Spirit of the Lord *is* upon me, because he hath anointed me to preach the gospel to the poor; he hath sent me <u>to</u> <u>heal</u> <u>the</u> <u>brokenhearted</u>, to preach deliverance to the captives, and recovering of sight to the blind, to set at liberty them that are bruised,

New International Version Lk. 4:18
"The Spirit of the Lord is on me, because he has anointed me to proclaim good news to the poor. He has sent me ___ ___ ___ _____ to proclaim freedom for the prisoners and recovery of sight for the blind, to set the oppressed free,

❶ Hasn't your heart been broken?

❷ How many times has your Saviour healed it?

❸ This precious truth and the actual words of Isaiah that your Saviour read in the synagogue are scrubbed from the pages of the NIV because they were erroneously taught that Luke omitted it.

The NIV falls short of the glory of God once again.

Available from

Learn more, get the book: WHICH BIBLE WOULD JESUS USE? The Bible Version Controversy Explained and Resolved By Jack McElroy
www.JackMcElroy.com

NIV's Dr. Luke Covers up 1ˢᵗ-Century Malpractice

MEDICAL MALPRACTICE

****

King James Bible Luke 8:43	New International Version Luke 8:43
And a woman having an issue of blood twelve years, **which had spent all her living upon physicians**, neither could be healed of any,	And a woman was there who had been subject to bleeding for twelve years, ____ ___ ____ ___ ___ _____ ____ _____ but no one could heal her.

❶ Everyone knows Luke is "the beloved physician" (Col. 4:14) and Luke's Gospel is written through the eyes of a 1st-century doctor.

❷ The NIV's Dr. Luke OMITS a critical piece of the REAL Dr. Luke's testimony. The woman was getting ripped off by empty PROMISES of healing while PAYING for poor performance from her docs.

❸ Strangely, the NIV's Luke (who KNEW the facts of the case) **fails to disclose the TRUTH.** Even though the evangelist Mark in ALL versions (including the NIV) say:

> "She had suffered a great deal under the care of many doctors **and had spent all she had,** yet instead of getting better she grew worse." NIV Mark 5:26

❹ In contrast, the KJB's real Dr. Luke reports the WHOLE TRUTH.

What the NIV corrupts, the KJB makes plain.

Available from

CHICK
PUBLICATIONS

amazon

nook

Learn more, get the book: WHICH BIBLE WOULD JESUS USE? The Bible Version Controversy Explained and Resolved By Jack McElroy www.JackMcElroy.com

Photo: Alpha Stock Images, http://alphastockimages.com/

NIV's Salvation Testimony Omission

****

King James Bible Luke 23:42	New International Version Luke 23:42
And he said unto **Jesus, <u>Lord</u>**, remember me when thou comest into thy kingdom.	Then he said, "**Jesus,** ____ remember me when you come into your kingdom."

❶ The thief knew who <u>the man</u> "Jesus" was. Everybody heard of his fame.

❷ But calling Jesus "<u>Lord</u>" (in the King James Bible, NOT in the NIV) elevated his statement from head knowledge to a salvation confession.

> That if thou shalt **confess with thy mouth the <u>Lord</u> Jesus**, and shalt believe in thine heart that God hath raised him from the dead, thou shalt be saved. Romans 10:9

❸ The NIV folks trusted a few flawed manuscripts that omit the key component of the thief's confession...

Then they published a defective narrative... Again.

Available from

WHICH **BIBLE WOULD JESUS USE?** The Bible Version Controversy Explained and Resolved

JACK MCELROY

Learn more, get the book: WHICH BIBLE WOULD JESUS USE? The Bible Version Controversy Explained and Resolved By Jack McElroy
www.JackMcElroy.com

81

NIV Scrubs Jesus' Omnipresence

****

The King James Bible John 3:13	New International Version John 3:13
And no man hath ascended up to heaven, but he that came down from heaven, *even* the Son of man **which is in heaven**.	No one has ever gone into heaven except the one who came from heaven—the Son of Man.

❶ The King James reading shows that Jesus lived in heaven and on earth **SIMULTANEOUSLY**.

❷ Not only can the Lord be in heaven and on earth but so can you ... **in him:**

> **And hath raised *us* up together, and made *us* sit together in heavenly *places* in Christ Jesus:** Ephesians 2:6

❸ The NIV folks dumped the rest of the verse because **they chose manuscripts** whose creators seemingly couldn't figure out how the Son of Man who was then on earth could also be in heaven.

Once again, the NIV folks made the wrong choice.

Learn more, get the book: WHICH BIBLE WOULD JESUS USE? The Bible Version Controversy Explained and Resolved By Jack McElroy
www.JackMcElroy.com

Available from

NIV Labels Your Lord with Words of Devils

✱✱✱

King James Bible John 6:69	**New International Version John 6:69**
And we believe and are sure that **thou art <u>that</u> <u>Christ</u>, <u>the</u> <u>Son</u> of the living God.**	We have come to believe and to know that **you are ____ _____ the Holy One of God."**

This is Peter's answer to the Lord's question; "Will ye also go away?"

It's his bold and powerful confession that Jesus IS (1) the Christ and (2) the Son of the living God.

The title "the Holy One of God" appears two other times (in any Bible) when it is spoken **BY DEVILS**:

> Saying, Let *us* alone; what have we to do with thee, thou Jesus of Nazareth? art thou come to destroy us? I know thee who **thou art, the Holy One of God**. Mark 1:24 KJB

> Saying, Let *us* alone; what have we to do with thee, *thou* Jesus of Nazareth? art thou come to destroy us? I know thee who **thou art; the Holy One of God**. Luke 4:34 KJB

The NIV folks believe Peter (speaking under the authority of the Holy Ghost) invoked the words of devils. Wow.

What the NIV corrupts, the KJB makes plain.

Available from

Learn more, get the book: WHICH BIBLE WOULD JESUS
USE? The Bible Version Controversy Explained and
Resolved By Jack McElroy www.JackMcElroy.com

83

NIV Abridges Gospel of John

****

King James Bible John 5:4
For an angel went down at a certain season into the pool, and troubled the water: whosoever then first after the troubling of the water stepped in was made whole of whatsoever disease he had.

New International Version John 5:4

❶ Verse 3 says sick people waited for the moving of the water. Verses 5–7 cover the infirm man's lament about no one to help him into the pool. **BUT...**

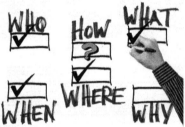

❷ Unless you had the explanation of John 5:4, you'd never know **HOW** they got healed.

❸ Would your Lord leave you in the dark about **HOW** they got healed?

The NIV; found deficient and defective once again.

Available from

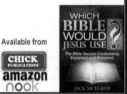

NIV Doctrinal Error: No Judgment for Christians

****

King James Bible John 5:24
Verily, verily, I say unto you, He that heareth my word, and believeth on him that sent me, hath everlasting life, **and shall not come into <u>condemnation</u>**; but is passed from death unto life.

New International Version John 5:24
"Very truly I tell you, whoever hears my word and believes him who sent me has eternal life and **will not be <u>judged</u>** but has crossed over from death to life.

❶ The NIV's Jesus says believers **will NOT be judged**.

❷ The real Jesus (as presented in the KJB) says **NO SUCH THING**. He says that believers will **NOT BE CONDEMNED. Big Difference.**

❸ That's because **believers WILL be judged at the judgement seat of Christ...**

> For **we must all appear before the judgment seat of Christ**; that every one may receive the things *done* in *his* body, according to that he hath done, whether *it be* good or bad. 2 Cor. 5:10 KJB

❹ Even the NIV says so, thereby contradicting itself...

> For **we must all appear before the judgment seat of Christ,** so that each of us may receive what is due us for the things done while in the body, whether good or bad. 2 Cor. 5:10 NIV

Makes you wonder; do they even read their own translations or check cross-references?

NIV Editors: John 7:53–8:11 Not Original; But Won't Eliminate it

****

without first hearing him to find out what he is doing?"

⁵²They replied, "Are you from Galilee, too? Look into it, and you will find that a prophet⁵ does not come out of Galilee."

[The earliest and most reliable manuscripts do not have John 7:53-8:11.]

⁵³Then each went to his own home.

8 But Jesus went to the Mount of Olives. ²At dawn he appeared again in the temple courts, where all the people gathered around him, and he sat down to teach them. ³The teachers of the law and the Pharisees brought in a woman caught in adultery. They made her stand before the group ⁴and said to Jesus, "Teacher, this woman was caught in the act of adultery. ⁵In the Law Moses commanded us to stone such women. Now what do you say?" ⁶They were using this question as a trap, in order to have a basis for accusing him.

But Jesus bent down and started to write on the ground with his finger. ⁷When they kept on questioning him, he straight-

Why not?

Because they know that if they did it will be too noticeable.

No publisher wants to make his Bible SO different from the King James Bible (the de facto standard) that customers will take notice and doubt its authority. BUT…

If John 7:53–8:11 never happened, why put it in the Bible in the first place?

Why not be honest, remove it and RENUMBER the verses? Not a chance. That'll leave a gaping hole. Everyone would question it.

Despite what they really believe the original text said, they just put in the note, <u>created doubt about what God said</u>, and marketed the "Bible" anyway.

The NIV: Just another cheap knockoff.

Available from

CHICK
PUBLICATIONS

amazon
nook

Above: Scan of John 8 in the Thompson Chain Reference Bible New International Version © 1978

What the NIV's Peter Forgot to Tell the Crowd

****

King James Bible Acts 2:30	New International Version Acts 2:30
...God had sworn with an oath to him, **that of the fruit of his loins, according to the flesh,** he would **raise up <u>Christ</u> to sit** on his throne;	... God had promised him on oath ___ __ __ ___ __ __ ___ ___ __ __ that he would **place <u>one</u> <u>of</u> <u>his</u> <u>descendants</u>** on his throne.

❶ **The NIV's Peter** said one of David's descendants would end up on the throne. David had lots of descendants. **No big deal.** Moreover, a descendant is not necessarily one who shares the same DNA (i.e., an adopted child can be regarded as in the direct line of descent depending on the law in a particular jurisdiction). **Worse, the Lord Jesus Christ isn't mentioned once in the NIV's verse.   BUT...**

❷ **The KJB's Peter** proclaimed that the promise to David was fulfilled in that:
1. **The Christ** would share his DNA and...
2. **The Christ** would sit on his throne.
Now that's a big deal and a fulfillment of a big promise!

The NIV misses relevant details... once again.

NIV Nixes Paul's Testimony in Acts 9

****

Don't you love hearing testimonies about how the Lord works in someone's life and how they got saved? But look what the NIV does to the biblical narrative about the moment Paul believed on Christ:

❶ In <u>verse 5</u>, Paul used the name "Lord" generically because he didn't know the identity of who was speaking to him:

> And he said, Who art thou, Lord? And the Lord said, **I am Jesus** whom thou persecutest: *it is* hard for thee to kick against the pricks. KJB Acts 9:5

****

King James Bible Acts 9:6	New International Version Acts 9:6
And he trembling and astonished said, <u>Lord</u>, what wilt thou have me to do? And the Lord *said* unto him, Arise, and go into the city, and it shall be told thee what thou must do.	__ __ _____ ____ _____ ____ ____ ____ ___ ____ ____ _____ "Now get up and go into the city, and you will be told what you must do."

❷ But then, **AS REVEALED in the KJB's verse 6**, he calls Jesus "Lord" in the sense of Romans 10:9:

> That **if thou shalt confess with thy mouth the <u>Lord Jesus</u>**, and shalt believe in thine heart that God hath raised him from the dead, **thou shalt be saved**. Romans 10:9 KJB

What the NIV fails to teach, the KJB makes plain.

NIV Flirts with Heresy

✲✲

King James Bible Acts 13:33	**New International Version Acts 13:33**
God hath fulfilled the same unto us their children, in that he hath raised up Jesus again; as it is also written in the second psalm, Thou art my Son, **this day have I <u>begotten</u> <u>thee</u>.**	he has fulfilled for us, their children, by raising up Jesus. As it is written in the second Psalm: "You are my Son; today I have **become <u>your</u> <u>father</u>.**"

❶ <u>Adoptionism</u> is a 2ⁿᵈ-century heresy teaching that Jesus earned and was granted supernatural powers by God and so **was adopted as the Son at his baptism**. Further, he was raised from the dead and **adopted into the Godhead** as a reward for His character and great accomplishments.[1]

❷ <u>Incarnational Sonship</u> i.e. Jesus **became the son** of God at birth is another heresy found here as well.

> Two Ancient Heresies

~ ~

If Jesus wasn't the son of God before that day and **from eternity** then he was just a man—not God in the flesh—and **COULDN'T die for your sins. In the King James Bible, the begetting of Jesus by God the Father refers to Jesus' resurrection from the dead:**

- And from Jesus Christ, *who is* the faithful witness, *and* the first begotten of the dead, and the prince of the kings of the earth. Revelation 1:5 KJB

- And he is the head of the body, the church: who is the beginning, the firstborn from the dead; that in all *things* he might have the preeminence. Colossians 1:18 KJB

This doctrinal corruption disqualifies the NIV from even being close to qualifying as God's book.

Available from

Learn more, get the book: WHICH BIBLE WOULD JESUS USE? The Bible Version Controversy Explained and Resolved By Jack McElroy www.JackMcElroy.com

CHICK PUBLICATIONS
amazon
nook

WHICH BIBLE WOULD JESUS USE
The Bible Version Controversy Explained and Resolved
JACK MCELROY

1.   See: https://carm.org/adoptionism

NIV Guts Apostles' Letter to Gentiles

****

King James Bible Acts 15:24
Forasmuch as we have heard, that certain which went out from us have troubled you with words, subverting your souls, saying, *Ye must* be circumcised, and keep the law: to whom we gave no *such* commandment:

New International Version Acts 15:24
We have heard that some went out from us without our authorization and disturbed you, troubling your minds by what they said.___ ____ __ _____ ___ _____ ___ __ __ ____ __ _ ____ _____

❶ There aren't many things more critical than the NT revelation of salvation by grace. Keeping the law doesn't cut it.

❷ The Judaizers were spreading this FALSE DOCTRINE and the Apostles wrote a letter to the gentiles to counter it.

❸ The NIV <u>falsifies</u> the true contents of the letter.

Trust Me

What the NIV distorts, the KJB makes plain.

Available from

Learn more, get the book: WHICH BIBLE WOULD JESUS USE? The Bible Version Controversy Explained and Resolved By Jack McElroy www.JackMcElroy.com

NIV Lies About "The Original Greek"

JESUS SPOKE HEBREW

BUSTING THE "ARAMAIC" MYTH

* *

King James Bible Acts 21:40

And when he had given him licence, Paul stood on the stairs, and beckoned with the hand unto the people. And when there was made a great silence, he spake unto them in the **Hebrew** tongue...

New International Version Acts 21:40

Having received the commander's permission, Paul stood on the steps and motioned to the crowd. When they were all silent, he said to them in **Aramaic:**

Here's an interlinear look at the passage...

Acts 21:40 And <de> when he had given <epitrepo> him <autos> licence <epitrepo> Paul <Paulos> stood <histemi> on <epi> the stairs <anabathmos>, and beckoned <kataseio> with the hand <cheir> unto the people <laos>. And <de> when there was made <ginomai> a great <polus> silence <sige>, he spake <prosphoneo> unto [them] in **the Hebrew <Hebrais> tongue** <dialektos>, saying <lego>

Since when does Hebrew = Aramaic (i.e., Syrian)?

Josephus says that Hebrew was spoken in 1st-century Israel.
Minge documents that Hebrew was widely spoken in that area at that time, **while Aramaic did not become popular till much later.**[1]

The NIV staff did NOT translate the word "Hebrew" accurately from their own Greek Text because they were taught that Jesus (Acts 26:14) and Paul (Acts 21:40) spoke Aramaic and NOT Hebrew—despite what it says "in the Original Greek!"

So much for "accurately" rendering the "Original Greek."

Available from

WHICH BIBLE WOULD JESUS USE?
The Bible Version Controversy Explained and Resolved

CHICK PUBLICATIONS

amazon

nook

Learn more, get the book: WHICH BIBLE WOULD JESUS USE? The Bible Version Controversy Explained and Resolved By Jack McElroy
www.JackMcElroy.com

1. https://www.amazon.com/Jesus-Spoke-Hebrew-Busting-Aramaic/product-reviews/0957986807

Was Phoebe a Woman Deacon?

****

She's only mentioned one time, but it sounds like she was a real nice sister with a stellar reputation as a servant.

Here's how the New International Version described her in 1983:

I commend to you our sister Phoebe, <u>**a servant**</u> of the church in Cenchrea	NIV ©1983 Romans 16:1

Good for Phoebe! She got her name in the Bible!

How cool is that?

But there's one more thing about her you need to know and that's coming up soon, but first,

The church she belonged to the church was in Cenchrea, a suburb of Corinth It had deacons. And they had certain qualifications.

Here's how the New International Version described them in 1983:

Deacons, likewise are to be **men** worthy of respect…	NIV ©1983 1 Timothy 3:8
A deacon must be the **husband** of one wife…	NIV ©1983 1 Timothy 3:12

In summary, the ©1983 NIV taught us two things back in 1983:

   (1)   **Phoebe was a servant and (2) Deacons have to be Men. Okay, Got it.**

Great Bible lesson from the ©1983 NIV!

BUT … And you knew there was going to be "but" … the NIV got updated in 2011. And one thing's for sure, like Dylan said many years ago, "the times they are a changin. It's true…

Times change and people change; there are cultural changes, ideological changes and even Christian world views changes.
And so, apparently does the NIV.

But what's odd is how the new group of NIV folks presented <u>these</u> <u>same</u> <u>verses</u> only 28 years later.

Here's how the New International Version ©2011 describes Phoebe now…

Page 1

NIV Section

I commend to you our sister Phoebe, **a deacon**[a][b] of the church in Cenchreae.	NIV ©2011 Romans 16:1

Our sister Phoebe has been promoted. She's now a deacon. Again, good for her. They say hard work pays off and it sure has for Phoebe.

And notice that they were careful to "footnote" their new translation:
- a. Romans 16:1 Or *servant*
- b. Romans 16:1 The word *deacon* refers here to a Christian designated to serve with the overseers/elders of the church in a variety of ways; similarly in Phil. 1:1 and 1 Tim. 3:8,12.

BUT wait, according to the 1983 NIV and there are about 400 million of them out there[1] she can't be a deacon because we were clearly taught that **a deacon has to be a man. Uh-oh Now what?**

It's not a problem for the new group of intrepid NIV translators. They just made a couple of really clever "adjustments" to the word of God...

deacons are to be worthy of respect ...	NIV ©2011 1 Timothy 3:8
A deacon must be faithful to his wife ...	NIV ©2011 1 Timothy 3:12

Notice how they completely changed the requirement that a deacon be a man.

Brilliant! Finally, women break through the glass ceiling in the local church and get a leadership role. They just needed a little tweak in Bible words to do it. It's one thing to be politically correct but we're dealing with the Bible here.

What do you think the Lord think of their little charade?

The Truth? Nothing changed about Phoebe but the new staff at the NIV production studio. Phoebe ALWAYS was a servant just like it says in the KJB and the 1983 NIV.

I commend unto you Phebe our sister, which is <u>a servant</u> of the church which is at Cenchrea:	KJB Romans 16:1

And what you didn't know about Phoebe is what it says in a note about her in the KJB, she delivered Paul's letter to the Romans!

To God only wise, *be* glory through Jesus Christ for ever. Amen. *Written to the Romans from Corinthus, and **sent by Phebe servant of the church at Cenchrea**.*	KJB Romans 16:27

The NIV ... Changing doctrine with impunity.

Available from

1. http://www.faithnews.cc/?p=14291

NIV Provides Justification for Flagellation Ritual

****

King James Bible 1 Corinthians 9:27

But **I keep under my body**, and bring it into subjection: lest that by any means, when I have preached to others, I myself should be a castaway.

New International Version 1 Cor. 9:27

No, **I strike a blow to my body** and make it my slave so that after I have preached to others, I myself will not be disqualified for the prize.

<u>Self-flagellation</u> is flogging or beating as a religious discipline.

You're thinking, "Nah, no one would see that in the verse." Au contraire…

Dr. Kent L. Yinger, Adjunct Professor of New Testament Studies, George Fox Evangelical Seminary says in the Journal of Religion & Society:

"On occasion, this verse has been painted as the chief fountainhead of more severe ascetic practices, such as flagellation."[1]

Did the Apostle Paul mean "**strike a blow**" to his own body OR "**keep under his body**"?

That depends on which Bible is telling you the truth.

Good Friday observance by a Kapampangan Catholic devotee in Barangay (barrio) San Pedro Cutud in San Fernando, Pampanga, Philippines. This is done for forgiveness of sins, fulfilling vows or to express gratitude for favors granted.

Photo: istolethev, Creative Commons Attribution 2.0 Generic license

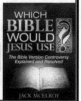
Learn more, get the book: WHICH BIBLE WOULD JESUS USE? The Bible Version Controversy Explained and Resolved By Jack McElroy www.JackMcElroy.com

Yinger, Kent L., "Paul and Asceticism in 1 Corinthians 9:27a" (2008). George Fox Evangelical Seminary. Paper 9.http://digitalcommons.georgefox.edu/gfes/9

Isn't It Great to Know God ACCEPTS YOU Because You're "In the Beloved?"

* *

King James Bible Ephesians 1:6	New International Version Ephesians 1:6
To the praise of the glory of his grace, wherein **he hath made us accepted in the beloved.**	to the praise of his glorious grace, which he has freely given us in the One he loves.
We are accepted because He put us "in Christ".	**The NIV fails to tell you WHAT you got because of His grace.**

IN a trial, there is nothing more comforting than to know that you ARE accepted in the beloved.

and now, in Christ Jesus, ye being once afar off became nigh in the blood of the Christ... Ephesians 2:13

What kind of Bible FAILS to teach you in Eph. 1:6 that you're accepted by God now that you're in Christ?

Available from

Learn more, get the book: WHICH BIBLE WOULD JESUS USE? The Bible Version Controversy Explained and Resolved By Jack McElroy www.JackMcElroy.com

Illustration: Mrs. Paul (Kay) Friederichsen, *God's Truth Made Simple*, p. 249.

The NIV's Selfie Salvation

****

King James Bible Ephesians 4:24	New International Version Eph. 4:24
And that ye **put on the new man**, which after God is created in righteousness and true holiness.	and to **put on the new self**, created to be like God in true righteousness and holiness.

"The new man" of the King James Bible is none other than the indwelling Lord Jesus Christ ...

But put ye on **the Lord Jesus Christ**, and make not provision for the flesh, to fulfil the lusts thereof.
Romans 13:14 (KJB)

Pretty important distinction, don't you think?

The NIV's "new self" sounds more like renovation than regeneration.

Available from

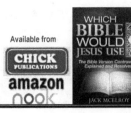

Learn more, get the book: WHICH BIBLE WOULD JESUS USE? The Bible Version Controversy Explained and Resolved By Jack McElroy
www.JackMcElroy.com

NIV Brazenly Restructures Church Government

****

King James Bible 1 Timothy 3:1
This is a true saying, If a man desire **the office** of a **bishop**, he desireth a good work.

New International Version 1 Tim. 3:1
Here is a trustworthy saying: Whoever aspires to be **an overseer** desires a noble task.

King James Bible 1 Timothy 3:13
For they that have used **the office** of **a deacon** well purchase to themselves a good degree, and great boldness in the faith which is in Christ Jesus.

New International Version 1 Tim. 3:13
Those who have served well gain an excellent standing and great assurance in their faith in Christ Jesus.

According to the KJB, a local church has **two offices**; Bishop (a.k.a. Pastor) and Deacon. **The men who serve in these offices ARE the elders of a church. There is no "office" of elders.**

According to the NIV, there no longer are ANY "offices" in the church.

And they swear to us that NO DOCTRINES are affected ... Sure they aren't.

Learn more, get the book: WHICH BIBLE WOULD JESUS USE? The Bible Version Controversy Explained and Resolved By Jack McElroy
www.JackMcElroy.com

Available from

The NIV and Sister Wives

Sister Wives is an American reality television series broadcast on The Learning Channel (TLC) that documents the life of a polygamist family, which includes patriarch Kody Brown, his four wives, and their 18 children.

****

King James Bible 1 Timothy 3:2	New International Version 1 Tim. 3:2
A bishop then must be blameless, **the husband of one wife**, vigilant, sober, of good behaviour, given to hospitality, apt to teach;	Now the overseer is to be above reproach, **faithful to his wife**, temperate, self-controlled, respectable, hospitable, able to teach,

❶ **Every man** should be faithful to his wife; bishops included.

❷ **BUT** one of the Biblical qualifications for a bishop is that he be the husband of **ONE wife.**

❸ **No polygamist** is qualified to be a bishop as is made CLEAR by the King James Bible. **Another truth you can't find in the NIV.**

The NIV falls short of the glory of God ... again.

Available from

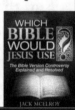

Learn more, get the book: WHICH BIBLE WOULD JESUS USE? The Bible Version Controversy Explained and Resolved By Jack McElroy
www.JackMcElroy.com

NIV's God Reduced to Man's Level

****

King James Bible Titus 1:2
In hope of eternal life,
which **God, that <u>cannot</u> lie**,
promised before the world began;

New International Version Titus 1:2
in the hope of eternal life, which
God, who <u>does</u> <u>not</u> lie,
promised before the beginning of
time

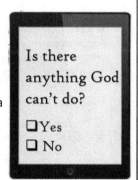

❶ People say that there's nothing God cannot do. And it's true in a sense but not entirely. Scripture says the Lord "**cannot lie**" as is **CLEARLY** seen in the King James Bible.

❷ That the NIV's God "**does not lie**" is merely a statement of fact **about his past performance**.

❸ But like the mutual fund prospectus says, "**Past performance is no guarantee of future results.**"

❹ There's a huge difference between **<u>does</u> <u>not</u>** and **<u>cannot</u>**.

❺ The Lord won't lie to you because, by his own confession, <u>he can't.</u>

What the NIV obscures, the KJB makes plain.

Available from

Learn more, get the book: WHICH BIBLE WOULD JESUS
USE? The Bible Version Controversy Explained and
Resolved By Jack McElroy www.JackMcElroy.com

amazon
nook

NIV Fails to Teach How to Get God's Approval

****

King James Bible 2 Timothy 2:15	2011 New International Version 2 Tim. 2:15
Study to shew thyself approved unto God, a workman that needeth not to be ashamed, rightly dividing the word of truth.	**Do your best** to present yourself to God as one approved, a worker who does not need to be ashamed and who correctly handles the word of truth.

❶ "Study" as a verb can mean to "make an effort to achieve" as seen in this KJB cross-reference:

"And that ye **study** to be quiet… 1 Thes. 4:11 KJB

❷ And it's true that the KJB translators translated the same Greek word as "diligence" in 3 other places: 2 Timothy 4:9; 2 Timothy 4:21; Titus 3:12.

❸ Here's why they didn't in 2 Timothy 2:15:

Although some say "study" is nothing more than a synonym for "diligence," what they don't tell you is the Italian Diodati 1602 says "studiati," the French Martin 1744 says "ETUDIE," the 2010 Reina Valera Gomez Spanish says "Estudia," and the 2014 Romanian Fidela says "studiaza." More importantly …

❹ The English word "study" can also mean: "Application of the mind to the acquisition of **learning; mental labor, reading and reflection** directed to learning…" References go back to circa 1300.[1]

This is evidenced in a KJB cross-reference:

"And further, by these, my son, be admonished: of making many books *there is* no end; and much **study** *is* a weariness of the flesh. Eccl. 12:12 KJB

But the NIV says to "Do your best."

To which any thinking person asks: "AT WHAT?" and "HOW?"

Whether you're "dividing the word of truth" or "correctly handling the word of truth" the ONLY way to do it is to … **STUDY.**

"Do your best" works with little kids, but it's a built-in excuse for failure without explaining AT WHAT and HOW for teens & adults.

Want God's approval?

Study the Book.

Learn more, get the book: WHICH BIBLE WOULD JESUS USE? The Bible Version Controversy Explained and Resolved By Jack McElroy www.JackMcElroy.com

Available from

1. Oxford English Dictionary   Photo; https://www.flickr.com/photos/wfryer/5230738432

NIV
Contradicts
Itself

THE RED BUTTON IS TRUE

THE BLUE BUTTON IS FALSE

****

King James Bible Hebrews 2:16	New International Version Heb. 2:16
For verily **he took not on** *him the nature of* angels; but he took on *him* the seed of Abraham.	For surely **it is not angels he helps**, but Abraham's descendants.

❶ **The NIV states** that the Lord **DOES NOT "HELP"** angels.

❷ **The NIV CONTRADICTS** itself in Daniel 10:13 where the archangel Michael does "help" another angel:

> But the prince of the Persian kingdom resisted me twenty-one days. Then Michael, one of the chief princes, **came to help** me, because I was detained there with the king of Persia. **Daniel 10:13 NIV**

❸ **The King James Bible says nothing about helping anyone in Hebrews 2:16. It's a reference to Jesus' incarnation.**

The NIV needlessly creates a confusion causing contradiction... again.

NIV's God Changes His Mind about Sarah's Faith

****

King James Bible Hebrews 11:11

<u>**Through faith also Sara**</u> herself received strength to conceive seed, and was delivered of a child when she was past age, because she judged him faithful who had promised.

New International Version Hebrews 11:11

NIV ©1984

By faith Abraham, even though he was past age—and Sarah herself was barren—was enabled to become a father because he considered him faithful who had made the promise.

NIV ©2011

And by faith even Sarah, who was past childbearing age, was enabled to bear children because she considered him faithful who had made the promise.

~ ~

The God of the NIV abruptly changed his mind in 2011 and decided to bring Hebrews 11:11 in line with what the God of the King James Bible has said for over 400 years.

Who knows WHAT the God of the NIV will say next?

Learn more, get the book: WHICH BIBLE WOULD JESUS USE? The Bible Version Controversy Explained and Resolved By Jack McElroy
www.jackmcelroy.com

Available from

CHICK PUBLICATIONS

amazon

nook

NIV Muddies Pastor's Primary Responsibility

✳✳✳

King James Bible 1 Peter 5:2
<u>Feed</u> <u>the</u> <u>flock</u> of God which is among you, taking the oversight thereof…

New International Version 1 Peter 5:2
<u>Be</u> <u>shepherds</u> of God's flock that is under your care, serving as overseers…

❶ Peter is talking to elders. Telling them to "BE SHEPHERDS" is meaningless—they ALREADY ARE.

❷ FEEDING the flock of God is a charge and a responsibility.

❸ Instructing a shepherd that his JOB is TO FEED the flock can make an incompetent shepherd into a competent one.

❹ Only the King James Bible makes this clear.

Sheep beget sheep. Well-fed sheep multiply…

Exactly what's supposed to happen.

Available from

Learn more, get the book: WHICH BIBLE WOULD JESUS USE? The Bible Version Controversy Explained and Resolved By Jack McElroy
www.JackMcElroy.com

Illustration: *God's Relief for Burdens*, Mrs. Paul (Kay) Friederichsen, p. 136.

NIV Finally Gets 1 John 2:16 Right

✔

****

©1984 NIV	©2011 NIV	KJB 1611
"For everything in the world— the cravings of sinful man, the lust of His eyes and the boasting of what he has and does— comes not from the Father but from the world."	"For everything in the world— **the lust of the flesh,** **the lust of the eyes,** and **the pride of life**— comes not from the Father but from the world."	For all that *is* in the world, **the lust of the flesh,** and **the lust of the eyes,** and **the pride of life,** is not of the Father, but is of the world.

The NIV folks said this after making the change …

"Has anyone really improved on the KJV rendering of these three expressions, to which the updated NIV returns? The language still communicates…"[1]

No kidding. That's exactly what KJB believers have been saying all along.

Available from

Learn more, get the book: WHICH BIBLE WOULD JESUS USE? The Bible Version Controversy Explained and Resolved By Jack McElroy
www.JackMcElroy.com

CHICK PUBLICATIONS
amazon
nook

1 Updating the New International Version of the Bible: Notes from the Committee on Bible Translation, https://www.biblegateway.com/niv/Translators-Notes.pdf

NIV Sadly Omits
WHY You Love God

★★★

| **King James Bible 1 John 4:19** | **New International Version 1 John 4:19** |
| We love **him**, because he first loved us. | We love ___ because he first loved us. |

❶ The NIV staff **was taught** that God NEVER wanted the word "him" in 1 John 4:19. They were taught that some forger added it after John wrote his epistle. They call it "scribal gap-filling."

❷ Nonsense, our Lord Jesus Christ IS the greatest demonstration of love. "God commendeth his love toward us, in that, while we were yet sinners, Christ died for us" and now that "the love of God is shed abroad in our hearts by the Holy Ghost," "we love **HIM** because he first loved us."

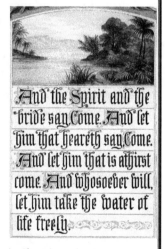

And the Spirit and the bride say, Come. And let him that heareth say, Come. And let him that is athirst come. And whosoever will, let him take the water of life freely.

❸ Contrary to their apologetics, every saved sinner (who got saved as an adult), with the right Bible, **has been taught of God since the Apostle John wrote it**, that the reason we love God is precisely because he first loved us.

The NIV misses the point again.

Learn more, get the book: WHICH BIBLE WOULD JESUS USE? The Bible Version Controversy Explained and Resolved By Jack McElroy
www.JackMcElroy.com

Available from

CHICK
PUBLICATIONS

amazon
nook

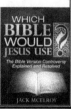

WHICH
BIBLE
WOULD
JESUS USE
The Bible Version Controversy
Explained and Resolved
JACK MCELROY

NIV's Devil
All Powerful

****

King James Bible 1 John 5:19

And we know that we are of God, and **the whole world lieth in wickedness.**

New International Version 1 Jn. 5:19
We know that we are children of God, and that **the whole world is under the <u>control</u> of the evil one.**

"Sympathy for the Devil" is the title of a 1968 film by Jean-Luc Godard featuring the Rolling Stones in the process of recording the song of the same name. Like the **NIV Devil,** the lyrics picture a powerful, transgenerational Devil ultimately controlling human atrocities.

But notice...The KJB mentions no such thing.
The NIV staff must have published this whole-world-controlled "evil one" nonsense without considering these two Scriptures:

...to the intent that the living may know that
the <u>most</u> <u>High</u> <u>ruleth</u> in the kingdom of men, and giveth it to whomsoever he will... Daniel 4:17

And <u>Jesus</u> came and spake unto them, saying,
<u>All</u> <u>power</u> <u>is</u> <u>given</u> <u>unto</u> <u>me</u> in heaven and in earth. Mat. 28:18.

The whole world DOES lie in wickedness and the lying Devil has his part in it. He just doesn't "control" it.

The NIV; Scripturally wrong again.

Available from

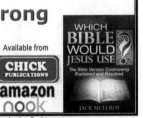

Learn more, get the book: WHICH BIBLE WOULD JESUS USE? The Bible Version Controversy Explained and Resolved By Jack McElroy www.JackMcElroy.com

Image: https://en.wikipedia.org/wiki/Sympathy_for_the_Devil#/media/File:Rolling_Stones_Sympathy_for_the_Devil.jpg

Who Stood Where?

* *

King James Bible Rev. 13:1	New International Version Rev. 13:1
<u>And</u> <u>I</u> <u>stood</u> **upon the sand of the sea**, and saw a beast rise up out of the sea, having seven heads and ten horns…	<u>And</u> <u>the</u> <u>dragon</u> <u>stood</u> **on the shore of the sea.** And I saw a beast coming out of the sea. He had ten horns and seven heads…

Outrageously different.

It's either the Apostle John OR the dragon—
Hence the Bible version controversy.

And they laugh at you when you defend the integrity of your Lord's words in the KJB.

Learn more, get the book: WHICH BIBLE WOULD
JESUS USE? The Bible Version Controversy
Explained and Resolved By Jack McElroy
www.JackMcElroy.com

Available from

amazon

nook

NIV: Everyone Wins

****

King James Bible Revelation 21:24	New International Version Rev. 21:24
And the nations <u>**of them which are saved**</u> shall walk in the light of it: and the kings of the earth do bring their glory and honour into it.;	The nations _ _____ ____ ___ _____ will walk by its light, and the kings of the earth will bring their splendor into it,

They'll argue, "Read vs 27 in the NIV, it also affirms that not all will enter, only those that are written in the book of life."

Nothing impure will ever enter it, nor will anyone who does what is shameful or deceitful, but only those whose names are written in the Lamb's book of life. Rev. 21:27 NIV

In 1996, Oprah gave everyone in her audience a trip to Disney World.[1]

True, BUT what they're missing is that the KJB defines WHOSE names are written in the book of life i.e., "them that are saved." **The NIV is mute here on HOW someone gets their name into the book of life.**

That the NIV is defective is NO surprise. but...

The agenda that everyone wins works for little kids sporting events and television shows.

It's not true in real life or in the real Bible.

Learn more, get the book: WHICH BIBLE WOULD JESUS USE? The Bible Version Controversy Explained and Resolved By Jack McElroy
www.JackMcElroy.com

Available from

CHICK PUBLICATIONS

amazon
nook

NIV Blows Cross-Reference; Makes Lucifer Jesus

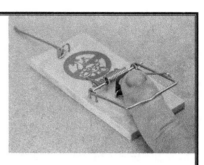

Reference	King James Bible	New International Version
Isaiah 14:12	How art thou fallen from heaven, **O <u>Lucifer</u>, <u>son of the morning</u>!**...	How you have fallen from heaven, **O <u>morning star</u>,** son of the dawn!...
Revelation 22:16	**I Jesus** have sent mine angel to testify unto you these things in the churches. **I am … the bright and <u>morning star</u>**	**"I, Jesus**, have sent my angel to give you this testimony for the churches. **I am … the bright <u>Morning Star</u>."**
	<u>Lucifer</u> is son of the morning. <u>Jesus</u> is the morning star in the KJB.	BOTH Jesus AND Lucifer are called "morning star" in the NIV.

The distinction is clear in the King James Bible

How can you TRUST a Bible that misses the difference between your Saviour and Lucifer?

Available from

Learn more, get the book: **WHICH BIBLE WOULD JESUS USE?** The Bible Version Controversy Explained and Resolved By Jack McElroy www.JackMcElroy.com

NIV Mistakes Book for Tree

****

King James Bible Rev. 22:19	New International Version Rev. 22:19
And if any man shall take away from the words of the book of this prophecy, God shall take away his **part** out of **the book of life**, and out of the holy city, **and *from* the things** which are **written** in this book.	And if anyone takes words away from this scroll of prophecy, God will take away from that person any **share** in **the tree of life** and in the Holy City, _____ which are **described** in this scroll.

❶ There is CURRENTLY no known Greek N.T. manuscript that says "book." Its support comes from Latin witnesses of Revelation. **Why not Greek?** Possibly because "the Greek Church did not accept the canonicity of the book of Revelation until 397 AD whereas the Latin Church already accepted the canonicity as early as in 150 AD."[1] Plus...

❷ No one ever had a "share" in the "Tree of Life." It's not something you own, like shares of stock. It was for food and will be again.

❸ No one gets access to "the tree of life" unless they FIRST get their part in the "book of life." **And Revelation 22:19 is the ONLY place in Scripture where you're explicitly warned that taking away from...**

"the words of prophecy of this book" gets you removed from "the book of life."

Available from

Learn more, get the book: WHICH BIBLE WOULD JESUS USE? The Bible Version Controversy Explained and Resolved By Jack McElroy
www.JackMcElroy.com

1. http://www.kjvtoday.com/home/book-of-life-or-tree-of-life-in-revelation-2219

NIV Dumps Verses...

Translators Take Big Risk

These 16 verses (containing 258 words) are IN the King James Bible but NOT in the New International Version.

****

Matthew 17:21	Mark 9:44	Luke 17:36	Acts 15:34
Matthew 18:11	Mark 9:46	Luke 23:17	Acts 24:7
Matthew 23:14	Mark 11:26	John 5:4	Acts 28:29
Mark 7:16	Mark 15:28	Acts 8:37	Romans 16:24

The translators and editors of the NIV were taught that God never wanted these verses in his Bible in the first place, so they eliminated them. **BUT...**

IF the Lord's Bible SHOULD contain those verses and words as he's had them appear in billions of King James Bibles over the past 400 years, then those 16 missing verses are <u>very</u> <u>important</u> <u>to</u> <u>God</u>.

Plus, the NIV's underlying Greek text has about 8,000 differences from the KJB's underlying Greek text.[1]

Do you think the editors or translators of the NIV ever feared this verse?

Therefore, behold, <u>I</u> <u>am</u> <u>against</u> the prophets, saith the LORD, that <u>steal</u> <u>my</u> <u>words</u> every one from his neighbour. Jeremiah 23:30

1 See: Dr. J.A. Moorman, *8,000 differences Between the N.T. Greek Words of the King James Bible and the Modern Versions.*

NIV's God Flips; Changes Mind and Position

CHANGE
WE CAN BELIEVE IN
CAN'T

****

The words in any Bible version represent the God behind that particular Bible.

The God behind the NIV is shown to be unstable, unreliable, and given to change. Look how he changed his mind and views in a mere 16 years...

Position and Ref.	NIV © 1995	NIV © 2011
Divorce Mal. 2:16	"I hate divorce" says the LORD God of Israel	"The man who hates and divorces his wife...
History 2 Sam. 21:19	Elhanan ... killed Goliath...	... Elhanan killed the brother of Goliath...
Faith Heb. 11:11	By faith Abraham,...	And by faith even Sarah,
Jesus' Character Mark 1:41	Filled with compassion, Jesus	Jesus was indignant.
Office of Deacon Rom. 16:1	I commend to you our sister Phoebe, a servant...	I commend to you our sister Phoebe, a deacon...

The NIV... peddling "CHANGE" we CAN'T believe in.

What should you do with the God of the NIV?

"...meddle not with them that are given to change:" Prov. 24:21

Available from

Learn more, get the book: WHICH BIBLE WOULD JESUS USE?
The Bible Version Controversy Explained and Resolved By
Jack McElroy www.JackMcElroy.com

Have You Taken the Archaic Language Test?

Though I speake with the tongues of men & of Angels, and haue not charity, I am become as sounding brasse or a tinkling cymbal 2 And though I haue the gift of prophesie, and vnderstand all mysteries and all knowledge: and though I haue all faith, so that I could remooue mountaines, and haue no charitie. I

****

Which column is from the NIV and which from the King James Bible?

2 Chr 13:22	annotations	story
Ps 58:7	blunted	cut in pieces
Ps 93:4	breakers	waves
Ex 35:22	brooches	bracelets
Is 57:4	brood	children
Dan 10:6	burnished	polished
I Ki 7:6	colonnade	porch
Song 2:12	cooing	voice
Gen 18:8	curds	butter
Gen 40:6	dejected	sad
I Pet 4:4	dissipation	riot
Pro 28:12	elation	glory
Rom 2:20	embodiment	form
Pro 23:10	encroach	enter
Is 30:17	flagstaff	beacon
Is 59:13	fomenting	speaking
Is 27:9	fruitage	fruit
Gen 14:1	goyim	nations
Hab 1:6	impetuous	hasty
Gen 6:4	Nephilim	giants
Est 1:6	porphyry	red
Is 20:3	portent	wonder
Acts 13:8	proconsul	deputy
Jude 12	qualm	fear
Song 1:13	sachet	bundle
Est 3:12	satraps	lieutenants
I Ki 21:5	sullen	sad
2 Ki 7:10	tethered	tied
2 Tim 1:7	timidity	fear
Song 7:5	tresses	galleries
1 Sam 14:19	tumult	noise
2 Ki 24:1	vassal	servant
Num 34:5	wadi	river

Wouldn't it be easier to use the Bible without the archaic language?

Right column is the King James Bible

Available from

CHICK PUBLICATIONS

amazon

nook

WHICH BIBLE WOULD JESUS USE?

Learn more, get the book: WHICH BIBLE WOULD JESUS USE? The Bible Version Controversy Explained and Resolved By Jack McElroy www.JackMcElroy.com

Adapted from work by Laurence Vance, www.vancepublications.com

NIV's Odd Staffing Choice

****

"Virginia Ramey Mollenkott, best known for her 'God of the Breasts' interpretation of El Shaddai, spent her 44-year professional career teaching college level English literature and language, but developed specializations in feminist theology and lesbian, gay, bisexual and transgender theology during the second half of that career.

Mollenkott served as an assistant editor of Seventeenth Century News from 1965 to 1975, **and as a stylistic consultant for the New International Version of the Bible for the American Bible Society from 1970 to 1978.**

A Democrat and trans-religious Christian, Mollenkott lived with her domestic partner Judith Suzannah Tilton at Cedar Crest Retirement Village until Judith's death in February 2018; together they co-grandmothered Mollenkott's three granddaughters.

She earned her B.A. from fundamentalist Bob Jones University in 1953, her M.A. at Temple University in 1955, and her Ph.D. at New York University in 1964. She received an honorary Doctorate in Ministries from Samaritan College in 1989.**"**[1]

Think: Infiltration.

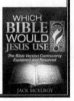
1. https://en.wikipedia.org/wiki/Virginia_Ramey_Mollenkott

NIV Goes Catholic

****

Sure...The Roman Catholic Church is on record forbidding Bible reading in the language of the people.

And sure...
They view the King James Bible as a "Paper Pope"— an unapproved and faulty translation of the Scriptures.

But Strangely...
The "Protestant" Bible version they DO approve of is...

The New International Version

Catholic Book Publishing puts out a **Catholic approved** edition of the Psalms (http://tinyurl.com/h5wzzwb)

The NIV folks custom-fit the text of the Psalms so that wouldn't offend the sensitivities of the Roman Catholic Church, which says:

> "**The belief in the Bible as the sole source of faith is unhistorical, illogical, fatal to the virtue of faith, and destructive of unity.**"[1]

One wonders what is in the Catholic "approved" NIV that's NOT approved in the KJB?

Available from

Learn more, get the book: WHICH BIBLE WOULD JESUS USE? The Bible Version Controversy Explained and Resolved By Jack McElroy
www.JackMcElroy.com

1.   http://www.newadvent.org/cathen/12495a.htm

Top 3 "Funny Things" About the NIV

****

| The King James Bible... **is a formal equivalency translation** where the translators "convey the meaning of each particular word"[1] **so you can know WHAT God SAID.** | The New International Version... is a **dynamic equivalence translation** employing a "balance between word-for-word and thought-for-thought."[2] "The first concern of the translators has been the accuracy of the translation and its fidelity to the **thought of the biblical writers...**"[3] |

❶ The "biblical writers" are the penmen of the author; the Holy Ghost. The NIV's mischief arises as they <u>attempt</u> to tell you what God is THINKING instead of what he SAYS.

❷ **Who's qualified to know WHAT the Lord is <u>THINKING</u>?**

And here's the really funny thing...

❸ Sometimes the NIV translators weren't even sure WHAT God meant...

"Despite their expertise they [the NIV translators] frequently found themselves **FAR FROM CERTAIN** about the **MEANING** intended by the Holy Spirit, the primary Author of Scripture."[4]

Shouldn't a Bible just tell you WHAT your Lord SAID instead of what someone THINKS he MEANT?

Available from

Grace to You, https://tinyurl.com/yae3tbge, 2. https://tinyurl.com/y6ukmvnt, 3 https://tinyurl.com/y7ot9xza, 4. https://tinyurl.com/y9ywdkgc

Did Jesus Create All Things or Not?

****

That all depends on which Bible tells the truth.

	KJB	NIV
John 1:3	All things were **made by him**;	**Through him** all things were made
John 1:10	He was in the world, and the world was made **by him...**	He was in the world, and though the world was made **through him...**
Col. 1:16	For **by him** were all things created...all things were created **by him**, and for him:	For **in him** all things were created... all things have been created **through him** and for him.
1 Cor. 8:6	and one Lord **Jesus Christ, by whom are all things**, and we by him.	there is but one Lord, Jesus Christ, **through whom all things came** and through whom we live.
Eph. 3:9	... God, who created all things **by Jesus Christ:**	... God, **who created all things**
Heb. 1:2	Hath in these last days spoken unto us by his Son, whom he [God] hath appointed heir of all things, **by whom** also he [God] made the worlds;	but in these last days he has spoken to us by his Son, whom he [God] appointed heir of all things, and **through whom** also he [God] made the universe.

They'll argue that Hebrews 1:2 says "God" made the worlds. Right. All the worlds were made "by" God. And since Jesus is God, the worlds were made "by" him.

They say your choice of a Bible version doesn't really matter because it's just a preference. And besides, they supposedly don't affect doctrine anyway. But here's a question they don't ever consider ...

Does God have a preference or is he forced to accept all "conservative" versions no matter what they say?

Available from

Learn more, get the book: WHICH BIBLE WOULD JESUS USE? The Bible Version Controversy Explained and Resolved By Jack McElroy
www.JackMcElroy.com

The English Standard Version— A Fixer-Upper

Introduction

****

If the ESV is God's Bible, why did he wait till 2001 to put it out there?

Of course, that's a question that applies to all new versions, isn't it? Anyway, the ESV's got kind of a weird origins story, so here goes ...

The ESV was produced to solve a problem.

Evangelicals were getting freaked out by the revisions to the New International Version. For some reason, their concern was triggered when the NIV began incorporating gender-inclusive language into the text (what a surprise).

Bible Researcher Michael D. Marlowe says:

> The English Standard Version (ESV) ... had its roots in discussions that took place before the May 1997 meeting called by James Dobson at Focus on the Family headquarters to resolve the [gender] inclusive NIV issue.
>
> The night prior to the meeting, critics of regendered language gathered in a Colorado Springs hotel room to discuss the next day's strategy. During the course of the evening it became clear their concerns with the NIV **extended beyond gender issues.**[1]

Evidently, they realized they had more to be concerned about than just gender. Then they had a brainstorm.

---

1. http://www.bible-researcher.com/esv.html

The group discussed the merits of the Revised Standard Version, first published in 1952 by the National Council of Churches and recently replaced by the New Revised Standard Version, a regendered update.

Some months later, Trinity Evangelical Divinity School professor Wayne Grudem and Crossway President Lane Dennis entered into negotiations with the National Council of Churches to use the 1971 revision of the Revised Standard Version as the basis for a new translation.

An agreement was reached in September 1998 allowing translators freedom to modify the original text of the RSV as necessary **to rid it of de-Christianing translation choices.**[2]

Isn't it interesting that they had to rid a Bible of "de-Christianing translation choices"?

Why would Bible translators "de-Christianize" a Bible in the first place? Sounds like a pretty shaky foundation to rebuild on.

In fact, it almost sounds like the ESV was a fire repair job.

Was the publisher able to successfully "fix and flip" it? You be the judge.

As you will see in this section, the ESV can't be God's Bible because it contains errors of fact, history, geography, and science.

How can the Lord possibly be behind such a questionable project?

I don't think he is.

I think his competition is.

---

2. Ibid.

ESV Corrupts Gen. 3:16... Pits Wives against Husbands

****

Genesis 3:16 King James Bible
Unto the woman he said, I will greatly multiply thy sorrow and thy conception; in sorrow thou shalt bring forth children; and **thy desire** ***shall be*** <u>**to**</u> **thy husband**, and he shall rule over thee.

Genesis 3:16 English Standard Version
To the woman he said, "I will surely multiply your pain in childbearing; in pain you shall bring forth children. **Your desire shall be** <u>**contrary**</u> <u>**to**</u> **your husband**, but he shall rule over you."

By inserting the word "<u>contrary</u>" into the translation (which no other version does) they have set up an **adversarial relationship** between husband and wife where they **compete for leadership** <u>instead of</u> cooperate as a team.

It's one thing for them to have a private interpretation of Scripture, it's quite another when they put their words into your Lord's mouth.

Available from

Learn more, get the book: WHICH BIBLE WOULD JESUS USE? The Bible Version Controversy Explained and Resolved By Jack McElroy
www.JackMcElroy.com

121

ESV Shock: Did Pharaoh Have Sex with Sarah?

****

King James Bible Genesis 12:19
Why saidst thou, She *is* my sister? so **I might have taken** her to me to wife: now therefore behold thy wife, take *her*, and go thy way...

English Standard Version Gen. 12:19
Why did you say, 'She is my sister,' so that **I took her** to be my wife? Now then, here is your wife. Take her and go!"

<u>**According to the Scripture of truth**</u> (KJB), the Lord stopped Pharaoh from defiling Sarah.

<u>**According to the ESV's false narrative**</u>, Pharaoh actually "took" her as his wife.

Even the corrupt Contemporary English Version erroneously (but plainly) states he married her:

> "Why did you make me believe she was your sister? **Now I've married her.** Take her and go! She's your wife." **Gen. 12:19 CEV**

Evidently, the God of the ESV was too slow or impotent to do anything to stop Sarah's defilement.

The ESV: unprofitable, polluted and defiled.

Available from

Learn more, get the book: WHICH BIBLE WOULD JESUS USE? The Bible Version Controversy Explained and Resolved By Jack McElroy www.JackMcElroy.com

ESV Destroys OT Type of Christ with Jewish Mythology

****

King James Bible Leviticus 16:10
But the goat, on which the lot fell to be **the scapegoat**, shall be presented alive before the LORD, to make an atonement with him, *and* to let him go for a **scapegoat** into the wilderness.

English Standard Version Lev. 16:10
but the goat on which the lot fell for **Azazel** shall be presented alive before the LORD to make atonement over it, that it may be sent away into the wilderness to **Azazel**.

❶ **The King James Bible's** scapegoat goes into the wilderness **carrying away** with him the sins of the people and typifying the sacrifice of Christ who **takes away** the sins of the world.

❷ According to the Jewish Encyclopedia, "Most modern scholars...have accepted the opinion...stated by Naḥmanides [1194–1270, Spanish rabbi and scholar and one of the leading authors of Talmudic literature in the Middle Ages] that **Azazel belongs to the class of 'se'irim,' goat-like demons,** jinn haunting the desert, to which the Israelites were wont to offer sacrifice."[1]

❸ **The ESV perpetuates Naḥmanides' myth and obscures the type,** saying the goat is "**for Azazel**" and is sent "**to Azazel**."

Your sins (and theirs through Christ) were never sent to a devil in the wilderness but were removed:

"As far as the east is from the west," *Psa. 103:12*

"cast into the depths of the sea," *Micah 7:19*

and "remembered no more." *Heb. 8:12.*

Learn more, get the book: WHICH BIBLE WOULD JESUS USE?
The Bible Version Controversy Explained and Resolved By
Jack McElroy www.JackMcElroy.com

Available from
CHICK PUBLICATIONS
amazon
nook

1 http://www.jewishencyclopedia.com/articles/2203-azazel

ESV's "Cut and Paste" Misses N.T. Revelation

****

King James Bible Leviticus 26:12	English Standard Version Lev. 26:12
And I will walk **among** you, and will be your God, and ye shall be my people.	And I will walk **among** you and will be your God, and you shall be my people.

Leviticus 26 describes God's conditional promise to Israel to walk **among** them. The KJB and the ESV agree. BUT...

Notice below how the KJB reveals God dwelling **in you** when the Lord **"quotes"** himself and applies the verse to New Testament believers...

King James Bible 2 Cor. 6:16	English Standard Version 2 Cor. 6:16
...for **ye** are the temple of the living God; as God hath said, **I will dwell in them**, and walk **in** *them*; and I will be their God, and they shall be my people.	...For we are the temple of the living God; as God said, "I will make my dwelling **among them** and walk **among them**, and I will be their God, and they shall be my people.

We are **indwelt** by the Father:
> One God and Father of all, who *is* above all, and through all, and **in you** all. Ephesians 4:6 KJB

We are **indwelt** by the Son:
> To whom God would make known what *is* the riches of the glory of this mystery among the Gentiles; which is Christ **in you**, the hope of glory: Colossians 1:27 KJB

We are **indwelt** by the Holy Spirit:
> Know ye not that ye are the temple of God, and *that* the Spirit of God dwelleth **in you**? 1 Corinthians 3:16 KJB

Words, including prepositions, really do matter.

As he often does, the Lord <u>coins new words</u> and <u>new</u> <u>revelation</u> when he quotes the OT in the New. Something you don't see here in the ESV.

There's nothing like the KJB to reveal New Testament truth to God's children.

Learn more, get the book: WHICH BIBLE WOULD JESUS USE? The Bible Version Controversy Explained and Resolved By Jack McElroy
www.JackMcElroy.com

Available from

amazon
nook

ESV Nixes Samson Miracle

****

King James Bible Judges 15:19	English Standard Version Jud. 15:19
But God clave an hollow place that *was* **in the jaw**, and there came water thereout…	And God **split open the hollow place that is at Lehi**, and water came out from it…

 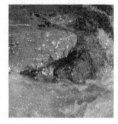

A fter killing 1,000 men with the jawbone of an ass, Samson prayed the Lord would give him water.

Miracle #1 was that no one hit Samson with an arrow or spear.
Miracle #2 was that God provided him drink out of the same jawbone.

Water out of the ground? Too easy. The Lord had already provided water from a rock to Moses and the children of Israel.
Water from an ass's jawbone as revealed in the real Bible?

Priceless.

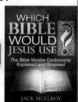

ESV Misses 3,000-Year-Old Diagnosis Revealed in the KJB

<u>Hemorrhoids</u> — **The disease no one talks about.**
And yet it affects 80% of the US population at one time or another.

✱✱✱

King James Bible 1 Samuel 5:9	**English Standard Version 1 Samuel 5:9**
And it was *so*, that, after they had carried it about, the hand of the LORD was against the city with a very great destruction: and he smote the men of the city, both small and great, and they had **emerods in their secret parts.**	But after they had brought it around, the hand of the LORD was against the city, causing a very great panic, and he afflicted the men of the city, both young and old, so that **tumors broke out on them.**

❶ Unlike the ESV, the King James has been reporting about <u>hemorrhoids</u> for over 400 years. **They're nasty.**

❷ You can't walk right, poop right, clean up right and they're painful in the extreme, especially at night. They can bleed, get infected, turn gangrenous, and in rare cases, cause death due to bleeding.

❸ <u>Tumors</u> can be anywhere, painless, small, benign, and insignificant.

☑ Unlike the ESV, the King James Bible has been medically and scientifically accurate for over 400 years.

And they swear to us that the ESV is an "accurate" translation. Nonsense.

Learn more, get the book: WHICH BIBLE WOULD JESUS USE? The Bible Version Controversy Explained and Resolved By Jack McElroy www.JackMcElroy.com

Available from

50,070 or 70; Which is it?
****

King James Bible 1 Samuel 6:19
And he smote **the men of Bethshemesh, because** they had **looked into the ark** of the LORD, **even** he smote of the **people fifty thousand and threescore and ten men [50,070]:** and the people lamented, because the LORD had smitten *many* **of the people** with a great slaughter.

English Standard Version 1 Samuel 6:19
And he struck some of the men of Beth-shemesh, because they looked upon the ark of the LORD. He struck **seventy men [70]** of them, and the people mourned because the LORD had struck **the people** with a great blow.

Apologist Gleason Archer suggests: (1) the text became "garbled" due to Hebrew grammar, (2) Josephus claimed 70, and (3) "a few" Hebrew manuscripts say 70.[2]

Dan Wallace's NET version footnote says: "The number 50,070 is **surprisingly large, although it finds almost unanimous textual support** in the MT [Hebrew Text] and in the ancient versions."[2]

The truth? Two groups died. The 70 "men" **BECAUSE** they "looked into the ark" and **EVEN** another 50,000 "of the people" "living in and near Beth-shemesh, or coming thither from all parts"[3]

Where did they come from?

Cross-references explain that they came from the **SUBURBS:**

> And Ain with her suburbs, and Juttah with her suburbs, *and* **Bethshemesh with her suburbs**; nine cities out of those two tribes. Joshua 21:16 KJB

> And Ashan with her suburbs, and **Bethshemesh with her suburbs:**
> 1 Chronicles 6:59 KJB

(The ESV conveniently says "pasturelands," thereby removing the indication that the population was spread out in suburbs.)

So why would the ESV folks change the text as written?

Simple; it's too hard for them to believe.

Available from

Learn more, get the book: WHICH BIBLE WOULD JESUS USE? The Bible Version Controversy Explained and Resolved By Jack McElroy www.JackMcElroy.com

1 Gleason Archer, Encyclopedia of Bible Difficulties, P. 169; 2. https://netbible.org/bible/1+Samuel+6; 3. Matthew Poole's Commentary.

KJB Exposes ESV Error

****

King James Bible 2 Samuel 21:19	English Standard Bible 2 Sam. 21:19
And there was again a battle in Gob with the Philistines, **where Elhanan** the son of Jaareoregim, a Bethlehemite, **slew** *the brother of* **Goliath** the Gittite, the staff of whose spear was like a weaver's beam.	And there was again war with the Philistines at Gob, and **Elhanan** the son of Jaare-oregim, the Bethlehemite, **struck down** ___ _____ ___ **Goliath** the Gittite, the shaft of whose spear was like a weaver's beam.

❶ **Dr. Charles Ryrie sees an error in the Hebrew text:**

> "The Hebrew text attributes the slaying of Goliath to Elhanan, in contradiction of 1 Samuel 17:50…There is evidence of a copyist's error (cf. 1 Chr. 20:5), and it is probable that Elhanan killed 'the brother of' Goliath."

❷ **Here's an explanation of HOW and WHY the KJB translators added words *in italics* that capture the true meaning of the Hebrew from author David Jackson:**

> "In the text, immediately before the word Goliath, the small Hebrew word *'êṭ* is present.
>
> This is what is called an indicator of the accusative case, meaning the object of the verb 'slew.'
>
> **In English there is normally no need to translate it.**
>
> In Hebrew it would typically signify Goliath himself, but can also mean 'with'. This is how Jewish commentators understand it.
>
> **Elhanan slew the one who was 'with Goliath.'** And of course, 1Chronicles 20:5 says explicitly that he slew the brother of Goliath.
>
> **The KJV italics are not merely an inference; they are picking up the 'êṭ telling us Elhanan killed someone other than Goliath.**
>
> **There is no 'copyist error' involved."**

David Jackson

The truth about Dr. Ryrie's "copyist's error" and the ESV's slavish following of faulty scholarship has been hidden in plain sight in billions of KJB's for over 400 years.

Available from

WHICH BIBLE WOULD JESUS USE

Learn more, get the book: WHICH BIBLE WOULD JESUS USE? The Bible Version Controversy Explained and Resolved By Jack McElroy www.JackMcElroy.com

CHICK PUBLICATIONS

amazon

1. See: David Jackson, *The Hidden Wisdom of the King James Bible*, p.121; 2. *The Ryrie Study Bible Expanded Edition* p.520

128

ESV Teaches Roman Catholic Theology

Worshiping "The Real Presence," Christ in the Eucharist

****

King James Bible 1 Kings 7:48	English Standard Version 1Kngs 7:48
And Solomon made all the vessels that *pertained* unto the house of the LORD: the altar of gold, and the table of gold, whereupon the **shewbread** *was*,	So Solomon made all the vessels that were in the house of the LORD: the golden altar, the golden table for the **bread of the Presence,**

Stephen Beale, a freelance writer in Providence, RI, **who was raised as an evangelical Protestant and converted to Catholicism, says:**

"The Eucharist is among those 'concealed wonders and choice treasures' in the Old Testament..."

"In ancient Israel, the **Bread of the Presence** was set out on a golden table in the tabernacle as 'a memorial of the oblation of the Lord' (Leviticus 24:7). The bread was to be before the presence of God continually... **When the table that held the bread was carried out of the tabernacle, it was veiled.** In fact, when the tabernacle was moved, all the vessels in it were carefully wrapped. ... **Does not this all sound quite familiar?** Indeed, it's harder to imagine a more obvious precedent for the devotion and reverence with which Catholics of today treat the Eucharist."[1]

And they have the nerve to swear that Bible versions DON'T affect doctrine.

1. https://catholicexchange.com/nine-ways-the-eucharist-is-hidden-in-the-old-testament

Why Joseph Stalin Would "Prefer" ESV Over KJB

****

He murdered anywhere from 20—60 million men, women, and children during a brutal 30-year reign.

If he were to pick a Bible version, no doubt he'd choose the ESV over the KJB because it says what he needed to hear.

King James Bible Psalm 9:17	English Standard Version Ps. 9:17
The wicked shall be **turned into hell,** *and* all the nations that forget God.	The wicked shall **return to Sheol,** all the nations that forget God.

According to world-famous textual critic Bruce Metzger, the Hebrew, *Sheol* (שאול, Sh'ol) is the "abode of the dead," the "underworld," **"the common grave of humankind,"** or "pit."[1]

Good thing for Stalin the King James Bible wasn't translated accurately. Otherwise, he would have gone to **hell** instead of "common grave of humankind."

> The ESV's Sheol: No fear of God, no judgment, no hell, and no justice.

Did Stalin get away with genocide, or is the King James Bible right—again?

1 Metzger & Coogan (1993) *Oxford Companion to the Bible*, p. 277.

ESV Publishes Gross Error

$2+2=5$

****

King James Bible Psalm 10:4–5	English Standard Version Ps. 10:4–5
The wicked, through the pride of his countenance, will not seek after God: God is not in all his thoughts.	In the pride of his face **the wicked** does not seek him; all his thoughts are, "There is no God."
His ways are <u>always</u> <u>grievous</u>; thy judgments are far above out of his sight: as for all his enemies, he puffeth at them.	His ways <u>prosper</u> <u>at</u> <u>all</u> <u>times</u>; your judgments are on high, out of his sight; as for all his foes, he puffs at them.

Anyone; over the age of 30 has been around the block enough to know that the ways of the wicked DO NOT "PROSPER AT ALL TIMES."

How can Christian leaders, who know SO much, be SO wrong in their choice and recommendation of the defective ESV?

Available from

CHICK
PUBLICATIONS

amazon

nook

WHICH BIBLE WOULD JESUS USE?
The Bible Version Controversy Explained and Resolved
JACK McELROY

Learn more, get the book: WHICH BIBLE WOULD JESUS USE? The Bible Version Controversy Explained and Resolved By Jack McElroy
www.JackMcElroy.com

ESV Goes Harry Potter

****

King James Bible Prov. 17:8	English Standard Version Prov. 17:8
A **gift** *is as* a **precious stone** in the eyes of **him that hath it**: whithersoever it turneth, it prospereth.	A **bribe** is like a **magic stone** in the eyes of **the one who gives it**; wherever he turns he prospers.

❶ Gifts are not always bribes or evil. They can:
- **Win you friends. Prov. 19:6**
- **Bring you before great men. Prov. 18:16**
- **Pacify the anger of an adversary. Prov. 21:14**
- **In business, free gifts are offered as incentives to deals, subscriptions, etc.**

❷ The ESV limits the proverb to bribes, which are typically illegal or dishonest.

❸ However, the ESV also introduces the disturbing idea that an occult magic stone brings prosperity. The KJB intimates NO SUCH THING.

Does this sound like something your Lord would say?

The ESV...not all it's cracked up to be.

Learn more, get the book: WHICH BIBLE WOULD JESUS USE? The Bible Version Controversy Explained and Resolved By Jack McElroy
www.JackMcElroy.com

Available from

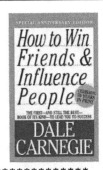

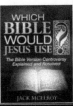

ESV Says Don't Kill Your Kid

****

King James Bible Proverbs 19:18	English Standard Version Prov. 19:18
Chasten thy son while there is hope, and **let not thy soul spare for his crying.**	Discipline your son, for there is hope; **do not set your heart on putting him to death.**

The same Hebrew word is translated differently here, teaching different things. Neither is wrong. **But the English text of Scripture must be established. Which one is it?**

The ESV's translation option was known to the KJB translators. They noted it in the margin of the 1611:

"for his crying. or, to his destruction, or, to cause him to die."

And it was translated similarly by Wycliffe in 1380:

"but sette thou not thi soule to the sleyng of hym."

However, that's NOT what they put in the text. But why? ...

Although the ESV reader is warned against vindictive chastisement it falls short of the KJB's **concise** "how-to" instruction that chastening should be both stern and in moderation (the KJB text says nothing about chastening in rage i.e., setting "your heart on putting him to death").

Which of the two instructions does the Lord want to appear in the English text of Proverbs 19:18? That's easy...

The one that's appeared in billions of KJBs over the past 400 years.

Available from

Learn more, get the book: WHICH BIBLE WOULD JESUS USE? The Bible Version Controversy Explained and Resolved By Jack McElroy www.JackMcElroy.com

ESV's Nonsensical Parenting Advice

****

King James Bible Proverbs 23:13–14
Withhold not correction from the child: for if thou beatest him with the rod, he shall not die. Thou shalt beat him with the rod, and shalt **deliver his soul from <u>hell</u>**.

English Standard Version Proverbs. 23:13–14
Do not withhold discipline from a child; if you strike him with a rod, he will not die. If you strike him with the rod, **you save his soul from <u>Sheol</u>**.

Textual critic Dr. Bruce Metzger (who assembled editions of the Greek NT text underlying almost all modern versions) says:

> In Hebrew, Sheol (שאול, Sh'ol) is the **"abode of the dead"** the **"underworld,"** **"the common grave of humankind"** or **"pit."**[1]

News Flash for Dr. Metzger: We're ALL headed for a hole in the ground.

If you discipline your children; will that save them from **"the common grave of humankind?"** Or will your correction hopefully save them from a life of sin, misery and finally hell?

What kind of "Bible" can't teach you how to deliver your child from hell?

Available from

Learn more, get the book: WHICH BIBLE WOULD JESUS USE? The Bible Version Controversy Explained and Resolved By Jack McElroy www.JackMcElroy.com

1. Metzger & Coogan (1993) *Oxford Companion to the Bible*, p 277. See: http://www.statemaster.com/encyclopedia/Sheol#_ref-oxford_0

KJB Proven Scientifically Accurate ... Once Again

* *

King James Bible Proverbs 30:28	English Standard Version Prov. 30:28
The spider taketh hold with her hands, and is in kings' palaces.	**the lizard** you can take in your hands, yet it is in kings' palaces.

Scholars are divided and say you can translate the Hebrew word both ways. **BUT ONLY ONE** of the above can be what God means to say.

Here are the facts...

	Spiders	Lizards
Population	**Over 50,000 species** http://www.spidersworlds.com/types-of-spiders/	**Over 6,000 species** https://en.wikipedia.org/wiki/Lizard
Smallest	**.01"** http://www.guinnessworldrecords.com/world-records/smallest-spider/	**.75"** http://animals.mom.me/five-smallest-lizards-world-2724.html

Estimates: Up to *1 million* spiders per acre of land on earth.

—https://www.ranker.com/list/10-amazing-things-about-spiders/analise.dubner

Survey: Of North Carolina homes: Spiders in 100% of them.

—Washington Post March 28, 2017

It's easy for kings to have a lizard-free palace. Not so with spiders. EVERYBODY has house spiders. NOT everybody has house lizards.

The empirical evidence shows the KJB to be scientifically true ... again.

Available from

Learn more, get the book: WHICH BIBLE WOULD JESUS USE? The Bible Version Controversy Explained and Resolved By Jack McElroy www.JackMcElroy.com

Ebenezer Scrooge "Prefers" ESV Over KJB

****

Ebenezer Scrooge

If Dickens' fictional character was to pick a Bible, no doubt he'd "prefer" the ESV over the KJB because it says what he wants to hear. Here's why...

He feared being forgotten:

"At one of these a lonely boy was reading near a feeble fire; and Scrooge sat down upon a form, and wept to see his poor forgotten self as he used to be."[1]

- The King James Bible delivers his worst nightmare.

- The ESV gives him what he wants. See for yourself...

King James Bible Ecclesiastes 8:10	English Standard Version Ecclesiastes 8:10
And so I saw **the wicked buried,** who had come and gone from the place of the holy, **and they <u>were</u> <u>forgotten</u>** in the city where they had so done: this is also vanity.	Then I saw **the wicked buried**. They used to go in and out of the holy place **and <u>were</u> <u>praised</u>** in the city where they had done such things. This also is vanity.

What do you think God really says about the wicked?

Available from

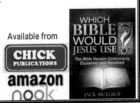

CHICK
PUBLICATIONS

amazon

nook

Learn more, get the book: WHICH BIBLE WOULD JESUS USE? The Bible Version Controversy Explained and Resolved By Jack McElroy www.JackMcElroy.com

1. http://www.open-bks.com/library/classics/dickens_charles_carol/carol-41-42.html

ESV Removes Your Lord's Ability to Think

Thoughts of

****

King James Bible Jeremiah 29:11	English Standard Version Jer. 29:11
For I know **the thoughts that I think** toward you, saith the LORD, thoughts of peace, and not of evil, to give you an expected end.	For I know **the plans I have** for you, declares the LORD, plans for welfare and not for evil, to give you a future and a hope.

❶ The KJB tells you that, like you, GOD THINKS (present tense).

❷ That means he can and does THINK new thoughts all the time.

❸ Team ESV advances its own agenda and erases your Lord's ability to THINK.

Your God is the Living and True God who is more dynamic and wonderful than the ESV's static God ever was.

ESV Historical Omission: Nixes Reference to Trade Shows

****

King James Bible Ezekiel 27:12
Tarshish was thy merchant by reason of the multitude of all kind of riches; with silver, iron, tin, and lead, they traded **in thy fairs**.

English Standard Version Ezekiel 27:12
"Tarshish did business with you because of your great wealth of every kind; silver, iron, tin, and lead they exchanged for your wares.

Ezekiel 27:14 King James Bible
They of the house of Togarmah traded **in thy fairs** with horses and horsemen and mules.

Ezekiel 27:14 English Standard Version
From Beth-togarmah they exchanged horses, war horses, and mules for your wares.

Ezekiel 27:16 King James Bible
Syria was thy merchant by reason of the multitude of the wares of thy making: they occupied **in thy fairs** with emeralds, purple, and broidered work, and fine linen, and coral, and agate.

Ezekiel 27:16 English Standard Version
Syria did business with you because of your abundant goods; they exchanged for your wares emeralds, purple, embroidered work, fine linen, coral, and ruby.

<u>Today</u>, the world's largest industrial fair is held every year in Hannover, Germany.[1]

<u>Back in the day</u>, the world's largest industrial fair was held every year in Tyrus. Tyrus is called a "mart of nations" in Isa. 23:3.

Just one more truth you can't find in the ESV.

Available from

Learn more, get the book: WHICH BIBLE WOULD JESUS USE? The Bible Version Controversy Explained and Resolved By Jack McElroy www.JackMcElroy.com

1.   https://www.exhibitionstand.contractors/en/news/21/HANNOVER-MESSE-2019-Hannover-Germany

ESV Excludes "Messiah" from Book of Daniel

G. Schirmer's Editions
of
Oratorios and Cantatas

THE MESSIAH
An Oratorio
For Four-Part Chorus of Mixed Voices,
Soprano, Alto, Tenor, and Bass Soli
and Piano
by
G. F. HANDEL

****

King James Bible Daniel 9:26
And after threescore and two weeks **shall Messiah be cut off, but not for himself:** and the people of the prince that shall come shall destroy the city and the sanctuary...

English Standard Version Daniel 9:26
And after the sixty-two weeks, **an anointed one** shall be cut off and **shall have nothing.** And the people of the prince who is to come shall destroy the city and the sanctuary...

❶ This is a translator's choice (same Hebrew word). However...

❷ ANY reader of Daniel 9:26 in the KJB sees plainly that the "Messiah" will die "but not for himself." He will die for his people.

❸ ANY reader of Daniel 9:26 in the ESV is left to figure out
(A) who or what "AN" anointed one is. And
(B) whoever this anointed one is, he/she/it "shall have nothing" (whatever that means).

What the ESV obscures, the King James Bible makes perfectly clear.

Available from

CHICK
PUBLICATIONS

amazon
nook

WHICH
BIBLE
WOULD
JESUS USE
The Bible Version Controversy
Explained and Resolved
JACK MCELROY

Learn more, get the book: WHICH BIBLE WOULD JESUS USE? The Bible Version Controversy Explained and Resolved By Jack McElroy
www.JackMcElroy.com

Fruitcakes or Booze; Which Did They Love?

King James Bible Hosea 3:1
... love a woman beloved of *her* friend, yet an adulteress, according to the love of the LORD toward the children of Israel, who look to other gods, and love **flagons of wine**.

English Standard Version Hosea 3:1
... love a woman who is loved by another man and is an adulteress, even as the LORD loves the children of Israel, though they turn to other gods and love **cakes of raisins**."

The Hebrew words **CAN** be translated as "flagons of wine" OR "cakes of raisins." **BUT ...**

Speaker & author Dr. Phil Stringer says:
❶ "Many words or phrases have more than one possible meaning. This is called *polysemy*. Hebrew, Greek, and English are polysemetic languages." [1]

❷ "The proper meaning is determined by 'context.'"
"Hosea 3:1 [in the ESV] is linguistically possible but it is a **nonsense translation**. Why? God condemns Israel for drunkenness in chapter 1, 2, 3, 4, and 5 of Hosea. **He is clearly doing the same in Hosea 3:1! But an anti-KJB bias makes some people willing to grasp at any possible translation as long as it is different from the KJB.**" [2]

❸ **Which is it**? Exactly what billions of KJBs have been saying for over 400 years—**flagons of wine**.

It's the ESV that's the fruitcake version here.

Learn more, get the book: WHICH BIBLE WOULD JESUS USE? The Bible Version Controversy Explained and Resolved By Jack McElroy www.JackMcElroy.com

Available from

CHICK PUBLICATIONS

amazon

nook

WHICH BIBLE WOULD JESUS USE?
The Bible Version Controversy Explained and Resolved

JACK MCELROY

H. D. Williams, M. D., Ph.D. *Word-for-Word Translating of The Received Texts* pp 149-150; 2. Ibid.

ESV Goes "Birther"... Challenges Jesus' Origin

WHERE'S THE BIRTH CERTIFICATE?

****

King James Bible Micah 5:2
But thou, Bethlehem Ephratah, *though* thou be little among the thousands of Judah, *yet* out of thee shall he come forth unto me *that is* to be ruler in Israel; whose goings forth *have been* from of old, **from everlasting**.

English Standard Version Micah 5:2
But you, O Bethlehem Ephrathah, who are too little to be among the clans of Judah, from you shall come forth for me one who is to be ruler in Israel, whose coming forth is from of old, **from ancient days**.

❶ Micah 5:2 is a reference to Jesus' **birth AND origin**.

❷ Ancient days is not even REMOTELY CLOSE to everlasting.

❸ The words "from everlasting" link the Lord Jesus Christ (via cross-reference) **to his position as God:**
> Before the mountains were brought forth, or ever thou hadst formed the earth and the world, even
> **from everlasting to everlasting, thou *art* God**. Psa. 90:2KJB

❹ Psalm 90:2 reads the same in the ESV, but they lost the cross-reference with their translation in Micah and worse, stripaway a proof of your Saviour's deity.

Questioning a politician's birth is one thing, but casting doubt on the origin of the Lord Jesus Christ is outrageous.

Learn more, get the book: WHICH BIBLE WOULD JESUS USE? The Bible Version Controversy Explained and Resolved
By Jack McElroy www.JackMcElroy.com

Available from

ESV Publishes Known Genealogy Error— Experts Blame God

****

King James Bible Matthew 1:10	English Standard Version Matt. 1:10
And Ezekias begat Manasses; and Manasses begat **Amon**; and Amon begat Josias;	and Hezekiah the father of Manasseh, and Manasseh the father of **Amos**, and Amos the father of Josiah,

❶ There is no one named "Amos" in the Lord's genealogy and all the experts know it. "Amos" is a <u>known</u> <u>error</u> for "Amon."

❷ They claim that the evangelist Matthew made the error by referring to some random genealogical lists instead of the Old Testament.

Here's proof...

404 error: File not found

❸ Dr. Roger L. Omanson, who worked as a translation consultant for United Bible Societies (publisher of the Greek NT underlying modern Bible versions) for nearly thirty years, wrote:

> "'**Amos**' is most likely the original reading. '**Amos**' is however, an error for '**Amon**,' the name of the King of Judah."[1]

> "According to Davies and Allison ... the name Amos 'may represent <u>a corruption</u> in **Matthew's** <u>source</u> or in the post Matthean textual tradition, **Or** <u>perhaps Matthew simply made an error</u>.'"[2]

Who'd use a Bible with errors? Surely not the Lord Jesus.

Available from

Learn more, get the book: WHICH BIBLE WOULD JESUS USE? The Bible Version Controversy Explained and Resolved By Jack McElroy www.JackMcElroy.com

CHICK
PUBLICATIONS

amazon
nook

1. Roger L. Omanson, *A Textual Guide to the Greek New Testament* (Stuttgart: German Bible Society, 2006), pgs. 1–2. 2. Ibid.

143

ESV Nullifies Your Saviour's Promise

****

King James Bible Matthew 5:22	English Standard Version Mat. 5:22
But I say unto you, That whosoever is angry with his brother **without a cause** shall be in danger of the judgment…	But I say to you that everyone who is angry with his brother _____ __ _____ will be liable to judgment…

The Lord made the exact some PROMISE three times:

Heaven and earth shall pass away, but my words shall not pass away. Matthew 24:35; Mark 13:31; Luke 21:33.

❶ The critics say Jesus NEVER said the words "without a cause" in Mat. 5:22 because they can't find them in their flawed and corrupt preferred manuscripts. They speculate that it is "much more likely that the word was added by copyists in order to soften Jesus extreme demand."[1]

❷ How odd. Because the "shorter text has the effect of forbidding anger, which would **contradict other Scriptures** (Ephesians 4:26, Psalms 4:4) and the Lord's own example (Mark 3:5)."[2] Moreover…

❸ "The Lord Jesus was angry on a few occasions (Mark 3:5), but he always had a cause. **When the phrases removed, the scholars are accusing Jesus Christ of sin.**"[3]

The ESV's excision of "without a cause" (which the Lord OBVIOUSLY said) makes the promise of God to preserve all his words of none effect.

Photo: Distant Shores Media/Sweet Publishing, CC BY-SA 3.0

1. Roger Omanson *A Textual Guide to the Greek New Testament* p. 6; 2. Wilbur Pickering; *Identity of the New Testament Text IV* p.332; 3. David Hoffman *The Common Man's Reference Bible*, p. 1408.

ESV Clueless on Demonic Hierarchy

****

King James Bible Matthew 17:21	English Standard Version Mat. 17:21
Howbeit **this kind** goeth not out but by **prayer** **and** **fasting**.	___ ___ ___ ___ ___ ___ ___ ___ ___ ___ ___

❶ These are the very <u>words</u> of the Lord Jesus Christ.
They don't appear in the ESV.

❷ They're missing because the ESV folks were taught that the Lord never wanted this verse in the Bible in the first place.
And they bought the head fake.

❸ <u>Yet</u> this verse teaches that **some devils are more powerful than others** and require more preparation to drive them out.

❹ Two things are required to deal with them: **<u>prayer</u> AND <u>fasting</u>**.

❺ **This missing truth** in the ESV has been in print for over 400 years in billions of King James Bibles.

When it comes to the solution to serious demonic possession...

The ESV shows up empty.

Available from

Learn more, get the book: WHICH BIBLE WOULD JESUS USE? The Bible Version Controversy Explained and Resolved By Jack McElroy
www.JackMcElroy.com

ESV Scientifically Inaccurate Again

****

King James Bible Matthew 14:30
But when **he saw the wind boisterous**, he was afraid; and beginning to sink, he cried, saying, Lord, save me.

English Standard Version Mat. 14:30
But when **he saw the wind** _____, he was afraid, and beginning to sink he cried out, "Lord, save me."

NO one ever "**sees**" the wind. You "**see**" **the result** of wind.

The experts are divided on this one because KNOW that the Greek word for "boisterous" could have been dropped from their "preferred" manuscript.

Plus, the KJB's reading is biblically consistent: The wind bloweth where it listeth, and thou hearest the sound thereof, but canst not tell whence it cometh, and whither it goeth: so is every one that is born of the Spirit. John 3:8 KJB

Modern version apologists will argue ...
"Yeah, but that's the way we speak today." So what?

Does anybody care about how GOD SPEAKS today?

Unlike the scholars, God doesn't speak foolishly nor does he make scientific mistakes.

Available from

Learn more, get the book: WHICH BIBLE WOULD JESUS USE? The Bible Version Controversy Explained and Resolved By Jack McElroy www.JackMcElroy.com

Embarrassing ESV Error Revealed

****

The ESV makes your Lord contradict himself in his conversation with the rich young ruler.

What follows are parallel passages:

	King James Bible	English Standard Version
Matthew 19:17	And he said unto him, **Why callest thou me good?**...	And he said to him, "**Why do you ask me about** what is good?...
Mark 10:18	And Jesus said unto him, **Why callest thou me good?**...	And Jesus said to him, "**Why do you call me good**
Luke 18:19	And Jesus said unto him, **Why callest thou me good?**...	And Jesus said to him, "**Why do you call me good?**...

Would the Lord use a Bible that contradicts itself?

<u>Yes</u>—if he uses the ESV.

<u>NO</u>—if he uses the King James Bible.

The Lord magnifies his word above all his name.

How could he possibly recommend the ESV?

Available from

Learn more, get the book: WHICH BIBLE WOULD
JESUS USE? The Bible Version Controversy
Explained and Resolved By Jack McElroy
www.JackMcElroy.com

Shock: ESV Staff Loses Bible Verse

⑬But woe ⁿto you, scribes and Pharisees, hypocrites! For you °shut the kingdom of heaven in people's faces. For you ᵖneither enter yourselves nor allow those who would enter to go in.²⑮Woe to you, scribes and Pharisees, hypocrites! For you travel across sea and land to make a single ᵠproselyte, and when he becomes a proselyte, you make him twice as much a ʳchild of ˢhell⁴ as yourselves.　　**Mat. 23 ESV Where is verse 14?**

On November 21, 1980, 350 million people around the world tuned in to television's popular primetime drama "Dallas" to find out <u>who shot J.R. Ewing</u>, the character fans loved to hate.[1]

Who Shot Matthew 23:14 in the ESV?

The scan above of Matthew 23 in the ESV Study Bible clearly shows something is terribly wrong. **What happened to verse 14?** How did the ESV staff lose verse 14; a misprint perhaps? We see verses 13 and 15 but NOT 14. Preschool kids know 14 follows 13.

But wait...

Although footnoted, the ESV creators don't think verse 14 is part of the written record, else it would be IN the text. **What's odd is that it IS recorded in the NASB, NKJV, HCSB, and the real Bible (KJB).** **BUT** If verse 14 shouldn't be there, why don't they just renumber the verses?

Wouldn't that be the HONEST thing to do?

Available from

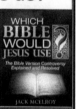

Learn more, get the book: WHICH BIBLE WOULD JESUS USE? The Bible Version Controversy Explained and Resolved By Jack McElroy
www.JackMcElroy.com

1.　http://www.history.com/this-day-in-history/millions-tune-in-to-find-out-who-shot-j-r

ESV Omits Another Historical FACT

****

King James Bible Matthew 27:24	English Standard Version Matthew 27:24
When Pilate saw that he could prevail nothing, but *that* rather a tumult was made, he took water, and washed *his* hands before the multitude, saying, I am innocent of the blood of this **just** person: see ye *to it*.	So when Pilate saw that he was gaining nothing, but rather that a riot was beginning, he took water and washed his hands before the crowd, saying, "I am innocent of this man's blood; see to it yourselves."

Jesus was innocent, guiltless, blameless, law-abiding, and "**just**." And Pilate knew it.

Pilate knew EXACTLY what he was saying and WHY (even if the ESV folks don't) and chose his words well. According to *Black's Law Dictionary*, "Just" means **"Right; in accordance with law and justice."**

Jesus was <u>just</u> and declared to be so by Imperial Rome's governor of the land. Plus, this narrative is found NOWHERE else in Scripture.

They'll say it's only one insignificant word and means nothing. But …

Is the FACT that Jesus was declared "Just" insignificant to the Lord?

1.   https://thelawdictionary.org/just/

149

ESV Scraps Fulfilled Prophecy in Matthew

* *

King James Bible Matthew 27:35	English Standard Version Mat. 27:35
And they crucified him, and parted his garments, casting lots: **that it might be fulfilled which was spoken by the prophet,** They parted my garments among them, and upon my vesture did they cast lots.	And when they had crucified him, they divided his garments among them by casting lots.

❶ Fulfilled prophecy is one of the greatest proofs of the authenticity of God's words.

❷ The ESV folks **were trained to believe** that the Lord **NEVER WANTED** this reference to fulfilled prophecy in the book of Matthew in the first place.

❸ They **were trained to believe** that some unknown men wantonly (and in violation of the Scripture) added these 25 words later on.

❹ They **were trained to believe** that these words the Lord has been using and blessing for over 400 years (and in multiple languages) to prove the authenticity of Scripture **AREN'T God's words, BUT men's.**

Sadly, with all their training, they were deprived a "Bible" education.

Available from

Learn more, get the book: WHICH BIBLE WOULD JESUS USE? The Bible Version Controversy Explained and Resolved By Jack McElroy www.JackMcElroy.com

ESV Strips Your Lord of His Power in Matthew 28

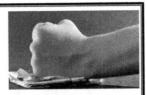

★★★

King James Bible Mat. 28:18
And Jesus came and spake unto them, saying, All **power** is given unto me in heaven and in earth.

English Standard Version Mat. 28:18
And Jesus came and said to them, "All **authority** in heaven and on earth has been given to me.

The Greek word ἐξουσία can be translated as "power" or "authority." **And the KJB translators did so elsewhere BUT NOT HERE**. Why? Because...

❶ Positions of authority are impotent, ineffective, and vulnerable if those that have it can't exercise it.

❷ Do you know what you need to exercise authority? **Power.**

❸ There's no question that Jesus has authority to do whatsoever he would. More importantly, **he was given the power to do so.**
A nuance you don't get in Matthew 28 from the ESV (or any of its cousins, including the NKJV.)

It's pretty clear which "version" the Lord has his hand on, isn't it?

Available from

Learn more, get the book: WHICH BIBLE WOULD JESUS USE? The Bible Version Controversy Explained and Resolved By Jack McElroy
www.jackmcelroy.com

ESV Inserts Known Citation Error in Bible

God Cares about Accuracy

✱✱

King James Bible Mark 1:2
As it is written in
the prophets,
Behold, I send my messenger
before thy face, which shall
prepare thy way before thee.

English Standard Version Mark 1:2
As it is written in
Isaiah the prophet,
"Behold, I send my messenger
before your face, who will
prepare your way,

❶ **The ESV creators KNOW that the citation is from Malachi and Isaiah** yet they allow their text to say: "As it is written in Isaiah the prophet."

❷ **Some textual experts believe Mark made a mistake in his original Autograph, others, that he loosely cited the OT reference.**[1] **These lame excuses are given to ignore 96%+ of existing Greek manuscripts without the citation error that say "prophets."**

❸ **The true, errorless reading is found the KJB.**
Here are the cross-references in Malachi and Isaiah:

As it is written in the prophets, **Behold, I send my messenger before thy face**, which shall prepare thy way before thee.
➤**Malachi 3:1 KJB**

The voice of him that crieth in the wilderness, **Prepare ye the way** of the LORD, make straight in the desert a highway for our God.
➤ **Isaiah 40:3 KJB**

If they willingly choose error over truth here, how can you be sure they haven't chosen other errors also?

Available from

Learn more, get the book: WHICH BIBLE WOULD JESUS USE? The Bible Version Controversy Explained and Resolved By Jack McElroy www.JackMcElroy.com

1.   See: Philip W. Comfort, *New Testament Text and Translation Commentary*, page 93.

ESV Geography Error Revealed

****

After our Lord and Savior healed Peter's mother-in-law he went about all **Galilee** preaching and teaching. **ALL** Bible versions **(including the ESV)** say that Jesus was in **Galilee.**

ESV Mark 1:39
"And he went throughout all **Galilee**, preaching in their synagogues and casting out demons."

Then, the ESV contradicts itself in the parallel passage in Luke by saying Jesus was in Judea about 70 miles south.

ESV Luke 4:44
"And he was preaching in the synagogues of **Judea**."

Of course, there is NO error in the King James Bible...

And he preached in their synagogues throughout all **Galilee**, and cast out devils." Mark 1:39 KJB

And he preached in the synagogues of **Galilee**." Luke 4:44 KJB

❶ The textual critics who created the ESV's underlying text believe Luke made the geography error in the original autograph which was later "fixed" by unknown, unnamed scribes from unknown places.[1]

❷ And the ESV folks just closed their eyes and trusted the genetically modified text provided to them by the textual critics.

The Lord Jesus Christ would NEVER use a Bible with a geography error in it.

Available from

1.   For details see: Philip W. Comfort, *New Testament Text and Translation Commentary*, page 180

ESV Makes Your Saviour Contradict Himself

	Mark 6:8	Luke 9:3	Matthew 10:10
KJB Instruction	**Take ONE staff** **Agrees**	**Take ONE staff** **Agrees**	**Take ONE staff** **Agrees**
King James Bible	And commanded them that they should take nothing for their journey, **save a staff only**…	And he said unto them, Take nothing for your journey, **neither staves**…	Nor scrip for your journey, neither two coats, neither shoes, **nor yet staves**…
ESV Instruction	**Take ONE staff** **Agrees**	**Take NO staff** **Disagrees**	**Take NO staff** **Disagrees**
ESV English Standard Version	He charged them to take nothing for their journey **except a staff**…	And he said to them, "Take nothing for your journey, **no staff**…"	no bag for your journey, nor two tunics nor sandals **nor a staff**…

Mark says that Jesus instructed his disciples to take **ONLY ONE staff**. The KJB and ESV **Agree**. But then…

The ESV makes Jesus contradict himself in Luke and Matthew by telling his disciples not to take ANY staffs.

The God of the ESV contradicts himself.
The God of the KJB doesn't.

Available from

ESV Claims It's Difficult to Get Saved

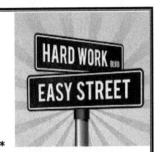

✱✱✱✱✱✱✱✱✱✱✱✱✱✱✱✱✱✱✱✱✱✱✱✱✱✱✱✱✱✱✱✱✱

King James Bible Mark 10:24	English Standard Version Mark 10:24
And the disciples were astonished at his words. But Jesus answereth again, and saith unto them, Children, **how hard is it** **for them that trust in riches** to enter into the kingdom of God!	And the disciples were amazed at his words. But Jesus said to them again, "Children, **how difficult it is** _____ _____ _____ _____ **to enter the kingdom of God!"**

The reason "**for them that trust in riches**" doesn't appear in the ESV is because its translators and editors believe the Lord **NEVER** wanted it to appear in Mark 10:24 in the first place—Even though **the Lord has had it appear** in King James Bibles billions of times over the past 400 years.

Trusting in riches is one thing, trusting Christ is another … and it's EASY.

In this passage, ESV is corrupting the doctrine of salvation by grace.

Available from

WHICH BIBLE WOULD JESUS USE
The Bible Version Controversy Explained and Resolved
JACK MCELROY

CHICK PUBLICATIONS

amazon
nook

Photo: https://www.tradingacademy.com/resources/financial-education-center/financial-images.aspx

ESV Ends Gospel of Mark in Defeat

****

The ESV folks were taught that Mark 16:9–20 is NOT authentic. And that verses 9–20 were **ADDED by random men AFTER it was written.**

They weren't TAUGHT that verses 9–20 are found in every extant:[1]
- Greek manuscripts—about 1,700 except three, and one of them (the infamous Sinaiticus) is a proven forgery at this point.
- Greek Lectionary—about 2,000 of them.
- Latin manuscript—about 8,000 of them except one.
- Syriac manuscript except one.
- Coptic manuscript except one.

The ESV's Gospel of Mark ends with "trembling," "astonishment," and fear:

> And they went out and fled from the tomb, for **trembling** and **astonishment** had seized them, and they said nothing to anyone, for they were **afraid**. Mark 16:8 ESV

Here's some of what the ESV folks think should be left out that you find (without dubious footnotes and brackets) in the KJB...

[9] Now when Jesus was risen early the first day of the week, he appeared first to Mary Magdalene...

[11] And they, when they had heard that he was alive...

[12] After that he appeared in another form unto two of them...

[14] Afterward he appeared unto the eleven... after he was risen.

[15] And he said unto them, Go ye into all the world, and preach the gospel to every creature.

[19] he was received up into heaven, and sat on the right hand of God.

[20] And they went forth, and preached every where...

Would your Lord leave his followers trembling, bewildered, and afraid? OR by following a few defective manuscripts...

Did the ESV surpress proofs of the Lord's resurrection, ascension, exaltation, and Great Commission?

Available from

Learn more, get the book: WHICH BIBLE WOULD JESUS USE? The Bible Version Controversy Explained and Resolved By Jack McElroy www.JackMcElroy.com

1. Wilbur N. Pickering, *Identity of the New Testament Text III*, p. 203.

Should You Go into all the World and Preach the Gospel?
ESV Advises Caution

"The Great Commission is not an option to be considered; it is a Command to be obeyed."
- Hudson Taylor

****

King James Bible Mark 16:15
And he said unto them, Go ye into all the world, and preach the gospel to every creature.

English Standard Version Mk 16:15
[[And he said to them, "Go into all the world and proclaim the gospel to the whole creation.]]

The ESV folks DON'T BELIEVE Jesus' instruction as recorded in the book of Mark is authentic.

They were taught that verses 9–20 were **ADDED by men** in violation of the Lord's command NOT to ADD TO or TAKE AWAY FROM his words, which means all 12 verses ARE NOT SCRIPTURE. So, they double brackets the verses and say this in an ESV Study Bible footnote:

"Some ancient manuscripts of Mark's Gospel contain these verses and others do not, **which presents a puzzle for scholars…**
Many think this shows to be a later addition.
In summary, vv. 9–20 should be read with caution… **And no point of doctrine is affected** by the absence or presence of vv. 9–20.)"[1]

❶ What they DON'T tell you in the footnote is that the verses are in…

- Every extant Greek manuscript—about 1,700 except three, and one of them (the infamous Sinaiticus) is a proven forgery at this point.
- Every extant Greek Lectionary—about 2,000 of them.
- Every extant Latin manuscript—about 8,000 of them except one.
- Every extant Syriac manuscript except one.
- Every extant Coptic manuscript except one.

❷ Nowhere else in Scripture does the Lord say to "Go into all the world, and preach the gospel." **Nobody gets saved without THE GOSPEL.**

❸ Why do critics and ESV folks insist on rejecting this passage? Because their agenda is to defend their darling "oldest and best" manuscripts at all costs.

❹ So are the last 12 verses of Mark authentic? **YES…**

They're just as authentic today as recorded on the pages of BILLIONS of King James Bibles as they were when first spoken by the Lord Jesus Christ almost 2,000 years ago.

Available from

WHICH BIBLE WOULD JESUS USE

CHICK PUBLICATIONS

amazon
nook

Learn more, get the book: WHICH BIBLE WOULD JESUS USE? The Bible Version Controversy Explained and Resolved By Jack McElroy www.JackMcElroy.com

1. *ESV Study Bible* (2008), Crossway p. 1933.

ESV Corrupts
Christmas Message

****

King James Bible Luke 2:14	English Standard Version Luke 2:14
Glory to God in the highest, and on earth peace, <u>good</u> <u>will</u> toward men.	"Glory to God in the highest, and on earth peace **among those with whom he is pleased!"**

❶ God expressed his "**good will**" by sending Jesus to redeem men from the curse of the law.

❷ God was pleased with the Lord Jesus Christ <u>alone</u>:
"This is my beloved son, in whom I am well pleased."

As for the rest...

❸ Didn't the Lord Jesus come because God was NOT pleased with men?

CHRIST IS OUR "PROPITIATION"
(TURNS AWAY WRATH)

❹ Doesn't the Scripture say **there is none good** but God only?

❺ Doesn't the Scripture say **there is none righteous**, no not one?

❻ Didn't Jesus come to call **sinners** to **repentance**?

❼ Didn't he come to **seek and save that which was lost**?

How could a "Bible" miss the real meaning of Christmas and be so theologically wrong?

Available from

Learn more, get the book: WHICH BIBLE WOULD JESUS USE? The Bible Version Controversy Explained and Resolved By Jack McElroy
www.JackMcElroy.com

CHICK PUBLICATIONS

amazon
nook

WHICH BIBLE WOULD JESUS USE?
The Bible Version Controversy Explained and Resolved
JACK McELROY

Illustration: Mrs. Paul (Kay) Friederichsen, *God's Will Made Clear*, p. 14.

ESV Error: Your Saviour Needed a Sin Offering

****

King James Bible Luke 2:22, 24	English Standard Version Luke 2:22
And when the days of **her** purification according to the law of Moses … And to offer a sacrifice according to that which is said in the law of the Lord, A pair of turtledoves, or two young pigeons	And when the time came for **their** purification according to the Law of Moses… and to offer a sacrifice according to what is said in the Law of the Lord, "a pair of turtledoves, or two young pigeons."

According to the law of Moses in Leviticus 12:6, the sacrifice and the purification were **for the WOMAN**:

> And when the days of **her purifying** are fulfilled, for a son, or for a daughter, she shall bring a lamb of the first year for a burnt offering, and a young pigeon, or a turtledove, **for a sin offering**, unto the door of the tabernacle… KJB

The ESV says the same, thereby contradicting itself:
> "And when the days of **her purifying** are completed, whether for a son or for a daughter… ESV

If your Saviour needed a sin offering (like it says in the ESV — i.e., "their"), then he couldn't be the PERFECT sacrifice for OUR SINS.

The ESV is the darling of many professional Christians...

But with all of its errors, you have to wonder WHY?

Available from

Learn more, get the book: WHICH BIBLE WOULD
JESUS USE? The Bible Version Controversy
Explained and Resolved By Jack McElroy
www.JackMcElroy.com

ESV Adds Two Fictitious Characters to Your Lord's Genealogy

****

King James Bible Luke 3:33	OT Ref.	English Standard Version Luke 3:33
Amminadab son of…	Ruth 4:19	Amminadab son of…
Aram [Ram] son of…	Ruth 4:19	
	No Reference	**Admin** son of…
	No Reference	**Arni** son of…
Esrom [Hezron] son of…	Gen 46:12	Hezron son of…
Phares son of…	Gen 46:12	Perez son of…
Juda	Gen 29:35	Judah

Admin and Arni do not appear in the Old Testament genealogy of Christ. The ESV followed the Greek text of the United Bible Societies (UBS). Textual expert and author of *Identity of the New Testament Text* Dr. Wilbur Pickering said:

"UBS has presented the evidence in their apparatus in such a way as to obscure the fact that **no Greek MS has the precise text they have printed** … In Metzger's presentation of the UBS Committee's reasoning in this case he writes, 'The Committee adopted what seems to be the least unsatisfactory form of text.'"

"Is this not a good candidate for 'chutzpah' of the year? The **UBS editors concoct their own reading** and proclaim it 'the least unsatisfactory'! And just what might be 'unsatisfactory' about the reading of 97% of the MSS except that it doesn't introduce any difficulties?"[1]

Jack McElroy   Will Kinney

At right is **Arni** Isaksson **"The Ice Viking"** Icelandic Welterweight. **He has no more a place in Christ's genealogy than the ESV's Arni.**

At left is my friend Will Kinney. He is **Admin** of FB page *King James Bible Debate*. **Brother Will has no more a place in Christ's genealogy than the ESV's Admin.**

The ESV; turning truth into a dime store novel.

Available from

1 http://www.walkinhiscommandments.com/Pickering/Miscellaneous/Luke%203%20revisited.r.pdf.

ESV Teaches You to Separate from Your Saviour, Contradicts Self

****

❶ The English Standard Version AND the King James Bible report that the Lord Jesus Christ **came to bring <u>division</u> in Luke**:

Luke 12:51 KJB	Luke 12:51 ESV
Suppose ye that I am come to give peace on earth? I tell you, Nay; but rather **<u>division</u>:**	Do you think that I have come to give peace on earth? No, I tell you, **but rather <u>division.</u>**

❷ **But in Titus, we see something entirely different from the ESV:**

Titus 3:10: KJB	Titus 3:10 ESV
A man that is **<u>an heretick</u>** after the first and second admonition reject;	As for a person who stirs up **<u>division</u>**, after warning him once and then twice, **<u>have nothing more to do with him</u>,**

❸ Someone who causes division **is not** the same as a heretic.

❹ The ESV then tells you to have nothing to do with a person who causes division, thereby contradicting itself:

Contrary to what we've been taught, **differences in translations DO matter. They matter A LOT.**

Should you separate from your Saviour? That depends on which Bible teaches the truth.

Learn more, get the book: WHICH BIBLE WOULD JESUS USE? The Bible Version Controversy Explained and Resolved By Jack McElroy www.JackMcElroy.com

Who Did Jesus Cast Out of the Temple?

****

<u>Testimonies need to be precise</u>. The KJB's Luke says the Lord cleaned house. But the ESV **omits this key fact** in Luke's testimony ...

King James Bible Luke 19:45	**English Standard Version Luke 19:45**
And he went into the temple, and began to cast out them that sold **therein, and them that bought**;	And he entered the temple and began to drive out those who sold _____ ___ ___ _____,

The experts claim that there was a conspiracy among born again Christian scribes to add the words to Luke's gospel. They claim that these scribes were guilty of "borrowing the words from Matthew 21:12 and Mark 11:15 to **fill out the sentence**."[1]

<u>Proof? None given.</u> The "scribes" have no names. Was it one man, a group or a cabal? They don't know. When did the "borrowing" occur? They don't know. Where did "they" do it? Unknown.

<u>Nonsense</u>. Luke gave the same testimony as Matthew and Mark. As billions of KJBs and almost all Greek NT manuscripts[2] testify. Nobody added anything to it.

So who did Jesus cast out of the temple? That depends on which Bible tells...

The whole truth and nothing but the truth. And God is watching.

Available from

Learn more, get the book: WHICH BIBLE WOULD JESUS USE? The Bible Version Controversy Explained and Resolved By Jack McElroy www.JackMcElroy.com

1 Philip W. Comfort, *New Testament Text and Translation Commentary*, page 225. 2. See:Wilbur Pickering, *The New Testament*, p. 35.

ESV Peddles A Strange Doctrine

****

King James Bible John 1:18	English Standard Version John 1:18
No man hath seen God <u>at **any** time</u>; the <u>**only** begotten</u> <u>Son</u>, which is in the bosom of the Father, he hath declared *him*.	No one has ever seen God; _ ____ ___ <u>the **only** God</u>, who is at the Father's side, he has made him known.

They tell us that modern Bible versions don't affect doctrine. But what strange doctrine is this...

❶ The ESV adopted a textual variant teaching that the Word (vs. 1) is "the <u>only</u> God" and this "<u>only</u> God" reveals to us "the Father."

❷ Anybody taking the ESV at face value would believe that "the Father" can't be God simply because the Word already is "the <u>only</u> God." <u>How</u> <u>strange</u>.

❸ Sadly, the translators of modern versions actually learned <u>sound</u> <u>doctrine</u> from the King James Bible before they started corrupting it in their new versions.

Evidently, much learning hath made them mad.

The ESV; weighed in the balance and found wanting.

Available from

Learn more, get the book: WHICH BIBLE WOULD JESUS USE? The Bible Version Controversy Explained and Resolved By Jack McElroy
www.JackMcElroy.com

amazon
nook

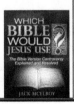

163

Another ESV Geography Error Exposed

★★★

King James Bible John 1:28	**English Standard Version Jn 1:28**
These things were done in **Bethabara** beyond Jordan, where John was baptizing.	These things took place in **Bethany** across the Jordan, where John was baptizing.

❶ **Bethany** (hometown of Mary, Martha, and Lazarus) was "nigh unto Jerusalem, about fifteen furlongs off:" (John 11:18) that's less than 2 miles from Jerusalem. **It's nowhere near the Jordan River, which is 21 miles away.**

❷ **Bethabara** was northeast of Jerusalem, near Jericho and Bethhogla (Joshua 15:6) and "beyond" Jordan.[1]

Textual critic Dr. Philip Comfort says: "But Origen [of Alexandria, c. 184–253], could not locate any 'Bethany' by the Jordan when he traveled to Palestine. However, there was a town called Bethabara in the vicinity, which, <u>according to local tradition</u>, was the site of John's baptism."[2]

❸ The locals gave Origen the straight skinny back then. And the plain truth is still available today to anyone with a KJB.

If the ESV can't get geography right, what else did they get wrong?

Available from

Learn more, get the book: WHICH BIBLE WOULD JESUS USE? The Bible Version Controversy Explained and Resolved By Jack McElroy www.JackMcElroy.com

1. https://biblebento.com/maps/BL213.html 2. Philip W. Comfort, New Testament Text and Translation Commentary, page 258.

ESV Dumps Omnipresence Doctrine in John 3:13

★★

John 3:13 King James Bible
And no man hath ascended up to heaven, but he that came down from heaven, *even* the Son of man **which is in heaven.**

John 3:13 English Standard Version
No one has ascended into heaven except he who descended from heaven, the Son of Man.

❶ These are the very words of the Lord Jesus Christ.

❷ He claims to be on the earth AND in heaven AT THE SAME TIME.

WHY is this missing in the ESV?

Because the ESV folks were TRAINED to believe that the Lord never wanted this part of the verse in the Bible in the first place.

Yet the Lord has had it in print for over 400 years in billions of King James Bibles.

Their mantra is that versions don't affect doctrine... but we all know better than that.

Learn more, get the book: WHICH BIBLE WOULD JESUS USE? The Bible Version Controversy Explained and Resolved By Jack McElroy
www.JackMcElroy.com

Available from

amazon

nook

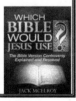

165

ESV Spams John 3:16

✱✱

King James Bible John 3:16
For God so loved the world, that he gave his **only begotten** Son, that whosoever believeth in him should not perish, but have everlasting life.

English Standard Version John 3:16
For God so loved the world, that he gave **his only** Son, that whoever believes in him should not perish but have eternal life.

The ESV says God gave his only son. And yet...

❶ Angels are called **"sons of God."** Job 38:7, Job 2:1

❷ If you're saved, you're not only a **"son"** of God but also **one of many "sons" of God.** "Beloved, now are **we the sons of God."** 1 John 3:2

❸ The Jesus of the ESV in John 3:16 is no different than you—

Just another son.

T he compound word they chose to half translate is **"monogenes"** – **"monos"** meaning **"only"** and **"genes"** meaning "to beget" or **"generate."** Taken together they mean **only begotten.**

Your lineage or generations go back to Adam.   **No big deal.**

The lineage (generation) of the Lord Jesus Christ is GOD.

That's a big deal.

Here's the doctrinal point...

1. There are lots of religious groups that teach that Jesus was nothing more than a mere man—**certainly NOT God in the flesh.**
2. If Jesus is no different from you, how could he ever save you?

Did the ESV creators make a mistake or are they just spamming you?

Available from

CHICK PUBLICATIONS

amazon
nook

WHICH **BIBLE** WOULD JESUS USE
The Bible Version Controversy Explained and Resolved
JACK McELROY

Learn more, get the book: WHICH BIBLE WOULD JESUS USE? The Bible Version Controversy Explained and Resolved By Jack McElroy www.JackMcElroy.com

Photo: https://www.flickr.com/photos/stevendepolo/3532199679 Attribution 2.0 Generic (CC BY 2.0)

ESV Modifies Gospel in John 3:36

****

King James Bible John 3:36	English Standard Version John 3:36
He that believeth on the Son hath everlasting life: and **he that believeth** not the Son shall not see life; but the wrath of God abideth on him.	Whoever believes in the Son has eternal life; **whoever does not obey** the Son shall not see life, but the wrath of God remains on him.

❶ **The option to translate the Greek word as "obey" was known to the KJB translators** (it was so translated in the Geneva Bible in 1560) and rejected. **But why?**

❷ **The ESV here presents a confusing form of salvation.** It's by faith in the first part but conditioned on works in the last part of the verse.

❸ **How much obedience is enough?** What if a believer DOESN'T ALWAYS obey? Is the wrath of God stayed when someone believes but lost when they disobey? **Which is correct?**

When it comes to translation choices, default to the book with a 400-year history of results and billions of copies in distribution.

Available from

Learn more, get the book: WHICH BIBLE WOULD
JESUS USE? The Bible Version Controversy
Explained and Resolved By Jack McElroy
www.JackMcElroy.com

CHICK
PUBLICATIONS

amazon
nook

WHICH
BIBLE
WOULD
JESUS USE?
The Bible Version Controversy Explained and Resolved

JACK MCELROY

ESV Strips Your Saviour of His Title

* *

King James Bible John 4:42
And said unto the woman, Now we believe, not because of thy saying: for we have heard him ourselves, and know that this is indeed **the Christ,** the Saviour of the world.

English Standard Version John 4:42
They said to the woman, "It is no longer because of what you said that we believe, for we have heard for ourselves, and we know that this is indeed ___ ___ the Savior of the world."

The ESV folks believe that the Lord NEVER WANTED the title "the Christ" to appear in John 4:42 in his Bible in the first place.

Yet his exalted title "the Christ" has been IN PRINT in John 4:42 for more than 400 years in billions of King James Bibles.

This is the ONLY place in scripture where common folks make this appellation, and you can't find it in the ESV.

There are lots of saviors in the world, but ONLY ONE Lord Jesus who is "the Christ."

Only an inferior quality "Bible" would strip your Saviour of his title in John 4:42.

Available from

Learn more, get the book: WHICH BIBLE WOULD JESUS USE? The Bible Version Controversy Explained and Resolved By Jack McElroy
www.JackMcElroy.com

Who "Fed" the 5,000?

****

King James Bible John 6:11	English Standard Version John 6:11
And Jesus took the loaves; and when he had given thanks, **he distributed to the disciples**, and the disciples to them that were set down; and likewise of the fishes as much as they would.	**Jesus then** took the loaves, and when he had given thanks, **he** _____ **distributed them** to those who were seated. So also the fish, as much as they wanted.

Everybody agrees that Jesus did the miracle to feed the 5,000 MEN. However, it's the HISTORICAL narrative we're concerned with here.

❶ The ESV says that Jesus personally distributed the food.

❷ The KJB says Jesus **distributed to the disciples** who then fed the crowd which may have been as high as 20,000 including women and children. Think, division of labor.

BOTH cannot be historically accurate. Which one is correct?

❸ The parallel passages (Matthew 14:19, Mark 6:41 and Luke 9:16) in **BOTH** Bibles say Jesus distributed **to his disciples FIRST** who then distributed the loaves and fishes to the people.
Which means, the ESV CONTRADICTS itself. And...

❹ The **LAME EXCUSE** speculated by the textual critics who created the ESV's underlying text is that John **OMITTED this critical part of the narrative** in his original autograph which was later "fixed" by unknown, unnamed scribes from unknown places ... **Sure thing.**

Does historical accuracy mean anything anymore?

Available from

Learn more, get the book: WHICH BIBLE WOULD JESUS USE? The Bible Version Controversy Explained and Resolved By Jack McElroy www.JackMcElroy.com

ESV Doctrinal Error in Book of John

****

King James Bible John 6:47	English Standard Version John 6:47
Verily, verily, I say unto you, He that **believeth <u>on me</u>** hath everlasting life.	Truly, truly, I say to you, **whoever believes** __ __ has eternal life.

❶ <u>The Jesus of the KJB is crystal clear</u>.
Only those who believe <u>**ON HIM**</u> have everlasting life.

❷ <u>The Jesus of the ESV</u> says "**WHOEVER BELIEVES**" **HAS** eternal life— **NOT** a true statement and **NOT** what God said in John 6:47.

❸ <u>The ESV corrupts the doctrine of salvation here.</u> Most folks **BELIEVE** in God: Deists, for example. Devils too (the devils also believe, and tremble. James 2:19).

Yet most folks, deists or devils, do not have eternal life.

This is just another reason why...

If Jesus came to your church, he wouldn't bring or use an ESV.

ESV Erases Jesus' Miracle Escape in John

King James Bible John 8:59
Then took they up stones to cast at him: but Jesus hid himself, and went out of the temple, **going through the midst of them, and so passed by.**

English Standard Version John 8:59
So they picked up stones to throw at him, but Jesus hid himself and went out of the temple. _____
_____ ___ _____ __ _____ ____
__ _____ __.

❶ The ESV and KJB both say Jesus "hid himself." And both recount this story in the book of Luke.

❷ Here, only the KJB explains HOW the Lord passed through the midst of the crowd without getting stoned—miraculously.

❸ Why did the ESV delete it here?
Textual critic Philip W. Comfort claims (and stop me if you've heard this one before):

> "Later scribes could not resist adding a little extra drama to the narrative, and so they borrowed from Luke 4:30..."[1]

Who were they? What were their names? When? Where did they live? Proof? None provided. Mere scholarly speculation.

❹ **This miracle appears twice in the KJB and once in the ESV.**

How can Christian leaders, who know SO much, be SO wrong in their choice and recommendation of the ESV?

Available from

1. Philip W. Comfort, *New Testament Text and Translation Commentary*, p. 292.

ESV Forgery in John 9:35

****

King James Bible John 9:35
Jesus heard that they had cast him out; and when he had found him, he said unto him, Dost thou believe on **the <u>Son</u> <u>of</u> <u>God</u>?**

English Standard Version John 9:35
Jesus heard that they had cast him out, and having found him he said, "Do you believe in **the Son of Man**?"

**<u>Question:</u> Who has the power to heal a man born blind...
THE SON OF <u>GOD</u> or THE SON OF <u>MAN</u>?**

- The Lord just healed a man that had been blind from birth.
- **"The Son of Man"** phrase is **NEVER USED** elsewhere in John as the object of the verb "believe."[1]
- Only the Lord Jesus Christ, **God in the flesh,** had the **power** to heal a man born blind.
- Jesus **SAID** he was **"the son of God"** and accepted **WORSHIP** from the man three verses later.

The King James Bible's "Son of God" is authentic.

The ESV's "Son of Man" is a forgery.

Available from

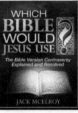

Learn more, get the book: WHICH BIBLE WOULD JESUS USE? The Bible Version Controversy Explained and Resolved By Jack McElroy
www.JackMcElroy.com

1.Philip W. Comfort, *New Testament Text and Translation Commentary*, p. 293.

Was Caiaphas a Co-Conspirator?

****

King James Bible John 11:50	English Standard Version John 11:50
Nor consider that it is expedient **for us**, that one man should die for the people, and that the whole nation perish not.	Nor do you understand that it is better **for you** that one man should die for the people, not that the whole nation should perish."

Historical testimonies matter. Especially since this is a prophecy.

Author and textual critic, Dr. Philip W. Comfort asserts:

"It seems odd that Caiaphas, the high priest, would address the Sanhedrin as if he were an outsider telling them, 'it is better for you **[instead of "us"]** that one man should die.' This reading, therefore **was changed** by substituting *us* for *you* or dropping the pronoun completely."[1]

Changed? By who, you ask? No answer. When? No answer. He further opines: "Caiaphas was an outsider, for he had been appointed by the Romans to be the high priest and therefore was considered by many Jews not to be the true high priest."[2]

Nonsense. Caiaphas was no outsider. He was the High Priest and son-in-law of former High Priest, Annas. He was an integral part of the whole conspiracy and plot to frame the Lord from the get-go. **What he was "considered" by "many Jews" is mere speculation.**

What did Caiaphas really say? That depends on which Bible REPORTS the whole truth and nothing but the truth.

Available from

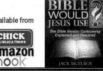

Learn more, get the book: WHICH BIBLE WOULD JESUS USE? The Bible Version Controversy Explained and Resolved By Jack McElroy www.JackMcElroy.com

1.   Philip W. Comfort, *New Testament Text and Translation Commentary*, p. 301. 2. Ibid.

ESV Deadens Proof of Your Lord's Resurrection

****

King James Bible Acts 1:3	English Standard Version Acts 1:3
To whom also he shewed himself alive after his passion **by many <u>infallible</u> proofs**, being seen of them forty days...	He presented himself alive to them after his suffering **by many_____ proofs**, appearing to them during forty days...

<u>Infallible means</u> incapable of making mistakes or being wrong. Synonyms include perfect, impeccable, precise, accurate, unfailing, and unerring.

No margin of error

<u>Infallible means</u> the proofs of your Lord's resurrection are dependable, trustworthy, reliable, sure, and certain.

The ESV's choice to present the text <u>without</u> the word "infallible" is clearly defective and deficient.

But it does follow the wording of the corrupt Revised Standard Version from which the ESV came.

Learn more, get the book: WHICH BIBLE WOULD JESUS USE? The Bible Version Controversy Explained and Resolved By Jack McElroy www.JackMcElroy.com

Available from

CHICK PUBLICATIONS

amazon

nook

WHICH BIBLE WOULD JESUS USE? The Bible Version Controversy Explained and Resolved

JACK MCELROY

ESV Doctrinal Error on Baptism Exposed

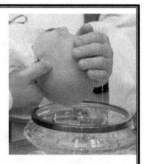

Is There a Bible Verse That Specifically Excludes Infant Baptism?

****

There is...IF you believe ...
King James Bible Acts 8:37
And Philip said, **If thou believest with all thine heart**, thou mayest. And he answered and said, **I believe** that Jesus Christ is the Son of God.

There Is not ... IF you believe ...
English Standard Version Acts 8:37
— — — — — — — — — —
— — — — — — — ——— — —
— — — — —— — — —— — —
— — — — — —.

❶ The staff of the ESV was taught that God never wanted Acts 8:37 in his Bible in the first place. Which is odd because...

❷ This is the **ONLY** time in the entire Bible where a personal confession of faith is a prerequisite for Baptism.

❸ The King James Bible **CLEARLY teaches** that you must personally **BELIEVE** on the Lord Jesus Christ **FIRST**.

❹ This is a big doctrinal problem and an error of omission in the ESV.

So can you baptize babies? **That all depends on WHICH Bible is true.**

They say Bible translations don't affect ANY cardinal doctrines of the faith...

Whose faith are they talking about?

Learn more, get the book: WHICH BIBLE WOULD JESUS USE? The Bible Version Controversy Explained and Resolved By Jack McElroy
www.JackMcElroy.com

Available from

amazon
nook

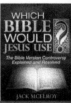

Why Every Version Must Compare Itself to the King James Bible

****

Here are a couple of screenshots of searches of Acts 8:37 in the NIV and ESV...

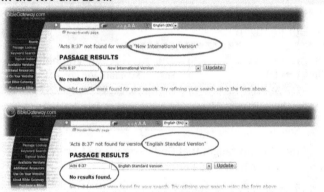

The NIV and ESV remove Acts 8:37 (and many other verses) because the creators were taught God **NEVER** wanted it in his Bible. But ...

❶ They'll **NEVER** renumber the remaining verses, mainly because the verses have appeared in the KJB (the most famous and most believed Bible on Earth) for over 400 years. And ...

❷ If they renumbered all the verses of the Bible (which would be the HONEST thing to do), then EVERYBODY would notice and would soon recognize these versions for what they really are ...

Nothing but cheap, defective knockoffs

Available from

Learn more, get the book: WHICH BIBLE WOULD JESUS USE? The Bible Version Controversy Explained and Resolved By Jack McElroy www.JackMcElroy.com

ESV Introduces You to Holy Mother Church

****

King James Bible Acts 9:31	English Standard Version Acts 9:31
Then had **the churches** rest throughout all Judaea and Galilee and Samaria, and were edified…	So **the church__** throughout all Judea and Galilee and Samaria had peace and was being built up.

❶ Some may say this is trivial. It isn't. Sometimes, singular and plural distinctions ARE critical, as shown here.

❷ The ESV staff was **trained** to think that "**churches**" is a corruption. It isn't. It's the truth. They know (or should know) that it sets a precedent for **one universal church**.

❸ Roman Catholics are taught that "**the Church**" is a dispenser of grace through the sacramental system.

❹ Every Catholic kid is (or used to be) taught "the Nicene Creed."[1] It includes this:

> "We believe in one holy catholic and apostolic Church."[1]

❺ The creators of the ESV's underlying Greek text included **Roman Catholic Jesuit Cardinal Carlo Martini.**

The goal of the Church **(although most fundamentalists and evangelicals are too blind to see it)** has always been to reincorporate "the separated brethren." The ESV is little more than a tool toward that end.

Available from

WHICH BIBLE WOULD JESUS USE?
The Bible Version Controversy
Explained and Resolved

CHICK
PUBLICATIONS

amazon

nook

Learn more, get the book: WHICH BIBLE WOULD JESUS USE? The Bible Version Controversy Explained and Resolved By Jack McElroy www.JackMcElroy.com

JACK MCELROY

http://www.vatican.va/archive/ccc_css/archive/catechism/credo.htm

What Did Paul & Barnabas Really Say at Lystra?

****

King James Bible Acts 14:15
… We also are men of like passions with you, and preach unto you that ye should turn from these vanities unto (the) living God, which made heaven, and earth …

English Standard Version Acts 14:15
"… We also are men, of like nature with you, and we bring you good news, that you should turn from these vain things to (a) living God, who made the heaven and the earth …

At issue: "How does God want his word to appear in English?"

❶ They'll argue that "the" or "a" mean the same thing. **Nonsense.**

❷ **"The" is a definite article.** "'The' is the one and only *definite article* in English, which means that it refers to, or introduces, a particular, specific noun."[1] Here it's specifically referring to THE LIVING GOD. The accurate "original Greek" underlying the KJB not only HAS the Greek definite article, **but has it twice for added emphasis**. It literally says "unto THE God THE living."

❸ **"A" is an indefinite article.** Which "refer[s] to, or introduce[s], an **unspecified noun … when we're not referring to a particular person**, place, thing or idea…"[2] Since there is no indefinite article ("a" or "an") in Greek AND the defective Greek text behind the ESV has NO definite article, the ESV folks added it (as all translators do) for their translation to make sense. BUT look at the result …

Since when did your Lord turn into an "unspecified" person? How degrading.

1. https://study.com/academy/lesson/indefinite-and-definite-articles-definition-and-examples.html; 2. Ibid

ESV Creators...
Willingly Ignorant

****

King James Bible Acts 17:26	English Standard Version Acts 17:26
And hath made **of one blood** all nations of men for to dwell on all the face of the earth...	And he made **from one man** every nation of mankind to live on all the face of the earth...

Philip W. Comfort, senior editor of Bible reference at Tyndale House Publishers and editor for the New Living Translation says:

> "The one substance from which God made all people **was not named by Paul**...Various modern translators have supplied 'man' (NLT, HSCB and NET) ..."[1]

Nonsense. The substance was "blood." It's clearly stated in the KJB and over 95% of all extant Greek NT manuscripts (but who's counting?).

More importantly, their own Greek text says "he made from one _____." **From (or of) one what? They don't know.** So they made up the word "man" and inserted it into the text. And P.S., they didn't even put it in italics so you'd know it was added.

<u>The truth was staring at them</u> not only on the pages of the KJB but also in every other Reformation-era Bible. But they're willingly ignorant of the truth because...

Sadly, they've been trained to believe in a text with a fabricated history and proven error.

Available from

Learn more, get the book: WHICH BIBLE WOULD JESUS USE? The Bible Version Controversy Explained and Resolved By Jack McElroy
www.JackMcElroy.com

CHICK
PUBLICATIONS

amazon

nook

1. Philip W. Comfort, *New Testament Text and Translation Commentary*, p. 403.

ESV Confuses Work of the Spirit with Light

****

King James Bible Ephesians 5:9 (For **the fruit of the <u>Spirit</u>** *is* in all goodness and righteousness and truth;)	English Standard Version Eph. 5:9 (for **the fruit of the <u>light</u>** is found in all that is good and right and true)

❶ The Holy Spirit is alive. He can and <u>does</u> produce fruit in the life of the believer.

❷ Light isn't alive. It illuminates, but it <u>can't</u> produce fruit in the life of the believer.

❸ The reading of "light" isn't new; it was available to the King James translators (in the Roman Catholic Douay-Rheims Bible 1582-1610)—but they soundly rejected it.

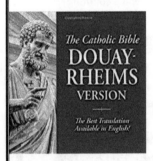

"For **the fruit of the light** is in all goodness, and justice, and truth;"
Douay-Rheims Bible Eph. 5:9

The ESV's latest and greatest scholarship is just a rerun of an old Roman Catholic Bible.

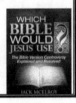

ESV's Jesus Drops the Ball

✱✱✱✱✱✱✱✱✱✱✱✱✱✱✱✱✱✱✱✱✱✱✱✱✱✱✱✱✱✱✱✱✱

King James Bible Philippians 2:6	English Standard Version Phil. 2:6
Who, being in the form of God, thought it not robbery **to be equal with God**:	who, though he was in the form of God, did not count equality with God **a thing to be grasped**,

The KJB plainly says: that Jesus (a) **is** (i.e., "being") in the form of God, and (b) he **is** equal with God.

The ESV cryptically says: Jesus (a) **"was"** in the form of God (did he lose his deity when he became man?), and (b) that equality with God was **NOT** a thing to be grasped. Was/is he equal with God or not?

You'd have thought the ESV's Jesus would **WANT** to "**grasp**" equality with God since that's what he is (a truth made clear in the KJB). **But no, we get confusion instead.**

The experts admit...

> "**The precise meaning of the enigmatic term** ἁρπαγμός [rendered 'a thing to be grasped'] in Phil 2:6 is a question that has been the subject of much debate in New Testament studies."[1]

They continue to debate what the KJB has made clear for over 400 years. Sad.

1. https://bible.org/article/meaning-philippians-26-overlooked-datum-functional-inequality-within-godhead

181

Memory Verse or Mantra? ESV Sings Different Tune

****

King James Bible Philippians 4:13	English Standard Version Phil. 4:13
I can do all things	I can do all things
through Christ	**through him**
which strengtheneth me.	who strengthens me.

The true Scripture sets your heart on the ONLY one who has the POWER to strengthen you.

The KJB identifies him as CHRIST.

The ESV never identifies WHO strengthens you, only referring to "him" (although they'll say everyone "knows" its Jesus).

Can the ESV rightly be called "Scripture"?

Christian educators and leaders have dumped the tried and proven standard English Bible replacing it with confusing and contradictory versions thereby changing a powerful Scripture meditation into an empty mantra.

How sad.

Available from

Learn more, get the book: WHICH BIBLE WOULD JESUS USE? The Bible Version Controversy Explained and Resolved By Jack McElroy
www.JackMcElroy.com

Chopped!
ESV Cuts
the Blood from
Colossians 1:14

****

King James Bible Col. 1:14	English Standard Version Col. 1:14
In whom we have redemption **through his blood,** even the forgiveness of sins:	in whom we have redemption, ___ ___ ___ the forgiveness of sins.

HOW and WHY Colossians 1:14 got chopped…

❶ After the NT was completed, the true text was corrupted by the elimination these important words (by mistake or on purpose).

❷ The corrupted reading found its way into a number of manuscripts **that were ignored by believers as false**.

❸ The corruption was revived in the 19th century and has been "**preferred**" by the new versions ever since 1881. **WHY?**

❹ One of the **arbitrary** rules of modern textual criticism is that the "**shorter reading (*Lectio brevior*) is to be preferred.**"[1] The creators of the ESV followed the rule here and eliminated the **shed blood of your Saviour in Colossians 1:14**.

Do you think the Lord "<u>prefers</u>" his blood be chopped out of the verse?

1. Canons of textual criticism, http://www.skypoint.com/members/waltzmn/CanonsOfCrit.html

Textual Critics Say There Are Two Kinds of Greek Textual Variants, Longer and Shorter

****

(The longer text)	(The shorter text)
King James Bible Col. 1:14 In whom we have redemption **through his blood**, even the forgiveness of sins:	**English Standard Version Col. 1:14** In whom we have redemption, _____ ____ _____ the forgiveness of sins.

❶ **Doctrine Affected:** Forgiveness of sins through the shed blood of the Lord Jesus Christ; without it, we have neither redemption nor forgiveness.

❷ They could have chosen manuscripts that **do include** his precious blood in this verse, **but they didn't**.

❸ The **ESV** creators **chose** to follow manuscripts that **eliminated** the precious blood of the Lord Jesus Christ from this verse because:

❹ Textual critics arbitrarily teach that shorter readings are "original."

❺ The blood of Christ is mentioned in verse 20 so Paul never would have said it in verse 14. So, it's redundant.

Here's what they missed:

Since the blood of Christ is so important, why wouldn't your Lord REPEAT himself for emphasis like he does SO OFTEN in other Scriptures?

Moreover, since he is the author...

Why would the Holy Ghost shorten this critical declaration?

Learn more, get the book: WHICH BIBLE WOULD JESUS USE? The Bible Version Controversy Explained and Resolved By Jack McElroy www.JackMcElroy.com

Available from

184

ESV Transgenderism

Was Nymphas a man or a woman?

That all depends on…

WHICH Bible reports the TRUTH.

****

King James Bible Colossians 4:15	English Standard Version Col. 4:15
Salute the brethren which are in Laodicea, and Nymphas, and the church which is in **his** house.	Give my greetings to the brothers at Laodicea, and to Nympha and the church in **her** house.

Billions of King James Bibles and over 99% of all extant Greek manuscripts (but who's counting) say "**he**" was a **man**.

The ESV, following Modern Greek New Testament critical speculation, says no…
he was a **woman**.

Knowing what HE knows…

Do you really think your Lord would leave Nymphas' gender to speculation?

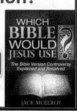

Was <u>God</u> Manifest in the Flesh or Not?

****

King James Bible 1 Tim 3:16	English Standard Version 1 Tim. 3:16
And without controversy great is the mystery of godliness: **God was manifest in the flesh...,**	Great indeed, we confess, is the mystery of godliness: **He** was manifested in the flesh...".

❶ **The King James Bible reading is doctrinal proof of the incarnation** (that your Saviour is God who took on flesh as a man). **And yet...**

❷ The ESV creators believe the Lord **NEVER** wanted the word **"God"** to appear in the Bible in 1 Tim. 3:16 but instead wrote the cryptic word **"He."**

❸ They were taught that orthodox Christians (like you) CORRUPTED the Scripture by substituting the word "God" for "He." **And yet...**

If the Lord has the word **"God"** appear on the pages of the KJB and in other Reformation era Bibles for over 400 years, **then** the Lord has made and continues to make a monumental error by allowing this "corruption" to be printed literally billions of times. **Or...**

The ESV creators are overthrowing the TRUTH as presented by the KJB (and all Reformation Bibles) for hundreds of years.

In so doing, they present an incompetent God who can't make up his mind about what he wants his Bible to say.

Truly disgusting.

Available from

Learn more, get the book: WHICH BIBLE WOULD JESUS USE? The Bible Version Controversy Explained and Resolved By Jack McElroy
www.JackMcElroy.com

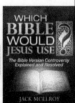

ESV's "Writer" Omits Words of Psalm 8:6 in Hebrews

****

King James Bible Hebrews 2:7
Thou madest him a little lower than the angels; thou crownedst him with glory and honour, **and didst set him over the works of thy hands:**

English Standard Version Heb. 2:7
You made him for a little while lower than the angels; you have crowned him with glory and honor, ___ ____ __ __ ___ __ ___ __ __ ____

The KJB's Paul quoted ALL of Psalm 8:6 in Hebrews 2:7:
Thou madest him to have dominion <u>over the works of thy hands;</u>...Psalm 8:6 KJB

The ESV's "writer"[1] (they're not sure if it was Paul) quoted only PART of Psalm 8:6 in Hebrews 2:7 even though he had it:
You have given him dominion <u>over the works of your hands;</u> Psalm 8:6 ESV

The Conclusion:

The Apostle Paul of the King James Bible and the "writer" of Hebrews in the ESV must be TWO DIFFERENT MEN **because they** SAY DIFFERENT THINGS.

Only the TRUE Bible contains ALL of God's holy words.

Available from

Learn more, get the book: WHICH BIBLE WOULD JESUS USE? The Bible Version Controversy Explained and Resolved By Jack McElroy
www.JackMcElroy.com

1.   See Philip W. Comfort, *New Testament Text and Translation Commentary*, p. 696-7.

ESV Contradicts Self

****

King James Bible Heb 9:3-4
And after the second veil, the tabernacle which is called **the Holiest of all; Which had the golden censer, and the ark of the covenant** overlaid round about with gold...

English Standard Version Hebrews 9:3-4
Behind the second curtain was a second section called **the Most Holy Place, having the golden altar of incense and the ark of the covenant** covered on all sides with gold...

In Exodus 30:6, the ESV (correctly) puts **the altar of incense "in front of the veil"** leading to the Holy of Holies.

Sadly, in Hebrews 9, the ESV (incorrectly) puts it in the Holy Place— i.e., the Holy of Holies; **thereby contradicting their own Bible.**

Holy of Holies | Holy Place

Ark of Covenant | Altar of Incense | Menorah | Table of Shewbread | Veil | Door

Want to avoid the ESV confusion?
KJB (correctly) places the altar of incense in front of the holy of holies in Exodus 30.

In Hebrews 9 it is the **golden censer** (used on the day of atonement Lev. 16:12) that was stored **behind the veil and IN the Holy of Holies.**

The ESV scholarly?
Bah.

Can You Grow Up into Salvation?

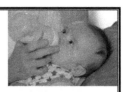

****

King James Version 1 Peter 2:2
As newborn babes, desire the sincere milk of **the word**, that ye may **grow** _ _ _ _____ thereby.

English Standard Version 1 Peter 2:2
Like newborn infants, long for the pure spiritual milk, ___ ____ that by it you may **grow up into salvation**—

First of all, what happened to "the word" being the agent of growth?

Textual critic, Philip W. Comfort claims that the KJB reading came about because **"scribes must have"** deleted the phrase "grow into salvation" because the "oldest and best" manuscripts contain it:

> "At some point in the history of the text, scribes **must have** found it **difficult to conceive** of how one could 'grow into salvation,' because salvation **is normally considered** as an initial gift accompanying regeneration…"[1]

Who did it? He doesn't say. When? He doesn't know. But the story fits their narrative.

Why isn't the phrase in the KJB?

❶ Peter is writing to "born again" believers who need to grow, **BUT NOT "into salvation."** How is it even possible?

❷ **The phrase was known to KJB translators and rejected.** Not surprisingly, the ESV reads close to the works-based righteousness promoting Roman Catholic Douay-Rheims Bible:

> As newborn babes, desire the rational milk without guile, that thereby **you may grow <u>unto salvation</u>**: Douay-Rheims 1 Peter 2:2

❸ All evangelicals (including the creators of the ESV), know salvation is a free gift obtained **in a moment of time** and NOT something that's **earned over time.** Yet …

❹ They'll make an argument for it because 65% of Greek manuscripts include the phrase, **even though doctrinally erroneous on its face.**

The ESV; confusing Bible studies since 2001.

Available from

Learn more, get the book: WHICH BIBLE WOULD JESUS USE? The Bible Version Controversy Explained and Resolved By Jack McElroy www.JackMcElroy.com

1.   Philip W. Comfort, *New Testament Text and Translation Commentary*, p. 739.

ESV Reduces Your Lord to Wishing

****

King James Bible 2 Peter 3:9

The Lord is not slack concerning his promise, as some men count slackness; but is longsuffering to us-ward, **not willing** that any should perish, but that all should come to repentance.

English Standard Version 2 Peter 3:9

The Lord is not slow to fulfill his promise as some count slowness, but is patient toward you, **not wishing** that any should perish, but that all should reach repentance.

❶ **Men wish.**

❷ **God wills.**

❸ **Does the Lord need to throw pixie dust and wish upon a star to get what he wants?**

How demeaning.

Do we serve a wishy-washy God, or is the ESV a wishy-washy Bible?

Available from

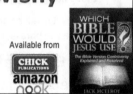

Learn more, get the book: WHICH BIBLE WOULD JESUS USE? The Bible Version Controversy Explained and Resolved By Jack McElroy www.JackMcElroy.com

Photo: https://www.flickr.com/photos/jessicatam/4177468736 jessicahtam Attribution 4.0 International (CC BY 4.0)

What They Don't Tell You About 1 John 5:7-8

****

King James Bible 1 John 5:7-8

[7] For there are three that bear record in heaven, **the Father, the Word, and the Holy Ghost: and these three are one.**
[8] **And there are three that bear witness in earth,** the Spirit, and the water, and the blood: and these three agree **in one.**

English Standard Version 1 John 5:7-8

[7] For there are three that testify ___

_____ ___ ___ ___ ___ ___
_____ ___ ___ ___ ___ ___
___.

[8] _____ ___ ___ ___ ___ ___
_____ ___ _____ the Spirit and the water and the blood; and these three agree ___ ___

These verses present a clear picture of a single Godhead made up of three that are one—i.e., **"three ARE one,"** commonly known as "The Trinity." It's also an important witness to the deity of the Lord Jesus Christ.

And yet the experts say it's NOT authentic because there isn't enough Greek manuscript support for the passage.

The UBS 4 Greek NT lists 8 manuscripts (out of about 500) that contain the passage, four in the text [61 (16th c), 629 (14th c), 2318 (18th c), 918 (16th c)], and four in the margin [88 (16th c), 221 (15–16th c), 429 (16th c), 636 (16th c)]. **True enough**.

<u>But what they mostly DON'T tell</u> you is that New Testament Greek AND other language manuscripts are commonly referred to as **"witnesses"** to the text; the Latin being especially important. The Reformation-era translators knew this when they assembled the traditional text for printing.

In a trial, shouldn't you consider the testimony from ALL the witnesses? (Note the language above: "bear witness" [KJB]; "testify" [ESV]. Let's hear what the other witnesses have to say...

Bible Version Secrets Exposed

❶ It is estimated that 95% of the Vulgate manuscripts containing 1 John (over 1,000) contain the verse.

❷ Well known early Christian writers and Councils (Carthage and Lateran) cited the passage. Here are citations proving that the passage existed, was believed authentic, was used widely **and not a medieval forgery**:

200 AD	**Tertullian** wrote: "which three are one."
Circa 250 AD	**Cyprian** of Carthage, a 3rd-century Church leader, wrote, **"And again, of the Father, Son, and Holy Spirit it is written: 'And the three are One.'"** The Cyprian citation refutes the theory of a 4th century interpolation against the Arians and dates to more than a century before any extant Epistle of John manuscripts.
350 AD	**Athanasius the Great**, 20th bishop of Alexandria, referred to it in the disputation with Arius and alluded to the verse in the *Synopsis of Scripture:* "John says, **And the three are one.**"
380 AD	**Priscillian** of Avila, Spain said. "As John says and **there are three which give testimony on earth the water the flesh the blood and these three are in one and there are three which give testimony in heaven the Father the Word and the Spirit and these three are one in Christ Jesus**"
484 AD	**Council of Carthage** appealed to it when debating the Arian belief (Arians didn't believe in the deity of Jesus Christ). **The Council was attended by hundreds of Bishops.** Their Confession of Faith included this: "here is proof from the testimony of John the evangelist. For he says: **There are three who bear witness in heaven, the Father, the Word and the Holy Spirit, and these three are one.**"
6th century	**Fulgentius** of Ruspe (468–533) a church father in North Africa used the verse in the doctrinal battles. "For St. John the apostle, testifieth saying, **There are three that bear witness in heaven, the Father, the Word, and the Spirit, and these three are one.**"

ESV Section

❸ **1 John 5:7 is found in** manuscripts used by believers in other languages as well—

- The earliest Old Latin manuscripts from the 5th to 7th century
- The Romaunt or Occitan New Testaments dating back to the 12th century
- The Tepl, an old German translation from the 14–15th centuries.
- The old French translations first appearing in the 13th century.
- The old German translations, which first appeared in the 13th and 14th centuries
- Spanish Bibles beginning in Valencia in 1478

❹ It's appeared in English-language Bibles for over 600 years. It's appeared in Reformation-era Bibles throughout the world as well.

❺ World-class Greek scholar Eugenius Bulgaris (1716–1806) showed that the abbreviated Greek text (as it is translated in the ESV) is ungrammatical. And the full text as it appears in the KJB is grammatically correct.

And finally, they constantly **REPEAT WITHOUT CHECKING** the two popular fake stories used to defend the deletion of the passage that **turn out to be SCHOLARLY MYTHS**

Myth #1 "…Erasmus promised to insert the verse in his Greek New Testament if a Greek manuscript were produced that included the passage." Modern textual critic Bruce Metzger claimed—
"At length such a copy was found—or made to order."

Myth #2 Author Erika Rummel in her 1986 book *Erasmus' Annotations* said, "Erasmus challenged Edward Lee to find a Greek manuscript that included 1 John 5:7. This story was repeated by James White in 1995 in his book *The Truth about the KJV-Only Controversy*."

Page 3

Both myths have been debunked.

H.J. de Jonge, the Dean of the Faculty of Theology at Rijksuniversiteit (Leiden, Netherlands), **has refuted both myths.** de Jonge, a recognized specialist in Erasmian studies, refuted the myth of a promise in 1980, stating that Metzger's view on Erasmus' promise "has no foundation in Erasmus' work. Consequently it is highly improbable that he included the difficult passage because he considered himself bound by any such promise."

He has also refuted the new myth of a challenge (which Rummel devised in reaction to the burial of the promise myth).[1]

But most importantly...

The passage is a thorn in the side of Jehovah Witnesses, Unitarians, Deists, modernists, as well as evangelicals and fundamentalists, whose "Bible" is the nonexistent "Original Autographs."

The Lord has had it appear in the world's best-selling, most published, most read, most memorized, most believed, most trusted Bible in the history of mankind.

1 John 5:7–8 as it's appeared in BILLIONS of King James Bibles over the past 400 years is not a coincidence or a mistake.

The words are AUTHENTIC.
God's Bible doesn't contain errors.

Learn more, get the book: WHICH BIBLE
WOULD JESUS USE? The Bible Version Controversy
Explained and Resolved
By Jack McElroy www.JackMcElroy.com

Available from

1. https://www.wayoflife.org/reports/a-defense-of-1-john.php

Page 4

ESV Turns Unclean Bird into a Prophet

King James Bible Revelation 8:13
And I beheld, and heard **an angel** flying through the midst of heaven, saying with a loud voice, Woe, woe, woe, to the inhabiters of the earth …!

English Standard Version Rev. 8:13
Then I looked, and I heard **an eagle** crying with a loud voice as it flew directly overhead, "Woe, woe, woe to those who dwell on the earth…"

 ALL Bible versions say that the eagle is an unclean bird. **INCLUDING the ESV…**

"And these you shall detest among the birds; they shall not be eaten; they are detestable: **the eagle**, the bearded vulture, the black vulture, Leviticus 11:13 **ESV**

What's **deeply troubling** is that the ESV has this unclean bird proclaiming the future and announcing WOE on the earth.

- Billions of King James Bibles say <u>Angel</u>.
- The ESV says <u>Eagle</u>.

The Lord CAN speak through any beast (e.g., Balaam's ass) but here we're presented a choice; an unclean bird or one of his holy angels.

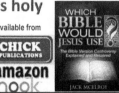

ESV Introduces Cartoon Character Into Scripture

****

King James Bible Revelation 16:7	English Standard Version Rev. 16:7
And **I heard <u>another out of</u> the altar** say, Even so, Lord God Almighty, true and righteous *are* thy judgments.	And **I heard** _____ ___ **the altar saying**, "Yes, Lord God the Almighty, true and just are your judgments!"

❶ <u>**They'll protest**</u> that the KJB reading has no Greek manuscript support— very true. The KJB reading is supported by a Latin vulgate and Coptic manuscript while theirs is supported by only four Greek witnesses. And ...

❷ <u>**They'll never admit**</u> that they CAN'T prove that Revelation was originally penned in Greek.

❸ <u>**They'll ignore**</u> the WITNESS of the <u>billions</u> KJB and other **Reformation-era Bibles the Lord has had this reading appear in.** And ...

<u>**So, who spoke?**</u>

A talking altar? Of course not. It was simply <u>**another**</u> angel (see context). Plus, only LIVING CREATURES speak in scripture including Balaam's ass and the serpent.

They'll object that the "image of the beast" spoke in Rev. 9:13 but the image was given "life" by the beast. **Altars don't talk; angels do.**

That kind of nonsense only happens in cartoons and ... The ESV.

Available from

Gideons Caught Adding to the Bible!

****

1. The Gideons[1] place **ESV Bibles** in hotel rooms.

2. The ESV **does not contain 17 verses** found in the King James Bible.[2]

3. The Gideons were allowed **to add those 17 missing verses** into a special version of the ESV.[3]

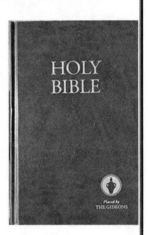

If the English Standard Version is the true Bible, then aren't the Gideons guilty of adding to God's word ... and therefore under a curse?

If the King James Bible is the true Bible then isn't the ESV guilty of taking away from God's word ... and therefore under a curse? (See Revelation 22:18 in ANY Bible.)

And they say your concern about Bible versions is a "hobby-horse."

Who's kidding who?

Available from

Learn more, get the book: WHICH BIBLE WOULD JESUS USE? The Bible Version Controversy Explained and Resolved By Jack McElroy www.JackMcElroy.com

1. http://tinyurl.com/jb8pcoa; 2. http://tinyurl.com/y47x5hu2; 3. http://tinyurl.com/y288qkxy

Introducing...

The ESV Vatican Version

****

Finally, a "Protestant" Bible that doubles as a Roman Catholic Bible—fully endorsed by Holy Mother the Church. (Presently only available in India.)[1]

CONTENTS

Nihil Obstat
✠ Bishop J. Susaimanickam
Sivagangai, India

Imprimatur
✠ Oswald Cardinal Gracias
Archbishop of Bombay
President, Conference of Catholic Bishops of India
May 4, 2017

Nihil Obstat: "The certification by an official censor of the Roman Catholic Church that a book has been examined and found to contain nothing opposed to faith and morals."

Imprimatur: "A license to print or publish especially by Roman Catholic episcopal authority."

Once the Roman Church persecuted those who left it. **Think: *Inquisition*.**

Today, they call them *Separated brethren*— a term the Roman Catholic Church uses to refer to baptized members of other Christian traditions. **Think: *One World Church*.**

The ESV; positioning to become the One World Church "Bible" —while clueless Christian leaders sleep at the wheel.

Available from

CHICK PUBLICATIONS

amazon

nook

WHICH **BIBLE WOULD** JESUS USE?
The Bible Version Controversy Explained and Resolved
JACK McELROY

Learn more, get the book: WHICH BIBLE WOULD JESUS USE?
The Bible Version Controversy Explained and Resolved By
Jack McElroy www.JackMcElroy.com

1. http://atcbooks.in/product/esv-ce-english-standard-version-catholic-edition-regular-hb/

The New King James Version

Introduction

****

The New King James Version is an interesting piece.

As modern versions go, it's better than the rest because at least it's *generally* from a text that has been handed down to believers throughout the centuries.

But why did it need to be produced in the first place?

NKJV is dangerous because it was intended to be a "transition Bible" by its publisher/creator. As you will see documented, its goal was to move King James Bible believers to a modern version.

You **would** want to move King James users to the New King James exclusively if it truly was the best translation of the best text, but that turns out not to be the case, as you will see.

Most people believe that the new King James is just the old King James with updated verbiage. Another thing that turns out not to be the case.

If they had not jacked the name "King James," their Bible would've had a difficult time being accepted in fundamental and conservative churches.

However, from a marketing standpoint, their ploy was extremely clever. They took a great name and so titled their creation.

They also got folks like Jerry Falwell and other well-known names at the time to hype the product. Great idea for someone looking to move books.

The problem is, it's not about moving product; it's about dealing with the very words of the living God … and that's not something to be trifled with.

This is a big section because the NJKV is such a deceptive book.

What Was the Serpent's Offer to Adam and Eve?

****

King James Bible Genesis 3:5	New King James Version Gen. 3:5
For God doth know that in the day ye eat thereof, then your eyes shall be opened, **and ye shall be <u>as gods</u>,** knowing good and evil.	For God knows that in the day you eat of it your eyes will be opened, **and you will be <u>like God</u>,** knowing good and evil."

❶ **Adam and Eve were ALREADY LIKE GOD.**
And God said, Let us make man in our image, **after our <u>likeness</u>... Gen. 1:26 KJB**

This *is* the book of the generations of Adam. In the day that God created man, **in the <u>likeness</u> of God** made he him; Gen. 5:1 KJB

❷ **The temptation was to be autonomous gods.** Just as the Lord states in the KJB.

❸ **The wording of the NKJV ("like God") matches** the NIV, NLT, NASB, ESV, and HCSB.

Proving once again that...

The New King James is nothing more than a cleverly disguised and deceitfully marketed modern version.

Available from

Learn more, get the book: WHICH BIBLE WOULD
JESUS USE? The Bible Version Controversy Explained
and Resolved By Jack McElroy
www.JackMcElroy.com

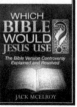

amazon
nook

Image: https://wellcomecollection.org/works?wellcomeImagesUrl=/

Who Built Nineveh?

****

King James Bible Genesis 10:11
Out of that land went forth
Asshur, and builded Nineveh, and
the city Rehoboth, and Calah,

**New King James
Version Gen. 10:11** From that land **he
[Nimrod]*** went to Assyria and built
Nineveh, Rehoboth and Calah

❶ **The text in each Bible is significantly different.**
It's important because the integrity of the word of God is at stake.
One Bible has a historical error, the other does not.

❷ Either Nimrod or Asshur founded Nineveh (**near modern-day Mosul,
Iraq**): same city, two different men. **It can't be both.**

❸ The dispute over who founded Nineveh has raged for over 2,500
years.
Jewish historian Josephus thought Ashur. Fifth century BC Greek
physician Ctesias thought Nimrod.

❹ **That it can be translated either way is not in dispute.** The KJB even
includes the alternate rendering "Or, *he went out into Assyria*" in a
side note. However, **footnotes and side notes DO NOT CARRY the
same AUTHORITY as the TEXT.**

❺ The KJB translators' understanding of textual and secular history led
them to the conclusion that **Asshur built Nineveh.**

So **which Bible is historically correct?** The fact that Asshur built
Nineveh has appeared in literally billions of King James Bibles
(and previous English Bibles) for over 400 years. Therefore…

If the KJB is factually and historically wrong, then the Lord Jesus Christ
(who allowed this error to appear in the world's best-selling, most
published, most read, most memorized, most believed, most trusted
Bible in the history of mankind) has a lot of explaining to do.

If the NKJV is factually and historically wrong, then God would NEVER
use it because…

God's Bible doesn't contain errors.

Available from

Learn more, get the book: WHICH BIBLE WOULD JESUS
USE? The Bible Version Controversy Explained and
Resolved By Jack McElroy www.JackMcElroy.com

*"Cush begot Nimrod. ¹⁰ And the beginning of his kingdom was Babel, in the land of Shinar ¹¹ From that land he went to Assyria and built Nineveh. NKJV

NKJV Obscures Prophetic Reference in Genesis 22:8

****

King James Bible Gen. 22:8	**New King James Version Gen. 22:8**
And Abraham said, My son, **God will provide ___ himself** a lamb for a burnt offering: so they went both of them together.	And Abraham said, "My son, God will provide **for Himself** the lamb for a burnt offering." So the two of them went together.

The NKJV isn't wrong, just deficient. **The KJB has a double meaning:**

1. That God will provide a lamb for his sacrifice and
2. That *himself* refers back to God **meaning that the lamb will be God himself,** referencing Christ's deity. This was how M. R. DeHann (1891–1965) founder of the *Radio Bible Class,* and co-editor *Our Daily Bread* understood the verse.[1]

Some object that *himself* is actually an archaic expression which means "for himself," as seen in Luke 12:33 in the KJB:

Sell that ye have, and give alms, **provide yourselves bags** which wax not old.

However:

❶ A cross reference, speaking of Christ, demonstrates the interpretation as presented: *Who* [Christ] *gave himself* a ransom for all. 1 Timothy 2:6 KJB

❷ The option to translate like the NKJV was known to the KJB translators because it was presented by John Wycliffe in 1380 **but they rejected it**:

Abraham seide, My sone, God schal puruey to hym the beeste… Wyc Gen. 22:8

IF they wanted to translate it that way, they could have… but didn't.

❸ They broke the tradition of ALL previously printed English Bibles:

Coverdale	God shall prouyde him a shepe for the brent offerynge.
Matthews Bible	god wyll prouyde hym a shepe for sacrifice.
Great Bible	God wyll prouyde him a shepe for sacrifyce.
Geneva	God will prouide him a lambe for a burnt offering:
Bishops	My God wyll prouide ___ a beast for burnt sacrifice:

❹ "God doesn't simply provide a lamb for himself (ESV), he provides himself, in Christ, as the lamb…observe that will provide, yireh, contains ra'a, and could be given as…'God will choose himself worthy as the lamb for an offering, his son' or '… God will choose himself [in] his son as the lamb for an offering.'"[2]

The NKJV obscures the deity of Christ reference by its translation choice.

1. https://claudemariottini.com/2006/01/17/rereading-genesis-228-the-sacrifice-of-isaac-and-the-preacher-2/. 2. David Jackson, *Fitly Spoken* Exploring The Language of The King James Bible Vol.1 pgs.

Is "Thou Shalt Not Kill" a KJB Translation Error?

****

King James Bible Exodus 20:13	New King James Version Ex.20:13
Thou shalt not **kill.**	You shall not **murder**.

❶ **Modern version apologists pretend people are "confused"** by the KJB wording "thou shalt not kill." They insist it should say "murder" because no one today understands what *kill* really means.

❷ **Their distinction is unnecessary.** Grade schoolers taught the 10 Commandments know it has nothing to do with killing animals, accidents, or self-defense.

❸ That it includes **the crime of "murder"** is obvious and proven by the Lord Jesus' reference to the commandment:

"Jesus said, Thou shalt do no murder…," Mat. 19:18

No confusion in this headline

❹ **"Kill" is a general term. It has a broad application.** It applies to murder (as seen in modern versions) but isn't restricted to murder. **Hence, the need to translate as "thou shalt not kill.**

❺ Murder is a legal term describing **unlawful killing** of a human being. **BUT what is "lawful" is sometimes at odds with the law of God.** For example:

❻ **Abortion is KILLING BUT NOT MURDER according to the state** because the state says it's LEGAL.

Abortion doctors do not murder but they kill, thereby violating the 6th commandment.

Will they get off on Judgment Day? No, because the commandment told them not to KILL.

❼ **The Pharisees KILLED Jesus but did not MURDER him** because what they did wasn't against Roman law. Will they get off on Judgement Day? **No, because the commandment told them not to KILL.**

How should Exodus 20:13 read?
Just like it has for over 400 years.
"Thou shalt not kill."

Available from

Photo: David Berkowitz -www.marketersstudio.com/ cropped

Where Did God Tell Moses to Put the Book of the Law?

****

King James Bible Deut. 31:26
Take this book of the law, and put it **IN THE SIDE** of the ark of the covenant of the LORD your God, that it may be there for a witness against thee.

New King James Version Deut. 31:26
"Take this Book of the Law, and put it **BESIDE** the ark of the covenant of the LORD your God, that it may be there as a witness against you;

The Book of the Law was extremely important because God's people would live or die based on their obedience to the precepts contained therein.

❶ No doubt God would make sure it was placed <u>IN</u> <u>a</u> <u>secure</u> <u>place</u>.

❷ If it were placed **"IN THE SIDE"** of the ark of the covenant, it wouldn't get lost.

Bible in the side of a pocketbook

❸ If it was placed **"BESIDE"** the ark of the covenant, it could easily get lost because the ark was frequently moved and even captured by the Philistines.

Was the Lord careless about where he told Moses to place the book, OR did he instruct him to put it in a secure place?

Bible beside a pocketbook

Not surprisingly, the NKJV reads like it's modern version cousins:

"...beside the ark..." NIV
"...beside the ark..." NASB

The New King James; following the wrong model, once again.

More NKJV Nonsense Contradicts Self About Death

RUBBISH

****

King James Bible 2 Samuel 14:14	New King James Version 2 Sam. 14:14
For we must needs die, and *are* as water spilt on the ground, which cannot be gathered up again; **neither doth God respect *any* person**: yet doth he devise means, that his banished be not expelled from him.	For we will surely die and *become* like water spilled on the ground, which cannot be gathered up again. Yet <u>**God**</u> <u>**does**</u> <u>**not**</u> <u>**take**</u> <u>**away**</u> a life; but He devises means, so that His banished ones are not expelled from Him.

❶ **Once again, the NKJV says something entirely DIFFERENT from the KJB,** thus putting to bed the "It's an updated language King James Bible" excuse.

❷ **God does take away life,** and EVERYONE ON EARTH knows it.

❸ **This fact is clearly stated in the King James Bible:**
> The LORD killeth, and maketh alive: he bringeth down to the grave, and bringeth up. 1 Samuel 2:6 KJB

❹ **Moreover, the NKJV contradicts itself:**
> For what is the hope of the hypocrite, Though he may gain *much,* If <u>**God**</u> <u>**takes**</u> <u>**away**</u> **his life**? Job 27:8 NKJV

Proving once again that the NKJV is not a "revision" of the real King James Bible but just an impostor.

Available from

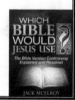

NKJV Prints Historical Error—Disqualifies Self

****

King James Bible 2 Kings 23:29
In his days Pharaohnechoh king of Egypt **went up against** the king of Assyria to the river Euphrates: and king Josiah went against him…

New **King James Version 2 Kings 23:29**
In his days Pharaoh Necho king of Egypt **went to the aid** of the king of Assyria, to the River Euphrates; and King Josiah went against him…

Contrary to the NKJV's assertion, Pharaoh and "the king of Assyria" were enemies in 609 BC because the "king of Assyria" was in fact the King of Babylon who had conquered Assyria.

"As the chronology of Eusebius and Jerome represents, Cyaraxes the Mede took Nineveh in 609–608 BC, or, according to the Armenian chronicle, apud Eusebius, in 608–607 BC, then **Necho's expedition (circa 609 BC) was really directed <u>against</u> a king of Assyria** in the strict sense."[1]

Enemies don't AID each other.

The **King James Bible** recounts **true history.**

The **New King James Version** recounts history that never happened.

How many errors of fact does it take to disqualify the NKJV as the word of truth?

Available from

amazon

nook

WHICH BIBLE WOULD JESUS USE
The Bible Version Controversy Explained and Resolved!

JACK McELROY

Learn more, get the book: WHICH BIBLE WOULD JESUS USE? The Bible Version Controversy Explained and Resolved By Jack McElroy www.JackMcElroy.com

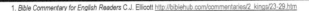

1. *Bible Commentary for English Readers* C.J. Ellicott http://biblehub.com/commentaries/2_kings/23-29.htm

NKJV Corrupts Prayer of Jabez

****

King James Version 1 Chronicles 4:10

And Jabez called on the God of Israel, saying, Oh that thou wouldest bless me indeed, and enlarge my coast, and that thine hand might be with me, and that thou wouldest keep me from evil, **that it may not grieve me!**...

New King James Version1 Chron. 4:10

And Jabez called on the God of Israel saying, "Oh, that You would bless me indeed, and enlarge my territory, that Your hand would be with me, and that You would keep *me* from evil, **that I may not cause pain!"**...

❶ The prayer of Jabez is all about Jabez and his selfish prayer. But who can blame him?

❷ Somehow it became a best-selling book. Who knows why?

❸ The NKJV SAYS something ENTIRELY out of context & different from the King James Bible.

❹ **BOTH can't be the words of God OR even the words of Jabez.**

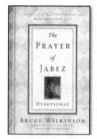

NY Times **Bestseller**

The New King James—a cleverly disguised King James Bible knockoff.

Learn more, get the book: WHICH BIBLE WOULD JESUS USE? The Bible Version Controversy Explained and Resolved By Jack McElroy
www.JackMcElroy.com

Available from

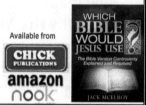

NKJV Footnote Treachery Exposed

****

King James Bible 1 Chronicles 20:3	New King James Vers. 1 Chron. 20:3
And he brought out the people that *were* in it,	And he brought out the people who *were* in it,
and cut *them* with saws...	**and put *them* to work**[a] with saws...

~ ~

NKJV Footnote: [a]Septuagint reads *cut them.*

1. This would lead one to believe that the King James reading **DID NOT** come from the Hebrew Masoretic Text (MT) but the Greek Septuagint.
2. This implies that the **KJB's reading is NOT original** but from a Greek translation and therefore in error.

~ ~

But the King James reading <u>did</u> come from the Hebrew Masoretic Text as seen in these modern version footnotes:

1. English Standard Version (**ESV**) "Hebrew *he sawed.*"
2. New Revised Standard Version (**NRSV**): "Heb. *and he sawed.*"
3. New Living Translation (**NLT**) "Hebrew reads *and cut them with saws...*"

The Amplified Bible's note gives you the real reason **WHY** the **NKJV** broke ranks with the **King James Bible...**

4. Amplified Bible: "MT reads *cut with saws,* ...**Due to the brutality implied by the reading *cut*, most expositors** <u>prefer</u> **to** <u>reject</u> **it as an early scribal error...**"

Apparently, the NKJV staff <u>didn't</u> <u>believe</u> "the original Hebrew" so they "corrected" it to say what they wanted.

Available from

Image: By A74ir89 [CC BY-SA 4.0 (https://creativecommons.org/licenses/by-sa/4.0)], from Wikimedia Commons

NKJV Staff Appalled, Change Translation

****

King James Bible 1 Chronicles 20:3
And he brought out the people that *were* in it, **and <u>cut</u> *them*** with saws, and with harrows of iron, and with axes. Even so **dealt** David with all the cities of the children of Ammon....

New King James Version 1 Chron. 20:3
And he brought out the people who *were* in it, **and <u>put</u> *them* <u>to work</u>** with saws, with iron picks, and with axes. So David did to all the cities of the people of Ammon...

King James Bible 2 Samuel 12:31
He also brought out the people who were in it, and **<u>set</u> <u>them</u> <u>under</u>** saws, sharp iron instruments, and iron axes, **and made them <u>pass</u> <u>through</u> <u>the</u> <u>brickkiln</u>**.

New King James Version 2 Sam. 12:31
And he brought out the people who *were* in it, and **<u>put</u> <u>them</u> <u>to work</u>** with saws and iron picks and iron axes, **and made them <u>cross</u> <u>over</u> <u>to</u> <u>the</u> <u>brick</u> <u>works</u>**.

❶ Cutting with saws and passing through a kiln **IS NOT** the same as putting someone to work and making them "**cross over**" (cross over what?) "to the brick works."

❷ The NKJV Staff was so appalled by King David's actions they just **rejected** the "original Hebrew" Masoretic Text . The Amplified Bible footnote says: "**MT reads** *cut with saws*, ... Due to the brutality implied by the reading *cut*, most expositors <u>prefer</u> <u>to</u> <u>reject</u> <u>it</u> as an early scribal error..."

❸ David was a "man of war." And because he shed much blood, the Lord nixed him from building a house for his name.

❹ The King James Bible reports the good, the bad, and the ugly. but it always reports **THE TRUTH**. Unlike what they tell us...

The NKJV is more than a KJB Language update.

Available from

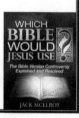

NKJV Erroneously Says Israel Without Hope

* *

King James Bible 1 Chronicles 29:15	New King James Version 1 Chron 29:15
For we *are* strangers before thee, and sojourners, as *were* all our fathers: our days on the earth *are* as a shadow, and *there is* **none abiding**.	For we *are* aliens and pilgrims before You, As *were* all our fathers; Our days on earth *are* as a shadow, **And without hope**.

❶ The KJB elsewhere translates מִקְוֶה: "miqweh" as "hope." **BUT not here. WHY?** Because...

❷ Contrary to the NKJV's announcement, Israel ALWAYS had HOPE. Their HOPE was their God; whether here or hereafter.
AS it says in NKJV ...

O Lᴏʀᴅ, **the hope of Israel**,
All who forsake You shall be ashamed... Jeremiah 17:13a **NKJV**

❸ Believers on Christ have HOPE today. It's the heathen who have NO HOPE.

Clearly deficient and defective, the New King James drops the ball again.

NKJV Doesn't Get the 1%ers

****

King James Bible Proverbs 1:32	New King James Version Prov. 1:32
For the turning away of the simple shall slay them, and **the prosperity of fools shall** destroy them.	For the turning away of the simple will slay them, And **the complacency of fools** will destroy them;

❶ Call it nitpicking but **complacency ≠ prosperity.**

❷ Some of the biggest FOOLS on earth are prosperous. These 1%ers include bankers, businessmen, tycoons, political operatives, and New World Order control freaks of all sorts.

❸ But they are anything but **complacent.**

❹ **Their prosperity is <u>exactly</u> what destroys them** because in their prosperity they don't need or want God. And many deny his existence. "The fool hath said in his heart, *There is* no God." Ps 14:1 KJB

❺ And the NKJV reads like the New International Version:
"and the **complacency** of fools will destroy them; Prov. 1:32 NIV

Showing once again that the NKJV is... just another copycat modern version.

NKJV Insults Christian Businessmen

****

King James Bible Proverbs 11:16
A gracious woman retaineth honour: and **strong** **_men_** retain riches.

New King James Version Prov. 11:16
A gracious woman retains honor, But **ruthless** **_men_** retain riches.

❶ **Strong and ruthless DO NOT mean the same thing.**

❷ What the NKJV translators misunderstand is that **ALL** successful Christian businessmen **MUST have the following strengths:**

☑ **Character**—to compete honestly in the market.

☑ **Integrity**—to keep just weights and balances.

☑ **Conviction**—about the value of their product or service.

☑ **Self-discipline**—to work more and earn less NOW while taking the long view of wealth creation.

☑ **Fearlessness**—to take advantage of opportunities despite the risks.

☑ **Endurance**—to admit and recover from their mistakes.

☑ **Patience**—to deal with menacing frustrations and crushing reversals yet persevere because the cause is worth it.

The NKJV folks confuse small business with crony capitalism.

Available from

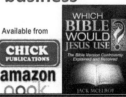

Learn more, get the book: WHICH BIBLE WOULD JESUS USE? The Bible Version Controversy Explained and Resolved By Jack McElroy www.JackMcElroy.com

NKJV Misses WHO Gets Hurt by Talebearers

****

King James Bible Proverbs 18:8
The words of a talebearer *are* as **wounds**, and they go down into the innermost parts of the belly.

New King James Version Prov. 18:8
The words of a talebearer *are* like **tasty trifles**, And they go down into the inmost body.

❶ These verses SAY and MEAN different things.

❷The KJB reader identifies with **the PAIN** they have felt and can **internalize the PAIN** they've inflicted by talebearing.
The Lord can use the verse to <u>comfort</u> and <u>reprove</u> the believer.

❸The NKJV reader is <u>separated</u> from the Lord's comfort and <u>spared</u> God's reproof by the **externalization** of this verse.

The NKJV reads similar to the New International Version:
        "The words of a gossip are like choice morsels..." Prov. 18:8 NIV

Proving once again that the NKJV is... just another defective modern version.

Available from

Learn more, get the book: WHICH BIBLE WOULD
JESUS USE? The Bible Version Controversy
Explained and Resolved By Jack McElroy
www.JackMcElroy.com

NKJV's Practical and Meteorological Error

****

King James Bible Proverbs 25:23	New King James Version Prov. 25:23
The north wind **driveth away** rain: so *doth* **an angry countenance** a backbiting tongue.	The north wind **brings forth** rain, And a backbiting tongue an angry countenance.

A blogger, relying on the NKJV and/or its modern version cousins, says ...

"This particular proverb creates a problem for us—in that in Israel the north wind **does not bring** rain. It is the southeastern winds that do that task. Some think that because of this that this proverb may be one Solomon learned from Egypt, because that particular area does have rain originate out of the north wind."[1]

This proverb creates NO PROBLEM for King James Bible Believers. Here's why ...

That the proverb *could be* translated either way is unquestioned. (The 1611 KJB's side note agrees with the NKJV rendering.)

Then why did the KJB translators choose the opposite for the text?

❶ **Because it is internally consistent** with the rest of Scripture:
Fair weather cometh out of the north Job 37:22 KJB

The wind goeth toward the south, and turneth about unto the north
Ecclesiastes 1:6

❷ **Because it's meteorologically correct,** as pointed out by the blogger. And finally,

❸ **Because a backbiting tongue does not always "bring forth" an angry countenance**. Men often enjoy it. **And everybody knows it.**

Not surprisingly, NKJV mimics the New American Standard Bible:

"The north wind **brings forth** rain, And a backbiting tongue, an angry countenance." Proverbs 25:23 NASB

The NKJV fails again.

1.   https://www.calvarychapeljonesboro.org/proverb-a-day/how-to-stop-gossip-in-its-tracks-proverbs-2523

NKJV Matches Modern Versions

****

King James Bible Ecclesiastes 3:11	New King James Version Ecclesiastes 3:11
He hath made every thing beautiful in his time: also he hath set <u>the world</u> in their heart, so that no man can find out the work that God maketh from the beginning to the end.	He has made everything beautiful in its time. Also He has put <u>eternity</u> in their hearts, except that no one can find out the work that God does from beginning to end.

<u>WORLD</u> is not the same as <u>ETERNITY</u>. The option to translate "'ō·w·lām" as everlasting or eternity was rejected by the KJB translators here. **But Why?...**

❶ **It is still translated by Jews today as "world."**

❷ **If he put eternity in men's hearts,** they would know the high and lofty One that inhabiteth eternity (Isaiah 57:15), but they don't.

❸ <u>Eternity</u> **in men's hearts? Not a chance.** Who's got time? Everyone's trying to get to tomorrow. Men LOVE the world and all that's in it. **That's WHY it's so hard to reach them with the gospel.**

❹ **What's in men's hearts?** The lust of the flesh, and the lust of the eyes, and the pride of life…. (1 John 2:16)

❺ **Which is why** "they should seek the Lord, if haply they might feel after him, and find him." (Acts 17:27)

❻ <u>Eternity</u> **is the exact reading of the NIV, ESV, NASB, NLT, and HCSB.** So much for the NKJV "updating" the real King James Bible.

The NKJV: Just another modern version … in disguise.

Available from

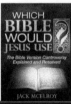

Learn more, get the book: WHICH BIBLE WOULD JESUS USE? The Bible Version Controversy Explained and Resolved By Jack McElroy www.JackMcElroy.com

NKJV vs KJB: Who's Lying under Oath?

****

King James Bible Isaiah 9:3	New King James Version Isaiah 9:3
Thou hast multiplied the nation, and **not increased** the joy…	You have multiplied the nation *And* ___ **increased** its joy…

The testimonies above are contradictory. Only one is true.

You, the jury, must decide who's lying and who's telling the truth.

The Evidence

❶ The KJB's reading comes **from the Hebrew Masoretic text** itself.

❷ The NKJV editors got their reading **from the margin** of the Masoretic text.

❸ Not surprisingly, the NKJV reads like the 1885 Revised Version:

> "Thou hast multiplied the nation, **thou hast increased** their joy…"

❹ They tell us the NKJV is an updated version of the KJB that eliminates "archaic, obsolete, or unnatural" words.[1] **But…**

In many ways, the NKJV's translation is more like its modern version cousins than the KJB.

Available from

Learn more, get the book: WHICH BIBLE WOULD JESUS USE? The Bible Version Controversy Explained and Resolved By Jack McElroy
www.JackMcElroy.com

amazon
nook

---

1. http: thenkjvbible.com/; See also http://www.kjvtoday.com/home/not-increased-the-joy-or-increased-the-joy-in-isaiah-93

NKJV Misses God's Target Audience

****

King James Bible Jeremiah 27:2	New King James Version Jer. 27:2
Thus saith the LORD to me; Make **thee** bonds and yokes, and put them upon **thy** neck,	"Thus says the LORD to me: 'Make for **yourselves** bonds and yokes, and put them on **your** neck

 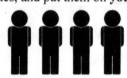

❶ Both "thee" and "thy" are singular. God is clearly speaking to Jeremiah in the King James Bible.

❷ The NKJV indicates he's speaking to Jeremiah AND many others.

❸ Even other modern versions get it right:
... "Make a yoke... and put it on **your** neck. NIV
... "Make **yourself** ... and put them on **your** neck. ESV
... "Make for **yourself** ... and put them on **your** neck, NASB

❹ If the NKJV is so wrong and confused about singular and plural, what else is it confused about?

Just another erroneous reading from the NKJV.

Learn more, get the book: WHICH BIBLE WOULD
JESUS USE? The Bible Version Controversy
Explained and Resolved By Jack McElroy
www.JackMcElroy.com

Available from

What Swallowed Jonah?

****

❶ **The KJB and the NKJV <u>both</u> say the same thing in the book of Jonah...**

Now the LORD had prepared **<u>a great fish</u>** to swallow Jonah. And Jonah was in the belly of the fish three days and three nights. Jonah 1:17

BUT...

❷ **The King James Bible provides <u>further</u> <u>revelation</u> as spoken by the Lord Jesus Christ defining the kind of great fish that swallowed Jonah.**

For as Jonas was three days and three nights in **<u>the whale's</u>** belly; so shall the Son of man be three days and three nights in the heart of the earth. Matt. 12:40 KJB

❸ **The NKJV NEVER tells you <u>what</u> <u>kind</u> of "great fish" swallowed Jonah...**
For as Jonah was three days and three nights in the belly of **<u>the great fish</u>,** so will the Son of Man be three days and three nights in the heart of the earth. Matt. 12:40 (NKJV)

There's nothing like a "New" King James Version to corrupt a kid's Bible story.

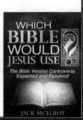

NKJV Claims Way to Eternal Life Difficult

****

King James Bible Matthew 7:14
Because strait *is* the gate, and **narrow *is* the way**, which leadeth unto life, and few there be that find it.

New King James Version Mat. 7:14
Because narrow *is* the gate and **difficult *is* the way** which leads to life, and there are few who find it.

❶ **"The way" is "narrow." So narrow, in fact, that it's comprised of the Lord Jesus Christ ALONE. Note the cross-reference:**

> Jesus saith unto him, I am the way, the truth, and the life: no man cometh unto the Father, but by me. **John 14:6.**

❷ **Coming to him is not "difficult." Even a drowning man or child can come.**

❸ **Turns out that a cocktail of 130 Christians came up with this "difficulty" nonsense. The NKJV was commissioned in 1975...**

> "130 respected Bible scholars, church leaders, and lay Christians worked for seven years to create **a completely new, modern** translation of Scripture..."[1]

The NKJV may be "new" and "modern," but it sure is second-rate.

Available from

Learn more, get the book: WHICH BIBLE WOULD JESUS USE? The Bible Version Controversy Explained and Resolved By Jack McElroy
www.JackMcElroy.com

1. https://www.biblegateway.com/versions/New-King-James-Version-NKJV-Bible

NKJV Error... Blames Common Neurological Disorder on Demons

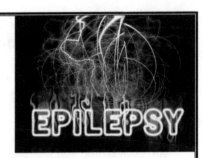

****

King James Bible Matthew 17:15, 18

[15]Lord, have mercy on my son: **for he is lunatick,** and sore vexed: for ofttimes he falleth into the fire, and oft into the water.

[18] And Jesus **rebuked the devil; and he departed out of him**: and the child was cured from that very hour.

New King James Bible Mat. 17:15, 18

[15] "Lord, have mercy on my son, **for he is an epileptic** and suffers severely; for he often falls into the fire and often into the water.

[18] **And Jesus rebuked the demon, and it came out of him**; and the child was cured from that very hour.

According to the Epilepsy Foundation, epilepsy is the fourth most common neurological disorder and affects people of all ages.[1]

Sometimes academics get carried away with their own brilliance. **The NKJV folks boldly and recklessly** stepped out of their bounds and made a medical diagnosis **with absolutely no training**.

The boy's problem was that he was possessed by a devil as is clearly stated in **the KJB, the world's most accurate Bible**.

Just more idle scholarly speculation from the NKJV.

1. https://www.epilepsy.com/learn/about-epilepsy-basics/what-epilepsy

New King James Swings and Misses

****

King James Bible Matthew 20:20	New King James Version Matthew 20:20
Then came to him the mother of Zebedee's children with her sons, **worshipping _him_**, and desiring a certain thing of him.	Then the mother of Zebedee's sons came to Him with her sons, **kneeling down** and asking something from Him.

❶ The NKJV editors and staff preferred to translate this passage using the words "**kneeling down**."

   That's one option.

❷ The King James Bible translators preferred the other option; "**worshiping him**."

❸ The King James Bible describes the **event <u>and</u>** the **intent**.

❹ The NKJV describes the **event <u>but missed</u>** the **intent**.

Which of the two translation options does the Lord prefer?

Available from

Learn more, get the book: WHICH BIBLE WOULD
JESUS USE? The Bible Version Controversy
Explained and Resolved By Jack McElroy
www.JackMcElroy.com

amazon
nook

NKJV Jesus Commands the Impossible

****

King James Bible Matt. 28:19	New King James Version Matt. 28:19
Go ye therefore, and **TEACH** all nations, baptizing them in the name of the Father, and of the Son, and of the Holy Ghost:	Go therefore and **MAKE DISCIPLES** of all the nations, baptizing them in the name of the Father and of the Son and of the Holy Spirit,

The Jesus of the NKJV says "make disciples" of all nations.

MISSION: IMPOSSIBLE
ROGUE BIBLE

The Problem: According to Scripture, you can't "make disciples" because ALL disciples today are born again believers made so by the operation of God through the new birth NOT by anyone "making" them disciples.

The Proof: ONLY born again believers can be baptized, which is mentioned in Matthew 28:19 in both Bibles.

The Jesus of the KJB says "TEACH all nations." This is something you CAN do. In summary...

The Jesus of the NKJV commands you to do what you can't.
The Jesus of the KJB commands you to do what you can.

Making disciples is God's work, not yours.

Available from

Learn more, get the book: WHICH BIBLE WOULD JESUS USE? The Bible Version Controversy Explained and Resolved By Jack McElroy
www.JackMcElroy.com

CHICK PUBLICATIONS

amazon

nook

WHICH
BIBLE
WOULD
JESUS USE
The Bible Version Controversy Explained and Resolved
JACK MCELROY

NKJV Insinuates Doubting Mary

****

Does God care about which English words are used to represent him in the Bible? You bet he does.

Notice the subtle difference in meaning between "shall" and "can."

****

King James Bible Luke 1:34	New King James Version Luke 1:34
Then said Mary unto the angel, How **shall** this be, seeing I know not a man?	Then Mary said to the angel, "How **can** this be, since I do not know a man?"

❶ **"Can"** and **"may"** are used to ask for permission. **"Can"** is commonly used to reference **ability and capability**—i.e., Can you speak English? Can he swim?

Hence, Mary asking "How **can** this be?" makes her appear to **doubt** the angel's words (i.e., **Is God ABLE to do this?**).

❷ However, **"shall"** or **"will"** refers to the future. Mary **BELIEVES** it shall happen, but asks "how" shall it be done.

Not surprisingly, the NKJV reading is like the New American Standard Bible:

> "Mary said to the angel, "How **can** this be, since I am a virgin?" NASB Luke 1:34

Showing once again that the NKJV is just another defective, deceptive, but cleverly marketed modern version.

Available from

Learn more, get the book: WHICH BIBLE WOULD JESUS USE? The Bible Version Controversy Explained and Resolved By Jack McElroy www.JackMcElroy.com

NKJV Changes John the Baptist's Instructions

****

King James Bible Luke 3:14

And the soldiers likewise demanded of him, saying, And what shall we do? And he said unto them, **Do violence to no man**, neither accuse *any* falsely; and be content with your wages.

New King James Version Lk. 3:14

Likewise the soldiers asked him, saying, "And what shall we do?" So he said to them, "**Do not intimidate anyone** or accuse falsely, and be content with your wages."

1. <u>DO VIOLENCE</u> is not the same as <u>INTIMIDATE</u> in any language.

2. It's one thing for someone to scare you. It's another to get punched in the face.

CHANGE
WE ~~CAN~~ BELIEVE IN
CAN'T

3. It's the difference between verbal abuse and felonious assault.

4. The New King James Version SAYS and MEANS something ENTIRELY different than the real King James Bible.

All the hype about the New King James presenting the same KJB text in contemporary language is just that—hype.

Learn more, get the book: WHICH BIBLE WOULD JESUS USE? The Bible Version Controversy Explained and Resolved By Jack McElroy www.JackMcElroy.com

Available from

CHICK PUBLICATIONS

amazon
nook

WHICH BIBLE WOULD JESUS USE?
The Bible Version Controversy Explained and Resolved
JACK MCELROY

NKJV Hides Devil's Tactics...
Leaves You Vulnerable

* *

King James Bible Romans 1:25
Who **changed** the truth of God **into** a lie, and worshipped and served the creature more than the Creator...

New King James Version Rom 1:25
who **exchanged** the truth of God **for** the lie, and worshiped and served the creature rather than the Creator....

❶ The real King James Bible WARNS you that ungodly and unrighteous men **will KNOWINGLY** twist the truth **INTO** a lie.
  In short, they are "perps" (perpetrators).

❷ The Devil is the ultimate perp since he changed God's truth into a lie by adding the word NOT in Gen 3:4: "Ye shall **not** surely die."

❸ The NKJV in turns the "perps" into near victims who simply **EXCHANGED** God's truth **FOR** a lie.

❹ Not surprisingly, the NKJV reads like the New American Standard Bible: **"They _exchanged_ the truth of God _for_ a lie..."** NASB Rom. 1:25

Proving once again that the NKJV is... just another defective modern version.

Learn more, get the book: WHICH BIBLE WOULD JESUS USE? The Bible Version Controversy Explained and Resolved By Jack McElroy
www.JackMcElroy.com

Available from

amazon
nook

NKJV Staff Misses Key NT Truth

****

King James Version Romans 3:22	New King James Version Rom. 3:22
Even the righteousness of God which is by **faith of** Jesus Christ unto all and upon all them that believe...	even the righteousness of God, through **faith in** Jesus Christ, to all and on all who believe...

The word "Faith" in Scripture can mean a religion as well as trust or confidence in someone or something.

❶ The Old Testament religion that Jesus practiced was the **faith of** God.

> For what if some did not believe? shall their unbelief make the **faith of** God without effect? Romans 3:3

Prepositions Matter

❷ The Lord Jesus Christ inaugurated **a new religion** with him as the focus. The Bible calls it the "**faith of Jesus Christ.**"

❸ By it, you get the righteousness of God, justification, and the promise of life eternal. Jesus Christ presents himself as the sole object of hope for any man to have everlasting life.

> Knowing that a man is not justified by the works of the law, but by the **faith of** Jesus Christ, Galatians 2:16

❹ Every man needs to believe this truth and "**change their religion**" from faith in themselves or any construct of man to the "**faith of Christ**" to be saved.
Our faith "in him," although necessary, is secondary.

The NKJV misses this distinction.

Available from

Learn more, get the book: WHICH BIBLE WOULD JESUS USE? The Bible Version Controversy Explained and Resolved By Jack McElroy
www.JackMcElroy.com

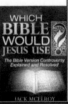

NKJV Sides with the ESV Catholic Edition Against KJB

****

King James Bible Romans 11:30–32	New King James Version Rom. 11:30–32
For as ye in times past have **not believed** God, yet have now obtained mercy through their **unbelief**: Even so have these also now **not believed**, that through your mercy they also may obtain mercy. For God hath concluded them all in **unbelief**, that he might have mercy upon all.	For as you were once **disobedient** to God, yet have now obtained mercy through their **disobedience**, even so these also have now been **disobedient**, that through the mercy shown you they also may obtain mercy. For God has committed them all to **disobedience**, that He might have mercy on all.

❶ The damning sin of mankind SINCE Adam's disobedience (Rom. 5:19) has been UNBELIEF. <u>Disobedience is the result of UNBELIEF.</u>

❷ They'll argue that the word COULD be translated "disobey" (an option known but REJECTED by the KJB translators).

Interestingly, the NKJV reads like the ESV Catholic Edition:

For just as you were at one time **disobedient** to God but now have received mercy because of their **disobedience**, so they too have now been **disobedient** in order that by the mercy shown to you they also may now receive mercy. For God has consigned all to **disobedience**, that he may have mercy on all.

Romans 11:30—32 ESV Catholic Edition

Whose side is the NKJV on anyway?

NKJV Confuses Things with People

HATERS GONNA HATE

****

King James Bible 2 Tim. 3:3	New King James Version 2 Tim. 3:3
Without natural affection, trucebreakers, false accusers, incontinent, fierce, **despisers of those that are good**,	unloving, unforgiving, slanderers, without self-control, brutal, **despisers of ___ ___ ___ good**,

1. Even in the last days (context) men still love things that are good. No one despises good health, good food, good business, a good family, etc.

2. They despise <u>people</u> that are good. That's because it's "good people" who push back and reprove their works. They can't stand them. That's why some despise you for being a Christian.

3. The NKJV reads like it's modern version cousins:

"...not loving good"   ESV
"...haters of good"   NASB

   Proving once again that, in some ways ...

The New King James is a cleverly disguised modern version.

Available from

amazon
nook

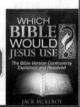

WHICH **BIBLE** WOULD JESUS USE
The Bible Version Controversy Explained and Resolved
JACK MCELROY

Learn more, get the book: WHICH BIBLE WOULD JESUS USE? The Bible Version Controversy Explained and Resolved By Jack McElroy
www.JackMcElroy.com

230

Are You "Saved" or "Being Saved?"

****

King James Bible 1 Cor. 1:18
For the **preaching** of the cross is to them that perish foolishness; but unto us which **are saved** it is the power of God.

New King James Version 1 Cor. 1:18
For the **message** of the cross is foolishness to those who are perishing, but to us who **are being saved** it is the power of God.

They swear to us that modern translations don't affect the fundamental doctrines of the faith but...

❶ The new birth happens in a moment of time. It's not a process. You're either saved OR lost. There is no middle ground.

❷ The NKJV and its modern version cousins present salvation as a "process" here instead of a fixed event by their translation CHOICE.

❸ ALL English Bibles previous to the KJB say "are saved." So where did this alternate choice translation come from?

❹ The NKJV reads like the apostate 1881 Revised Version.

> **"The Revised Version, brings out the true meaning of these words.** Instead of reading 'them that perish' and 'us which are saved,' we ought to read 'them that are perishing,' and 'us which are being saved.'
>
> That is to say, the Apostle represents the two contrasted conditions, **not so much as fixed states**, either present or future, **but rather as processes** which are going on, and are manifestly, in the present, **incomplete."**[1]

The NKJV repackaged the corrupt 1881 Revised Version's view of salvation.

1.   Commentator Alexander Maclaren (1826 – 1910) https://biblehub.com/sermons/auth/maclaren/perishing_or_being_saved.htm

NKJV Turns Followers of Christ into Actors

****

King James Bible 1 Cor. 11:1	New King James Version 1 Cor. 11:1
Be ye **followers** of me, **even as I also am of Christ.**	**Imitate** me, **just as I also imitate Christ.**

❶ **The real KJB** has Paul exhorting believers to be **followers**.

❷ **Following a leader** (who is one by example) allows the follower to retain their own identity, originality, and God-given creativity. Eventually, they can become leaders.

❸ **The NKJV reduces "followers" of Christ into "imitators."**

> "No man was ever great by imitation."
> –Samuel Johnson

❹ **Imitators** have no depth. It's not long before others see the imitator for what he really is, **a copycat, an actor** in a play. All show and no substance. **And Copycats make bad leaders.**

❺ Naturally, the NKJV reads like the English Standard Version:

Be **imitators** of me, as I am of Christ. 1 Cor.11:1 ESV

The NKJV? It's just another modern version imitation.

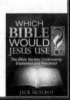

NKJV Hides Bible Corruption

****

King James Bible 2 Cor. 2:17	New King James Version 2 Cor. 2:17
For we are not as many, which **corrupt** the word of God…	For we are not, as so many, **peddling** the word of God…

❶ Corrupt **is NOT** the same as peddle.
According to Oxford University Press, "**peddle**" means:
"Try to sell (something, especially small goods) by going from place to place."[1]

❷ The KJB teaches that MANY men were **corrupting** the word of God. Even the marginal note from the 1611 KJB says:
"Or, *deal deceitfully with.*" **Wouldn't the Devil have an interest in <u>cleverly</u> packaging poison into God's word?**

❸ The warning was about **MANY** Bible corruptors. There's nothing wrong with selling (peddling) Bibles including making a profit on them unless you're a free-market hating leftist.

The Lord gave first-century believers a "heads up" about men corrupting his WORDS even while they were being written.

Shouldn't we be on the lookout for corrupted Bibles today?

Available from

CHICK
PUBLICATIONS

amazon

nook

Learn more, get the book: WHICH BIBLE WOULD JESUS USE? The Bible Version Controversy Explained and Resolved By Jack McElroy www.JackMcElroy.com

1 https://en.oxforddictionaries.com/definition/peddle

Who Will Raise You from the Dead?

****

King James Bible 2 Corinthians 4:14	New King James Version 2 Cor. 4:14
Knowing that he which raised up the Lord Jesus shall raise up us also (by) Jesus, and shall present *us* with you.	knowing that He who raised up the Lord Jesus will also raise us up (with) Jesus, and will present *us* with you..

The NKJV is clear about two things in this verse:
1. That God the Father "raised" Jesus from the dead.
2. That Jesus **DOES NOT** participate in your resurrection.
BUT...

According to the King James Bible, **BOTH** God the Father **AND** the Lord Jesus Christ will raise you up on the last day as it says in John 6:40:

"…every one which seeth the Son, and believeth on him, may have everlasting life: and (I) will **raise him up** at the last day." John 6:40 KJB

Not surprisingly, the NKJV reads like the NIV:

"… the one who raised the Lord Jesus from the dead will also raise us (with) Jesus…" 2 Cor.4:14 NIV

Proving once again that the NKJV is... just another modern version.

Available from

Learn more, get the book: WHICH BIBLE WOULD JESUS
USE? The Bible Version Controversy Explained and
Resolved By Jack McElroy www.JackMcElroy.com

What's the NKJV Verse You Can't Use with an Unbeliever?

****

King James Bible Ephesians 2:8–9
For by grace **are ye saved** through faith; and that not of yourselves: *it is* the gift of God: Not of works, lest any man should boast.

New King James Version Eph. 2:8–9
For by grace **you have been** saved through faith, and that not of yourselves; *it is* the gift of God, not of works, lest anyone should boast.

Both translations are addressed to believers and are (they say) technically accurate. Call it nitpicking, but "updating" the translation from the KJB is problematic. Here's why:

❶ The NKJV's "you have been saved" doesn't give assurance that you are saved NOW. Assurance of salvation is a serious problem for some folks.

❷ The KJB's salvation is always present tense. Not so with the NKJV. Moreover ...

❸ A soul winner can use this versatile KJB verse to explain to the unconverted **HOW** they can be saved (you ARE saved through faith). Not so with the NKJV.

The NKJV is sold as a language upgrade to the real King James (even though it really isn't) but it's a downgrade here.

Looks like they released it without debugging it first.

The NKJV: Just another Bible "upgrade" we can do without. Available from

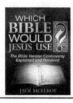

NKJV: You're a Slave

★★

King James Bible Ephesians 6:5	New King James Version Eph. 6:5
Servants, be obedient to them that are *your* masters according to the flesh, with fear and trembling, in singleness of your heart, as unto Christ;	**Bondservants**, be obedient to those who are your masters according to the flesh, with fear and trembling, in sincerity of heart, as to Christ;

The NKJV translators chose to use the word **BONDSERVANT** instead of **SERVANT** thereby **restricting the verse to an audience of slaves. Which you aren't.**

❶ **Bondservants are slaves.** Slaves work without pay.

❷ **Servants** choose to work and are compensated.

> bond·serv·ant
>
> /ˈbän(d)ˌsərvənt/ ◀))
>
> *noun*
>
> a person bound in service without wages.
> • a slave or serf.

❸ In spite of all the "spiritual" sounding sermons we've heard about being a "slave" sold out to Christ, the truth is that you WERE a servant of sin (Rom. 6:17).
BUT NOW you're are a servant of righteousness and a grateful servant of the Lord Jesus Christ.

The Lord Jesus Christ made you FREE indeed despite what the NKJV says.

Available from

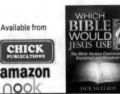

Learn more, get the book: WHICH BIBLE WOULD JESUS USE? The Bible Version Controversy Explained and Resolved By Jack McElroy
www.JackMcElroy.com

NKJV Weakens Key Evangelism Verse

****

King James Bible Philippians 2:16
Holding forth the word of life; that I may rejoice in the day of Christ, that I have not run in vain, neither laboured in vain.

New King James Version Phil. 2:16
holding fast the word of life, so that I may rejoice in the day of Christ that I have not run in vain or labored in vain.

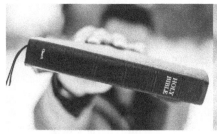 

Should you:
"Hold forth" **your Bible and shout it from the housetops?**

Or Should you:
"Hold fast" **and cling to your Bible hiding it under a bushel?**

The New King James Version comes up short again.

Learn more, get the book: **WHICH BIBLE WOULD JESUS USE? The Bible Version Controversy Explained and Resolved By Jack McElroy**
www.JackMcElroy.com

Available from

amazon
nook

NKJV Channels RC Douay-Rheims Bible

Q. Who Was Marcus?

****

King James Version Colossians 4:10	New King James Version Colossians 4:10
Aristarchus my fellowprisoner saluteth you, and Marcus, **sister's son** to Barnabas, (touching whom ye received commandments: if he come unto you, receive him;)	Aristarchus my fellow prisoner greets you, with Mark the **cousin** of Barnabas (about whom you received instructions: if he comes to you, welcome him),

❶ The King James Bible says Marcus was Barnabas' nephew.

❷ The NKJV says Marcus was Barnabas' cousin.

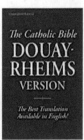

Interestingly, **The NKJV** mirrors the Roman Catholic Douay-Rheims Bibles:

> Aristarchus, my fellow prisoner, saluteth you, and Mark, the **cousin german [first cousin] of Barnabus**, touching whom you have received commandments; if he come unto you, receive him: Col. 4:10 Douay-Rheims Bible

At the end of the day, the NKJV is... just another modern version.

Available from

Learn more, get the book: WHICH BIBLE WOULD JESUS USE? The Bible Version Controversy Explained and Resolved By Jack McElroy
www.JackMcElroy.com

NKJV Restructures Baptist Church Government

****

King James Bible 1 Timothy 3:1
This is a true saying, If a man desire **the office of a bishop**, he desireth a good work.

New King James Version 1 Tim. 3:1
This *is* a faithful saying: If a man desires **the position of a bishop**, he desires a good work..

King James Bible 1 Timothy 3:13
For they that have used **the office of a deacon** well purchase to themselves a good degree, and great boldness in the faith which is in Christ Jesus.

New King James Version 1 Tim. 3:13
For those who have **served well as deacons** obtain for themselves a good standing and great boldness in the faith which is in Christ Jesus.

Most Baptist churches and the KJB, have **two offices:** Bishop (a.k.a. Pastor) and Deacon. **The men who serve in these offices ARE the elders of a church. There is no "office" of elders.**

According to the NKJV, there are no longer ANY "offices" in the church. Even a Junior Church teacher holds a "position."

And they swear to us that NO DOCTRINES are affected ... Sure they aren't.

Available from

Learn more, get the book: WHICH BIBLE WOULD JESUS USE? The Bible Version Controversy Explained and Resolved By Jack McElroy
www.JackMcElroy.com

NKJV Obliterates Baptist Distinctive

****

King James Bible 1 Timothy 3:1
This is a true saying, If a man desire **the office** of a bishop, he desireth a good work.

New King James Version 1 Tim. 3:1
This *is* a faithful saying: If a man desires **the position** of a bishop, he desires a good work..

King James Bible 1 Timothy 3:13
For they that have used **the office** of a deacon well purchase to themselves a good degree, and great boldness in the faith which is in Christ Jesus.

New King James Version 1 Tim. 3:13
For those who have **served well as deacons** obtain for themselves a good standing and great boldness in the faith which is in Christ Jesus.

In most Baptist churches and the KJB, there are **two offices:** Bishop (a.k.a. Pastor) and Deacon. **The men who serve in these offices ARE the de facto elders of a church. There is no "office" of elders.**

There are the Eight Baptist Distinctives—easily remembered by the acrostic "BAPTISTS."[1]

Biblical Authority
Autonomy of the Local Church
Priesthood of the Believer
Two Ordinances

Individual Soul Liberty
Saved, Baptized Church Membership
Two Offices [Bishop & Deacons]
Separation of Church and State

According to the NKJV there no longer are ANY "offices" in the church.

Proving once again that the NKJV isn't a "New" King James Bible.

Available from

Learn more, get the book: WHICH BIBLE WOULD JESUS USE? The Bible Version Controversy Explained and Resolved By Jack McElroy
www.JackMcElroy.com

1.   http://www.garbc.org/about-us/beliefs-constitution/baptist-distinctives/

240

NKJV Obscures the Truth About False Science

****

King James Version 1 Timothy 6:20	New King James Version 1 Timothy 6:20
O Timothy, keep that which is committed to thy trust, avoiding profane and vain babblings, and oppositions of <u>science</u> falsely so called:	O Timothy! Guard what was committed to your trust, avoiding the profane *and* idle babblings and contradictions of **what is** falsely called <u>knowledge</u>—

Knowledge is a collection of facts and/or information that can be either true or false. True science is "empirical" (based on evidence) and follows the scientific method.

"Science" falsely so-called says:

- The earth is not a special creation but a Big Bang accident.
- Men descended from monkeys.
- Oil comes from dead dinosaurs.
- Pharmaceuticals can heal you.
- Vaccinations confer immunity.
- Climate Change is a fact.

Much of what is called "science" is pseudoscience with an AGENDA; a distinction totally HIDDEN by the NKJV.

The NKJV reading of "knowledge" is the same as the NIV, ESV, NASB, and a host of others.

What to do with the New King James Version?

As with all modern versions... #JustWalkAway.

Available from

amazon
nook

Learn more, get the book: WHICH BIBLE WOULD JESUS USE? The Bible Version Controversy Explained and Resolved By Jack McElroy
www.JackMcElroy.com

"Science" or "Knowledge" in 1 Timothy 6:20?

****

King James Bible 1 Timothy 6:20	New King James Version 1 Tim. 6:20
O Timothy, keep that which is committed to thy trust, avoiding profane *and* vain babblings, and oppositions of **science falsely so called**:	O Timothy! Guard what was committed to your trust, avoiding the profane *and* idle babblings and contradictions of **what is falsely called knowledge**

They say the NKJV is more accurate because the Greek word "gnosis" (literally "to know") can ONLY be translated as "Knowledge." And it is so translated in 28 of the 29 times it appears in in the KJB. **BUT not here. Why?**

❶ The translation choice was known to the KJB translators because it appeared in the Roman Catholic Rheims NT published in 1582, **and they rejected it**.

❷ Some claim that "science" as a discipline was not used as it is today back in 1611. **YET ...**
According to the Oxford English Dictionary, the

English word "science" also means:
"knowledge acquired by study; acquaintance with or mastery of any **department of learning**."

"By the late 14th century, **science** meant, in English, **collective knowledge**."[1] Which is just like we understand the word "science" today.

This is seen in this KJB cross-reference:
"Children in whom *was* no blemish, but well favoured, and skilful in all wisdom, and cunning **in knowledge, and** understanding **science**, and such as *had* ability in them to stand in the king's palace..." Daniel 1:4 KJB

Real **"Science" is systematized "knowledge"** derived from observation, study, experimentation, and demonstration. 1 Tim. 6:20 in the KJB is a specific **warning** as to what's been going on for years.

And you don't have to be a rocket knowledgist to figure it out.

Available from

Learn more, get the book: WHICH BIBLE WOULD JESUS USE? The Bible Version Controversy Explained and Resolved By Jack McElroy www.JackMcElroy.com

1. http://theconversation.com/the-weighty-history-and-meaning-behind-the-word-science-48280;

NKJV Nonsense about Persecution

****

King James Bible 2 Tim. 3:12	New King James Version 2 Tim. 3:12
Yea, and all **that will live godly** in Christ Jesus shall suffer persecution.	Yes, and all **who desire to live godly** in Christ Jesus will suffer persecution.

The Greek word in question, *thelontes* occurs 7 times in the NT. And even the KJB translates it as "desire" three out of those seven times.

But not here. Why?

❶ The KJB phrase "will live godly" indicates <u>ACTION</u>.

❷ Actually living godly in the face of the world will get you persecuted because men love darkness and don't want their deeds reproved either by your example or your words. In short, they will push back.

❸ The instruction in the NKJV is that anyone who simply <u>desires</u> to "live godly," will suffer persecution.

❹ <u>Nonsense</u>. Nobody gets persecuted for their heart's desire. They get persecuted for what they DO. Moreover...

The NKJV reads like its modern version cousins:

"desire to live a godly life"   ESV
"desire to live godly"   NASB

Demonstrating once again that...

The New King James is just a cleverly disguised modern version.

NKJV Counterfeits Hebrews 3:16 Publishes Factual Error

★★★

King James Bible Heb. 3:16	New King James Bible Heb. 3:16
For **some**, when they had heard did provoke: **HOWBEIT NOT ALL** that came out of Egypt by Moses.	For who having heard rebelled? Indeed, **WAS IT NOT ALL** who came out of Egypt led by Moses?

WAS IT NOT ALL? Asks the NKJV. NO, IT WASN'T.

Joshua and Caleb, for instance; probably their households and **certainly** the thousands of children under 20 years old, **DID ENTER the Promised Land.**

❶ **The NKJV** suggests that "ALL" who came out of Egypt rebelled.

❷ The Scripture of truth in **the King James Bible** plainly says "SOME," NOT ALL of the Israelite who left Egypt rebelled against God. **A grade schooler who reads Exodus can see that.**

❸ **The NKJV contradicts BOTH the KJB and the Old Testament.**

It's easy to spot a fake when you compare it to the truth.

Available from

Learn more, get the book: WHICH BIBLE WOULD JESUS USE? The Bible Version Controversy Explained and Resolved By Jack McElroy www.JackMcElroy.com

NKJV Eliminates Deity of Christ Proof Text

PROOF

ELIMINATED!

****

King James Bible 1 John 3:16
Hereby perceive we **the** love *of God*, **because he** laid down His life for us: and we ought to lay down our lives for the brethren.

New King James Version 1 John 3:16
By this we know___ love, __ __ **because He** laid down **His** life for us. And we also ought to lay down *our* lives for the brethren.

E veryone knows this verse is referring to the Lord Jesus Christ, who laid down his life for us. BUT …

ONLY the King James Bible IDENTIFIES him as GOD in this passage. Note the words "because he" is referring to "God" who laid down his life for us. Therefore, <u>Jesus</u> = <u>God</u>.

They'll argue that *"of God"* is in Italics. Interestingly, the 1611 edition was not italicized. No matter, italicized words ARE part of the text.

And you don't find this clearly written doctrinal truth in this verse in the NKJV.

Learn more, get the book: WHICH BIBLE WOULD JESUS USE? The Bible Version Controversy Explained and Resolved By Jack McElroy
www.JackMcElroy.com

Available from

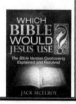

Designer Who Dressed Melania Trump for White House Portrait Tells Critics to "Go to Hell"

****

O ther designers outright refused to dress Trump but Italian designer Stefano Gabbana told his critics and detractors **"I don't care!!"**

"He defended the FLOTUS and told Instagram trolls who chided him for working with her to 'go to hell.'"[1]

And his critics know exactly what he means. That's because everybody knows what it means. And yet...

The NKJV translators substituted the word "Hades" (which hardly ANYONE uses) for "Hell" which EVERYBODY uses and UNDERSTANDS.

King James Bible Revelation 1:18	New King James Version Rev. 1:18
I am he that liveth, and was dead; and, behold, I am alive for evermore, Amen; and have the keys of **hell** and of death.	I *am* He who lives, and was dead, and behold, I am alive forevermore. Amen. And I have the keys of **Hades** and of Death.

Not surprisingly, the NKJV matches the ESV:

behold I am alive forevermore, and I have the keys of Death and **Hades**. Rev. 1:18 ESV

Proving once again that...
Sometimes, New King James is just window-dressing.

Available from

Learn more, get the book: WHICH BIBLE WOULD JESUS USE? The Bible Version Controversy Explained and Resolved By Jack McElroy www.JackMcElroy.com

http://www.thewrap.com/designer-who-dressed-melania-trump-for-white-house-portrait-tells-critics-to-go-to-hell/

Missing from NKJV ...
WHY God Made All Things

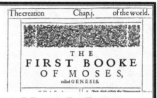

The creation   Chap.j.   of the world.

THE
FIRST BOOKE
OF MOSES,
called GENESIS.

****

King James Bible Rev. 4:11
Thou art worthy, O Lord, to receive glory and honour and power: for thou hast created all things, and **for thy pleasure** they are and were created.

New King James Version Rev. 4:11
You are worthy, O Lord, To receive glory and honor and power; For You created all things,
And **by Your will** they exist and were created.

❶ The King James Bible and the New King James Version DO NOT SAY or MEAN the same thing.

❷ The NKJV says God willingly created all things. Obviously. This is <u>not</u> news.

❸ The King James says God made <u>ALL</u> things <u>FOR</u> his pleasure. This is a revelation.

This is a **big picture verse.** With it, you can explain to anybody why God created the devil, angels, men, women, and all things in the heavens and on Earth.

And, more importantly, WHY he's so upset.

Only a defective Bible buries God's <u>PURPOSE</u> in creating all things
FOR HIS PLEASURE.

NKJV Decades Behind 400 Year-Old KJB

****

King James Bible Revelation 13:16	New King James Version Rev. 13:16
And he causeth all, both small and great, rich and poor, free and bond, to receive a mark **in** their right hand, or **in** their foreheads:	He causes all, both small and great, rich and poor, free and slave, to receive a mark **on** their right hand or **on** their foreheads,

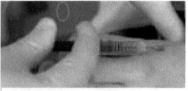

"A surgeon implants British scientist Dr. Mark Gasson in his left hand with an RFID microchip" (March 16, 2009)[1]

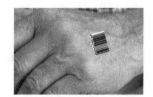

A mark ON hand

❶ Both the KJB and the NKJV say that the mark of the beast is found **ON or UPON** the right hand or forehead of those that received it.

Reference	King James Bible	New King James Version
Revelation 14:9	and receive *his* mark **IN** his forehead, or IN his hand	receives *his* mark **ON** his forehead or ON his hand,
Revelation 20:4	**UPON** their forehead and UPON their hand,	received *his* mark **ON** their foreheads or ON their hands.

❷ HOWEVER, only the KJB gives you greater insight into the fact that the mark of the beast will be **both UPON and IN** the right-hand and forehead.

❸ In short, the RFID chip will be inserted under the skin along with a mark on top of the skin for scanning.

For a modern, up to date Bible version, the NKJV is woefully inadequate.

Learn more, get the book: WHICH BIBLE WOULD JESUS USE? The Bible Version Controversy Explained and Resolved By Jack McElroy
www.JackMcElroy.com

Available from

CHICK PUBLICATIONS

amazon

nook

1.   https://en.wikipedia.org/wiki/Microchip_implant_(human)

NKJV Erases God's Name

****

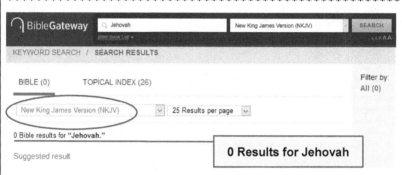

0 Results for Jehovah

❶ **The Lord's name has been revealed to you for over 400 years in the King James Bible:**

And I appeared unto Abraham, unto Isaac, and unto Jacob, by the name of God Almighty, but by my name **Jehovah** was I not known to them. **Exodus 6:3 (KJB)**

❷ **They say the NKJV removes the archaisms found in the King James Bible. Is your Lord's name now archaic?**

❸ **Not surprisingly, the New International Version erases it too:**

New International Version (NIV)

0 Bible results for "**jehovah**."

Demonstrating once again that the NKJV is just another modern version.

Available from

Learn more, get the book: WHICH BIBLE WOULD JESUS USE? The Bible Version Controversy Explained and Resolved By Jack McElroy
www.JackMcElroy.com

"The New King James Is So Much Easier to Understand"

****

Here's some of its vocabulary...

Alighting; Allays; Armlets; Befalls; Belial; Bleat; Bray; Buffet; Burnished; Caldron; Carrion; Chalkstones; Circumspect; Citron; Dainties; Dandled; Daubed; Dappled; Enmity; Entrails; Fallow; Festal; Fowlers; Fuller; Furlongs; Jackdaw; Mammon; Matrix; Paramours; Parapet; Pilfering; Pinions; plaited; Potentate; Potsherd; Poultice; Prattler; Prow; Pyre; Quadrans; Raze; Retinue; Rivulets; Rogue; Satiate; Shards; Sistrums; Skiff; Supplanted; Tamarisk; Terebinth; Timbrel; Tresses; Verdure; Verity; Waifs; Wane; Wend; and woof.

Some of these words are in the KJB and may require a dictionary to learn the meanings.

BUT...

Why are they in the NKJV? Isn't it supposed to be easier to understand because they dropped the "thees" and "thous"?

Easier? Sure it is.

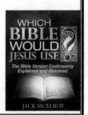

Available from

Learn more, get the book: WHICH BIBLE WOULD JESUS USE? The Bible Version Controversy Explained and Resolved By Jack McElroy
www.JackMcElroy.com

CHICK
PUBLICATIONS

amazon

nook

Photo Attribution: Alpha Stock Images - http://alphastockimages.com/

NKJV Dirty Tricks Revealed

****

Dirty Trick #1

One the objectives of the NKJV is to transition you <u>**FROM**</u> the King James Bible **TO** <u>**A**</u> modern version.

The Nelson promo found on the back cover says:

> **"And this is the perfect transition Bible if you are thinking about moving <u>from</u> the classic King James to <u>a</u> modern translation."**

This is very troublesome to say the least.

Dirty Trick #2

Even the New King James translators weren't sold on it. Some went on to translate other modern versions like the ESV, NLT, HCSB, and ISV.[1]

Why should you believe every word of the NKJV when even the guys that built it weren't sold on it?

Available from

Learn more, get the book: WHICH BIBLE WOULD JESUS USE? The Bible Version Controversy Explained and Resolved By Jack McElroy
www.JackMcElroy.com

Bible Version Secrets Exposed

The New King James question nobody asks...

Why Did It Need to Be Produced in the First Place?

****

Adapted from: WHICH BIBLE WOULD JESUS USE? Chapter 8, pp.127–128

Did the Lord decide that the 1611 Authorized Version he'd been blessing for 371 years [NKJV was published in 1982] just didn't cut it anymore?

When did the best-selling, most read Bible of all time become insufficient to meet the needs of his people?

Here's a theological question:
Do you believe that just because someone publishes a book with the title "Bible" on it that it has to be "God's will"?

How many things have you done that were definitely "God's will"?
Likewise, just because some academic, scholarly Christian contracts his translation services to a businessman, does it automatically follow that it's "God's will" just because he's agreed to work on a book titled "Bible"?

There have been well over 100 English Bible versions published in the last hundred years.

Do you think the Lord was behind them all? Even if their publishers and committee members did, that doesn't make it so.

Top brands distinguish themselves by setting a standard of quality that all pretenders to the throne must meet or be forever lost in the ordinary.

You always get what you expect from top brands because they consistently prove themselves dependable. Their quality doesn't change over time.

They give you confidence. That's why you trust them....

In marketing, this is known as "brand insistence."

BRANDING IS EVERYTHING

$1.25 $3.25

The reason there is such a thing as "King James Onlyism" is because the King James Bible is the <u>only</u> <u>brand</u> millions of folks have insisted on.

If the Lord chooses the NKJV, then he would be undermining the integrity of the brand that he established over 400 years ago.

Image credit: Amy Nadine Dix @amyndix

What's Wrong with the New King James Version?

****

Many things; but your best short answer comes from WHICH BIBLE WOULD JESUS USE? The Bible Version Controversy Explained and Resolved Chapter 8...

Even the editors who built the book aren't sold on it...

Their Bible has so much authority that the editors of the ©1982 NKJV actually encourage their readers to alter it as they see fit. You don't believe it? Here's what they said:

> It was the editors' conviction that the use of footnotes would encourage further inquiry by readers. They also recognized that it was easier for the average reader to delete something he or she felt was not properly a part of the text, than to insert a word or phrase which had been left out by the revisers.[1]

Look how their variant reading footnotes "encourage further inquiry" and make it "easier for the average reader to"...

• **"Delete"** the word "yet" from the text and present Jesus a liar like the NIV, NASB, ESV, and Holman Christian Standard (HCSB) do in John 7:8–10.

• **"Delete"** the phrase "without a cause," thereby presenting Jesus a sinner like the NIV does in Matthew 5:22 and Mark 3:5.

• **"Delete"** the proof text for the Trinity like the NIV, ESV, NASB, and HCSB do in 1 John 5:7–8.

• **"Delete"** the proof text for the Incarnation explicitly stating that God became a man like the NIV, ESV, and NASB do in 1 Timothy 3:16.

The revisers themselves aren't even sold on the Greek and Hebrew texts underlying the ©1982 NKJV. That's why they worded their comment as they did.[2]

If the folks who built the book aren't sold on it... why should you be?

Available from

Learn more, get the book: WHICH BIBLE WOULD JESUS USE? The Bible Version Controversy Explained and Resolved By Jack McElroy
www.JackMcElroy.com

amazon

nook

---

1. New King James Version, Old Time Gospel Hour edition, p. 1235. 2. McElroy, WHICH BIBLE WOULD JESUS USE? p.147

NKJV Editor Says
You're Handicapped

****

James D. Price B.S., M.Div, Ph.D. was Professor of Hebrew and Old Testament, Temple Baptist Seminary, 1972—2005. **He was also executive editor, Old Testament, New King James Version.** In his book *King James Onlyism: A New Sect*, he says:

> **"Anyone who limits his study of God's word to one <u>out</u>-<u>of</u>-<u>date</u> translation is unnecessarily restricted by his own <u>self</u>-<u>inflicted</u> <u>handicap</u>."**[1]

His statement means God has **NO STANDARD** when it comes to his words.

Look how Dr. Price's <u>teaching</u> makes your Lord contradict himself...

Mat. 18:22	How many times did Jesus say you should forgive your brother?
ESV	Jesus said to him, "I do not say to you seven times, but seventy-seven times." [77]
NASB	Jesus said to him, "I do not say to you, up to seven times, but up to seventy times seven." [490]
2 Sam. 15:7	How long did Absalom wait to talk to King David?
ESV	And at the end of **four years** Absalom said to the king… [4]
NASB	Now it came about at the end of **forty years** that Absalom [40]
Luke 10:1	How many did Jesus appoint in Luke 10?
ESV	After this the Lord appointed **seventy-two** others… [72]
NASB	Now after this the Lord appointed **seventy** others… [70]

And he thinks we're handicapped?

Available from

Learn more, get the book: WHICH BIBLE WOULD
JESUS USE? The Bible Version Controversy
Explained and Resolved By Jack McElroy
www.JackMcElroy.com

1. *King James Onlyism: A New Sect*, p.313.

NKJV Editor Exposed

****

James D. Price (B.S., M.Div, Ph.D.) was Professor of Hebrew and Old Testament, Temple Baptist Seminary, 1972—2005. He was also executive editor, Old Testament, New King James Version.

In an April of 1996 email, he admitted to author David Cloud that he is not committed to the Received Text and that he supports the modern critical text in general:

> "**I am not a TR** [Textus Receptus] **advocate**. I happen to believe that God has preserved the autographic text in the whole body of evidence that He has preserved, not merely through the textual **decisions of a committee of fallible men based on a handful of late manuscripts.** The modern critical text ... apparatus indicates where possible additions, omissions, and alterations have occurred....
> **I am not at war with the conservative modern versions**"[1]

Sounds like he thinks the KJB is a low-grade book, produced by translators not up to his caliber. At any rate...

Who builds a product they don't even believe in?

Available from

Learn more, get the book: WHICH BIBLE WOULD JESUS USE? The Bible Version Controversy Explained and Resolved By Jack McElroy
www.JackMcElroy.com

1.   http://www.wayoflife.org/database/what_about_new_king_james_version.html

NKJV's Dirty Little Secret Exposed

•••

The Deceptive Claim:

> "The Statement of Purpose issued by Thomas Nelson, publishers of the New King James Bible New Testament (1979), makes the following claim:

> "**Not to add to, take from, nor alter** the communication intended by the original translators, but to convey that communication in 20th century vocabulary and usage."[1]

The Truth:

In 1996, prolific author David Cloud corresponded via email with New King James Version Old Testament Executive Editor, Dr. James Price. Cloud says:

> "Dr. Price told me that the NKJV translators **DID NOT SOLELY FOLLOW** the Masoretic Hebrew text in the Old Testament of the NKJV but that **they introduced textual changes**.

> This is born out in the Preface to the NKJV, which says the New King James Bible **modifies the Masoretic Hebrew** with the **Septuagint**, the **Latin Vulgate**, "**a variety of ancient versions**," and the **Dead Sea Scrolls**."[2]

If you believed the NKJV is just an updated translation of the KJB text... you've been had.

Available from

Learn more, get the book: WHICH BIBLE WOULD
JESUS USE? The Bible Version Controversy
Explained and Resolved By Jack McElroy
www.JackMcElroy.com

1 http://www.wayoflife.org/database/what_about_new_king_james_version.html 2. Ibid.

Why You Shouldn't Trust the NKJV

****

Because even the team that built it didn't trust their own text...

The NKJV editors actually **encourage their readers to alter it as they see fit.** Here's what they said:

"It was the editors' conviction that the use of footnotes would encourage further inquiry by readers. They also recognized that it was easier for the average reader to delete something he or she felt was not properly a part of the text, than to insert a word or phrase which had been left out by the revisers."[1]

Their footnotes **"encourage further inquiry"** and make it **"easier for the average reader to"**...

• Delete the word **"yet"** from the text, **making Jesus a liar** like the NIV, NASB, ESV, and HCSB do in John 7:8–10.

• Delete the phrase **"without a cause,"** **making Jesus a sinner** like the NIV does in Matthew 5:22 and Mark 3:5.

• Delete the **proof text for the true nature of God** like the NIV, ESV, NASB, and HCSB do in 1 John 5:7–8.

If the professionals who built the NKJV aren't certain which words are God's and which are men's, why should you <u>trust</u> it?

Available from

WHICH BIBLE WOULD JESUS USE
The Bible Version Controversy Explained and Resolved
JACK McELROY

Learn more, get the book: **WHICH BIBLE WOULD JESUS USE? The Bible Version Controversy Explained and Resolved By Jack McElroy** www.JackMcElroy.com

CHICK PUBLICATIONS

amazon
nook

¹ New King James Version, Old Time Gospel Hour edition, p. 1235.

NKJV Gate

NKJV Insider Reveals True Goals—
(1) Bridge to Modern Versions
(2) Break Down Resistance of KJV Believers...

Introduction by Jack McElroy:

One of the biggest competitors to the true Bible (i.e., King James Bible) is the New King James Version. Based largely in part because people think it's just a modernization of the King James Bible.

Jack McElroy
www.jackmcelroy.com

They pitch it to us as coming from the same texts (which is pretty much true although not completely).

They promote it as a fifth revision (which it really isn't but it sounds good). Even if it were a revision, by whose authority did they undertake such a task?

Did the Lord feel it was necessary? No one ever asks that question.

Anyway, one of the best ways to uncover the truth about your competition is to listen to their salespeople.

In the following excerpt, you get the chance to read what a sales rep from Thomas Nelson (then publisher of the New King James Version) said its goals were.

The shocking revelation is that one of the purposes for the New King James Version is to break down the resistance of those who still revere the KJV and serve as a transitional bridge to eventually get people to accept **a** "more accurate Bible" (i.e., modern version).

Here's the inside scoop...

Reprinted with permission from:
What About the New King James Version?
Updated January 8, 2015 (first published March 9, 2003) (David Cloud, Fundamental Baptist Information Service, P.O. Box 610368, Port Huron, MI 48061, 866-295-4143, fbns@wayoflife.org) http://www.wayoflife.org/

THE MOST SIGNIFICANT PROBLEM THAT WE HAVE WITH THE NEW KING JAMES VERSION IS

THAT IT IS A BRIDGE TO THE MODERN VERSIONS.

In reality, therefore, the New King James Version is simply a bridge to the modern versions.

Those who move away from the standard King James Bible to the New King James are lulled into a sense of security that they have moved merely to an updated and improved King James, but actually they are being brainwashed to be weaned away from the King James and to accept the modern versions.

Kirk DiVietro, Pastor of Grace Baptist Church in Franklin, Massachusetts, was in one of the Thomas Nelson planning meetings that prepared the way for the publication of the New King James.

He testified to me that the Thomas Nelson representative plainly stated that **their goal with the NKJV was to create a bridge to the modern versions, to break down the resistance of those who still revere the KJV.**

Following is Bro. DiVietro's testimony as he gave it to me by e-mail on January 9, 2005:

"Over 20 years ago I attended a pre-publication meeting of the NKJV held by the Thomas Nelson People and hosted by the Hackman's Bible Bookstore in Allentown, PA.

I am personal friends with the owners who took great delight in seating me next to the brother of the main translator of the NIV. The meeting was attended by over 300 college professors and pastors.

At the meeting we were treated to a slide presentation of the history of the English bible and in particular the King James Bible and its several revisions.

During the presentation of the NKJV the **Thomas Nelson representative** made a statement which to the best of my memory was,

> "We are all educated people here.
>
> **We would never say this to our people**, but we all know that the King James Version is a poor translation based on poor texts.
>
> But every attempt to give your people a better Bible has failed.
>
> **They just won't accept <u>them</u>.**
>
> **So we have gone back and done a revision of the King James Version, a fifth revision.**
>
> **Hopefully it will serve as a transitional bridge to eventually get your people to accept a more accurate Bible."**

Because of the years, and because I did not write it down, I cannot give you the speaker's name and I cannot promise you that this is word for word correct, but the meeting so seared my spirit that I have never picked up and opened a NKJV.

I can tell you that this is absolutely the substance and nearly the exact words of what was said.

Now you know how sinister and deceptive the New King James Version really is.

Learn more, get the book: WHICH BIBLE WOULD JESUS USE? The Bible Version Controversy Explained and Resolved By Jack McElroy
www.JackMcElroy.com

Available from

The Holman Christian Standard Bible/Christian Standard Bible

Introduction

****

The Holman Christian Standard Bible, now retitled as the Christian Standard Bible, is just another imposter pretending to be a "Christian Standard."

The HCSB/CSB is published by LifeWay, a nonprofit agency of the Southern Baptist Convention.

Like the evangelicals who were concerned with the NIV's plan to produce an "inclusive language" revision that would make the NIV less accurate but more acceptable to feminists, the Southern Baptists were looking to buy the rights to something they could be more comfortable with than the NIV, which they had used up to that point.

Unable to buy any rights, they decided to produce their own Bible. In 2004, they introduced the Holman Christian **Standard** Bible. It was revised in 2009. Then they changed the name to Christian **Standard** Bible in an effort to prove to the world that it IS some sort of **standard**.

All without proof, of course.

BUT, you have to be different to copyright and market a new Bible. So ...

Let me introduce you to a pagan god called Yahweh.

Bible researcher Michael Marlowe explains:

> The Tetragrammaton [YHWH] occurs 6,828 times in the Hebrew Bible. Nearly all English versions follow the ancient tradition of rendering the Divine name as "the Lord." The King James Version makes only four exceptions (Exodus 6:3, Psalm 83:18, Isaiah 12:2, and Isaiah 26:4), where it renders the name as "Jehovah."

HCSB Teaches Christians to Worship Pagan God

Jehovah? or Yahweh?

****

King James Bible Exodus 6:3	Holman Christian Standard Bible Ex. 6:3
And I appeared unto Abraham, unto Isaac, and unto Jacob, by the name of God Almighty, but by my name **JEHOVAH** was I not known to them.	I appeared to Abraham, Isaac, and Jacob as God Almighty, but I did not reveal My name **Yahweh** to them.

The "<u>**tetragrammaton**</u>" consists of four Hebrew consonants, יהוה (YHWH). The controversy is over how the letters should be pronounced. The only way to know is to add vowels.

Obviously, different names identify different people.

❶ They tell us it should be YaHWeH (they add an "a" & "e").

What they DON'T tell you (or don't know) is …

❷ The word "Yahweh" **HAS NEVER BEEN FOUND** in **ANY HEBREW MANUSCRIPT** or ANY major English Bible prior to the HCSB.

<u>And yet…</u>

❸ Biblical scholar Nehemiah Gordon cites **over 1,000 Hebrew manuscripts <u>with</u> the name YeHoWaH—i.e. "Jehovah"—clearly spelled out.**[1]

---

1 https://www.nehemiaswall.com/1000-manuscripts-yehovah

Page 1

❹ How do we KNOW it's not Yahweh?

Not only are there over 1,000 Hebrew manuscripts that SPELL IT OUT, but the pronunciation is found in what's known as "Theophoric names."

They're names that combine the name of God with another word to create a new name as seen in this chart to the right.

These familiar names begin with "Yeh" (Jeh in English) as in "Jehovah" and are NOT derivatives of Yahweh.

Chart (left to right, top to bottom): Yeho'achaz, Yeho'adah, Yehoash, Yeho'adan, Yehozavad, Yehotzadak, Yehochanan, Yehoram, Yehoyada, Yehosheva, Yehoyakhin, Yehoshav'at, Yehoyakim, Yehoshua, Yehonadav, Yehoshafat, Yehonatan, **Yehovah**

http://seekingtruth.info

❺ So, where did this Yahweh character come from and WHO is he?

Not surprisingly, 19th-century scholars played *Scrabble* with the Tetragrammaton by inserting various vowels into the name, thereby producing many iterations; one of which is Yahweh.

The problem?

❻ By so doing, they linked their newly coined "Yahweh" name to pagan gods like Jove (a.k.a. Jupiter [Acts 14:12], Yaho, Yahu, Yave, because they sound like Yahweh depending on the language).

In ancient Latin, Jove was pronounced, "YO Way." Sound familiar?

So, when anyone calls on "Yahweh," they're unknowingly calling the name of a pagan god.

Not exactly the "Hebrew nugget" they make it out to be, is it?

Available from

Learn more, get the book: WHICH BIBLE WOULD JESUS USE? The Bible Version Controversy Explained and Resolved By Jack McElroy www.JackMcElroy.com

Image: http://seekingtruth.info/blog/hebrew-theophoric-names-and-the-name-of-god/

Page 2

HCSB Confuses Dog with Money

****

King James Bible Deut. 23:18
Thou shalt not bring the hire of a whore, or **the price of a dog**, into the house of the LORD thy God for any vow: for even both these are abomination unto the LORD thy God.

Holman Christian Standard Bible Deut. 23:18
Do not bring a female prostitute's wages or **a male prostitute's earnings** into the house of the LORD your God to fulfill any vow, because both are detestable to the LORD your God.

According to author David W. Daniels,

"The word 'dog' (keleb) is translated 'dog' all through the Old Testament. It means 'dog,' plain and simple." [1]

Why the difference in the Holman Christian Standard Bible (now called The Christian Standard Bible)?

Daniels says, **"This <u>isn't</u> <u>translating</u>. This <u>is</u> <u>interpreting</u>.** They placed their opinion into the text, instead of the words God preserved. A true translator won't let his personal opinions or interpretations stop him from accurately transferring the Bible concept to the target language."

The HCSB is just another wannabe that's nobody's "standard."

Learn more, get the book: WHICH BIBLE WOULD JESUS USE? The Bible Version Controversy Explained and Resolved By Jack McElroy
www.JackMcElroy.com

Available from

CHICK PUBLICATIONS

amazon

nook

WHICH BIBLE WOULD JESUS USE
The Bible Version Controversy Explained and Resolved
JACK MCELROY

1. https://www.chick.com/bc/2015/15_bibles.asp

HCSB Misunderstands the World System

* *

King James Bible 1 Kings 22:38	Holman Christian Standard Bible 1 Kings 22:38
And *one* washed the chariot in the pool of Samaria; **and the dogs licked up his blood; and they <u>washed</u> <u>his</u> <u>armour</u>**; according unto the word of the LORD which he spake.	Then someone washed the chariot at the pool of Samaria. **The dogs licked up his blood, and the <u>prostitutes</u> <u>bathed</u> in it**, according to the word of the LORD that He had spoken.

Kim Kardashian #VampireFacial

❶ It's always been the rich and/or ruling elites who've been obsessed with blood rituals thinking that's the ticket to the fountain of youth.

❷ Prostitutes are abused souls turning tricks just to live for another day.

❸ BUT the real Bible says **NOTHING** about bathing prostitutes.

The truth has been in print for over 400 years in the King James Bible.

Learn more, get the book: WHICH BIBLE WOULD JESUS USE? The Bible Version Controversy Explained and Resolved By Jack McElroy
www.JackMcElroy.com

Available from

CHICK PUBLICATIONS

amazon

nook

WHICH **BIBLE** WOULD JESUS USE?
The Bible Version Controversy Explained and Resolved
JACK MCELROY

Image: http://news.nationalpost.com/life/style/why-the-wealthy-believe-the-fountain-of-youth-flows-with-blood-and-are-spending-thousands-to-satiate-their-lust

Does Proverbs 11:30 Encourage You to Win Souls or Not?

****

<u>Yes</u>, if you believe the….
King James Bible Proverbs 11:30
"The fruit of the righteous *is* a tree of life; and

he that winneth souls *is* wise."

<u>No</u>, if you believe the…
Holman Christian Standard Bible Prov. 11:30
"The fruit of the righteous is a tree of life,

but violence takes lives."

Same verse; but they couldn't be more different.

And they have the nerve to tell you:

"Your stand on Bible versions causes division!"

Is there not a cause?

Available from

Learn more, get the book: WHICH BIBLE WOULD JESUS USE? The Bible Version Controversy Explained and Resolved By Jack McElroy
www.JackMcElroy.com

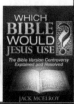

Which Way Did
Barney and Saul Go?

****

King James Bible Acts 12:25
And Barnabas and Saul **returned from** Jerusalem, when they had fulfilled *their* ministry, and took with them John, whose surname was Mark.

Christian Standard Bible Acts 12:25
After they had completed their relief mission, Barnabas and Saul **returned to Jerusalem**, taking along John who was called Mark.

❶ A Bible should have no errors to qualify as the word of God. And yet …

❷ EVERYBODY KNOWS (including the NIV, ESV, and NASB) Barnabas and Saul were returning **FROM** Jerusalem and going **TO** Antioch.

❸ Sadly, the scholars behind the Christian Standard Bible (A.K.A. the Holman Christian Standard Bible) broke ranks with fellow scholars and followed manuscripts that contain the error.

Printing this KNOWN ERROR in their Bible makes a mockery out of the word of God.

Available from

Learn more, get the book: WHICH BIBLE WOULD JESUS USE? The Bible Version Controversy Explained and Resolved By Jack McElroy
www.JackMcElroy.com

CHICK PUBLICATIONS

amazon

nook

HCSB: You're Nothing but a Slave

****

King James Bible 2 Timothy 2:24	Holman Christian Standard Bible 2Tim. 2:24
And **the servant** of the Lord must not strive; but be gentle unto all *men*, apt to teach, patient,	**The Lord's slave** must not quarrel, but must be gentle to everyone, able to teach, and patient,

❶ The notion that we are slaves found in modern Bible versions comes from Greek dictionary creator and lexographer Gerhard Kittel (1888–1948) who said:

> "The word *doulos* means slave, the meaning is so unequivocal, no study of history is necessary." [1]

❷ However, "Kittel was modernistic in his approach to the Bible, denying that it is the infallible Word of God."[2]

Gerhard Kittel

❸ **Slaves don't volunteer to be slaves.** You came to Christ willingly.
And whosoever will, let him take the water of life freely. Revelation 22:17 KJB

❹ **You're not a slave** because Christ has made you FREE.
If the Son therefore shall make you free, ye shall be free indeed. John 8:36 KJB

❺ **You willingly volunteered to serve your Lord.** In him, we are adopted sons of God who voluntarily become servants as an expression of our love to him.

The HCSB is an insult to the Lord and to believers on him.

Available from

Learn more, get the book: WHICH BIBLE WOULD JESUS
USE? The Bible Version Controversy Explained and
Resolved By Jack McElroy www.JackMcElroy.com

1 https://www.gty.org/library/sermons-library/GTY129/servant-or-slave 2. David Cloud, *The Modern Bible Version Hall of Shame*, p. 140.

The Bible Version Controversy Summed Up in One Photo

Title page and insert from the 2017 *Christian Standard Bible*. The Bible was formerly titled: *Holman Christian Standard Bible (HCSB)*.

The *Christian Standard Bible* folks ADMIT that the text in their BRAND NEW Bible Version is "not final." (And it still isn't.)

① The King James <u>text</u> has been settled for more than 400 years.

② The experts who bring you <u>ALL</u> modern Bible versions <u>STILL</u> haven't figured out which words are God's and which are men's.

How sad.

Learn more, get the book: WHICH BIBLE WOULD JESUS USE? The Bible Version Controversy Explained and Resolved By Jack McElroy
www.JackMcElroy.com

Available from

The New American Standard Bible—

The Version for Smart Kids

Introduction

****

The NASB hit the street in 1971. The New Testament first appeared in 1963. It was billed as a conservative, literal revision of the American Standard Version (1901).

They pitched it as a version for **"serious"** Bible study by **"serious students"** of the Bible.

Used to "correct" the so-called dated and deficient King James Bible, it was taught in fundamentalist colleges like it really was the word of God—faithful to the (nonexistent) originals.

Yet, it needed a major face-lift in 1995.

Bible version researcher Will Kinney reports:

> The NASB keeps on changing from one edition to the next. The changes introduced in the 1995 NASB update where it differs from the 1977 edition affect 10,616 verses and directly affect 24,338 words.

> There are only 4,704 changes in capitalization, 32 in spelling, and 30 in italics. This makes 19,572 corrections involving word omissions, additions, transpositions, or substitutions to the text of the NASB 1977.

> There are 6,966 fewer words in the 1995 edition than there were in the 1977 NASB.

These are not all just different ways of saying the same thing—the NASB of 1995 has actually altered the text itself, by adding whole phrases which were not found in the 1977 edition.

Every example of these changes is documented in a book by Laurence M. Vance titled *Double Jeopardy*, published in 1998.[1]

Of course, it doesn't really matter anymore because this version is presently on life support, no longer making the grade.

It's been replaced by the newer version for smart kids called the ESV.

---

1. https://brandplucked.webs.com/everchangingnasbs.htm

Dr. Ryrie Finds Hebrew Text Error; Probably Corrected by KJB

* *

King James Bible 2 Samuel 21:19	New American Standard Bible 2 Sam. 21:19
And there was again a battle in Gob with the Philistines, **where Elhanan** the son of Jaareoregim, a Bethlehemite, **slew *the brother of*** Goliath the Gittite, the staff of whose spear was like a weaver's beam.	There was war with the Philistines again at Gob, **and Elhanan** the son of Jaare-oregim the Bethlehemite **killed ____ _____ __** Goliath the Gittite, the shaft of whose spear was like a weaver's beam.

The Ryrie Study Bible, Expanded Edition, states:
"**The Hebrew text** attributes the slaying of Goliath to Elhanan, **in contradiction of** 1 Samuel 17:50.

There is evidence of a copyist's error (cf. 1 Chr. 20:5), and **it is probable** that Elhanan killed '**the brother of**' Goliath."[1]

Dr. Ryrie is right. "It is probable" that Elhanan killed the brother of Goliath and NOT Goliath; just like it says in billions of KJBs for over 400 years.

Available from

Learn more, get the book: WHICH BIBLE WOULD JESUS USE? The Bible Version Controversy Explained and Resolved By Jack McElroy www.JackMcElroy.com

1. *The Ryrie Study Bible, Expanded Edition,* ©1986, 1994 Moody Bible Institute, p. 520.

NASB Kills Cross-Reference to Your Lord's Voice

****

King James Bible I Kings 19:12	New American Standard Bible 1 Kngs 19:12
And after the earthquake a fire; but the LORD was not in the fire: and after the fire <u>a still small voice</u>.	After the earthquake a fire, but the LORD was not in the fire; and after the fire <u>a sound of a gentle blowing.</u>

❶ **The Lord has a voice that you can recognize:**
My sheep hear **my voice**, and I know them, and they follow me: John 10:27 KJB

❷ **The cross-reference description of his voice** mentioned in John 10:27 is found in 1Kings 19:21 **IF you have a KJB.**

❸ **The NASB says <u>NOTHING</u> about a voice in 1 Kings 19:2**.

The NASB is a sad excuse for a Bible that can't even tell you how to recognize your Saviour's voice.

NASB's God
Gets Deceived

****

King James Bible Psalms 78:36	New American Standard Bible Psalms 78:36
Nevertheless **they did <u>flatter</u> him** with their mouth, and they lied unto him with their tongues.	But **they <u>deceived</u> Him** with their mouth And lied to Him with their tongue.

The impotent God of the NASB got deceived by Israel. How pathetic.

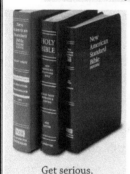

Get serious.

NASB⊠
Most literal, more readable.

❶ Can your Lord really be **DECEIVED** like the NASB says?

Or...

❷ Did the children of Israel **ATTEMPT to deceive** him with **FLATTERY** like the King James Bible says?

❸ Many leaders recommend the NASB for "**serious**" Bible study by "**serious students**" of the Bible.

Who's deceiving who?
Use "serious" Bible the Lord has endorsed for over 400 years.

Learn more, get the book: WHICH BIBLE WOULD JESUS USE? The Bible Version Controversy Explained and Resolved By Jack McElroy
www.JackMcElroy.com

Available from

WHICH
BIBLE
WOULD
JESUS USE
The Bible Version Controversy
Explained and Resolved
JACK MCELROY

How the NASB Calls Your Lord a Liar

* *

King James Bible Isaiah 38:8

Behold, I will bring again the shadow of the degrees, which is gone down in the sun dial of Ahaz, ten degrees backward. **So the sun returned ten degrees,** by which degrees it was gone down.

New American Standard Bible Is. 38:8

Behold, I will cause the shadow on the stairway, which has gone down with the sun on the stairway of Ahaz, to go back ten steps. So **the sun's shadow went back ten steps** on the stairway on which it had gone down.

A ccording to the King James Bible "the sun" returned 10,° by which degrees it was gone down. **Clearly, "the sun" reversed its course.**

E vidently, the NASB folks believe the Big Bang and Nebular Hypothesis Cosmologies and **don't believe the sun actually retraced his steps.** So, they conform the words to **THEIR BELIEF** and say that it was only **"the sun's shadow"** that went back.

Isn't this just another way of making your Lord a liar?

Available from

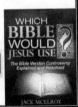

Learn more, get the book: WHICH BIBLE WOULD JESUS USE? The Bible Version Controversy Explained and Resolved By Jack McElroy
www.JackMcElroy.com

Photo: By liz west (Sundial) [CC BY 2.0 (http://creativecommons.org/licenses/by/2.0)], via Wikimedia Commons

Professors' Nonsensical Statement on Bible Versions

✴✴

King James Bible Jeremiah 10:5	New American Standard Bible Jer. 10:5
They *are* upright as the <u>palm tree</u>, but speak not: they must needs be borne, because they cannot go. Be not afraid of them; for they cannot do evil, neither also *is it* in them to do good.	Like a <u>scarecrow</u> in a cucumber field are they, And they cannot speak; They must be carried, Because they cannot walk! Do not fear them, For they can do no harm, Nor can they do any good.

❶ It doesn't take a genius to see that these two Bibles **SAY** and **MEAN** different things.

❷ **BOTH <u>cannot</u> be God's word.**

❸ And yet a couple of Fundamentalist professors from Bob Jones University tell us …

GOD'S WORD IN OUR HANDS "When we use a faithful conservative translation such as **the King James Version**, New King James Version, **the New American Standard Version**, or another version of demonstrated accuracy we can trust our Bible <u>as</u> the word of God. We can be confident that **we have God's word in our hands.**"[1]

Nonsense; nothing but scholarly doublespeak from the land of OZ.

Available from

CHICK
PUBLICATIONS
amazon
nook

Learn more, get the book: WHICH BIBLE WOULD
JESUS USE? The Bible Version Controversy Explained
and Resolved By Jack McElroy www.JackMcElroy.com

1. James B. Williams, Randolph Shaylor, *God's Word in Our Hands: The Bible Preserved for Us*, p. 422.

NASB Presents Two Gods

* *

King James Bible John 1:18	New American Standard Bible Jn. 1:18
No man hath seen **God** at any time; **the only <u>begotten</u> <u>Son</u>**, which is in the bosom of the Father, he hath declared him.	No one has seen **God** at any time; **the only <u>begotten</u> <u>God</u>,** who is in the bosom of the Father, he has explained him.

According to the NASB, there must be two; **the original one** and **the begotten one.**

Author and textual expert Dr. Wilbur Pickering says:

"Instead of 'the only begotten son' (as in over 99.5% of the Greek manuscripts), some five manuscripts (of inferior quality, objectively so) have 'an only begotten god', while another two (also inferior) have 'the only begotten god.'

… this alternative has appealed to many evangelicals who see in it a strong affirmation of the deity of Christ.

<u>But</u> if the God-part of the Christ was begotten in the womb of the virgin Mary, **then He is not eternally pre-existent; and in that event Christ could not be God the Son …** [How Ironic.]

… why follow … manuscripts of demonstrably inferior quality against 1,700 better ones? The original and therefore true reading is certainly 'the only begotten Son'".[1]

The NASB; theologically defective … again.

Available from

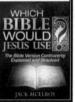

Learn more, get the book: WHICH BIBLE WOULD JESUS USE? The Bible Version Controversy Explained and Resolved By Jack McElroy www.jackmcelroy.com

1 http://www.walkinhiscommandments.com/Pickering/New%20Translation/John-ff-revised.pdf

NASB Jesus Lies

****

King James Bible John 7:8–10	New American Standard Bible Jn. 7:8–10
Go ye up unto this feast: **I go not up <u>yet</u> unto this feast;** for my time is not yet full come. When he had said these words unto them, he abode still in Galilee. But when his brethren were gone up, **then went he also up unto the feast**, not openly, but as it were in secret.	Go up to the feast yourselves; <u>I do not go</u> up to this feast because My time has not yet fully come." Having said these things to them, He stayed in Galilee. But when His brothers had gone up to the feast, **then He Himself also went up**, not publicly, but as if, in secret.

❶ The King James Bible accurately reports that the Lord said he **was not going up to the feast** <u>YET</u> because he did go up <u>later</u>.

❷ The Jesus of the NASB is telling a "<u>white lie</u>" by saying that he **was not going up** to the feast at all, only to go later.

> **WHITE LIES MATTER**

❸ **What's disturbing is that Fundamentalist academics seem to be oblivious to the obvious problem here.** Here's a quote from a Fundamentalist book justifying BOTH Bibles!

"When we use a **faithful conservative translation** such as the **King James Version**, New King James Version, **the New American Standard Bible,** or another version of **demonstrated accuracy** *we can trust our Bible as the word of God.* We can be confident that we have God's Word in our hands."[1]

Would your Saviour ever use a "faithful conservative translation" with "demonstrated accuracy" that makes him a liar?

Learn more, get the book: WHICH BIBLE WOULD JESUS USE? The Bible Version Controversy Explained and Resolved By Jack McElroy
www.JackMcElroy.com

Available from

CHICK PUBLICATIONS

amazon
nook

WHICH BIBLE WOULD JESUS USE?
The Bible Version Controversy Explained and Resolved
JACK MCELROY

1.   *God's Word in Our Hands*, Ambassador Emerald Publications, Greenville, SC. p. 422.

Blatant NASB
Error Exposed

****

King James Bible 1 Cor. 5:1
It is reported commonly *that there is* fornication among you, and such fornication as is **not so much as named** among the Gentiles, that one should have his father's wife.

New American Standard Bible 1 Cor. 5:1
It is actually reported that there is immorality among you, and immorality of such a kind as **does not exist** even among the Gentiles, that someone has his father's wife.

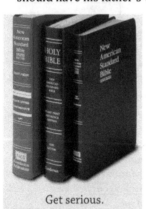

Get serious.

question the most faithful of all literal, word-for-word Bible translations, and now also the *ly for serious word-for-word study, see other English Bible compares. The Updated NASB* *r text, reference, study and specialty editions.*

NASB
Most literal, more readable.

❶ The NASB says this type of incest "does not exist" among the Gentiles. Are they kidding you?

❷ Every kind of sexual perversion has existed throughout history.

❸ And they tell us the NASB is for those who want to do "serious Bible study."

Seriously?

Available from

WHICH
BIBLE
WOULD
JESUS USE
The Bible Version Controversy
Explained and Resolved
JACK MCELROY

Learn more, get the book: WHICH BIBLE WOULD JESUS USE? The Bible Version Controversy Explained and Resolved By Jack McElroy www.JackMcElroy.com

NASB Needs to "Lawyer Up"

****

King James Bible Hebrews 9:16	New American Standard Bible Heb. 9:16
For where a **testament** *is*, there must also of necessity be the death of the testator.	For where a **covenant** is, there must of necessity be the death of the one who made it.

❶ **A testament** is the true declaration of a man's last will as to that which he would have to be done, **after his death.**[1]

❷ **A covenant** is an agreement or promise honored by two or more persons *while they are alive.*[2]

❸ **Clearly in error**, the NASB needs to hire a lawyer to explain the difference to the translators. And yet many Christian leaders recommend the NASB for "serious" Bible study by "serious students" of the Bible.

Get serious.

NASB⬛
Most literal, more readable.

The NASB: Seriously defective.

Available from

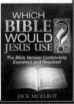

Learn more, get the book: WHICH BIBLE WOULD JESUS USE? The Bible Version Controversy Explained and Resolved By Jack McElroy
www.JackMcElroy.com

CHICK PUBLICATIONS

amazon
nook

1 See Black's Law Dictionary: http://heimatundrecht.de/sites/default/files/dokumente/Black%27sLaw4th.pdf 2. Ibid.

NASB Makes Elementary School Science Error

****

King James Bible James 3:12	New American Standard Bible Jas. 3:12
Can the fig tree, my brethren, bear olive berries? either a vine, figs? **so *can* <u>no</u> <u>fountain</u> both yield <u>salt water</u> and fresh.**	Can a fig tree, my brethren, produce olives, or a vine produce figs? **<u>Nor</u> can <u>salt</u> <u>water</u> <u>produce</u> <u>fresh</u>.**

A spring can't bring forth both salt and fresh water; But salt water <u>does produce fresh water</u> on a continual basis because most rain we get comes from <u>evaporated</u> <u>ocean</u> <u>saltwater</u>.

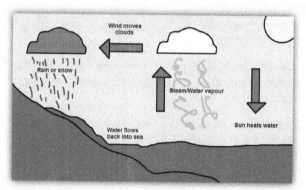

For all their smarts, the NASB translators must have skipped what's plain in a kid's science book. **God doesn't do errors. The NASB does.**

Unlike the NASB, King James Bible is scientifically accurate.

Available from

CHICK
PUBLICATIONS

amazon

nook

Learn more, get the book: WHICH BIBLE WOULD JESUS USE? The Bible Version Controversy Explained and Resolved By Jack McElroy www.JackMcElroy.com

Which Edition of the NASB Is Authentic?

****

The NASB ©1995 Has Almost 7,000 Words Less Than the ©1977 Edition. Yet we're taught...

Dr. R. Albert Mohler, Jr., President,
Southern Baptist Theological Seminary

"The New American Standard Bible has set the standard for faithful Bible translations for a generation. It is the favorite of so many who love the Bible and look for **accuracy** and clarity in translation. The New American Standard Bible should be close at hand for any serious student of the Bible. I thank God for this faithful translation."[1]

King James Bible believers are constantly accosted with the "which edition" question. Which makes us ask …

Which edition should a **"serious"** student of the Bible trust as accurately presenting the Word of God; the 1977 or 1995 NASB editions?

Did the Lord update "the originals?" Or were lots of new manuscripts discovered in those 18 years?

More importantly, does the Lord trust the NASB (either edition)?

Available from

CHICK
PUBLICATIONS

amazon
nook

WHICH
BIBLE
WOULD
JESUS USE
The Bible Version Controversy Explained and Resolved

Learn more, get the book: WHICH BIBLE WOULD JESUS USE? The Bible Version Controversy Explained and Resolved By Jack McElroy
www.JackMcElroy.com

1. http://www.lockman.org/nasb/endorsements.php

The New Living Translation—
The Paraphrase Pretending to Be a Bible
Introduction

****

Bible Researcher Michael D. Marlowe says:

> The *New Living Translation* is an extensive revision of
> Ken Taylor's Living Bible (published by Tyndale House in
> 1971). It was designed to improve the accuracy of Taylor's
> paraphrase.

> The press release also says that the NLT is an "entirely
> new translation," but an examination of the version shows
> that it inherits many renderings of the Living Bible which
> would probably not have been used by the NLT reviewers
> if they started from scratch.[1]

Gender-Neutralism and Egalitarianism

… the NLT carefully
avoids the use of "male-
oriented" language. In
Bible translations this
involves a suppression of
the male-oriented
language in the original
text by means of various circumlocutions and paraphrases.
We may suppose that in the NLT this was done in a late
editorial stage of the version's production, because it is
evident from the press release quoted above that it was
done without the cooperation or approval of some of the
scholars who worked on the version.[2]

---

1. http://www.bible-researcher.com/nlt.html
2. Ibid.

The preface of the NLT is less than frank about the reasons for this gender-neutral language. It claims that this style is necessary "to make the translation clear to a modern audience that tends to read male-oriented language as applying only to males" and that it is "driven by the concern to reflect accurately the intended meaning of the original texts."[3]

… when we examine the version, it seems that there was no real attempt by the NLT editors to reproduce the style of the original, or even the meaning of the text beyond a very basic and simplified level.[4]

Ah, the ol' "fake right" and "jab with the left" ploy.

And this doesn't even count some of the other weird stuff the NLT comes up with, as you will see in this section.

3. Ibid.
4. Ibid.

NLT Corrupts Prophetic Reference to Christ

****

King James Bible Genesis 22:18	New Living Translation Genesis 22:18
And **in thy** <u>seed</u> shall all the nations of the earth be blessed; because thou hast obeyed my voice.	And **through your** <u>descendants</u> all the nations of the earth will be blessed—all because you have obeyed me.

<u>The **seed**</u> of Abraham is the Lord Jesus Christ.

Now to Abraham and **his** <u>seed</u> were the promises made. He saith not, And to seeds, as of many; but **as of one**, And to **thy seed, <u>which is Christ</u>**. Gal. 3:16 KJB

<u>ONLY</u> <u>JESUS</u> has the **ability** and **power** to bless all nations.

<u>The **descendants**</u> of Abraham were all mere mortals incapable of saving themselves let alone "blessing all the nations."

<u>The NLT is a moneymaker</u> for Tyndale House Publishers. The Christian Booksellers Association ranks the NLT as the second most popular English version of the Bible based on unit sales.[1]

There's nothing wrong with making money selling a good product ... But one riddled with errors? That's a different story.

Available from

CHICK
PUBLICATIONS

amazon
nook

WHICH
BIBLE
WOULD
JESUS USE
The Bible Version Controversy
Explained and Resolved

Learn more, get the book: WHICH BIBLE WOULD JESUS USE? The Bible Version Controversy Explained and Resolved By Jack McElroy www.JackMcElroy.com

NLT Confuses Mildew with Leprosy

King James Bible Leviticus 13:47
The garment also that the plague of <u>**leprosy**</u> is in, *whether it be* a woollen garment, or a linen garment;

New Living Translation Lev. 13:47
"Now suppose <u>**mildew**</u> contaminates some woolen or linen clothing,

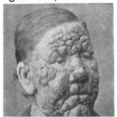

Leprosy needs to be cured.

Mildew needs to be cleaned.

Leprosy is a terrifying disease curable today but in times past only by miracle of God.

Mildew is an annoyance that's easily cleaned up — then and now; no miracle required. Home and Garden TV says: "**Mildew** is a surface fungi that can easily be identified as a patch of gray or even white fungus that is lying on the surface of a moist area. **Mildew is easily treated with a store-bought cleaner and a scrubbing brush.**"[1]

The NLT—tough on stains, not so hot on accuracy.

1.   https://www.hgtv.com/remodel/interior-remodel/mold-vs-mildew

Should You Win Friends or Win Souls?

****

King James Bible Proverbs 11:30	New Living Translation Prov. 11:30
The fruit of the righteous is a tree of life; and **he that winneth souls** is wise.	The seeds of good deeds become a tree of life; **a wise person <u>wins friends</u>.**

❶ Surely, "a wise person wins friends."

❷ And any wise soul winner is also a good friend maker.

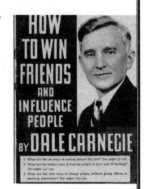

❸ BUT a BIBLICALLY wise person WINS SOULS.

❹ Which is something the NLT's proverb clearly DOESN'T SAY.

The King James Bible ... the soul winner's choice for over 400 years.

Learn more, get the book: WHICH BIBLE WOULD JESUS USE? The Bible Version Controversy Explained and Resolved By Jack McElroy
www.JackMcElroy.com

Available from

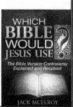

NLT Makes God Your Servant

****

| King James Bible Proverbs 16:3 Commit **thy works** unto the LORD, and **thy** <u>thoughts</u> shall be established. | New Living Translation Prov. 16:3 Commit **your actions** to the LORD, and **your** **plans** <u>will</u> <u>succeed</u>. |

Just because you commit "your actions" to the LORD doesn't mean he's going to bless "your plans" and give you success.

Anybody who knows the Lord and has ever accomplished anything in their lives knows that our plans don't always succeed nor is the Lord obligated to make them succeed.

The NLT is just pretending to be a Holy Bible.

Learn more, get the book: WHICH BIBLE WOULD JESUS USE? The Bible Version Controversy Explained and Resolved By Jack McElroy
www.JackMcElroy.com

Available from

CHICK PUBLICATIONS

amazon

nook

"Everybody Has A Plan Until They Get Punched in the Mouth."

****

King James Bible Proverbs 16:3	New Living Translation Prov. 16:3
Commit thy **works** unto the LORD, and **thy <u>thoughts</u>** shall be established.	Commit your **actions** to the LORD, and **your <u>plans</u> will succeed**.

That famous quote was said by "Iron" Mike Tyson, former undisputed world champion heavyweight professional boxer. Tyson is considered one of the best heavyweights of all time.[1]

❶ **The NLT puts the living God at your service. What a deal.**
All you have to do is commit your "actions" (whatever that means) to the Lord and he's on the hook to make your plans succeed!

❷ **And what happens if you fail?** You've probably already guessed … It'll be all your fault. You must not have committed hard enough.

❸ **The truth is plain.** And it's been plain for all to see for over 400 years in the KJB. There is NO guarantee of "success." BUT the Lord will guide you by establishing your thoughts.

The NLT was bad when it used to be The Living Bible and it's just as bad today.

Learn more, get the book: WHICH BIBLE WOULD JESUS USE? The Bible Version Controversy Explained and Resolved By Jack McElroy
www.JackMcElroy.com

Available from

amazon
nook

Photo Attribution: Brian Birzer http://www.brianbirzer.com Creative Commons Attribution 2.0 Generic

1. https://en.wikipedia.org/wiki/Mike_Tyson

NLT Publishes History Error

****

King James Bible Mark 6:22	New Living Translation Mark 6:22
And when **the daughter of** the **said Herodias** came in, and danced, and pleased Herod …	Then **his** daughter, also named **Herodias**, came in and performed a dance that greatly pleased Herod …

❶ Herodias was married to Herod Agrippa's brother Philip. The girl was the daughter of Herodias and Philip.

Herod Agrippa I — **Herodias** ┬ **Philip**
Acts 12:1-4, 20-23   Phillip's wife   Half-brother of
                 Mark 16:17   Herod Agrippa I Mark 6:17
                      Salome
                     Daughter of
                     Philip & Herodias

❷ ALL other versions (except the NET Bible) say that the girl who danced was <u>Herodias</u>' daughter (as opposed to Herod Agrippa's daughter).

According to first-century Jewish historian Josephus (c. 37 – c. 100):

> "Herodias was married to Herod [Philip], the son of Herod the Great … They had a daughter Salome, after whose birth Herodias … married Herod the Tetrarch [Agrippa I], her husband's brother by the same father."[1]

❸ If he came to your church, Jesus would **NEVER** use the New Living Translation **because he'd NEVER use an erroneous Bible.**

The NLT—still pretending to be a Holy Bible.

Available from

Learn more, get the book: WHICH BIBLE WOULD JESUS
USE? The Bible Version Controversy Explained and
Resolved By Jack McElroy www.JackMcElroy.com

1 *Antiquities* 18.5.3 136, http://www.josephus.org/JohnTBaptist.htm#Salome

They Swear Bible Versions Don't Affect Doctrine But...

****

King James Bible Mark 10:40	New Living Translation Mk 10:40
But to sit on my right hand and on my left hand **is not mine to give**; but it shall be given to **them** for whom it is **prepared**.	But **I have no right** to say who will sit on my right or my left. God has prepared those places for the **ones** he has **chosen**.

Questions:

1. **Has God already chosen** (before the foundation of the world) the individuals that will sit on the right and left hand of the Lord Jesus Christ?

                    Or

2. **Has the Lord yet to make up his mind?**
   Just because he has **prepared** those two positions doesn't necessarily mean he's chosen who gets them.

Both verses say different things; which of the two should you believe?

When it comes to doctrine, which Bible is your final authority?

Available from

NLT Overrides Your Saviour's Pronouncement

* *

King James Bible Luke 10:15

And thou, Capernaum, which art exalted to heaven, shalt be **thrust down to hell**.

New Living Translation Luke 10:15
"And you people of Capernaum, will you be honored in heaven? No, you will go down to **the place of the dead."**

The KJB is clear, concise, to the point, and frightening.

The NLT is fundamentally flawed. The real Jesus would never have said the folks of Capernaum would wind up in **"the place of the dead."**

The Lord spoke clearly and warned them that they'd end up in hell.

❶ The "place of the dead" is a cemetery.
❷ Hell is where the fire is.
❸ Everyone knows the difference.

The NLT; just pretending to be a Holy Bible.

Learn more, get the book: WHICH BIBLE WOULD JESUS USE? The Bible Version Controversy Explained and Resolved By Jack McElroy
www.JackMcElroy.com

Available from

amazon
nook

NLT Section

> # NLT Proves Catholic Doctrine ... You Can Save Your Own Soul
>
> ***
>
> | King James Bible Luke 21:19 | New Living Translation Luke 21:19 |
> |---|---|
> | In your **patience** <u>possess</u> ye your souls. | By standing firm, you will <u>win</u> your souls. |
>
> **REV. JAMES S. KERRIGAN, O.M.I.**
> AT
> **Sacred Heart Church**
> GROTON, MASS.
> **St. James Church**
> WEST GROTON, MASS.
> REV. OSCAR R. O'GORMAN, Pastor
> NOV. 2nd to NOV. 9th, 1941.
>
> **SAVE YOUR SOUL!**
> 1. Receive regularly the Sacraments of Penance and the Holy Eucharist.
> 2. Say your morning and evening prayers. Make acts of Faith, Hope and Charity every day; at night, before retiring, examine your Conscience and make an act of Contrition.
> 3. Attend Mass on all Sundays and Holy Days of Obligation.
> 4. If there exist any Church Societies in your parish, join at least one of them.
> 5. It is an obligation to contribute to the support of the Church, binding under sin.
> 6. You are obliged to avoid the Occasions of Sin; an occasion of sin is any person, place or thing which will likely lead you into sin.
> 7. Practice Daily Devotion to the Blessed Virgin: pray to her particularly for the grace of a Happy Death.
> 8. Remember: Death — Judgment — Heaven — Hell, and you will persevere to the end.
>
> Thew F. Sheehan Co., 22 Chauncy Street, Boston
>
> **The God of the KJB** says you <u>possess</u> your soul in patience.
>
> **The God of the NLT** says you can <u>WIN</u> your soul **by standing firm.**
>
> ## Which God is telling the truth?
>
> ## That depends on WHICH BIBLE you believe.
>
> Available from
>
> amazon
> nook
>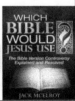
>
> Learn more, get the book: WHICH BIBLE WOULD JESUS USE? The Bible Version Controversy Explained and Resolved By Jack McElroy
> www.JackMcElroy.com

The New English Translation

Introduction

****

The first edition of The Holy Bible: New English Translation (the NET Bible) was published in 2001.

> The NET Bible is a completely new translation of the Bible with 58,506 translators' notes! It was completed by more than 25 scholars—experts in the original biblical languages—who worked directly from the best currently available Hebrew, Aramaic, and Greek texts.[1]

There are eight memes covering the NET Bible. The translators' notes give you a lot of insight into why they presented the critical text the way they did. That's helpful in formulating arguments against it.

You never know what you'll catch in the NET

Publisher or Perish

With all those scholars and all those notes, you can be sure you're going to get some interesting angles. For example:

In 1 Samuel 17:4, they boldly claim that Goliath, the champion of the Philistines, was close to 7 feet tall. He would barely make it as a center on a D-1 college basketball team today.

There are also a couple of memes covering the NET Bible's translation of Isaiah 7:14 stating that it was a young woman who would conceive, not a virgin as it says in just about all other Bible versions.

In the old days, when something smelled fishy it caused outrage and controversy. Sadly, that was then.

---

1. https://netbible.com/

NET Bible Creates Fake Eve

****

King James Bible Genesis 4:1
And Adam knew Eve his wife; and she conceived, and bare Cain, and said,
I have gotten a man from the LORD.

New English Translation Genesis 4:1
Now the man had marital relations with his wife Eve, and she became pregnant and gave birth to Cain. Then she said,
"I have created a man just as the LORD did!"

❶ The NET Bible was produced by a team of more than 25 scholars who are experts in the original biblical languages. And yet …

❷ **The NET Bible's Eve** is in serious error and is unacquainted with the facts of creation. **She never "created a man just as the Lord did."** She gave birth. **Not even close to the same thing.**
The Lord formed the man out of the dust of the earth and the woman from the man. Neither was born of a woman.

❸ **The real Eve,** as quoted in the King James Bible, wasn't ignorant of the facts. She never would've said what the NET Bible claims she said.

The NET Bible: Just another modern counterfeit version.

Available from

Learn more, get the book: WHICH BIBLE WOULD JESUS USE? The Bible Version Controversy Explained and Resolved By Jack McElroy
www.JackMcElroy.com

NET Bible Dumpster Dives, Finds Short Goliath

****

King James Bible 1 Samuel 17:4	**New English Translation 1 Sam. 17:4**
And there went out a champion out of the camp of the Philistines, named Goliath, of Gath, **whose height** *was* **six cubits and a span**.	Then a champion came out from the camp of the Philistines. His name was Goliath; he was from Gath. **He was close to seven feet tall**.

❶ **The King James Bible's Goliath** is **9' 9" tall** (6 cubits and a span). He was an awe-inspiring giant—a champion.

❷ **The NET Bible's Goliath** is **less than 7' tall**. He's not a giant. He's not even an NBA center. He's more like a small forward.

❸ The NET Bible authors got their stats from the spurious Septuagint (LXX) and one of the dumpster Dead Sea Scrolls which pegged his height at 6' 9."

All these NBA stars are or were taller than the NET Bible's Goliath:

YAO is 7' 5", SAMPSON 7'4", KAREEM 7'2", WILT and SHAQ 7'1", DUNCAN, EWING, GASOL, OLAJUWON, & PARISH at 7' 0". Even MLB's "The Big Unit" RANDY JOHNSON was 6' 10".

The NET Bible; still pretending to be a "Holy" Bible.

Available from

Learn more, get the book: WHICH BIBLE WOULD JESUS USE? The Bible Version Controversy Explained and Resolved By Jack McElroy www.JackMcElroy.com

amazon
nook

WHICH
BIBLE
WOULD
JESUS USE
The Bible Version Controversy Explained and Resolved
JACK MCELROY

NET Bible Flagrantly Cuts Your Saviour Out of Psalm 2

****

King James Bible Psalm 2:12	NET Bible Psalm 2:12
Kiss the Son, lest he be angry, and ye perish from the way, when his wrath is kindled but a little. Blessed are all they that put their trust in him.	**Give sincere homage!** Otherwise he will be angry, and you will die because of your behavior, when his anger quickly ignites. How blessed are all who take shelter in him!

❶ **The KJB sends out a clear warning** to the kings, rulers and people of the earth to **KISS the SON** lest he be angry.

❷ **The NET version says NOTHING** about the Son and **warns no one** to make peace with the SON.

❸ In this world, the Son of God is IGNORED ....

And the NET Bible follows suit by cutting him out of Psalm 2.

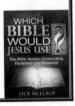
Photo: Vanishing South Georgia Photographs by Brian Brown

NET Bible Defect Exposed

****

Psalm 116:15 is a great encouragement to believers—especially when facing death or the death of a saved love one. But look at what the NET Bible does to it ...

King James Bible Psalm 116:15	NET Bible Psalm 116:15
Precious in the sight of the LORD is the **death** of his **saints**.	The LORD values the lives of his faithful followers.

❶ **Are you one of the Lord's saints?**
You are if you're born again.

❷ **Is your "death" or that of a saved loved one "precious" in the Lord's sight?**
It is if you believe the King James Bible.

❸ **Does Psalm 116:15 talk about death?**
It does if you believe the King James Bible.

T**hey tell us that using multiple versions gives us a clear understanding of God's word ...**

Who do you suppose made up that bit of fake news?

Available from

Learn more, get the book: WHICH BIBLE WOULD JESUS USE? The Bible Version Controversy Explained and Resolved By Jack McElroy www.JackMcElroy.com

Photo: Aqua Mechanical bigstock-a-chain-with-a-broken-rusted—37045324 Flickr

NET Bible Goes Apostate

✶✶

King James Bible Isaiah 7:14	**NET Bible Isaiah 7:14**
Therefore the Lord himself shall give you a sign; Behold, **a <u>virgin</u> shall conceive**, and bear a son, and shall call his name Immanuel.	For this reason the sovereign master himself will give you a confirming sign. Look, **this <u>young</u> <u>woman</u>** is about to conceive and will give birth to a son. You, young woman, will name him Immanuel.

❶ The NET Bible was produced by a team of translators under the direction of three professors from Dallas Theological Seminary. It claims to be non-sectarian, "inter-denominational" and **evangelical.**

❷ "The notes in the NET Bible further explain that, in the opinion of the editors, the Immanuel prophecy **was fulfilled** in the person of Isaiah's son Maher-shalal-hash-baz (8:1–4)."[1]

❸ **65 years ago** this Revised Standard (RSV) reading caused an outcry from Christian leaders. **No longer.**

❹ **Sound doctrine is under fire by new Bible versions like never before. And the response from mainstream Christian leaders?** Crickets.

The NET Bible: Just another <u>sound-doctrine-trashing</u> modern counterfeit.

Chicago Tribune Dec. 1, 195?

Part 1—Page 16   F

BAPTIST PASTOR BURNS PAGE OF REVISED BIBLE

Charges Challenge to Virgin Birth

Rocky Mount, N. C., Nov. 30 (AP) —A Baptist minister ripped a page out of the revised standard edition of the Bible tonight and burned it while his shivering congregation looked on outside the church.

The Rev. Martin Luther Hux had announced he planned to burn a copy of the revised edition of the Bible. But instead he tore out the page that bore the inscription in which the words "young woman" had been substituted for

Available from

CHICK PUBLICATIONS

amazon

nook

Learn more, get the book: WHICH BIBLE WOULD JESUS USE? The Bible Version Controversy Explained and Resolved By Jack McElroy www.JackMcElroy.com

1 http://www.bible-researcher.com/net.html

NET Bible Nixes Isaiah's Virgin Birth Prophecy

****

King James Bible **Isaiah 7:14**
Therefore the Lord himself shall give you a sign; Behold, **a virgin** shall conceive, and bear a son, and shall call his name Immanuel.

NET Bible **Isaiah 7:14**
For this reason the sovereign master himself will give you a confirming sign. Look, **this young woman** is about to conceive and will give birth to a son. You, young woman, will name him Immanuel.

King James Bible **Matthew 1:22–23**
Now all this was done, **that it might be fulfilled which was spoken of the Lord by the prophet**, saying, Behold, **a virgin** shall be with child, and shall bring forth a son, and they shall call his name Emmanuel, which being interpreted is, God with us.

NET Bible **Matthew 1:22–23**
This all happened so **that what was spoken by the Lord through the prophet would be fulfilled:** "Look! **The virgin** will conceive and bear a son, and they will call him Emmanuel," which means "God with us."

The NET Bible's Isaiah never said a word about a "virgin" conceiving, only a "young woman." Young women conceive all the time; virgins don't. But somehow the NET Bible's Matthew figured it out.

They swear modern versions don't affect doctrine. Nonsense.

Available from

Learn more, get the book: WHICH BIBLE WOULD JESUS USE? The Bible Version Controversy Explained and Resolved By Jack McElroy www.JackMcElroy.com

Photo: https://www.maxpixel.net/Prophet-Beard-Man-Old-762636

NET Bible Turns God's Promise into Threat and Kills NT Prophecy

****

King James Bible Hosea 13:14	NET Bible Hosea 13:14
I will ransom them from the power of the grave; I will redeem them from death: O death, I will be thy plagues; O grave, I will be thy destruction: repentance shall be hid from mine eyes.	Will I deliver them from the power of Sheol? No, I will not! Will I redeem them from death? No, I will not! O Death, bring on your plagues! O Sheol, bring on your destruction! My eyes will not show any compassion!

❶ Contrary to what they falsely teach us, all Bibles **DO NOT SAY or MEAN** the same thing.

❷ Sometimes they say **OPPOSITE things** as this comparison CLEARLY shows.

❸ **What's deeply troubling here** is that the NET Bible creators flip a promise of God into a threat and, worse, absolutely bury the cross-reference ...

> O death, where *is* thy sting? O grave, where *is* thy victory?
>
> 1 Corinthians 15:55

The NET version misrepresents the Lord...again.

Available from

Photo: Tim Evanson https://www.flickr.com/photos/timevanson/7237098046

NET Bible's
Luke Gets It Wrong

****

King James Bible Luke 23:34	NET Bible Luke 23:34
Then said Jesus, Father, forgive them; for they know not what they do. And they parted his raiment, and cast lots.	*[But Jesus said, "Father, forgive them, for they don't know what they are doing."]* Then they threw dice to divide his clothes.

❶ <u>Note the brackets</u>. That's because the NET Bible creators were taught that Luke **never** reported those words. They think the words were **forged** a hundred or so years later (although they say the words were probably "historically" true). **And yet ...**

❷ This is the ONLY time in the Bible where you'll find these words of your Saviour. If the Lord said these words, of course, Luke would report them. The NET Bible is making an error of OMISSION here.

Textual expert Dr. Wilbur Pickering says:

"The eclectic text currently in vogue (following less than 1% of the Greek manuscripts, of objectively inferior quality places within double brackets the first half of verse 34 ... **this way they deny that Luke wrote it, surely a perverse proceeding.**"[1]

❸ Billions of King James Bibles, and all Reformation-era Bibles **NEVER SPREAD ANY DOUBT** that ALL of Luke's words are authentic.

The NET Bible's presentation is a "perverse proceeding" indeed.

Available from

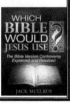

Learn more, get the book: WHICH BIBLE WOULD JESUS USE? The Bible Version Controversy Explained and Resolved By Jack McElroy www.JackMcElroy.com

1. http://www.walkinhiscommandments.com/Pickering/New%20Translation/Luke-ff-revised.pdf, p. 54.

The Message and Other Lesser-Known Versions

Introduction

****

The Message is one man's delusion, however well-intentioned he may have been, as to what God said.

The Message is a confusing mess.

Bible version researcher Michael Marlowe explains:

> In evaluating this version, the author's purpose and audience must be kept in mind. Unfortunately, the publisher has advertised it as a "translation from the original languages" that "accurately communicates the original Hebrew and Greek" and brings out "the subtleties and nuances of the Hebrew and Greek languages," being the work of a respected "exegetical scholar," etc., all of which gives an entirely false impression of the work.

> Instead, what we have here is a free paraphrase of the text, often very eccentric, with many unlikely renderings, lengthy insertions and omissions, and other problems; but to criticize this work for its many inaccuracies would be to miss the whole purpose of its author.

> [Eugene] Peterson's purpose in this is to present something new and provocative at every turn, something vivid and unusual, in order to stir up the dull minds of people who have become bored with their familiar Bibles.[1]

I guess for Peterson, the medium IS the message.

---

1. http://www.bible-researcher.com/themessage.html

307

CEV Soils Jeremiah 17

****

King James Bible Jeremiah 17:9	Contemporary English Version Jer. 17:9
The heart *is* deceitful above all *things*, and **desperately wicked**: who can know it?	**You people of Judah** are so deceitful that you even fool yourselves, and you can't change.

Verses 1–4 concern the sins of Judah. Then the Lord shifts gears (in the real Bible and other versions EXCEPT the CEV) and starts talking in general terms about men. **The CEV folks:**

<u>Claim</u> they want to put the "word of God" into the language of the people and it's a simplified version of the Bible designed for children and uneducated adults (at a fourth-grade reading level). YET …

<u>Claim</u> "The CEV is not a paraphrase. It is an accurate and faithful translation of the original manuscripts."[1]

<u>Claim</u> They were **"in constant prayer for the guidance of the Spirit of God, that guarantees the accuracy, integrity and trustworthiness of the CEV Bible"**[2]

Not a chance.

People don't get saved until they realize they're lost. And one of the great soul winning verses is Jeremiah 17:9 because the Holy Spirit uses it to awaken people to their lost condition.

What these guys are doing to God's word is disgraceful.

Available from

Learn more, get the book: WHICH BIBLE WOULD JESUS USE? The Bible Version Controversy Explained and Resolved By Jack McElroy www.JackMcElroy.com

1. https://www.bible.com/versions/392-cev-contemporary-english-version. 2. *Creating and Crafting the Contemporary English Version* American Bible Society, 1996.

The Message Bible Insults Your Saviour

****

King James Bible Psalm 22:16
For dogs have compassed me: the assembly of the wicked have inclosed me: **they pierced my hands and my feet.**

The Message Psalm 22:16
Now packs of wild dogs come at me; thugs gang up on me. **They pin me down hand and foot, and lock me in a cage—.**

Zechariah 13:6
And one shall say unto him, What are these **wounds in thine hands**? Then he shall answer, Those with which I was wounded in the house of my friends.

Zechariah 13:6
"...And if someone says, 'And so where did you get **that black eye**?' they'll say, **'I ran into a door at a friend's house.'**"

~~~~~~~~~~~~~~~~~~~~~~~~~~~~

David (Psalm 22) is foreshadowing the crucifixion. Zechariah is foreshadowing the 2nd coming.

~~~~~~~~~~~~~~~~~~~~~~~~~~~~

The verses above sound like they're describing a drunken frat party.

Isn't it upsetting when "a Bible" turns a fulfilled prophecy about your Saviour into a joke?

Learn more, get the book: WHICH BIBLE WOULD JESUS USE? The Bible Version Controversy Explained and Resolved By Jack McElroy
www.JackMcElroy.com

Available from

Q. When Is the King James Text NOT the King James Text?

A. When It Appears in a New Scofield Reference Bible.

THE NEW SCOFIELD REFERENCE BIBLE

****

King James Bible Proverbs 23:33
Thine eyes shall behold **strange women**, and thine heart shall utter perverse things.

New Scofield Reference Bible Pr. 23:33
Thine eyes shall behold **strange things,** and thine heart shall utter perverse things

King James Daniel 3:25
He answered and said, Lo, I see four men loose, walking in the midst of the fire, and they have no hurt; and the form of the fourth is like **the Son of God.**

New Scofield Reference Bible Dan. 3:25
He answered and said, Lo, I see four men loose, walking in the midst of the fire, and they have no hurt; and the form of the fourth is like **a son of the gods.**

Oxford University Press (who ALWAYS owned the copyright; Scofield <u>NEVER</u> <u>did</u>) can and does change the TEXT AND NOTES. Here they substituted the 1901 American Standard Version text.

Thine eyes shall behold **strange things … Prov. 23:33 (ASV)**

…and the aspect of the fourth is like **a son of the gods. Daniel 3:25 (ASV)**

What other lies are hidden in the New Scofield?

Available from

CHICK PUBLICATIONS
amazon

WHICH **BIBLE** WOULD JESUS USE
The Bible Version Controversy Explained and Resolved

Learn more, get the book: WHICH BIBLE WOULD JESUS USE? The Bible Version Controversy Explained and Resolved By Jack McElroy www.jackmcelroy.com

Did God Preserve His Words or Just the Message?

****

Dr. **Samuel E. Schnaiter,** MA, PhD, Bob Jones University, said …

"However, such promises of preservation in view of the wording variations must apply <u>only to the message</u> of God's Word, <u>not</u> its precise wording."[1]

Okay, here's The Lord's Prayer Matthew 6:7–13, from *The Message*:

Our Father in heaven,
Reveal who you are.
Set the world right;
Do what's best—as above, so below.
Keep us alive with three square meals.
Keep us forgiven with you and forgiving others.
Keep us safe from ourselves and the Devil.
You're in charge!
You can do anything you want!
You're ablaze in beauty!
Yes. Yes. Yes.

They tell us… "Strive not about words to no profit." But don't words matter to God?

Brethren, is there not a cause?

Available from

Learn more, get the book: WHICH BIBLE WOULD JESUS USE? The Bible Version Controversy Explained and Resolved By Jack McElroy www.JackMcElroy.com

1.Samuel Schnaiter, *The Relevancy of Textual Criticism to the Modern English Version Controversy for Fundamentalists*, A Dissertation (May 1980), p. 209.

They Tell Us That Different Translations Don't Affect Doctrine

****

King James Bible John 3:5
Jesus answered, Verily, verily, I say unto thee, Except a man be **born** _____ **of water** and of the Spirit, he cannot enter into the kingdom of God.

Douay-Rheims Bible John 3:5
Jesus answered: Amen, amen I say to thee, unless a man be **born <u>again</u> of water** and the Holy Ghost, he cannot enter into the kingdom of God.

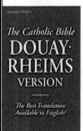

According to the Church of Rome, all Roman Catholics become "Born Again" when they are baptized as infants.

The addition of <u>just</u> <u>one</u> <u>word</u> justifies infant baptism.

Authors Fee and Strauss tell us: "This version was produced [when] several Roman Catholic scholars … sought refuge in northern France during the Elizabethan era. For all practical purposes, it became the 'KJV' of the English-speaking Roman Catholic Church through the mid-20th century."[1]

Their book is recommended reading for Christian college students. Any warning about doctrine? Perish the thought.

What a sad commentary on 21st Century Christian Education.

Available from

Learn more, get the book: WHICH BIBLE WOULD JESUS USE? The Bible Version Controversy Explained and Resolved By Jack McElroy www.JackMcElroy.com

1 Gordon Fee and Mark Strauss, *How to Choose a Translation for All Its Worth A Guide to Understanding and Using Bible Versions*, p. 137

"Work" or "Ambition" Which Did God Write?

****

King James Bible 1 Timothy 3:1
This is a true saying, If a man **desire <u>the office</u> of a bishop**, he desireth a **<u>good</u> <u>work</u>**.

The New English Bible 1 Tim. 3:1
To **aspire to leadership** is an honorable **ambition**.

A local church has two offices: Bishop (a.k.a. Pastor) and Deacon. **They ARE the elders of a church. There is no "office" of elders.**

The **<u>WORK</u>** of a Bishop-Pastor is difficult, time-consuming, and energy-draining. It requires intense passion and commitment or he won't be successful.

<u>A successful pastor</u> isn't motivated by an ambition for leadership. He knows that most of the time there is NO glory, NO thanks, and NO reward.

Yet these men Do the WORK because they're driven by a call of God for service. They don't do it for vainglory, position, or title.

There's nothing wrong with ambition BUT it is NOT the same as a **DESIRE** to do the hard but **GOOD WORK** of serving the church that God has purchased with his own blood.

They say criticizing Bible translations is nothing but a divisive hobbyhorse.

Nothing could be further from the truth.

Available from

Learn more, get the book: WHICH BIBLE WOULD JESUS USE? The Bible Version Controversy Explained and Resolved By Jack McElroy
www.JackMcElroy.com

amazon
nook

God Finally Gets with the Program

****

Qualifications for:	King James Bible	Contemporary English Version
Bishops 1 Tim. 3:2	**A bishop** then must be blameless, **the husband of one wife**	That's why <u>**officials**</u> **must** have a good reputation and **be faithful in marriage**.
Elders Titus 1:6	If any be blameless, **the husband of one wife**	<u>**they**</u> must have a good reputation and be **faithful in marriage**.
Deacons 1 Tim. 3:12	Let the **deacons** be the **husbands of one wife**	<u>**Church officers**</u> must be **faithful in marriage**

The CEV is produced and promoted by the American Bible Society:

"**Uncompromising simplicity** marked the American Bible Society's (ABS) translation of the Contemporary English Version (CEV) that was first published in 1995. The text is **easily read by grade schoolers**, second language readers, and **those who prefer the more contemporized form**. The CEV is **not a paraphrase**. It is **an accurate and faithful translation of the original manuscripts**."[1]

The CEV has everything some experts say Christians need:

- "Uncompromising simplicity"
- "Easily read by grade schoolers"
- "Those who prefer the more contemporized form"
- "Not a paraphrase"
- "An accurate and faithful translation of the original manuscripts."

According to the "**accurate and faithful**" CEV, God gets up-to-date by dropping the outdated KJB requirement for a pastor, bishop, overseer, elder or deacon (or whatever you call a church "official") <u>**TO BE MALE**</u>.

Retired Chaplain (Maj. Gen.) Lorraine Potter, the first female chaplain and female chief of chaplains in the Air Force

Nothing to see here folks, move along.

Available from

Learn more, get the book: WHICH BIBLE WOULD JESUS USE? The Bible Version Controversy Explained and Resolved By Jack McElroy www.JackMcElroy.com

CHICK PUBLICATIONS
amazon
nook

1 https://www.biblegateway.com/versions/Contemporary-English-Version-CEV-Bible/

Is the New Testament Anti-Semitic?

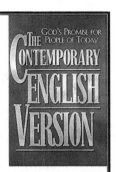

The creators of the Contemporary English Version evidently believe it is.
So they edited the text to make it politically correct.

	King James Bible	Contemporary English Version
John 5:15, 16	The man departed, and told **the Jews** that it was Jesus, which had made him whole. And therefore did **the Jews** persecute Jesus...	The man left and told **the leaders** that Jesus was the one who had healed him. **They** started making a lot of trouble for Jesus...
John 5:18	Therefore **the Jews** sought the more to kill him...	Now **the leaders** wanted to kill Jesus for two reasons...
John 10:31	Then **the Jews** took up stones again to stone him.	Once again **the people** picked up stones in order to kill Jesus.
John 11:8	*His* disciples say unto him, Master, **the Jews** of late sought to stone thee...	"Teacher," they said, **the people** there want to stone you to death...
John 19:7	**The Jews** answered him, We have a law, and by our law he ought to die, because he made himself the Son of God.	**The crowd** replied, "He claimed to be the Son of God! Our Law says that he must be put to death."

Tampering with God's words because they aren't "politically correct" can't be good, can it?

Available from

WHICH BIBLE WOULD JESUS USE
The Bible Version Controversy Explained and Resolved

Learn more, get the book: WHICH BIBLE WOULD JESUS USE? The Bible Version Controversy Explained and Resolved By Jack McElroy www.JackMcElroy.com

CHICK PUBLICATIONS

amazon

nook

JACK MCELROY

CEV Fails to Tell You HOW to Have Peace

****

King James Bible Isaiah 26:3
Thou wilt keep *him* in perfect peace, **whose mind is stayed on thee:** because he trusteth in thee.

Contemporary English Version Isaiah 26:3
The LORD gives perfect peace to those whose faith is firm.

Both Bibles promise *perfect peace*—But only one tells HOW to get it.

The KJB instructs you to:
Stay your mind on God, (as in, "stay" calm or "stay" in one place) and trust in God.

The battle for peace is in our minds. They wander. That's why we get into trouble. It's only when we bring "into captivity every thought to the obedience of Christ" (2 Corinthians 10:5) by staying focused on the Lord that we can obtain the perfect peace he promised.
In short, it takes effort. On the other hand...

The CEV doesn't instruct you to do anything. It just says that IF you somehow have a "firm faith" (whatever that means), God will GIVE you perfect peace. The CEV wrecks the Isaiah 26:3 promise.

Modern versions muddy the waters of doctrine and ANYBODY who's attended a multi-version Bible study knows it. But what's worse is that ...

Some Christian leaders act like words don't matter.

Available from

Learn more, get the book: WHICH BIBLE WOULD JESUS USE? The Bible Version Controversy Explained and Resolved By Jack McElroy www.JackMcElroy.com

Part Two:
Wisdom

Arguments, Answers and
The Big Picture for Critical Thinkers

Wisdom *is* the principal thing; *therefore* get wisdom: and with all thy getting get understanding. Proverbs 4:7

For the LORD giveth wisdom: out of his mouth *cometh* knowledge and understanding. Proverbs 2:6

There are 156 memes in part two:

- 27 demonstrate the superiority of the King James Bible.
- 18 cover original languages and translation.
- 10 discuss inspiration and preservation.
- 59 discuss critics, textual critics, and commentary.
- 12 answer the oft-repeated questions of where was the Bible before 1611? And which edition is authentic?
- 16 present Multi-version confusion—thereby demonstrating that God can't be like our leaders in recommending many versions because he is NOT the author of confusion.
- 14 encompass other memes, personal statements and comments from the author.

Inspiration and Preservation

Introduction

****

We hear all kinds of lessons about the inspiration of the original autographs and that the labels *inspiration* and *inerrancy* can't be applied to any copies.

Nonsense.

All the apostles and the Lord Jesus Christ used copies.

This section introduces a different take on the biblical definition of *inspiration* as well as the preservation of God's words as they appear in plain English on the pages of the King James Bible

They say that **NO** translation or copies are inspired. So...

Which ~~IS~~ WAS Inspired; the Original Autographs or the Scripture?

****

What the ALL Bible versions SAY:	What Autograph Onlyists TEACH:
All scripture **is given** by inspiration of God, and **is profitable** for doctrine…, 2 Timothy 3:16 KJB	All scripture **was given** by inspiration of God, and **is profitable** for doctrine…2 Timothy 3:16 as taught

Where does an Autograph Onlyist find Scripture that can:

❶ Be **READ TODAY**: "Did ye never **read** in the scriptures…" Mat 21:42 KJB

❷ Be **SEARCHED TODAY**: "**search** the scriptures…" John 5:39 KJB

❸ **SPEAK TODAY**: "For **what saith** the scripture?…" Rom. 4:3 KJB

❹ Be **BELIEVED IN TODAY**: "For the scripture saith Whosoever **believeth** on him shall not be ashamed." Rom. 10:11 KJB

❺ Be a **COPY of the Original**: "And he began to say unto them, This day is this **scripture fulfilled** in your ears." Lk. 4:21 KJB **Jesus read from a copy**.

❻ Be a **TRANSLATION of the Original** "And when he had given him licence, Paul … spake unto them in the **Hebrew** tongue, saying…" Acts 21:40 KJB **Acts was written in Greek**.

How can the original autographs (which no longer exist) be "profitable" (as God promised) to you today? The answer is easy…

The Originals <u>WERE</u> inspired. The Scriptures still <u>ARE</u>.

All you have to do is find the Bible that contains the inspired Scriptures. In English, It's the King James Bible.

Apostle Paul...
Copies of Scripture
ARE (present tense)
Given by Inspiration

****

Paul NEVER said that scriptures Timothy had known from a child were the "Original Autographs."

And that **from a child** thou hast known **the holy Scriptures**, which **are** able to make thee wise unto salvation through faith which is in Christ Jesus. **All Scripture is given [not was] by inspiration of God**, and is profitable for doctrine, for reproof, for correction, for instruction in righteousness: 2 Timothy 3:15–16 KJB

❶ The Apostle Paul called Timothy's **copies** of Scripture not only **holy** but also **given by inspiration.**

❷ The word "scripture(s)" appears in the Bible 53 times and **Never ONCE** is referring to the unavailable and nonexistent "Original Autographs."

❸ And yet, **2 Timothy 3:15–16** is always quoted to PROVE that ONLY the Original Autographs were inspired.

Many Christian teachers quote this Scripture out of context. What are they trying to prove?

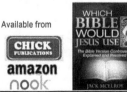

Proof: Translators Can Be Inspired

****

**Scripture says they can be, and so can you.
Job 32: 8 in the King James Bible says...**

INSPIRATION

What it REALLY means

> **But there is a spirit in man: and the inspiration of the Almighty giveth them understanding.**

~ ~ ~ ~ ~ ~ ~ ~ ~ ~ ~ ~ ~ ~ ~ ~ ~

"**Inspiration is a method** by which the Holy Ghost imparts understanding to men. **It's a ministry of the Holy Ghost.**

The context of 2 Timothy 3:16 (All scripture is given by inspiration of God, and is profitable for doctrine, for reproof, for correction, for instruction in righteousness...) **is present tense, not past.**

It's all about you, right now—just like it was all about Timothy when he got Paul's letter.

Every time you understand the meaning of Scripture, it is only by inspiration of the Almighty that you are given that understanding. It is a continual process."[1]

Just like the Lord gives you understanding by inspiration, even so gave he the KJB translators understanding by inspiration.

They claim translators can't be inspired but they must IGNORE Job 32:8 to do it.

1. *WHICH BIBLE WOULD JESUS USE?*, pp 242–244.   Image attribution: Alpha Stock Images - http://alphastockimages.com/

Which Would the Lord Want You to Have?

****

Circle one:

A.   Original Autographs

B.   King James Bible

And the answer is...

(B) King James Bible.

Why?

Because you can cross-reference the same words in the same language in both the Old and New Testaments. That's something no one possessing the Original Autographs could ever do.

> CHAP. I.
>
> 1 The Diuinitie, Humanitie, and Office of Ie-
> fus Chrift. 15 The teftimonie of Iohn. 39
> The calling of Andrew, Peter, &c.
>
> IN the beginning was the word, & the word was with God, and the word was God.
> 2 *The fame was in the beginning with God.

But that assumes you have God's words to cross-reference.

Heaven and earth shall pass away, but my **words** shall not pass away. Matthew 24:35 KJB

Heaven and earth shall pass away: but my **words** shall not pass away. Mark 13:31 KJB

Heaven and earth shall pass away: but my **words** shall not pass away. Luke 21:33 KJB

Available from

Learn more, get the book: WHICH BIBLE WOULD JESUS USE? The Bible Version Controversy Explained and Resolved By Jack McElroy www.JackMcElroy.com

WHY the Lord Didn't Preserve the Original Autographs

****

Because by so doing, he challenges men to BELIEVE his promises to preserve his words...

> The words of the LORD are <u>pure words</u>: as silver tried in a furnace of earth, purified seven times. **Thou shalt keep them**, O LORD; **thou shalt preserve them** from this generation for ever. Ps. 12:6-7 KJB

> Heaven and earth shall pass away, but my words **shall** <u>not</u> pass away. Mat. 24:35 KJB

<u>If you believe what he said</u> you will find that he indeed has kept his word to keep his words.

<u>If you don't believe</u> that he ever promised to keep his words you'll never find them.

✓ <u>Textual critics</u> **begin by NOT believing** God's promise to preserve his words but that they must recover and "reconstruct the original [autographs]."[1]

✓ <u>King James Bible believers</u> **begin by believing** God's promises to preserve his words and that you can find them all without error **in the BOOK.**

Which of the two "beliefs" pleases the Lord?

1. https://en.m.wikipedia.org/wiki/Textual_criticism_of_the_New_Testament

Did Your Lord Flunk the Bible Preservation Test?

****

The experts claim they're getting closer to the originals, but in the meantime, they teach us...

❶ ALL Bible versions have inaccuracies and errors including the King James Bible. They're just in different places. AND...

❷ There isn't ANY Bible in ANY language that is without error anywhere on earth.

Y et here's what your Lord said about preserving his words:

Heaven and earth shall pass away,
but my words shall not pass away. Mt. 24:35 KJB
Heaven and earth shall pass away:
but my words shall not pass away. Mr. 13:31 KJB
Heaven and earth shall pass away:
but my words shall not pass away. Lu. 21:33 KJB

The words of the LORD *are* **pure words**: *as* silver tried in a furnace of earth, purified seven times. Thou shalt keep them, O LORD, **thou shalt preserve them** from this generation **for ever**.

Ps. 12:6–7

❸ Their teaching means that the Lord FAILED to leave us with ANY **book** that is **The Standard** of absolute of truth.

How do you share your faith in a God like that?

Learn more, get the book: WHICH BIBLE WOULD JESUS
USE? The Bible Version Controversy Explained and
Resolved By Jack McElroy www.JackMcElroy.com

Available from

Illustration: Mrs. Paul (Kay) Friederichsen, *God's Truth Made Simple*, p. 192.

Former Bible School Dean Claimed KJB IS "The Inspired Word of God"

****

"**Dr. Bruce Lackey** (1930–1988) taught at Tennessee Temple University (Chattanooga, TN) for 19 years and was Dean of the Bible School from 1965 until the early 1980s ...
He was ... a diligent scholar who was proficient in the Greek language." (David Cloud, Way of Life Literature)

Why I Believe The Old
KING JAMES
BIBLE

Dr. Bruce Lackey

Dr. Lackey said:

"**It is correct to call <u>a translation</u> of the Bible 'the inspired Word of God,'** if it is a correct translation **from <u>uncorrupted</u> <u>manuscripts</u>** ...

"Any correctly translated scripture, in any version, would be correctly called the inspired Word of God, **if it is from <u>uncorrupted</u> <u>text</u>s** ...

"**I believe that the King James Version is** a correct translation of **<u>uncorrupted</u> <u>manuscripts</u>** in both Hebrew and Greek and is **worthy of being called the inspired Word of God.**"[1]

So why should they make fun of you for believing the same thing?

Available from

Learn more, get the book: WHICH BIBLE WOULD JESUS USE? The Bible Version Controversy Explained and Resolved By Jack McElroy
www.JackMcElroy.com

CHICK
PUBLICATIONS

amazon
nook

WHICH
BIBLE
WOULD
JESUS USE?
The Bible Version Controversy
Explained and Resolved

JACK MCELROY

1. Bruce Lackey, *Inspiration And Translation*, http://www.gotothebible.com/HTML/inspirationandtranslation.html

3 Reasons WHY Christian Academics Argue AGAINST the PRESERVATION of God's WORDS in a Book

****

Almost all Christian academics of this and the past five generations **have been taught** that all of God's authentic and infallible words cannot be found in any book in any language on the face of the earth.

Training vs. Education

They **were trained** to believe:
❶ that only the original autographs **were** inspired and inerrant.

❷ NO book on earth is inspired or inerrant **IN ANY LANGUAGE.**

❸ Finally, they're left without a Bible (meaning a book) and no promise of the certainty of the words of truth.

In contrast, King James Bible believers have **the presupposition** that after the invention of printing, God cared enough about his words to preserve them **in a place where they can be found.**
In short, they believe they're found <u>in a **book**.</u>

What's really tragic is that academics glory in the fact that they DON'T have a book.

If The Lord Preserved His Words in English ...

1. Could he do it?
2. Where would you find them?

****

King James Bible	English Standard Bible
2 Samuel 21:19	2 Samuel 21:19
And there was again a battle in Gob with the Philistines, **where Elhanan** the son of Jaareoregim, a Bethlehemite, **slew _the brother of_ Goliath** the Gittite, the staff of whose spear was like a weaver's beam.	And there was again war with the Philistines at Gob, and Elhanan the son of Jaare-oregim, the Bethlehemite, struck down ___ _____ __ Goliath the Gittite, the shaft of whose spear was like a weaver's beam.

The ESV says Elhanan killed Goliath.

Junior church kids know that's not true.

Would the "Holy Bible" contain the error?

Does God Preserve His "Words" (KJB) or the Poor and "Needy" (NASB) in Psalm 12:7?

Original 1611 KJB marginal note resolves issue.

Answers Questions

****

King James Bible Psalm 12:5–7
⁵ For the oppression of the poor, for the sighing of the needy, now will I arise, saith the LORD; **I will set him in safety** from him that puffeth at him.
⁶ **The words of the LORD are pure words**: as silver tried in a furnace of earth, purified seven times.
⁷ **Thou shalt keep them**, O LORD, **thou shalt preserve them** from this generation for ever.

New American Standard Bible Ps.12:5–7
⁵ "Because of the devastation of the afflicted, because of the groaning of the needy, Now I will arise," says the LORD; "**I will set him in the safety** for which he longs." ⁶ **The words of the LORD are pure words**; As silver tried in a furnace on the earth, refined seven times.
⁷ You, O LORD, **will keep them**; You will **preserve him** from this generation forever.

1. The debate has persisted for centuries. Calvin thought the Lord preserved the <u>poor</u>, Spurgeon (sermon on Psalm 12) and Wesley thought <u>words</u>.

2. The KJB and NASB differ in verse 7. The NASB team believes the verse is referring to the poor as mentioned in verse 5.

3. The KJB translators believed verse 7 referred to God's words as mentioned in verse 6. The proof is their marginal note on Proverbs 30:5. It cross-references Psalm 12:7 and three other verses.

4. <u>ALL</u> the cross-references cited in the 1611 KJB are to the words of LORD and **NOT** to the poor.

Page 1

> *Pfal. 12.7.
> and 18. 32.
> & 19. 8. &
> 119. 140.
> † Heb. puri-
> fied.
>
> 5 *Euery word of God† is pure: he is a shield vnto them that put their trust in him.
> 6 *Adde thou not vnto his words, left he reproue thee, and thou be found a

Above: **Proverbs 30:5–6** from the First Edition King James Bible 1611 A.D. with side note cross-referencing 4 verses talking about WORDS: Ps. 12:7; Ps. 18:32 (a misprint for Ps. 18:30), Ps. 19:8, and Ps. 119:140.

Note that the cross-references in the marginal note ALL refer to WORDS:

1. **Thou shalt keep <u>them</u>**, O LORD, **thou shalt preserve <u>them</u>** from this generation for ever. Psalm 12:7 KJB

2. *As for* God, his way *is* perfect: **the <u>word</u> of the LORD is tried:** he *is* a buckler to all those that trust in him. Psalm 18:30 KJB

3. **The <u>statutes</u>** of the LORD *are* right, rejoicing the heart: the commandment of the LORD *is* pure... Psalm 19:8 KJB

4. **Thy <u>word</u>** *is* very pure: therefore thy servant loveth it. Psalm 119:140 KJB

If the KJB translators (some of the best and brightest ever assembled) believed Psalm 12:7 contained God's promise to preserve his pure words. who's qualified to argue with them?

P.S. If the Lord doesn't FIRST <u>keep</u> <u>his</u> <u>words</u>, how can you trust him to keep the poor?

Available from

Learn more, get the book: WHICH BIBLE WOULD JESUS USE? The Bible Version Controversy Explained and Resolved By Jack McElroy
www.JackMcElroy.com

CHICK PUBLICATIONS
amazon
nook

WHICH BIBLE WOULD JESUS USE?
The Bible Version Controversy Explained and Resolved
JACK MCELROY

Page 2

King James Bible Superiority

Introduction

****

Maybe there's a reason the King James Bible…

- Is the "most influential and revered English Bible that has ever existed."[1]
- Is "probably the most beautiful piece of writing in all the literature of the world."[2]
- Is "rightly regarded as the most influential book in the history of English civilization."[3]
- "Has contributed 257 idioms to English, more than any other single source, including Shakespeare."[4]
- Has "more than 1,000 churches worldwide that subscribe to a statement of faith that this 400-year-old translation 'preserves the very words of God in the form in which He wished them to be represented in the universal language of these last days: English.'"[5]
- Is "still the best-selling book in the world."[6]

Doesn't it make sense that the Lord must be the author and promoter of the "best-selling" Bible ever printed?

If the KJB is factually and historically wrong, then the Lord Jesus Christ (who allowed error to appear in the world's best-selling, most published, most read, most memorized, most

---

[1] Leland Ryken, *The Legacy of the King James Bible: Celebrating 400 Years of the Most Influential English Translation* (Wheaton, IL: Crossway Books, 2011), 13. (

[2] David Sorenson, "The Most Influential Book in the World: How the King James Version Has Changed the World," Ministry 127, May 4, 2011, http://ministry127.com/christian-living/the-most-influential-book-in-the-world.

[3] Compton's Online Edition, downloaded from America Online, May 26, 1995.

[4] Ibid.

[5] Cited in Ron Grossman, "For Some Christians, King James Is the Only Bible," *Chicago Tribune*, March 12, 2011, http://articles.chicagotribune.com/2011-03-12/news/ct-met-king-james-20110311_1_king-james-Bible-translation-Bible-study-class.

[6] David Daniell, *The Bible in English: Its History and Influence* (New Haven, CT: Yale University Press, 2003), 427.

believed, most trusted Bible in the history of mankind) has a lot of explaining to do.

If the King James Bible isn't THE Holy Bible, then it's the best imposter in the history of mankind.

What did the Lord really say? You will find the right answer on the pages of the King James Bible.

The Lord has provided a book for you. It's brought forth good fruit for over 400 years

King James Only folks believe that the Lord himself has provided them with a book that contains ALL of his words and ONLY his words WITHOUT ERROR. They believe this because it's the brand the Lord Jesus Christ has been using mightily for over 400 years—the most memorized, most read, best-selling Bible of all time.

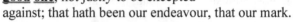

Like the KJB translators said in the Preface to the King James Version 1611:

> Truly, good Christian Reader, we never thought from the beginning that we should need to make a new translation ... but to make ... **out of many good ones <u>one principal good one</u>**, not justly to be excepted against; that hath been our endeavour, that our mark.

They said that their goal was **"to make ONE PRINCIPAL GOOD ONE"** —which they did.

It's been the one principal good one for over 400 years, and it still is.

For KJB believers, it isn't a preference, it's a conviction.

Did God Make a Terrible Mistake?

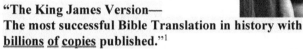

****

Bible Publisher Thomas Nelson (who should know) says:

> **"The King James Version—
> The most successful Bible Translation in history with billions of copies published."**[1]

Critics quickly dismiss this historical fact out of hand, <u>without giving a second thought to the obvious blessing and approval of God.</u>

The KJB is the best-selling, most published, most read, most memorized, most believed, most trusted Bible in the history of mankind. It has generated revivals, soul winning campaigns, and missionary efforts.

The Greek text that underlies it has been believed by God's children for nearly two thousand years.

If The KJB isn't THE STANDARD English Bible based on THE BEST Greek text, then God made a terrible mistake rolling it out in the first place.

In contrast, the **critical text** that underlies modern versions **has no history of use and appeared suddenly in the late 19th century.**

Since they can't deny its history and unparalleled influence on Western Civilization, they simply dismiss the KJB and move on. **A classic manipulation technique.**

Did God make a monumental error with the KJB or are the professional Christians that promote modern versions really that blind?

Learn more, get the book: WHICH BIBLE WOULD JESUS USE? The Bible Version Controversy Explained and Resolved By Jack McElroy www.JackMcElroy.com

Available from

1. https://www.amazon.com/King-James-Study-Bible/dp/141854714X accessed April 7, 2017

What's the One Thing KJB Critics Just Don't Get?

****

They tell us the King James Version... Died of "old age," including has **outdated language**, an **outdated text**, an **outdated knowledge** of the languages by the translators[1], a Greek text that was **not based on early manuscripts**, not **reliably edited**, and consequently **not trustworthy**[2], **thousands of errors**[3], is **filled with readings** created by overly zealous scribes[4], has (at least) 16 whole verses **NOT** found in "the Original Bible"[5], and more **drastically altered the Scriptures** than have modern translations.[6]

And yet after 400 years and billions of copies, the King James Bible is still the most widely read, believed, memorized, quoted, and distributed Bible on earth.

What they just don't get is...

"This is the Lord's doing, it is marvelous in our eyes." Ps. 118:23 KJB

Available from

Learn more, get the book: WHICH BIBLE WOULD JESUS USE? The Bible Version Controversy Explained and Resolved By Jack McElroy www.JackMcElroy.com

amazon
nook

---

[1] Norman Geisler, Bible Translations: Which Ones Are Best? Complete PowerPoint Library CD © 2008.
[2] Norman L. Geisler and William E. Nix, *A General Introduction to the Bible* (Chicago, IL: Moody Press,1968), 384.
[3] The Old Time Gospel Ministry, "The Authorized King James Version of the Bible," 4, citing Leslie R. Keylock, "The Bible that Bears His Name," *Moody Monthly* (July–August 1985), accessed December 2012, http://www.theoldtimegospel.org/about/akjvb4.html.
[4] Ibid.
[5] For list see: Jack McElroy, *WHICH BIBLE WOULD JESUS USE? The Bible Version Controversy Explained and Resolved* (Shirley, MA: McElroy Publishing, 2013, 2015), 95–97, 108.
[6] Daniel B. Wallace, "Why I Do Not Think the King James Bible Is the Best Translation Available Today," Bible.org, accessed January 1, 2016, http://tinyurl.com/nryj7bx

Which Bible Version
Do People Read Most?

****

The NIV outsells the King James Bible in Christian bookstores. But **when it comes to actually <u>READING</u> <u>the</u> <u>book</u>, the truth is revealed**...

A 2014 *Christianity Today* article cited a study advised by respected historian Mark Noll which concluded:

> "**The 55 percent who read the KJV easily outnumber the 19 percent who read the New International Version** (NIV). And the percentages drop into the single digits for competitors such as the New Revised Standard Version, New America Bible, and the Living Bible."[1]

Evidently...

❶ <u>**Cutting out thousands of words**</u> and 16 whole verses (and a pile of verse portions), which makes it shorter, and...

❷ <u>**Dumbing it down**</u> to make it easier to read, and...

❸ <u>**Substituting men's words for God's**</u> words so people can "understand it better" still ... **<u>doesn't</u> <u>get</u> <u>people</u> <u>to</u> <u>read</u> <u>it.</u>**

Maybe actually believing you have ALL of God's words WITHOUT ERROR is the reason why the KJB is the most–read Bible on Earth.

Available from

Learn more, get the book: WHICH BIBLE WOULD JESUS USE? The Bible Version Controversy Explained and Resolved By Jack McElroy www.jackmcelroy.com

1. http://www.christianitytoday.com/news/2014/march/most-popular-and-fastest-growing-bible-translation-niv-kjv.html

335

Bible Version Secrets Exposed

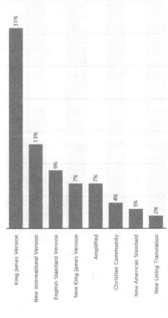

400+ Year-Old "Relic" Still Dominates Bible Reading

statista 🗲 The Statistics Portal
Statistics and Studies from more than 18,000 Sources

| Prices & Access | Our Services | Industries | Topics | Digital Markets | Consumer Markets | Infographics | Login |

Enter search term, e.g. mobile

Industries › Media & Advertising › Books & Publishing › Preferred Bible version in the U.S. 2017

What is the version or translation of the Bible you read most often?

- King James Version — 31%
- New International Version — 13%
- English Standard Version — 9%
- New King James Version — 7%
- Amplified — 7%
- Christian Community — 4%
- New American Standard — 3%
- New Living Translation — 2%

ABOUT THIS STATISTIC

The graph presents data on the popularity of the versions of the Bible read in the United States as of January 2017. During the survey, 31 percent of the respondents stated they most often read the King James Version of the Bible. During the same survey, 32 percent of respondents stated that they had never read the Bible, whilst 16 percent stated that they read the Bible every day. New ways of reading the Bible have begun to become popular, such as using the internet to access Bible content or searching for Bible verses on a smartphone. However, reading from a print version of the Bible still remains the most popular method.

Available from

CHICK PUBLICATIONS
amazon
nook

When will they finally realize the KJB is God's chosen vessel above all else?

Learn more, get the book: WHICH BIBLE WOULD JESUS USE? The Bible Version Controversy Explained and Resolved By Jack McElroy www.JackMcElroy.com

https://www.statista.com/statistics/299402/preferred-bible-version-usa/

Which Bible Should You Use?

****

First, you might want to look for the biggest stack.

An online search for the number of King James Bibles published has estimates that range from **hundreds of millions[1] as high as 5[2] to 6 billion.[3]**

Managing Editor for the highly-acclaimed National Public Television Program *Religion & Ethics NewsWeekly*, Kim Lawton said:

> No one knows exactly how many King James Bibles have been published over the centuries, **but experts say it's likely in the billions.[4]**

Bible Publisher Thomas Nelson (who ought to know) says:

> The King James Version—The most successful Bible translation in history **with billions of copies published.[5]**

Add in all the free and electronic copies it's no wonder that the estimates run into the billions. In contrast, the NIV (second in line) has over 450 million copies in print.[6]

Second, you might want to look for the one with a proven track record. If the Bibles were in NASCAR, and each year was a lap, you'd find that the King James Bible has made 400 laps around the track without a pit stop, unlike all the rest.

Third, you might want to look for the world's best-selling Bible that's had portions directly translated into scores, and possibly hundreds of foreign languages. Is there another with such an illustrious history?

But maybe your best bet is to just use the Bible the Lord would use if he came to your church tonight.

Which one? It's the same KJB he's been using and blessing for the past 400 years.

Available from

Learn more, get the book: WHICH BIBLE WOULD JESUS USE? The Bible Version Controversy Explained and Resolved By Jack McElroy www.JackMcElroy.com

---

[1] http://www.nytimes.com/2011/01/09/opinion/09sun3.html accessed April 7, 2017.
[2] Adam Nicholson, author of the national bestseller, *God's Secretaries: The Making of the King James Bible*, interview with Gwen Ifill, December 24, 2003, PBS Online NewsHour. http://www.pbs.org/newshour/bb/entertainment-july-dec03-nicolson_12-24/.
[3] http://www.independent.ie/entertainment/books/review-the-holy-bible-authorised-king-james-version-26710741.htm, accessed 4/717.
[4] http://www.pbs.org/wnet/religionandethics/2011/08/05/april-22-2011-king-james-bible-400th-anniversary/8666/, accessed April 7, 2017.
[5] https://www.amazon.com/King-James-Study-Bible/dp/141854714X, accessed April 7, 2017.
[6] http://www.faithnews.cc/?p=14291, accessed April 7, 2017.

King James Gay? Just More Fake News

****

One of the lamest accusations leveled at the King James Bible is that King James himself was a homosexual.

The facts are these:

❶ He had nothing to do with the translation of the KJB but to authorize it.

❷ **The father of 8 children**, King James was a very happily married man, who loved his wife.[1]

❸ **The charge** was invented by his political opposition **over 25 years after his death** in a book (*The Court and Character of King James*) published in 1651, supposedly written by Sir Anthony Weldon (1583–1648).

The Evidence? Like the unfounded and politically motivated accusations made against Judge Kavanagh, no one ever witnessed the dirty deeds they accused the King of.[2] Moreover, it's hard to convict someone of anything when you have no actual evidence.[3]

The truth? Politics as usual. He was straight.

Learn more, get the books: CAN YOU TRUST JUST ONE BIBLE by David W. Daniels and Jack McElroy and WHICH BIBLE WOULD JESUS USE? The Bible Version Controversy Explained and Resolved By Jack McElroy. Both are available from www.chick.com

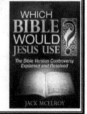

1 *Can You Trust One Bible*, David W Daniels and Jack McElroy, p. 22   2. Ibid., p. 26 Ibid., 3. P. 27 See also Stephen A. Coston's *King James Unjustly Accused*.

Some say ...
Believing ONLY the King James Bible Puts You in a "Cult"

If true, then one must ask ...

- When did the cult start?
- Who started it?
- What's the proper, legal name of the cult? Who named it?
- Like any cult, there has to be a leader. Who is it?
- Where are the meetings held?
- Do they swear an oath? To whom?
- What must one do "get in"?
- What code of ethics must be followed?
- Where are the foundational documents?
- Where is its doctrinal statement? Who wrote it?

Some further assert that in addition to cultish, KJB defenders are ungodly, dishonest, and bear false witness because they maintain the "myth" of a pure Bible in English.

Since when did believing an in-hand Bible in its entirety as God's authority become cultish?

Available from

CHICK
PUBLICATIONS

amazon
nook

WHICH
BIBLE
WOULD
JESUS USE

Learn more, get the book: WHICH BIBLE WOULD JESUS USE? The Bible Version Controversy Explained and Resolved By Jack McElroy www.JackMcElroy.com

Photo: "Village of the Damned" from a 1960 film of an alien invasion where women are impregnated by aliens in areas across the world.

Be Not Ignorant of "His" Devices

****

"**Problem-Reaction-Solution**"[1] is a geopolitical strategy the controllers of this world use to propagandize, deceive, manipulate, oppress and suck the life blood out of citizens like the parasites they are. Their purpose is profit.

They invent and incite a **problem**, calling it a **crisis**. Then, they control and orchestrate a **reaction,** finally, they provide their predetermined **solution**. The result? **Cash from chaos.**

In like manner, in the mid-19th century came cries to revise the King James Bible. But not from the people.

The "problem" they invented was that the KJB translation was (1) defective and (2) all the votes (i.e. newly "discovered" manuscripts) hadn't been counted.

"**The reaction**" was to form a committee to fix this unproved and nonexistent problem. (Propaganda)

"**The solution**" was the English Revised Version of 1885 with a new Greek text spawning scores of "new" and "more accurate" versions. The result? **Confusion from chaos.**
Who's really behind all this?

Confusion is his game; can you guess his name?

Available from

Learn more, get the book: WHICH BIBLE WOULD JESUS USE? The Bible Version Controversy Explained and Resolved By Jack McElroy www.JackMcElroy.com

1. Hegelian Dialectics and Conspiracy, https://www.biblebelievers.org.au/bb970219.htm

Top 3 KJB Errors

****

Here they are...	Strangely...
1. _____	After hundreds of years of
2. _____	searching, they still haven't found
3. _____	REAL errors. Surprised?

The so-called "errors" are <u>pretty lame</u> but fall into 3 categories...

❶ They don't LIKE the way a word has been translated in the King James so they call them translation errors—despite the superior scholarship of the translators.

❷ They CLAIM a word or passage wasn't "in the Original Autographs" so they call them errors—despite the fact that they don't have the Originals to prove it.

❸ They note printing, spelling, orthography, and other differences in various KJB editions so they call them errors—despite the fact that printing mistakes were corrected; spelling and word usage was modernized, and minor translation tweaks were made.

They simply IGNORE the fact that the underlying original language texts haven't changed in over 400 years. Besides...

They'll use any excuse they can to overthrow the authority of the ONE Standard English Bible the Lord has continually blessed for over 400 years.

Learn more, get the book: WHICH BIBLE WOULD JESUS USE? The Bible Version Controversy Explained and Resolved By Jack McElroy
www.JackMcElroy.com

Available from

KJB Drains the Swamp

****

No matter which of the thousands of editions of the King James Bible you choose …

1. **None present Jesus a liar** like the NIV, NASB, ESV, and HCSB do in John 7:8–10 by eliminating the word "**yet**" from the narrative.

2. **None present Jesus as a sinner** like the NIV does by saying he got angry without a cause in Matthew 5:22 and Mark 3:5.

3. **None** say **Elhanan killed Goliath** (instead of David) like the NASB, ESV, and HCSB say in 2 Samuel 21:19.

4. **None** say **Jesus was "indignant" instead of compassionate** at the leper looking to get healed like the NIV says in Mark 1:41.

5. **None call Jesus a begotten God** instead of begotten son like the NASB does in John 1:18.

6. **None contain known errors purposefully inserted into the text** like the ESV does in Matthew 1:7, 8, and 10.

7. **None eliminate 16 entire verses** like the Greek text underlying the NIV, NASB, ESV, and HCSB do.

8. **None eliminate the proof text for the Triunity of God** like the NIV, ESV, NASB, and HCSB do in 1 John 5:7–8.[1]

There's nothing like the King James Bible to clean up modern version corruption.

Available from

Learn more, get the book: WHICH BIBLE WOULD JESUS USE? The Bible Version Controversy Explained and Resolved By Jack McElroy
www.JackMcElroy.com

WHICH BIBLE WOULD JESUS USE?
The Bible Version Controversy Explained and Resolved
JACK MCELROY

CHICK PUBLICATIONS
amazon
nook

---

1. Jack McElroy *WHICH BIBLE WOULD JESUS USE*, pp. 161-162.

Some Scholars Believe the King James Bible is as Much a Dictionary and Lexicon as Vine or Thayer

****

Alexander W. McClure in *The Translators Revived* noted,

It was well remarked by Robertson, above a hundred years ago, that it [the King James Bible] may serve as a Lexicon of the Hebrew language, as well as for a translation[1]

The Old Masters who translated the King James Bible knew EXACTLY which English words PRECISELY conveyed what the Hebrew and Greek text said.

So, the next time you hear, "The Greek in this passage means such and such," remember that the Greek in that passage <u>also means exactly</u> what the King James translators said it means.

Learn more, get the book: WHICH BIBLE WOULD JESUS USE? The Bible Version Controversy Explained and Resolved By Jack McElroy
www.JackMcElroy.com

Available from

---

1. *The Translators Revived: A Biographical Memoir of the Authors of the English Version of the Holy Bible.* (New York: Board of Publications of the Reformed Protestant Dutch Church, 1855), p. 239.

What They Don't Tell You about Lexicons

****

Bible version researcher **Will Kinney** discovered these examples in different editions of Liddell and Scott's Greek-English Lexicon. **Look how they game you with definitions:**

KJB Reading	Liddell and Scott's 1887 edition
Unicorn	"Unicorn"
Lunatick	"moon struck or lunatic."
Only begotten	"Only begotten"

The 1887 definitions in L/S Lexicon AGREE with the KJB!

Modern Versions Read	Liddell and Scott's 1976 edition
Wild ox	"Wild ox"
Epileptic	"Epileptic"
Unique, Only, Single	"Unique, Only, Single"

By 1976, Liddell, Scott et al., are ALL DEAD— and so are their definitions. So, WHO redefined the words AND WHY?

Missionary to the Gypsy People in Romania, Peter Heisey says:

1. "**Lexicons are not exhaustive** of every possible meaning of a word (Yes that includes Kittel). And often it is the correct biblical meaning which isn't thoroughly dealt with.

2. **Lexicons are not contextual**, i.e., they do not necessarily give the meaning of a word in a specific biblical context, or in the context of the whole Bible.

3. **Lexicons are usually authored by unsaved men** who have not the Spirit of God.

4. **Lexicons tempt people to choose the first or most often used definition/meaning, and thus demean the work of the KJB translators** (under the good preserving hand of God) who were far more skilled than the lexicon author or the lexicon user."[1]

Lexicon definitions are CONSTANTLY used by Bible teachers to undermine the KJB under the guise of being more scholarly than the KJB translators. Sadly...

They're being gamed and they're clueless.

Learn more, get the book: WHICH BIBLE WOULD JESUS USE? The Bible Version Controversy Explained and Resolved By Jack McElroy www.JackMcElroy.com

Available from

amazon
nook

Proof: King James Translators were King James Onlyists

In the Preface to the 1611 First Edition the translators said …

T ruly, good Christian Reader, we never thought from the beginning that we should need to make a new translation … but to make … **out of many good ones <u>one</u> <u>principal</u> <u>good</u> <u>one</u>,** not justly to be excepted against; that hath been our endeavour, that our mark.

❶ They said their goal was **"to make ONE PRINCIPAL GOOD ONE"**—which they did.

❷ Their statement is "Onlyism" at its finest.

Jack McElroy   David W. Daniels

It's been the one principal good one for over 400 years and it still is.

Learn more, get the books: CAN YOU TRUST JUST ONE BIBLE by David W. Daniels and Jack McElroy and WHICH BIBLE WOULD JESUS USE? The Bible Version Controversy Explained and Resolved By Jack McElroy. Both are available from www.chick.com

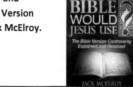

CHICK
PUBLICATIONS

Why <u>YOU</u> Are THE Problem for Modern Bible Versions

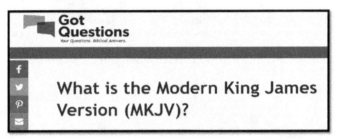

What is the Modern King James Version (MKJV)?

Question: "Why have there been so many attempts to create a more modern version of the KJV, and why have none of them truly replaced the KJV?"

Answer: "The problem is with the <u>powerful</u> <u>influence</u> the <u>King James</u> <u>Only</u> <u>Movement</u> still possesses."

"Their vehement loyalty is to the actual English text of the King James Version, not to the Textus Receptus, or to literal Bible translation.

The King James Only Movement's refusal to even consider any revisions/updates to the KJV and the venom they spew at anyone who even attempts to revise the KJV have prevented any of the modern versions of the KJV from replacing the KJV."[1]

It's working. Keep the faith.
Without the venom, of course.

Available from

Learn more, get the book: WHICH BIBLE WOULD JESUS
USE? The Bible Version Controversy Explained and
Resolved By Jack McElroy www.JackMcElroy.com

1. https://www.gotquestions.org/Modern-King-James-Version-MKJV.html

Top Four Reasons Why King James Bible Believers Are so Passionate

****

1. They're excited to see how the Lord has **fulfilled his promise** to preserve his words. The Lord is **faithful**.[1]

2. They know they are **preserved in a book**[2] so we can tell **what** they are and **where** they are.

3. They know that the book contains **all** of his words and **only** his words. His words are **certain**.[3]

4. They know the Lord provided them to us **without error**. His book is **inerrant**.[4]

> Most "prefer" a translation.
>
> Whereas...
>
> KJB believers are "passionate" about the truth.

No wonder they're inspired to read it, study it, memorize it, and believe it with all their hearts.

For them, believing the King James Bible isn't a preference... it's a conviction.

Available from

Learn more, get the book: WHICH BIBLE WOULD JESUS USE? The Bible Version Controversy Explained and Resolved By Jack McElroy www.JackMcElroy.com

[1] **Psalms 12:6–7:** The words of the LORD *are* pure words: *as* silver tried in a furnace of earth, purified seven times. Thou shalt keep them, O LORD, **thou shalt preserve them from this generation for ever.**

[2] **Hebrews 10:7:** Then said I, Lo, I come (**in the volume of the book it is written of me,**) to do thy will, O God.

[3] **Proverbs 22:21:** That I might make thee **know the certainty of the words of truth**; that thou mightest answer the words of truth to them that send unto thee?

[4] **Psalms 119:140:** Thy word *is* **very pure**: therefore thy servant loveth it.

7 Core Beliefs of King James Bible Believers

****

1. All Bible versions **SAY** and **MEAN** different things.

2. **Some differences matter**; they are significant and affect doctrine in text and translation.

CONVICTION NOT PREFERENCE

3. These differences create a **confidence problem** in the hearts of God's children about his words.

4. Sometimes modern Bible versions are contradictory and, worse; they actually contain **errors of fact and doctrine**.

5. God has **promised** to preserve his words.

6. God has **fulfilled his promise** by giving us **A BOOK** so we can know for sure **WHAT** they are and **WHERE** to find them.

7. The **King James Bible** is the repository of **ALL** of his words and **ONLY** his words without error.

Image: Alpha Stock Images - http://alphastockimages.com/

Top 3 Reasons Why King James Onlyists Are Crazy

****

① They're crazy enough to believe that God fulfilled his promise to preserve all of his pure words without error. And that those words are found in a book.

② They're crazy enough to believe in a textual lineage that their forefathers in the faith used and believed for thousands of years is TRUE.

③ They're crazy enough to believe that the Lord Jesus Christ is behind the 400+ year success of the best-selling, most published, most read, most memorized, most believed, most trusted Bible in the history of mankind.

What's really crazy is that some people call such a belief...
Heresy.

Learn more, get the book: WHICH BIBLE WOULD JESUS USE? The Bible Version Controversy Explained and Resolved By Jack McElroy
www.JackMcElroy.com

Available from

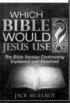

"Buck Up & Pick Teams" Choose your Translators

The King James Bible Translators Included:[1]

Lancelot Andrews, "His knowledge in Latin, Greek, Hebrew, Chaldee, Syriac and Arabic, besides **fifteen modern languages**, was so advanced that he may be ranked as one of the rarest linguists in Christendom ... A great part of five hours every day he spent in prayer."

John Bois, "**began to read Hebrew at the age of five**; admitted to St. John's College, Cambridge, at fourteen. sometimes studied Greek in the library from 4 a.m. until 8 p.m."

Dr. Miles Smith, "He **had Hebrew at his fingers' ends**; and he was so conversant with Chaldee, Syriac, and Arabic, that he made them as familiar to him as his native tongue."

Andrew Downes, "conversant and expert in the Chaldee, Syriac, and Arabic, that he made them as familiar to him, **almost, as his native tongue**; and had Hebrew also at his fingers' ends."

William Bedwell, "authored *Lexicon Heptaglotton* in seven folio volumes, including Hebrew, Syriac, Chaldee and Arabic."

Edward Lively, "one of the best linguists in the world."

Lawrence Chaderton, "familiar with the Latin, Greek, and Hebrew tongues, and was thoroughly skilled in them."

Dr. Richard Brett, "well versed in Latin, Greek, Hebrew, Chaldee, Arabic and Ethiopic.

Dr. Thomas Holland, "Another Apollos, mighty in the Scriptures..."

Dr. Richard Kilbye, "Regius Professor of Hebrew; expert in Greek."

Dr. John Reynolds, "his memory and reading were near to a miracle."

Are today's men really more qualified to translate God's word than those in 1611?

Available from

Learn more, get the book: WHICH BIBLE WOULD JESUS USE? The Bible Version Controversy Explained and Resolved By Jack McElroy www.JackMcElroy.com

1. *The Translators Revived: A Biographical Memoir of the Authors of the English version of the Holy Bible by Alexander Wilson M'Clure*

4 Questions Almost All <u>Non-King James Only</u> Folks Won't Answer

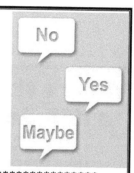

****

Bible version researcher Will Kinney has asked these questions to literally hundreds of folks over the years.

He says about 95% **can't bring themselves to admit** that they simply <u>do</u> <u>not</u> <u>believe</u> in the inerrancy of <u>**ANY**</u> Bible in <u>**ANY**</u> language, including "the" Hebrew and Greek.

Jack McElroy   Will Kinney

❶ "Do you personally believe that there is such a thing as a Bible in ANY language that is the complete (66 books in a single volume), inspired and 100% true and inerrant words of God?"

❷ "When other versions or translations differ from your 'inerrant Bible' either in the **text or meaning**, do you believe **the other versions are wrong and yours is right**?"

❸ "If you do then can you please give us **the specific name** of this infallible Bible you believe in or a link to where we can see it for ourselves so we can compare it to the Bible we are using now to see the differences and similarities?"

❹ "If you don't, then are you willing to be honest enough to admit it?"

Ask these questions of those who ridicule your faith in the King James Bible and see what happens.

Learn more about how you can defend the King James Bible, visit Will Kinney's website at http://brandplucked.webs.com/ and get the book: *WHICH BIBLE WOULD JESUS USE? The Bible Version Controversy explained and Resolved* by Jack McElroy www.JackMcElroy.com

Available from

CHICK PUBLICATIONS

amazon
nook

WHICH BIBLE WOULD JESUS USE?
The Bible Version Controversy Explained and Resolved
JACK MCELROY

What's the Difference Between a KJB Believer and a Modern Version User?

****

A King James Bible believer's faith is founded on a Bible you can actually point someone to with full confidence and assurance that the book contains ALL of God's words and ONLY God's words without error.

Whereas …

A modern version user believes:

1. ONLY the nonexistent original manuscripts were inerrant.

2. All Bibles have errors in them.

3. God's words are found somewhere in **competing, sometimes erroneous, and sometimes contradicting** readings that exist in a pile of manuscripts, versions, printed texts, translations and annotations that no one has yet determined for sure which words are authentic and which aren't.

KJB believers believe in a MOST HOLY book.

Modern version users believe in an ALMOST HOLY book.

Available from

Learn more, get the book: WHICH BIBLE WOULD JESUS USE? The Bible Version Controversy Explained and Resolved By Jack McElroy www.JackMcElroy.com

The Non-King James Onlyist's Dilemma

What to say to new converts about "the Bible" without "lying"?

****

Non-King James Onlyists are careful to tell the new convert that **"the Bible" IS the very word of God."** And it's inspired and inerrant.

The poor convert thinks it's a book. BUT soon the convert learns he's been tricked ...

The **ONLY** inerrant, and inspired Bible is **"The Original Bible"; The imaginary one made up of readings from the original manuscripts.**

The literal Bible they **HOLD IN THEIR HANDS** is just a generic and defective version of the real thing. Unfortunately, **it's neither inspired nor inerrant.**

And then doubt comes ...

What a terrible thing to do to a babe in Christ.

Our faith has no other foundation than the words in a Book. And it better not be a fictional book like "The Original Bible."

Available from

Learn more, get the book: WHICH BIBLE WOULD JESUS USE? The Bible Version Controversy Explained and Resolved By Jack McElroy
www.JackMcElroy.com

CHICK PUBLICATIONS

amazon
nook

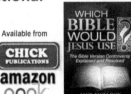

Top 4 Things to Believe If You're __NOT__ KJB Only

****

❶ __God decided to confuse his children__ by providing well over 100 Bible versions that say and mean different things.

❷ __God still isn't sure__ which Hebrew and Greek words are supposed to represent his truth.

❸ __God hid thousands of his authentic words__ from his own children for over 1,000 years only to reveal them to unbelieving higher critics in the late 19th century.

❹ __God has provided his children with defective Bibles for hundreds of years__ containing factual, historical, and geographical errors and only lately has cleaned up his act by providing Bibles based on "better manuscripts."

Does this sound like something your Lord would do?

Learn more, get the book: WHICH BIBLE WOULD
JESUS USE? The Bible Version Controversy
Explained and Resolved By Jack McElroy
www.JackMcElroy.com

Available from

CHICK
PUBLICATIONS

amazon
nook

WHICH
BIBLE
WOULD
JESUS USE
The Bible Version Controversy
Explained and Resolved

JACK MCELROY

Image: [like caramel!] https://www.flickr.com/photos/misskiller/3260650941

4 Things <u>Non</u>-King James Bible Believers Have in Common

****

Longtime Bible version researcher Will Kinney notes the following ...[1]

❶ They **DO NOT BELIEVE there IS** such a thing as a complete and inerrant Bible—**in any language**— anywhere on earth; because that's what they've been taught.

❷ Even if they say they do, most **won't show you a copy** of it or tell you exactly which one it is so you can go out and get one for yourself. Sadly, **they come up empty–handed.**

❸ Even though they DO NOT BELIEVE there is such a thing as an inerrant Bible, **most are not honest enough to admit it**. It's too painful and embarrassing.

❹ Even though they don't know for sure, **most won't** just say "**I don't know.**" BUT....

Wouldn't that be the honest answer?

Available from

Learn more, get the book: WHICH BIBLE WOULD JESUS USE? The Bible Version Controversy Explained and Resolved By Jack McElroy
www.JackMcElroy.com

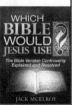

CHICK
PUBLICATIONS
amazon
nook

WHICH **BIBLE** WOULD JESUS USE
The Bible Version Controversy Explained and Resolved
JACK MCELROY

1.　See his work here: https://brandplucked.webs.com/kjbarticles.htm

6 Ways the KJB Compares to Modern Versions

****

❶ Both can be used to lead sinners to Christ.

❷ Both contain words and concepts hard to be understood **requiring study and sometimes a dictionary**.

❸ Both are **not always literal.**

❹ Both sometimes translate **identical** Greek words and phrases **differently**.

❺ **Both contain the words of God: However**, King James Bible believers **presuppose** that God cares enough about his words so that **ALL** of them can be found **WITHOUT ERROR** on the pages of **A BOOK, whereas** modern version creators have no such presupposition.

❻ Dallas Theo. Seminary's Dr. Dan Wallace says the Greek text underlying the KJB is "demonstrably inferior" in certain places to the Critical Text. **Yet,** Professor Maurice Robinson of Southeastern Baptist Theo. Seminary and author of *The New Testament in the Original Greek: Byzantine Textform*, says this about the Greek text underlying almost all modern versions:

> "…It can be demonstrated with success that **more than <u>100</u> whole <u>verses</u> … have <u>no</u> apparent <u>support</u> within the <u>Greek</u> manuscript <u>tradition</u>**; in most (if not all) cases, **<u>no</u> support <u>exists</u>** for such whole verses even within the versional or patristic traditions."[1]

The similarities of points 1–4 pale in comparison to the differences in points 5 & 6.

Available from

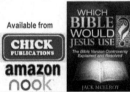

Learn more, get the book: WHICH BIBLE WOULD JESUS USE? The Bible Version Controversy Explained and Resolved By Jack McElroy www.JackMcElroy.com

1. Maurice A. Robinson, *Rule Nine, Isolated Variants, and the "Test Tube" Nature of the NA27/UBS4 Text: A Byzantine-Priority Perspective*, from Porter and Boda, *Translating the New Testament*, p. 33.

Is the King James Bible "Given by Inspiration of God" or Is It a Heresy to Believe So?

****

A Simple math test reveals the answer...

If	A=B
And	B=C
Then	A=C

IF the King James Bible is "Scripture,"
(and many refer to it as such.) And...

> "All scripture <u>is</u> given by inspiration of God...
> **2 Timothy 3:16**

Then the equation looks like this...

If	The King James Bible (A) = (B) Scripture
And	Scripture (B) = (C) given by inspiration of God
Then	The King James Bible (A) = (C) given by inspiration of God

Making the substitution, we get this...

"All **the King James Bible is given by inspiration of God**, and is profitable for doctrine, for reproof, for correction, for instruction in righteousness."

The answer is as easy as A—B—C

Available from

Learn more, get the book: WHICH BIBLE WOULD JESUS USE? The Bible Version Controversy Explained and Resolved By Jack McElroy
www.JackMcElroy.com

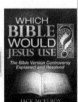

Translation and Original Languages

Introduction

****

The common objection we hear is that the full meaning of Greek and Hebrew words can't be accurately communicated in English.

They say "only the original Greek and Hebrew text can be regarded as the word of God. Something is always lost in translation. Always."[1]

Nonsense.

International deals are done all the time. Contracts are translated, agreements are reached, and lots of money exchanges hands based on the accurate translation "of the original."

This section addresses the translation issue as well as its cousin, the argument over original languages.

It covers some key translation choices like the word *Easter* in the KJB, the thee's and thou's of the King James Bible, the defective Greek teaching of *agape* and *phileo*, and the proper pronunciation of God's name (Jehovah vs. Yahweh).

---

[1] https://danielbwallace.com/2012/10/08/fifteen-myths-about-bible-translation/

They Say God's Inspired Words Can't Be Translated and Still Be God's Inspired Words

****

"Inspiration is claimed for original autographs, NOT for translation or copying.... But WE DO NOT claim for ANY copy or **ANY translation** the absolute, divine PERFECTION that was in the original autographs. **Inspiration refers to the original autographs.**"[1]

The EU's "Parliament" Building in France was designed to represent the Tower of Babel. The building is complete but is designed to look unfinished.

Right: European Parliament debate chamber.
Debates are translated into 24 different languages for Parliament members.[2]

If translation and interpretation is no problem for the world, why is it a problem for Bible translation?

Available from

Learn more, get the book: WHICH BIBLE WOULD JESUS USE?
The Bible Version Controversy Explained and Resolved By
Jack McElroy www.JackMcElroy.com

1. Dr. John R. Rice *Our God Breathed Book—The Bible*, pp. 68–69. 2. http://europa.eu/rapid/press-release_MEMO-13-825_en.htm

They Say a "Perfect Bible" Isn't Possible Because "No Translation Can Capture the Full Meaning of the Original Languages."

****

That's one of the excuses we hear for why multiple translations of the Bible in a language like English are not only preferable, but necessary.

The experts constantly tell us that our language (or any language for that matter) isn't equivalent to Hebrew or Greek. They teach that it's literally impossible to transfer the words from one language to another without losing some meaning in the process.

Their whole teaching is self-serving propaganda. Businessmen translate catalogs, brochures, and websites all the time. Business agreements and treaties are translated and signed, binding corporations and nations as well as putting trillions of dollars at risk.

Business
Translation Services

Christian biblical experts don't give God any credit. They think he hasn't been able to figure out how to transfer his inspired, living, and life-giving words from one language into another without error.

None of the experts want to defend any Bible (i.e., book) in particular because they have been taught that there are textual and/or translational errors in all of them. And there's nothing worse for a professional than to have egg on his face. So they'll avoid embarrassment at almost any cost.

That's why there are no NIV, ESV, NASB, HCSB Onlyists. They are afraid to commit to the Bible version they use. They need to be careful defending these versions because they never know when the copyright owner will pull the rug out from under them and change the text via a "new and improved" update.

The safe position is that only the autographs were without error. It's not only safe, it's politically correct. The designers of most institutional and church "statements of faith" are pretty clever. **They always refer to *"The Bible"*** generically—as a commodity—never as a Bible by brand name.

The only ones who don't are King James Bible Believers, who know that the Lord hasn't failed to deliver his words to his people.

Available from

Learn more, get the book: WHICH BIBLE WOULD JESUS
USE? The Bible Version Controversy Explained and
Resolved By Jack McElroy www.JackMcElroy.com

CHICK
PUBLICATIONS
amazon
nook

Why Jesus Never Used the Septuagint

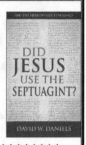

DID JESUS GET IT WRONG?

DID JESUS USE THE SEPTUAGINT?

DAVID W. DANIELS

****

The Septuagint (a.k.a. LXX) is a Greek translation of the Old Testament. "What is generally referred to as the LXX today are basically compilations of different Greek translations taken from Vaticanus, Sinaiticus and Alexandrinus, which do not perfectly coincide."[1] **Yet our teachers tell us that The Lord Jesus Christ and his disciples used it. Here are two reasons why they didn't...**

1

Genesis 5:26 King James Bible	**Genesis 5:26 Septuagint**
And Methuselah lived after he begat Lamech **782 years**.[2]	And Mathusala lived after his begetting Lamech **802 years**.[2]

This dating error (of plus 20 years, with others) in the LXX's Genesis causes Methuselah to **survive the flood by 14 years.**

2

1 Samuel 17:4 King James Bible	**1 Samuel 17:4 Septuagint**
And there went out a champion out of the camp of the Philistines, named Goliath, of Gath, **whose height** *was* <u>six</u> **cubits and a span**.	And there went forth a mighty man out of the army of the Philistines, Goliath, by name, out of Geth, **his height** *was* <u>four</u> **cubits and a span**.

❶ **The King James Bible's Goliath** is **9' 9" tall** (6 cubits and a span). He was an awe-inspiring giant—a champion.

❷ **The Septuagint's Goliath** at **6' 9" tall** isn't a giant. He's a small forward in the NBA.[3]

❸ David W. Daniels' book, *Did Jesus Use the Septuagint?* shows why the B.C. Septuagint "proofs" can't be trusted and that **Jesus read the same** <u>Hebrew</u> <u>Scriptures</u> **read by every other devout Jew.**

❹ The Lord Jesus Christ never used the Septuagint because (1) he knows the truth, and (2) he IS the TRUTH.

He'd NEVER use an erroneous Bible.

Available from

WHICH **BIBLE** WOULD JESUS USE?

Learn more, get the book: WHICH BIBLE WOULD JESUS USE? The Bible Version Controversy Explained and Resolved By Jack McElroy www.JackMcElroy.com

1. http://textus-receptus.com/wiki/Septuagint; 2. Numbers inserted for text for comparison 3. http://www.nba.com/fantasy/draft_kit/smallforwards1_15.html

Did God Influence the Word Choices of the King James Bible?

ABCDEFGHIJ
KLMNOPQR
STUVWXYZabc
defghijklmnopqrs
tuvwxyz0123456

****

Maybe there's a reason the King James Bible...

- Is the "most influential and revered English Bible that has ever existed."
- Is "probably the most beautiful piece of writing in all the literature of the world."
- Is "rightly regarded as the most influential book in the history of English civilization."
- "Has contributed 257 idioms to English, more than any other single source, including Shakespeare."
- Has "more than 1,000 churches worldwide that subscribe to a statement of faith that this 400-year-old translation '**preserves the very words of God** in the form in which He wished them to be represented in the universal language of these last days: English.'"
- Is "still the best-selling book in the world."
- "Lives on the ear, like music that can never be forgotten, like the sound of church bells."
- Is the only Bible whose words were heard simultaneously by 25% of the earth's population.

Doesn't it make sense that the Lord must be the author and promoter of the "best-selling" Bible ever printed? Maybe the book of the LORD IS the King James Bible to the exclusion of all others.

He's been displaying the same text for the past 400 years. In fact, he's so confident in it that he's had it reproduced billions of times.

If the King James Bible isn't <u>THE</u> <u>Holy</u> <u>Bible</u>, then it's the best imposter in the history of mankind.

Considering its influence, maybe the word choices made by those learned men are just as much His as theirs.

Available from

Learn more, get the book: WHICH BIBLE WOULD JESUS USE? The Bible Version Controversy Explained and Resolved By Jack McElroy www.JackMcElroy.com

For citations, see WHICH BIBLE WOULD JESUS USE? The Bible Version Controversy Explained and Resolved, pp. 117–119.

Top 5 Reasons Why You're Ahead of the Corinthians

****

Even though they had two "Original Autographs"...

1. **You've got the whole counsel of God**; both Old & New Testaments—in your own language—**they didn't.**

2. Those believers knew Greek about as well as you know English BUT **you have access to a dictionary of your language, which <u>they didn't.</u>**

3. **The Lord's all done with Ancient Greek.** Even the Greek guy at the sub shop has trouble with it. The people the Lord reached and taught using it are all dead.

4. **You're alive and teachable.** The Lord is using English and other current languages to teach his word today.

5. **God was involved in the translation of Paul's letters into English.**

~ ~

Want to know what it says in the "original Greek"? The same as what it says in the English ...

But only IF you have a Bible containing ALL of God's words and ONLY God's words.

Available from

Learn more, get the book: WHICH BIBLE WOULD JESUS USE? The Bible Version Controversy Explained and Resolved By Jack McElroy
www.JackMcElroy.com

CHICK PUBLICATIONS

amazon
nook

WHICH **BIBLE WOULD JESUS USE**
The Bible Version Controversy Explained and Resolved
JACK MCELROY

Want to be "One Up" on The Rest of Them?

Once you learn this <u>simple</u> <u>lesson</u>, you'll never hate the Thees and Thous again.
Here's all you have to remember…

T = 1 person or 1 group as in:	Y = 2 or more as in:
<u>t</u>hee, <u>t</u>hou, <u>t</u>hine, <u>t</u>hy	<u>y</u>e, <u>y</u>ou, <u>y</u>our

****

When it comes to personal pronouns, the KJB is faithful to the original Hebrew and Greek languages.[1] This distinction, is completely lost in modern English translations, <u>including the NKJV</u> is ENORMOUSLY significant. For example …

Luke 22:31–32 KJB And the Lord said, Simon, Simon, behold, Satan hath desired to have **YOU**, that he may sift **YOU** as wheat but I have prayed for **THEE**, that **THY** faith fail not: and when **THOU** art converted, strengthen **THY** brethren." **Satan desired to sift <u>ALL</u> the disciples (You) but Jesus prayed for Peter (thy).**	**Luke 22:31–32 ESV** Simon, Simon, behold, Satan demanded to have **YOU**, that he might sift **YOU** like wheat, but I have prayed for **YOU** that **YOUR** faith may not fail. And when **YOU** have turned again, strengthen **YOUR** brothers."
John 3:7 KJB Marvel not that I said unto **THEE**, **YE** must be born again." **The message was spoken to the individual Nicodemus <u>Thee</u>, but Ye applies to all.**	**John 3:7 ESV** Do not marvel that I said to you, '**YOU** must be born again.'
Matthew 26:64 KJB "Jesus saith unto him, **THOU** has said: nevertheless I say unto **YOU**, hereafter shall **YE** see the Son of man sitting on the right hand of power, and coming in the clouds of heaven." **Thou refers to the High Priest; <u>You/Ye</u> includes all those with the high priest.**	**Matthew 26:64 ESV** Jesus said to him, "**YOU** have said so. But I tell **YOU**, from now on **YOU** will see the Son of Man seated at the right hand of Power and coming on the clouds of heaven."

These distinctions occur throughout the Old and New Testaments and are missing in modern English translations. You could refer to the Greek Grammar OR you can just "see the original language" through the KJB.

Next time, why not use the "archaic" thees and thous to your advantage?

Available from

1. http://www.thekingsbible.com/KjvToday/Language.aspx

They Use "The Greek" to Undo the King's English and Yet ...

****

Look how clear things are to the experts at Logos Bible Software ...

"**O**ne of the great debates in the study of biblical Greek has to do with whether or not verbal 'tenses,' such as *aorist* and *imperfect*, actually communicate a temporal reference (indicating that the action of the verb taking place in the past, present or future) or whether they might not communicate something else entirely (aspect). Or do tenses sometimes convey time, sometimes, aspect and/or sometimes both?"[1]

Do they <u>really</u> know what they're talking about, or is it all Greek to them too?

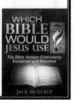
1. https://blog.logos.com/2008/04/free_greek_book/

Was all of the New Testament Originally Written in Greek?

****

You'd think so if you believed your teacher.
But did you know…

❶ Early Church historian Eusebius said …
> "Papias states: '**Matthew** put together the oracles [of the Lord] in **the Hebrew language**, and each one interpreted them as best he could.'" *Hist. Eccl.* 3.39

❷ Early church leader Irenaeus says:
> "**Matthew** also issued a written **Gospel among the Hebrews in their own dialect** while Peter and Paul were preaching at Rome and laying the foundations of the church." (*Adv. Haer.* 3.1.1)

❸ Robert B. Y. Scott (1899–1987), a clergyman of the United Church of Canada, Old Testament scholar, and former chairman of the Department of Religion at Princeton University, said:
> We come to the conclusion, therefore that the **Apocalypse** [**Book of Revelation**] as a whole **is a translation from Hebrew or Aramaic.** [*The Original Language of the Apocalypse* (U of Toronto Press, 1928)]

❹ Clement of Alexandria asserts that:
> The Epistle to the Hebrews was written by **Paul, to the Hebrews, in the Hebrew tongue.** (*Hypotyposes*, referred to by Eusebius in *Eccl. Hist.* 6:14:2)

Looks like "The Original Greek" turns out NOT to be "ALL THAT" after all.

Available from

Learn more, get the book: WHICH BIBLE WOULD JESUS USE? The Bible Version Controversy Explained and Resolved By Jack McElroy www.JackMcElroy.com

Why "Easter" is NOT a KJB Translation Error

✶✶

A nd when he had apprehended him, he put *him* in prison, and delivered *him* to four quaternions of soldiers to keep him; intending after **Easter** (Gr. Pascha) to bring him forth to the people. **Acts 12:4 King James Bible**

❶ **Some say**: That **since** the KJB translators translated the Greek word "Pascha" as "Passover" 28 of the 29 times it appears in the New Testament, "Easter" in Acts 12 was a CHOICE, not an ERROR. That's because "Easter" is defined as a "**festival of the Christian Church**" (a holiday) that took place **AFTER** the Resurrection, thereby reflecting a Christian observance and befitting the **traditional translation and meaning** of the word ...

The Oxford English Dictionary affirms this:
Easter is **"One of the great festivals of the Christian Church**, commemorating the resurrection of Christ, and corresponding to the Jewish Passover..."

❷ **Others say**: That Herod was celebrating the spring equinox holiday and the goddess Ishtar (later represented by the Saxon goddess Eostre from which Bede derived the name Easter) and intended to wait 'till the crowds died down after the holiday before delivering up Peter.

❸ **Either way:** The translation was a CHOICE, not an error.

~ ~

The folks who argue against the KJB translation are:

① Those who **object to the KJB's authority** as **THE** English speaker's standard Bible and so repeat worn–out propaganda.

② Those who want to **guilt you** into observing the Jewish Passover feast despite the N.T. admonition:

> Let no man therefore judge you in meat, or in drink, or in respect of an holyday, or of the new moon, or of the sabbath *days*: Colossians 2:16 KJB

The King James Bible is ALWAYS accurate despite the gainsayer's pronouncements.

Why Titus 2:13 Is Not a Translation Error in the KJB

****

King James Bible Titus 2:13	New American Standard Bible Titus 2:13
Looking for that blessed hope, and the glorious appearing of **the** great God and **our** Saviour Jesus Christ;	looking for the blessed hope and the appearing of the glory of **our** great God and Savior, **Christ Jesus,**

Some say: "The KJV provides an inferior translation … that unintentionally detracts from the presentation of Jesus Christ's full deity.[1]

❶ "It is argued that the KJV incorrectly translated this passage and violated the *Granville Sharpe Rule* of Greek grammar.

This rule states that the two nouns (*God* and *Savior*) refer to the same Person, Jesus Christ. They are correct in their understanding of this grammatical rule. They are incorrect in stating the *Authorized Version* has violated it."[2]

Granville Sharp (1735–1813)

❷ "The problem is not with the KJV, but rather a lack of understanding English grammar. In English, when two nouns are separated by the phrase *and our*, the context determines if the nouns refer to two persons or to two aspects of the same person."[3]

<u>Here's why the KJB translators got it right…</u>

❸ The grammar principle formulated by Sharp in the 18th century "was known in the 16th century and discussed by Theodore Beza in his 1598 edition of the Textus Receptus: 'We need to read this conjunctively because there is only one article; as more fully stated in Tit. 2.13, this place also [2 Peter 1:1] contains <u>a **clear** **testimony** of the divinity of Christ</u>.'"[4]

❹ The KJB translators could have translated these verses as does the NASB, but they didn't. One reason is because …

The NASB, has us looking for merely the "appearing of the <u>glory</u> of <u>our</u> great God" instead of the PERSONAL "<u>glorious</u> appearing of <u>the</u> great God and <u>our</u> Saviour Jesus Christ."

The NASB: Trying to fix what's already perfect.

Available from

1.   James White *The King James Only Controversy*, p. 254; 2. https://av1611.com/kjbp/faq/holland_tit2_13.html 3. Ibid. 4. KJV Today http://tinyurl.com/y2sjam9n

Defective Greek Teaching Exposed

****

❶ <u>They tell us</u> that hidden in "the original Greek" is a special usage of Greek words, AGAPE and PHILEO. They say AGAPE means "deep, intimate, selfless love" and PHILEO, a casual "friendly" love.

❷ <u>Yet ALL their versions</u> translate these two different Greek words as "love."

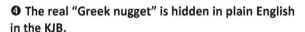

❸ <u>Actual research</u> proves that the words are used interchangeably and don't teach what they say.

BUT ...

❹ The real "Greek nugget" is hidden in plain English in the KJB.

"The English word 'charity' comes from the Latin 'caritas,' which means 'Christian love' as opposed to sexual love (*Online Etymological Dictionary*). Throughout history, Latin theologians such as Augustine have used 'caritas' as a term of art to refer specifically to Christian love (*On Christian Doctrine*, 3.10.16). **Whenever 'charity' appears in the KJV [24 times], it is in reference to Christian love toward fellow Christians.**"[1]

Another truth from the KJB they're blind to.

Available from

Learn more, get the book: WHICH BIBLE WOULD JESUS USE? The Bible Version Controversy Explained and Resolved By Jack McElroy www.jackmcelroy.com

1. http://www.kjvtoday.com/home/charity-or-love-in-1-corinthians-81-et-al

Top 3 Reasons Why KJB Translation Choices Are Correct

Should it be:
"Follow Christ" or "imitate Christ"? (1 Cor 11:1)

"Science" or "knowledge"? (1 Tim 6:20)

"Corrupt or peddle"? (2 Cor 2:17)

****

Some say a particular word as it appears in the King James Bible can be translated by a similar word as they appear in a modern version because they "mean the same thing." And that may be true ASSUMING THE BIBLE IS JUST LIKE ANY OTHER BOOK.
But the Bible is not like any other book.

The question nobody ever asks (or do they even care?) Is ...
What's the precise word that God wants to appear on the page?

❶ The presupposition of KJB believers is that God has provided us A BOOK with all his words and only his words without error.
Non-KJB believers have no such presupposition.

❷ Words have nuances and shades of meaning. The KJB wording has been selected and provided by God himself.
KJB believers don't correct it, they accept it.
Non-KJB believers have no such presupposition.

❸ Modern version translations have been tainted by 175 years of Higher and Lower Criticism along with compromised and/or corrupted "Bible study tools" (i.e., lexicons, Hebrew/Greek word studies, and ESPECIALLY commentaries).

IF you believe the King James Bible is GOD'S BOOK, then he's the one who made the final decision on which words appear in HIS BOOK.

HENCE, the choice for which synonym has already been made and it's your Lord's choice.

Thus, you can safely reject the corrector's (well–meaning) comments as irrelevant.

Available from

Learn more, get the book: WHICH BIBLE WOULD JESUS USE? The Bible Version Controversy Explained and Resolved By Jack McElroy
www.JackMcElroy.com

CHICK
PUBLICATIONS

amazon
nook

Does "The Greek" Teach That Mary Was a Perpetual Virgin?

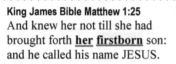

Roman Catholics were ALWAYS taught that Jesus NEVER had brothers or sisters. Seeming references to siblings are passed off as cousins.

****

King James Bible Matthew 1:25	English Standard Version Matthew 1:25
And knew her not till she had brought forth **her firstborn** son: and he called his name JESUS.	But knew her not until she had given birth to **a** _____ son. And he called his name Jesus.

❶ The King James Bible clearly teaches that Jesus was the <u>first son born</u> of Mary. Afterward, she had other children.

❷ In contrast, the ESV's Greek text matches up nicely with the Catholic Bible and reads like this…

> **New American Bible (Roman Catholic Bible)**
> He had no relations with her **until** she bore
> **a** _____ son, and he named him Jesus.
> Matthew. 1:25

❸ The footnote to the Catholic New American Bible says…

> "Until she bore a son … **The Greek word translated 'until' does not imply normal marital conduct after Jesus' birth, nor does it exclude it."**[1]

❹ A Catholic apologetics website says …

> "**Brother doesn't mean Brother…** From *An Expository Dictionary of New Testament Words*: *Adelphos* (the Greek word for "brother" in the New Testament): denotes a brother, **or near kinsman.**"[2]

Did Mary have other biological children? That depends on:

1. Whether or not someone's "gaming" you on what the "original Greek" means or more importantly …

2. Which Bible you believe.

Available from

Learn more, get the book: WHICH BIBLE WOULD JESUS USE?
The Bible Version Controversy Explained and Resolved By
Jack McElroy www.JackMcElroy.com

1. https://www.republicanoperative.com/t/five-biblical-proofs-that-jesus-did-not-have-brothers/8379 2. **Ibid.**

NIV: "We do not know if we should say Jahu or Yahweh or Jehovah."

****

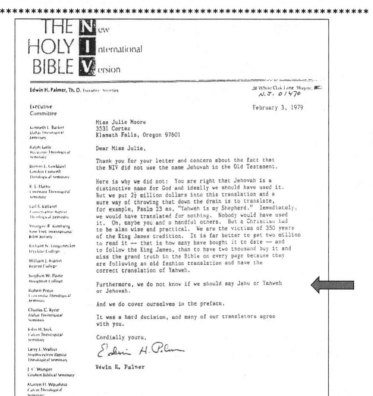

THE **N**ew
HOLY **I**nternational
BIBLE **V**ersion

Edwin H. Palmer, Th. D. Executive Secretary

30 White Oak Lane, Wayne, N.J.
N.J. 01470

Executive
Committee

February 3, 1979

Kenneth L. Barker
Dallas Theological Seminary

Ralph Latie
Nazarene Theological Seminary

Burton L. Goddard
Gordon Conwell Theological Seminary

R. L. Harris
Covenant Theological Seminary

Earl S. Kalland
Conservative Baptist Theological Seminary

Younger R. Kistberg
New York International Bible Society

Richard N. Longenecker
Wycliffe College

William J. Martin
Regent College

Stephen W. Paine
Houghton College

Robert Preus
Concordia Theological Seminary

Charles C. Ryrie
Dallas Theological Seminary

John H. Stek
Calvin Theological Seminary

Larry L. Walker
Southwestern Baptist Theological Seminary

J. C. Wenger
Goshen Biblical Seminary

Marion H. Woudstra
Calvin Theological Seminary

Miss Julie Moore
3531 Cortez
Klamath Falls, Oregon 97601

Dear Miss Julie,

Thank you for your letter and concern about the fact that
the NIV did not use the name Jehovah in the Old Testament.

Here is why we did not: You are right that Jehovah is a
distinctive name for God and ideally we should have used it.
But we put 2¼ million dollars into this translation and a
sure way of throwing that down the drain is to translate,
for example, Psalm 23 as, "Yahweh is my Shepherd." Immediately,
we would have translated for nothing. Nobody would have used
it. Oh, maybe you and a handful others. But a Christian had
to be also wise and practical. We are the victims of 350 years
of the King James tradition. It is far better to get two million
to read it -- that is how many have bought it to date -- and
to follow the King James, than to have two thousand buy it and
miss the grand truth in the Bible on every page because they
are following an old fashion translation and have the
correct translation of Yahweh.

Furthermore, we do not know if we should say Jahu or Yahweh
or Jehovah.

And we do cover ourselves in the preface.

It was a hard decision, and many of our translators agree
with you.

Cordially yours,

Edwin H. Palmer

Edwin H. Palmer

Seriously? And these are the experts?

Proof: God's Name is Jehovah NOT Yahweh

****

You can't get any better proof than OVER 1,000 Hebrew manuscripts calling out the name Yehovah.

Sadly, the scholars are hopelessly out of date. Even the encyclopedias claim God's name is Yahweh.

Author and researcher, **Nehemia Gordon** is the creator and host of the Hebrew Voices podcast, downloaded over 5 million times in 2017.

"Gordon holds a Masters Degree in Biblical Studies and a Bachelors Degree in Archaeology from the Hebrew University of Jerusalem. He has worked as a translator on the Dead Sea Scrolls and a researcher deciphering ancient Hebrew manuscripts."[1]

"Nehemia Gordon celebrates the incredible milestone of finding God's holy name **with full vowels in over 1,000 Hebrew Bible manuscripts.**

"The 1000th Hebrew Bible manuscript with the full vowels of God's holy name Yehovah, discovered earlier today (Jan 21, 2018)!"

"In less than one year, we have gone from five Hebrew Bible manuscripts with the full vowels Yehovah to (at the time of this post) 1,006!"[2]

Yahweh; the pagan God not found in ANY Hebrew scriptures.

Available from

Learn more, get the book: WHICH BIBLE WOULD JESUS USE? The Bible Version Controversy Explained and Resolved By Jack McElroy www.JackMcElroy.com

1 https://www.nehemiaswall.com/about-nehemia-gordon; 2 https://www.nehemiaswall.com/1000-manuscripts-yehovah

FOR IMMEDIATE RELEASE...
3:32 PM . . . DATELINE. . . NEW JERUSALEM . . .

Luminaries Shocked...
Translations No Longer
Considered Inspired or Inerrant

Moses and Apostle Paul Stunned, Saddened by News...

****

It is a well-established teaching by academia that **"no translation of the Scripture is infallible or inerrant."** This position has widespread acceptance and is taught in fundamental and evangelical Bible colleges and seminaries throughout the United States.

Moses and the apostle Paul were stunned to learn that their conversations which were spoken in Egyptian (see Moses' conversations with Pharaoh in Exodus) and in Hebrew (see  Paul's conversations with the Jews in Acts) respectively, are no longer considered infallible or inerrant because they were translated into Hebrew and Greek respectively.

When asked to comment, a visibly upset Moses protested,
"Of course, Pharaoh and I spoke Egyptian. It was our native tongue. Pharaoh would never have lowered himself to speak Hebrew."
"I have always maintained that the translation of our conversation into Hebrew as it appears in the book of Exodus (chapters 5-10) was not only complete but also infallible and inerrant."

Likewise, the apostle Paul was adamant about the inspiration of his translated conversation in Acts 21:40-22:21:

"I continue to stand by the position I've taken for nearly 2,000 years, the Greek translation (and subsequent translations) of the Hebrew words that I spoke are in fact my words and because they are Scripture, I regard them as infallible and inerrant."

If God inspired a translation from Egyptian into Hebrew and another from Hebrew into Greek, can't he provide one in any language he wants?

Available from

Are You TR Only or KJB Only?

****

I am both by default. But here's the kicker ...

I believe that the King James Bible **by virtue of its history and influence is the present-day determiner of the original language text.**

My view is similar to Edward Hills, who had a doctorate in Textual Criticism from Harvard:

> "the King James Version ought to be regarded not merely as a translation of the Textus Receptus but also **as an <u>independent variety</u> of the <u>Textus Receptus</u>.**"[1]

<u>The problem for TR Only folks</u> is that the question still remains ... "Which edition?" They point to Scrivener's Greek edition, which supposedly underlies the KJB as their preferred edition.

But in so doing, they are, by default defining their authentic TR edition to be determined by the text of the King James Bible.

It's like the time when Magic Johnson showed up at a tribute for Larry Bird. He wore his LA Lakers jersey but underneath he wore a Boston Celtics jersey. **They proclaim that they're TR only...**

But underneath, they're really KJB only.

Jack McElroy

Available from

Learn more, get the book: WHICH BIBLE WOULD JESUS USE? The Bible Version Controversy Explained and Resolved By Jack McElroy www.JackMcElroy.com

amazon
nook

1. https://www.wayoflife.org/reports/which_edition_of_received_text_should_we_use.html Photo: https://www.sportsmemorabilia.com/player/Larry_Bird

Which "Received Text" Edition Should We Follow?

****

Based on an article by David Cloud from Fundamental Baptist Information Service.[1]

There are a number of Greek Received Text editions at the base of all of the Protestant Reformation Bibles until the late 19th century.

❶ Erasmus published five editions (1516, 1519, 1522, 1527, 1535).

❷ Stephanus published four editions (1546, 1549, 1550, 1551).

❸ Beza published at least four (1556, 1582, 1688–89, 1598).

❹ The Elziver family printed two editions (1624, 1633).

❺ Others include the Complutensian Polyglot and Scrivener's in 1881.

The differences between the various editions of the Greek Received Text are extremely slight and cannot be compared to the differences found in the Alexandrian manuscripts.

According to Scrivener's extensive comparisons, there are only 252 places in which the Erasmus, Stephanus, Elzevir, Beza, and Complutensian Polyglot disagree sufficiently to affect the English translation. The 3rd edition of Stephanus and the 1st edition of Elzevir differ only 19 times in Mark. The editions of Beza differ from the 4th edition of Stephanus only 38 times in the entire New Testament.

Following are some of the most important of the differences between editions of the Greek Received Text:

1. https://www.wayoflife.org/reports/which_edition_of_received_text_should_we_use.html Page 1

Bible Version Secrets Exposed

Luke 2:22—Erasmus and Stephanus have "their purification," while Beza, Elzevir, and Complutensian have "her purification"

Luke 17:36—Erasmus and the first three editions of Stephanus omit this verse, while Beza, Elzevir, and the 4th edition of Stephanus include it.

John 1:28—Erasmus, Beza, Elzevir, and the 3rd and 4th editions of Stephanus have "Bethabara beyond Jordan," while the 1st and 2nd editions of Stephanus have "Bethany beyond Jordan."

John 16:33—Beza and Elzevir read "shall have tribulation," while Erasmus and Stephanus read "have tribulation."

Romans 8:11—Beza and Elzevir read "by His Spirit that dwelleth in you," while Erasmus and Stephanus read "because of His Spirit that dwelleth in you."

Romans 12:11—Beza, Elzevir, and the first edition of Erasmus read "serving the Lord," while Stephanus and the 2nd to the 5th editions of Erasmus read "serving the time."

1 Timothy 1:4—Erasmus, Beza, and Elzevir have "godly edifying," while Stephanus has "dispensation of God."

Hebrews 9:1—Stephanus reads "first tabernacle," while Erasmus and Beza omit "tabernacle."

James 2:18—The last three editions of Beza has "without thy works," while Erasmus, Stephanus, and the first edition of Beza have "by thy works."

Which edition of the Received Text should we follow today?

Edward F. Hills, who had a doctorate in modern textual criticism from Harvard, made the following important statement in regard to the KJB and the Received Text:

"The King James Version ought to be regarded not merely as a translation of the Textus Receptus but also as an independent variety of the Textus Receptus..."

Critics and Textual Criticism

Introduction

****

I've spent a lot of time reading, studying, and considering the arguments presented by modern textual critics as they assault the traditional text of the New Testament.

I believe their "history of the text" arguments are based on conjecture and speculation.

This large 50+ meme section answers a lot of objections that we get from folks who repeat the same (albeit sincerely believed) arguments we've heard a thousand times before.

The Insidious Priesthood of Christian Scholarship

****

S ome Christians elevate scholars to a sort of priesthood so that their subjective opinions become the oracles of God. Yet many of these scholars ...

❶ <u>CAUSE DIVISION</u> in the body of Christ by recommending competing and contradictory Bibles.
*Now I beseech you, brethren, **mark them which cause divisions** and offences contrary to the doctrine which ye have learned; **and avoid them.*** Rom. 16:17 KJB

❷ <u>Deceptively claim</u> ANY "conservative" translation IS the "Word of God" despite of the obvious textual and translational differences.
*Professing themselves to be wise, **they became fools**,* Rom. 1:22 KJB

❸ <u>Set themselves up as the authorities</u> above ANY Bible in ANY language for what God said and **subject the truth of God to their own opinions.**
*Therefore, behold, **I am against the prophets**, saith the LORD, that steal my words every one from his neighbour.* Jer. 23:30 KJB

❹ <u>DO NOT have a Bible</u> that they believe is inerrant and infallible and undermine the faith of young Christians by teaching their unbelief.
*and by **good words and fair speeches deceive the hearts** of the simple.* Rom. 16:18 KJB

❺<u>Use corrupt Hebrew & Greek lexicons</u> and tools that substitute the words of other scholars (some saved, many not) for the Holy words of God.
*But **they** measuring themselves by themselves, and comparing themselves among themselves, **are not wise**.* 2 Cor. 10:12 KJB

Surely ... men of high degree *are* a lie: to be laid in the balance, they *are* altogether *lighter* than vanity. Psalms 62:9 KJB

Available from

Learn more, get the book: WHICH BIBLE WOULD JESUS
USE? The Bible Version Controversy Explained and
Resolved By Jack McElroy www.JackMcElroy.com

Do You Know What Many Bible College and Seminary Professors Were Taught?

****

Textual Critic **Sir Richard Bentley** (1662–1742) said:

"The real text of the sacred writers **does not now** (since the originals have been so long lost) lie in **any MS.** [Manuscript] **or edition**, but is dispersed in them all."[1]

Just because Bentley was misinformed doesn't mean you have to be.

Bentley never believed in an inerrant, infallible, inspired "Holy Bible." His "Bible" contained a pile of conflicting manuscript readings. Which are authentic and which are not? The "experts" have yet to completely agree.

And sadly, this belief has resulted in over 100 competing and conflicting English versions.

On the other hand, you can believe God's promise …

> The **words** of the LORD are pure words: as silver tried in a furnace of earth, purified seven times. Thou shalt keep them, O LORD, **thou shalt preserve** them from this generation **for ever**. Psalm 12:6–7 KJB

God kept His promise to preserve his own words in a way that makes sense—**in a book you can actually read.**

But please, don't blame your professors or teachers…

They mean well. In their effort to uphold the tenets of modern textual criticism, they have been taught to follow others who have been misguided in their positions.

Unlike the critics, King James Bible believers know the Lord is clever enough to provide ALL of His Words in a book we can actually read.

Available from

Learn more, get the book: WHICH BIBLE WOULD JESUS USE?
The Bible Version Controversy Explained and Resolved By
Jack McElroy www.JackMcElroy.com

CHICK
PUBLICATIONS
amazon
nook

1. http://www.bible-researcher.com/tisch02.html

Christian Leaders Duped About Greek Text Behind Modern Versions

****

By good words and fair speeches, they deceive the hearts of the simple by assuring us that their thorough investigation is leading them to uncover the text of the original autographs.

Professor Maurice Robinson of NT Southeastern Baptist Theological Seminary & author of *Rule Nine, Isolated Variants, And The "Test Tube" Nature of the NA27/UBS4 Text* and *The New Testament in the Original Greek: Byzantine Textform* says this about the Greek text underlying almost all modern versions:

> "It is beyond question that the text presented in the current Nestle-Aland 27th and United Bible Societies 4th editions is regarded by many throughout the world as the closest possible approximation to the New Testament autographs or at least the best text that can be constructed by modern methods of New Testament textual criticism."[1]

BUT ...

> "It can be demonstrated with success that **more than 100 whole verses ... have no apparent support within the Greek manuscript tradition**; in most (if not all) cases, **no support exists** for such whole verses even within the versional or patristic traditions."[2]

Over 100 whole verses with NO Greek manuscript support?

What kind of deception is this?

Available from

Learn more, get the book: WHICH BIBLE WOULD JESUS USE? The Bible Version Controversy Explained and Resolved By Jack McElroy www.JackMcElroy.com

1. Stanley Porter & Mark Boda, *Translating the New Testament*, p. 27.   2. Ibid. p.33.

Beware of
Scholarly Vendors

****

<u>Scholars are vendors</u>. They sell you information. Sometimes their material is good and true and sometimes not.

They all have presuppositions and sometimes they have agendas.

But they're vendors; no different than any other professional vendor, including bankers, lawyers, doctors, engineers, judges, and scientists, electricians, plumbers and carpenters.

When they're wrong, vendors can cost you a lot of time, money, agita and sometimes, even your life.

But YOU are the ultimate decision-maker. It's up to you to decide how valid their product is.

One thing I've noticed over my 45-year business career is that sometimes really smart people come to some pretty dumb conclusions, and say some pretty stupid things. Notice...

> Dr. Kenneth L. Barker, one of the original NIV translators said, **"Most members of the committee on Bible translation (including myself) regard the footnotes as an important <u>part of the NIV text</u>."**[1]

<u>Nonsense</u>. Footnotes supplement information in the text. Biblical footnotes may help explain a text, give translational nuances or even cite alternate manuscript evidence. **BUT...**

Footnotes are not TEXT or any "part" of it.

Dr. Kenneth Barker is a smart man. But this comment, especially as it relates to Scripture, has to be...

One of the stupidest things I've ever heard.

Jack McElroy is a Born-Again Christian, businessman and entrepreneur with over 45 years of experience in various business disciplines. He is author of three books including *WHICH BIBLE WOULD JESUS USE? The Bible Version Controversy Explained and Resolved.* www.JackMcElroy.com

Jack McElroy

---

1. Kenneth Barker, *Accuracy Defined and Illustrated: An NIV Translator Answers Your Questions*, p.17

Don't Fall for the Footnote Ploy

* *

Loading up Bible versions with copious textual footnotes is a cunningly designed ploy used by academics that creates confusion in God's people and turns the situation to their advantage.

1. Modern version creators do not have ANY Bible in ANY language that they believe is inspired and inerrant.

2. What they do have are variant readings that, to varying degrees, THEY are unsure of. THEY decide which ones to put in the text and which to put in footnotes.

3. **All the while pretending that whether footnote or text, ALL readings have some degree of legitimacy.**

4. By so doing, they become the arbiter of what's authentic and what's not based on their own training and opinions.

Although they truly believe they're doing God's service, nothing could be farther from the truth.

What they really want is for you to:
(1) Doubt that God has preserved
his words in a book and …
(2) Trust them.

Available from

WHICH
BIBLE
WOULD
JESUS USE
The Bible Version Controversy
Explained and Resolved

JACK MCELROY

Learn more, get the book: WHICH BIBLE WOULD JESUS USE? The Bible Version Controversy Explained and Resolved By Jack McElroy www.JackMcElroy.com

New World Order (NWO) Insider Exposes Planned Bible Corruption in 1969

****

Dr. Richard Day (1927–1989) was a professor of Pediatrics the University of Pittsburgh and Mount Sinai Medical School in NY and **National Medical Director of Planned Parenthood** (1965–1968), which is funded by the government, the Rockefeller Foundation (since its inception in 1921), and private donors.

Dr. Lawrence Dunegan (1923–2004) was Practicing Pediatrician in Mt. Lebanon, PA, for over 34 years. The following is quoted from his recollections of a lecture he attended on March 20, 1969, at a meeting of Pediatricians.

The transcribed document, titled <u>NWO PLANS EXPOSED BY INSIDER in 1969</u>, outlines the complete destruction of the world based on the "New World System."[1]

> "**In order to do this, the Bible will be changed.** It will be rewritten to fit the new religion. Gradually, **key words will be replaced with new words having various shades of meaning.** Then the meaning attached to the new word can be close to the old word—and as time goes on, other shades of meaning of that word can be emphasized and then gradually that word replaced with another word.
>
> I don't know if I'm making that clear, but the idea is that everything in Scripture need not be rewritten, just key words replaced by other words. **The variability in meaning attached to any word can be used as a tool to change the entire meaning of Scripture**, and therefore make it acceptable to this new religion. **Most people won't know the difference;** and this was another one of the times where he said, '**the few who do notice the difference won't be enough to matter.**'"[2]

Some of us have noticed the difference and are shouting out the warning.

1 http://www.stopthecrime.net/docs/NWO%20Plans%20Exposed%20By%20Insider%20In%201969.pdf 2. Ibid.

New World Order Insider Said "The Churches Will Help Us"

****

Dr. Richard Day (1927–1989) was a professor of Pediatrics the University of Pittsburgh and Mount Sinai Medical School in NY and **National Medical Director of Planned Parenthood** (1965–1968), which is funded by the government, the Rockefeller Foundation (since its inception in 1921), and private donors.

Dr. Lawrence Dunegan (1923–2004) was Practicing Pediatrician in Mt. Lebanon, PA, for over 34 years. The following is quoted from his recollections of a lecture he attended on March 20, 1969, at a meeting of Pediatricians.

The transcribed document, titled NWO PLANS EXPOSED BY INSIDER in 1969, outlines the complete destruction of the world based on the "New World System."[1]

BLENDING ALL RELIGIONS

"Another area of discussion was Religion. This is an avowed atheist speaking. He said, 'Religion is not necessarily bad. A lot of people seem to need religion, with its mysteries and rituals - so they will have religion. But the major religions of today have to be changed because they are not compatible with the changes to come. **The old religions will have to go especially Christianity.** Once the Roman Catholic Church is brought down, the rest of Christianity will follow easily. **Then a new religion can be accepted for use all over the world**. It will incorporate something from all of the old ones to make it more easy for people to accept, and feel at home. Most people won't be too concerned with religion. They will realize that they don't need it...'"

"… He said, '**Some of you probably think the Churches won't stand for this,**' and he went on to say, '**the churches will help us!**' There was no elaboration on this, it was unclear just what he had in mind when he said, 'the churches will help us!'"[2]

The goal: Destroy Christianity by corrupting it....

Evangelist for 38 years, **Thomas Littleton says**; "We must now … face some hard facts, namely, that major institutions in the Southern Baptist Convention and Presbyterian Church of America are actually training LGBTQ activists and advocates for inclusion of sexual minorities **in the churches—in ministry positions and even as 'theologians'** of LGBTQ and Queer Theory.[3]

Available from

1 http://www.stopthecrime.net/docs/NWO%20Plans%20Exposed%20By%20Insider%20In%201969.pdf 2. Ibid. 3. https://thirtypiecesofsilver.org/2018/05/

KJV Only
Conspiracy Theory?

✳✳✳

The *Index librorum prohibitorum* (Latin, "List of Prohibited Books")
was a list of publications deemed heretical, or contrary to morality
by the Sacred Congregation of the Index (a former Dicastery of the
Roman Curia) and thus Catholics were forbidden to read them
without permission.[1]

"INDEX OF FORBIDDEN BOOKS, the reading of which is expressly forbidden by the Holy See. Any book or publication whose material constitutes a danger to the faith and morals of the reader is prohibited. Forbidden books would include:
1. Any non-Catholic edition or translation of the Holy Bible (for example the King James Version):"

＝＝＝＝＝＝＝＝＝＝＝＝＝＝＝＝＝＝＝＝＝＝＝＝＝＝＝＝＝＝＝＝＝＝＝＝＝＝＝

But today there is a "protestant" version
FULLY APPROVED by the Church of Rome— *The
English Standard Version Catholic Edition...*

Nihil Obstat
✠ Bishop J. Susaimanickam
Sivagangai, India

Imprimatur
✠ Oswald Cardinal Gracias
Archbishop of Bombay
President, Conference of Catholic Bishops of India
May 4, 2017

Nihil Obstat: "The certification by an official censor of the Roman Catholic Church that a book has been examined and found to contain nothing opposed to faith and morals."

Imprimatur: "A license to print or publish especially by Roman Catholic episcopal authority."

This ESV edition is presently only available in India.[2] But with enough
conditioning, maybe the "protestants" and evangelicals will finally
figure out who's their boss.

**Some say the Roman Catholic Church connection to modern bible
versions is a "KJV Only conspiracy theory."**

Maybe not so much.

Available from

Learn more, get the book: WHICH BIBLE WOULD JESUS USE?
The Bible Version Controversy Explained and Resolved By
Jack McElroy www.JackMcElroy.com

amazon
nook

1. https://en.wikipedia.org/wiki/Index_Librorum_Prohibitorum#cite_note-PFGrendler-1 ; 2. http://atcbooks.in/product/esv-ce-english-standard-version-catholic-edition-regular-hb/

Top 5 Reasons for the Bible Version Controversy

✳✳✳✳✳✳✳✳✳✳✳✳✳✳✳✳✳✳✳✳✳✳✳✳✳✳✳✳✳✳✳✳✳✳✳✳

King James Only Bible believers are sometimes called "divisive," and "cultists." They endure the insults because ...

❶ **KJB BELIEVERS KNOW** that the differences in Bible versions undermine the integrity and truthfulness of their Lord and Saviour Jesus Christ.

❷ **Christian leaders say the differences DON'T matter** and that the reliability of the Bible exists in the **"message"** and not the words. **KJB BELIEVERS KNOW** this is NOT true because ...

❸ The experts hypocritically spend countless man hours and literally millions of dollars **examining WORDS** and publishing versions that sometimes exhibit contradictory differences **making a mockery of Christianity's Holy Book**.

❹ The introduction of competing versions **has produced disbelief in ANY Bible** (meaning book) because Christians are taught **ALL** Bible translations have errors in them.

❺ Everybody who's ever attended a multiversion Bible study knows all versions sometimes **SAY and MEAN** different things and the differences **DO matter and DO affect doctrine**.

The differences matter—a lot.
If they didn't, there wouldn't be a
controversy in the first place.

Available from

Learn more, get the book: WHICH BIBLE WOULD JESUS USE? The Bible Version Controversy Explained and Resolved By Jack McElroy www.JackMcElroy.com

Photo: Photo by rawpixel on Unsplash

Hypocrisy and the "Imperfect Bible" Doctrine

****

Many Christian leaders hold up <u>a</u> Bible and say:

"The Bible is the inspired, inerrant and perfect Word of God!"

But what they **really believe and teach** about the book they claim to "believe in" is ...

❶ ONLY the Original Autographs "are" inspired and inerrant.

❷ ALL translations have errors and are imperfect.

❸ There is NO Bible on earth that contains ALL of God's words and ONLY God's words.

They boldly proclaim the "perfect" word of God" but possess an "imperfect" Bible instead.

<u>They profess FAITH</u> in a **perfect book**. But ...

<u>They possess DOUBT</u> that such a book exists.

Sadly, they've laid a defective foundation without realizing it.

Available from

Learn more, get the book: WHICH BIBLE WOULD JESUS USE? The Bible Version Controversy Explained and Resolved By Jack McElroy
www.JackMcElroy.com

Have You Ever Noticed Bible Version Hypocrisy?

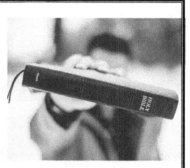

****

It's when someone holds up a Bible and SAYS ...

"I believe the Bible is the inerrant, infallible word of God."

Sounds great ... and believable. Until you ask them the "divisive" but honest question, "Which one?"

And then they don't or won't produce **ANY** Bible in **ANY** language that they believe contains **ALL** of God's words and **ONLY** God's words without error.

It seems like the ONLY folks who honestly believe their Bible contains ALL of God's words and ONLY God's words are ... King James Bible Believers.

Learn more, get the book: WHICH BIBLE WOULD JESUS USE? The Bible Version Controversy Explained and Resolved By Jack McElroy www.JackMcElroy.com

Available from

The Bold and Empty Statement of Faith in "The Bible"

****

Some Christian schools and churches boldly proclaim...

> "We believe the Bible to be the inspired Word of God, complete and without error in the original autographs."

❶ This honest and seemingly spiritual bit of sophistry is actually meant to deceive the hearts of the simple. The deception?

There never was a "Bible" containing the original autographs and they know it. They NEVER say this about a particular BOOK.

❷ Yet they declare that "the Bible"—i.e., "original autographs" was "inspired," "complete," and "without error."

❸ Which means that "The Bible" we now have (any version) is uninspired, incomplete, and contains errors.

By their OWN ADMISSION, their "holy book" is defective.

What an embarrassment to God and Christianity.

Learn more, get the book: WHICH BIBLE WOULD JESUS USE? The Bible Version Controversy Explained and Resolved By Jack McElroy
www.JackMcElroy.com

Available from

They Boldly Say ...

"I Believe the Bible is Inerrant!"

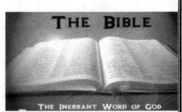

THE BIBLE

THE INERRANT WORD OF GOD

But they'll never tell you which one.

****

It happens ALL THE TIME. And yet ...

1. The word *Bible* means book.
2. The Bible today is one book.
3. The Hebrew Old and Greek New Testament Scripture are combined in one book called *the Bible*.
4. The one book has to be in **one** language to qualify as a "Bible" that speakers of the same language can be **search and study. How else can you compare Scripture with Scripture unless it's in one language?**

They can't show you "the Bible" they profess to believe in because they don't possess one. They've been taught that ONLY the originals are inspired and inerrant.

How can they HONESTLY tell people they believe in "the Bible" and not be able to show you the book they believe in?

The **God of MANY versions** not only says and means different things but sometimes says erroneous and contradictory things. Anyway ...

King James Bible believers know the real God has provided them A BOOK.

Available from

Learn more, get the book: WHICH BIBLE WOULD JESUS USE? The Bible Version Controversy Explained and Resolved By Jack McElroy www.JackMcElroy.com

What Most Fundamental Bible College and Seminary Professors Won't Ever Give You

****

They'll never give you...

A **book** in **ANY** language (including Koine Greek, Hebrew, Aramaic or English) with the words "Holy Bible" written on it that **they will certify is** the inspired, perfect, complete, pure (without error) words of God.

Here's why...

1. Because they believe the original words God inspired are now located in a big pile of original language manuscripts, ancient translations, and quotations of the text.

2. Because no matter what words they come up with, they don't have any—**not one**—original manuscript to compare them to and know for sure they're right.

Of this you can be sure...

Anyone who does hold a book (with the words "Holy Bible") in their hands in any language and really believes that the book is the pure word of the living God, being the complete holy scripture of truth without error, will be considered a fool at best <u>and a heretic at worst</u>.

If you believe that your Lord has given you a book containing all of his words and only his words ... will He think you a fool or a heretic? Available from

Learn more, get the book: WHICH BIBLE WOULD JESUS USE? The Bible Version Controversy Explained and Resolved By Jack McElroy
www.JackMcElroy.com

CHICK PUBLICATIONS
amazon
nook

4 Reasons Why You Never Meet NIV, ESV, or NKJV Onlyists

****

❶ The **scholars** who build the Greek and Hebrew texts underlying all modern versions and their English translations **believe that their texts may have errors in them.**

❷ Then they teach **pastors** and **students** that ONLY the (nonexistent) original autographs **"are"** inspired and inerrant.

Training vs. Education

❸ Who then teach that **NO book on earth** contains ALL of God's words and ONLY God's words without error.

❹ Finally, the poor Christian BELIEVES the scholars, their pastors, and teachers and gives up hope of EVER getting an inerrant Bible.

~ ~~

On the other hand ...

King James Bible believers **are sure** the Lord HAS preserved his words in a book that His children can hold in their hands.

Try witnessing to an atheist, agnostic, Jew, Hindu, Buddhist, or Muslim and tell them that your Bible is anywhere from 85–99.5% perfect.

Why should they ever believe you or your imperfect Bible?

Available from

Learn more, get the book: WHICH BIBLE WOULD
JESUS USE? The Bible Version Controversy
Explained and Resolved By Jack McElroy
www.JackMcElroy.com

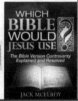

"Where Does Scripture Say the KJV is the Best or Only 'Holy' Bible?"

****

This <u>insincere</u> <u>question</u> is usually asked by folks who think you're a fool because you believe God preserved his pure words IN A BOOK instead of a cocktail of various and competing "readings" recommended by "experts" who sometimes <u>DON'T EVEN AGREE WITH EACH OTHER</u>.

Nonetheless, here's the answer:
The Scripture never says a word about the King James Bible.

BUT...The Scripture DOES condition us to be on the lookout for a BOOK. God mentions the word *book(s)* 196 times. Here are some of them ...

Ge 5:1	**the book** of the generations of Adam
Ex 24:7	**the book** of the covenant
Nu 21:14	**the book** of the wars of the LORD
De 29:21	**this book** of the law
Jos. 10:13	**the book** of Jasher
1 Ki 11:41	**the book** of the acts of Solomon
1 Ki 14:19	**the book** of the chronicles of the kings of Israel
1 Ki 15:23	**the book** of the chronicles of the kings of Judah?
Ezra 4:15	**the book** of the records
Es 10:2	**the book** of the chronicles of the kings of Media and Persia
Ps 69:28	**the book** of the living
Isa 34:16	**the book** of the LORD
Jer 32:12	**the book** of the purchase
Na 1:1	**The book** of the vision of Nahum
Mt 1:1	**The book** of the generation of Jesus Christ
Lu 3:4	**the book** of the words of Esaias the prophet
Lu 4:17	**the book** of the prophet Esaias
Ac 1:20	**the book** of Psalms
Ac 7:42	**the book** of the prophets
Ga 3:10	**the book** of the law
Phil 4:3	**the book** of life
Rev 20:12	**the books** were opened
Rev 20:12	and **another book** was opened, which is *the book* of life:

The Lord said, "Seek ye out of the book of the LORD and read..."

We found it—despite the "experts."

Available from

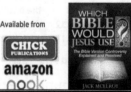

6 Ways Modern Bible Versions Mock God

★★

❶ **They charge him with lying.** Experts say God's words are still being dug out of a pile of ancient manuscripts but DO NOT EXIST in one place so that God's own children can believe them. God's promise to preserve his words is not only scriptural (Psa. 12:6–7) but also common sense. **Why inspire something that you don't preserve? Why play Hide and Seek with something of such great importance?**

❷ **They charge the Lord Jesus Christ with lying** in John 7:8-10.[1]

❸ **They charge the Lord Jesus Christ with sin** in Mt. 5:22 with Mark 3:5.[2]

❹ **They charge God with child abuse.** According to the textual critics who created the modern version texts, God's true words were hidden for more than 1,500 years. **What kind of God keeps his pure words from his own children?**

❺ **They charge him with foolishness.** Only a fool or liar recommends contradictory and competing specifications, testimonies, and historical records and then claims they're all true.

❻ **They charge him with error in the original autographs.** Modern versions publish KNOWN errors of fact, geography, history, science, and genealogy. Who wants a **"holy" book** with errors?

And they say "God has blessed us with many versions." **Nonsense.**

Modern versions are a curse, not a blessing.

Available from

[1,2,3] Learn more, get the book: WHICH BIBLE WOULD JESUS USE? The Bible Version Controversy Explained and Resolved By Jack McElroy www.JackMcElroy.com

amazon

nook

Jack McElroy, *WHICH BIBLE WOULD JESUS USE?*, pp. 69–70. 2. Ibid. pp. 73–74.

Top 6 Reasons for the Bible Version Controversy

****

According to the experts, the King James Bible has real problems.

❶ "Few people realize, for example, that thousands of errors have been found in the KJV."—The Old Time Gospel Ministry, "The Authorized King James Version of the Bible," citing Leslie R. Keylock, "The Bible that Bears His Name," *Moody Monthly* (July–August 1985), accessed December 2012, http://www.theoldtimegospel.org/about/akjvb4.html.

❷ "I contend that the KJV has far more drastically altered the Scriptures than have modern translations."— Dallas Theological Seminary Professor Daniel B. Wallace, "Why I Do Not Think the King James Bible Is the Best Translation Available Today," Bible.org, accessed January 1, 2016, http://tinyurl.com/nryj7bx.

❸ "The problem is that the King James Bible is filled with readings which have been created by overly zealous scribes."—Dallas Theological Seminary Professor Daniel B. Wallace, ibid.

❹ "The KJV has added 16 whole verses NOT found in so-called "Original Bible." See: *WHICH BIBLE WOULD JESUS USE?*, pp. 95–97, 108.

❺ The Greek text behind NT of the KJV "was not based on early manuscripts, not reliably edited, and consequently not trustworthy. — Norman L. Geisler and William E. Nix, *A General Introduction to the Bible, p. 384.*

On the one hand we're told...
The King James Bible has **thousands of errors,** is **"filled"** with counterfeit words **"created"** by men, and its underlying text is **"not trustworthy."**

Yet, on the other hand, we are told...

❻ "When we use a faithful conservative translation such as the King James Version, New King James Version, the New American Standard Version, or another version of demonstrated accuracy we can trust our Bible as the word of God. We can be confident that we have God's word in our hands."— James B. Williams, Randolph Shaylor, *God's Word in Our Hands: The Bible Preserved for Us,* P. 422.

If we believe what we're told, that means...

"God's word" has **"thousands of errors"** is **"filled"** with counterfeit words, **"created"** by men, and its underlying text is **"not trustworthy."**

And they wonder why there's a controversy!

Available from

amazon
nook

Learn more, get the book: WHICH BIBLE WOULD JESUS USE? The Bible Version Controversy Explained and Resolved By Jack McElroy www.JackMcElroy.com

The 4 Root Causes of the Bible Version Controversy

****

❶ Evangelical and fundamental leaders are **STILL SEARCHING** for the readings from a nonexistent book known as "The Original Bible."

❷ **The wording of this "Original Bible" is a moving target.** It changes depending on which professional Christian leader you listen to.

❸ They all have an opinion as to which Bible they **PREFER** but will **NEVER** tell you which one is **WITHOUT ERROR** and **COMPLETE**.

❹ That's because **they don't believe ANY Bible in ANY language** contains **all** the words of God and **only** God's words **without error**.

That's why there are so many "versions." And why new ones get printed all the time.

On the other hand, King James Only folks believe that the Lord himself has provided them with a book that contains ALL of his words and ONLY his words WITHOUT ERROR.

They believe this because it's the brand the Lord Jesus Christ has been using mightily for over 400 years—The most memorized, most read, best-selling Bible of all time.

For KJB believers, it isn't a preference, it's a conviction.

Available from

Learn more, get the book: WHICH BIBLE WOULD JESUS USE? The Bible Version Controversy Explained and Resolved By Jack McElroy www.JackMcElroy.com

The Two Dirty Little Secrets of Modern Textual Criticism

"Get thee hence, Satan"

"Man shall-live--by every word that proceedeth out of the mouth of God."

THE CHRISTIAN

Specious arguments gratuitous assumptions guesses, surmises, conjectures, and the like, all aimed at destroying faith in the Word of God.

DESTRUCTIVE HIGHER CRITICISM

"Don't be a fool, man. How can you believe the Bible in the face of all this evidence?"

****

❶ **The textual critics know their two "go-to" manuscripts are error-filled but use them anyway.**

Everybody in the textual criticism business knows that Vaticanus and Sinaiticus contain errors of fact, spelling, grammar, history, and geography. They know that there are missing words, phrases, and verses that appear in parallel passages or elsewhere in Scripture.

Instead of just admitting their favorite manuscripts are corrupt …

❷ **The critics assert that God made those mistakes in the original autographs. They claim that later on, "pious scribes" fixed the errors in the original autographs to help God out OR the "pious scribes" just flat out added words and whole verses that God NEVER wanted in his Bible.**

The textual critics won't dump these manuscripts even when they know they contain error. They choose error rather than truth and say that's what God originally wrote.

They don't come right out and tell you, but most of them really believe that the Bible is a mere human book. No different than any of the classics.

By subtly suggesting (or sometimes saying outright in their own publications) that the human authors of Scripture made mistakes, they undermine the direct influence of the Holy Ghost in the production of the Bible.

Unbelieving textual critics are the brains and spirits behind ALL modern Bible versions.

Learn more, get the book: WHICH BIBLE WOULD JESUS USE? The Bible Version Controversy Explained and Resolved By Jack McElroy www.JackMcElroy.com

Available from

amazon nook

Modern Textual Criticism's Psychological Projection

****

Psychological projection is ascribing **to someone else** one's own thoughts, feelings, and in some cases, sins.

The political left uses this technique by making false accusations (racist fascist, sexist, misogynist, xenophobic, demeaning, divisive) to divert attention away from their own guilt and/or to avoid blame and punishment.

Think of all the names and accusations they make when pointing to conservatives and realize that they've got three fingers pointing right back at them.

Interestingly, modern textual critics project the "sins" of their corrupt Critical Text onto the Received Text and by extension the KJB.

Textual critic Dr. Bruce Metzger says the following are the types of errors occurring in the Greek New Testament (Textus Receptus) underlying the KJB:[1]

1. Spelling and Grammatical mistakes
2. History and Geography mistakes
3. Added words, phrases, and verses
4. Added words, phrases, and verses to harmonize Scripture
5. Alterations for doctrinal purposes

<u>Here's the Projection:</u>
These are the very types of errors (except they also <u>delete</u> words, phrases, and verses and <u>dis-harmonize</u> scripture) that are found in the NIV, ESV, NASB, HCSB, and almost all modern versions as I've demonstrated over and over again in many memes.

Don't fall for the projection.
Where they accuse the KJB of a textual error, be thankful; you caught them in a projection.

Learn more, get the book: WHICH BIBLE
WOULD JESUS USE? The Bible Version Controversy
Explained and Resolved
By Jack McElroy www.JackMcElroy.com

Available from

CHICK
PUBLICATIONS

amazon
nook

Jack McElroy

1. See chapter 7 of Dr. Metzger's book, *The Text of the New Testament—It's Transmission, Corruption and Restoration.*

Top 2 Reasons Why Modern Bible Versions Are an Embarrassment to God

****

1 They're based on a text that God supposedly hid from his own children for over 1,500 years and only revealed it to liberal (and apostate) textual critics in the 19th century.

Which means they cared more about God's words than he did.

2 Sometimes they say and mean different and even contradictory things.

Which makes your God the author of confusion.

In short, they make your Lord look incompetent.

Learn more, get the book: WHICH BIBLE WOULD JESUS USE? The Bible Version Controversy Explained and Resolved By Jack McElroy
www.JackMcElroy.com

Available from

Top 4 Faith-Killing Things Kids Are Taught in Bible College and Seminary

****

For over 100 years, fundamental and evangelical ministerial students were taught:

❶ **Unbelief in "The Bible."** There is **NO** Bible **(meaning BOOK)** on the face of the earth, in any language that contains all of God's words and only God's words without error.

If this true, then the Lord has **NOT** provided his own children with a Bible (meaning book) even after the invention of printing over 500 years ago.

❷ **No single Bible is sufficient** (in ANY language) to know exactly which words are God's and what they actually mean.

If this true, then our Lord leaves his own children uncertain as to what his actual words ARE—which means **the Lord purposely confuses** his children because many translations **SAY** and **MEAN** different things.

❸ **The New Testament Text believed by the church for over 15 centuries was deliberately and purposely corrupted for doctrinal reasons.**
If this true, then the Lord deceived born-again Christians (his children) by providing them a corrupted and doctrinally erroneous text for over 1,500 years.

❹ **The true text of the New Testament** was, for the most part, discovered and assembled in the latter half of the 19th century by unbelieving textual critics.

If this true, then the Lord violated his promise to preserve his words to all generations. (Psalms 12:6–7; 33:11)

And that's WHY there's a Bible version controversy.

Available from

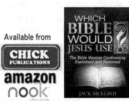

Learn more, get the book: WHICH BIBLE WOULD JESUS USE? The Bible Version Controversy Explained and Resolved By Jack McElroy www.JackMcElroy.com

CHICK PUBLICATIONS

amazon

nook

407

Modern Scholarship's Fake News Story

****

Modern scholars have invented and circulated a <u>BIZARRE</u> history of the biblical text that borders on disinformation.

Their narrative goes like this …

① <u>Born again Christians</u> (like you) lied and corrupted the New Testament Scriptures by adding <u>their</u> <u>own</u> <u>words</u> to it (to help God out) despite of His admonition **NOT to add to OR take away from** his words; even pronouncing a curse on those who do so.

② **Some obscure man** in Syria named Lucian **somehow** gathered, edited, published, and distributed this corrupted text in the third century.

③ **Somehow his work went viral**. This supposedly corrupted text spread all over the "known world" with no printing press, no mass media, with primitive communications and transportation systems.

④ **Somehow this text (traditional text)** became the basis of thousands of manuscripts used by unsuspecting and naive believers for almost 2,000 years.

⑤ **Somehow this text became basis of <u>ALL</u> the Reformation Bibles** of the 16th and 17th centuries including the King James Bible.

⑥ **God did an about-face and overrode this text** that deceived Christians for 1,800 years with a new text created by unbelieving scholars in the 19th century.

Do you really think your Lord would allow his own children to be deceived for almost two millennia about the location and authenticity of his words?

Available from

The Truth about the Two Bad Boy Manuscripts behind Modern Bible Versions

****

Almost all evangelical and fundamental professors and pastors are taught that Vaticanus and Sinaiticus are the "oldest and best" manuscripts "we" have. And in them "we" have "our" best representation of the "original text" of the Bible.

Here's what they **DON'T** get taught...

Jack McElroy with facsimiles of "the oldest and best."

John W. Burgon (1813–1888), who was the leading religious teacher of his time, said, "Vaticanus and Sinaiticus are two "**of the most scandalously corrupt copies extant.**"

They exhibit "**the most shamefully mutilated texts...**" and they contain "**the largest amount of fabricated readings, ancient blunders and intentional perversions of Truth.**"[1]

Almost ALL modern versions of the Bible default to the **corrupt readings** in these two manuscripts when they differ from the underlying text of the King James Bible.

Textual critics, big-name Christian leaders, professors, and pastors may trust them. But here's the question they'll never ask...

Why would Jesus ever trust these two defective and error filled manuscripts?

Available from

Learn more, get the book: WHICH BIBLE WOULD JESUS USE? The Bible Version Controversy Explained and Resolved By Jack McElroy
www.jackmcelroy.com

1. John William Burgon, *The Revision Revised: A Refutation of Westcott and Hort's False Greek Text and Theory* (1881).

Experts Abandon "Oldest and Best" Manuscripts

****

❶ ALL CURRENT English versions agree with the KJB that Sceva **had 7 sons.**

And there were <u>seven</u> sons of one Sceva... Acts 19:14 KJB

❷ ALL CURRENT English versions, BUT NOT ALL MANUSCRIPTS, say that the evil spirit prevailed **against** "them," meaning <u>all</u> <u>seven</u>.

❸ However, the "oldest and best" manuscripts (Vaticanus, Sinaiticus) say Sceva had only <u>2 sons</u>— a known error acknowledged by ALL.

❹ In 1966, the NASB agreed with "the oldest and best" manuscripts:

Jack McElroy with facsimiles of "the oldest and best."

Acts 19:16 King James Bible	Acts 19:16 Vaticanus, Sinaiticus ©1966 NASV
And the man in whom the evil spirit was leaped on them, and **overcame them**...	and the man in whom was the evil spirit leaped on them and **subdued** <u>both</u> of them...

But ... realizing the <u>egregious</u> <u>error</u> (<u>both</u> vs. <u>seven</u>) in their own "go to" manuscripts, the NASB staff later **CONVENIENTLY** changed their reading (since it OBVIOUSLY CONTRADICTS Acts 19:14) to agree with the KJB and most other versions.

Here's the point: **they swear to us that the FOUNDATION MANUSCRIPTS (Vaticanus, Sinaiticus) of modern version texts are of "excellent testimony."** Yet according to John W. Burgon (1813–1888), who was "the leading religious teacher of his time,"said, Vaticanus and Sinaiticus are two "of the most scandalously <u>corrupt</u> copies extant" ... They exhibit "the most shamefully <u>mutilated</u> <u>texts</u>" and they contain "the largest amount of <u>fabricated</u> readings, ancient <u>blunders</u> and intentional <u>perversions</u> of Truth."[1]

The experts make lame excuses defending them, but ...

When weighed in the balance, Vaticanus and Sinaiticus are always found wanting.

Available from

---

1. John William Burgon, *The Revision Revised: A Refutation of Westcott and Hort's False Greek Text and Theory*, (1881).

Which "Oldest and Best" Manuscripts Should You Follow in John 4:1?

****

~AD 200 Papyri	4th Century Manuscripts ~AD 350-375	Printed Bibles	Reading
P⁶⁶	Vaticanus	King James Bible	When therefore **the Lord** knew how the Pharisees had heard that **Jesus** made and baptized more disciples than John,
P⁷⁵		NASB	Therefore when **the Lord** knew that the Pharisees had heard that **Jesus** ...
	Sinaiticus	ESV	Now when **Jesus** learned that the Pharisees had heard that Jesus was making and baptizing more disciples than John
		NIV	Now **Jesus** learned that the Pharisees had heard that he was gaining and baptizing more disciples than John

❶ According to the experts, the readings of the King James Bible and the NASB go back to ~AD 200.

❷ The readings of the NIV and the ESV only go back to ~AD 350-375.

❸ When it comes to his children, "The Lord knoweth them that are his" (2 Timothy 2:19). When it comes to variant readings, the same truth applies ... The Lord knoweth them that are his.

And you'll find them all in the King James Bible.

Available from

NIV Committee Member Says KJV has Doctrinal Problems

★★★

Jack Pearl Lewis (1919–2018) Ph.D. in New Testament and Old Testament. He served as translation consultant and editorial committee member for the *New International Version.*

The Mantra: **"No doctrine is affected by modern translations."**

The Truth: **Lewis reveals what they REALLY believe** in his book, *The English Bible from KJV to NIV*. Chapter 3 is titled *"Doctrinal Problems in The King James Version"*. It covers 33 pages.

> "'Doctrine' means 'teaching,' and any failure to present the Word of God accurately, completely, and clearly in a translation is a doctrinal problem.[1]

> "If the same kind of fine-tooth comb that is expanded on the new translations is used on the KJV, we see that the problems of the KJV are as numerous and as serious as those of the new translations. The need for new translations lies in the inadequacies of the KJV".[2]

He doesn't want anybody examining new translations with a fine-tooth comb because you'll find doctrinal problems. Shouldn't God's word bear close doctrinal scrutiny? But there's more...

> "[the KJV] is not the original Bible. The translators worked neither by inspiration nor by special divine approval."[3]

Sure. God had nothing to do with it.

Available from

Learn more, get the book: **WHICH BIBLE WOULD JESUS USE?** The Bible Version Controversy Explained and Resolved By Jack McElroy www.JackMcElroy.com

---

1. Jack P. Lewis, *The English Bible from KJV to NIV*, p. 61; 2. Ibid, p.67; 3. Ibid p. 68

Facts Modern Versionists are Clueless About

****

Eldon J. Epp, STM, Harvard Divinity School PhD, Harvard University is one of the foremost figures in modern textual criticism. Here's what he said …

"we simply do not know how to make a definitive determination as to what the best text is; that we do not have a clear picture of the transmission and alternation of the text in the first few centuries…[1]

"…and, of course, we no longer think so simplistically or so confidently about recovering 'the New Testament in the Original Greek.'…[2]

Fact Check

Westcott-Hort, von Soden, and others had sweeping theories (which we have largely rejected) to undergird their critical texts, but we seem now to have no such theories and no plausible sketches of the early history of the text that are widely accepted."[3]

He just trashed over 100 years of seminary and Bible college propaganda that demotes the KJB as God's final authority for English-speaking people.

Available from

Learn more, get the book: WHICH BIBLE WOULD JESUS USE? The Bible Version Controversy Explained and Resolved By Jack McElroy
www.JackMcElroy.com

CHICK
PUBLICATIONS

amazon
nook

WHICH BIBLE WOULD JESUS USE
The Bible Version Controversy Explained and Resolved
JACK MCELROY

1. https://tinyurl.com/y7p3r7p9   2. https://tinyurl.com/ydfwxjcc   3. Ibid. p. 114.

The committee largely responsible for the Greek New Testament found in <u>most</u> modern Bible Versions.
Left to right, Klaus Junak, Matthew Black, Bruce Metzger, Alan Wikgren, Kurt Aland, Jesuit Priest Carlo M. Martini.

Modern Versions' Greek NT Committee Unsure Which Words Are God's

<u>Note the blackboard letters</u>. "By means of the letters A, B, C, and D, enclosed within {braces} at the beginning of each set of textual variants the Committee has sought to indicate the **relative degree of certainty**, arrived at the basis of internal considerations as well as of external evidence, for the reading adopted as the text. **The letter <u>A</u> signifies that the text is <u>virtually</u> certain**, while <u>B</u> indicates that there is <u>some degree of <u>doubt</u></u>. The letter <u>C</u> means that there is a **considerable** degree of **doubt** whether the text or the apparatus contains the superior reading, while <u>D</u> shows that there is a <u>very high</u> degree of <u>doubt</u> concerning the reading selected for the text."[1]

They built a Greek New Testament text that **sometimes:** (1) Is **"virtually certain,"** (2) Contains **"some degree of doubt,"** (3) Has a **"considerable degree of doubt,"** (4) Has a very **"high degree of doubt." Wow**.

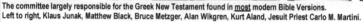

Modern versions: men's words or God's? Sometimes, it's a roll of the dice.

Available from

Learn more, get the book: WHICH BIBLE WOULD JESUS USE? The Bible Version Controversy Explained and Resolved By Jack McElroy www.JackMcElroy.com

CHICK
PUBLICATIONS
amazon
nook

[1] *Der Text Des Neuen Testaments* by Kurt Aland, Barbara Aland p.44

The Devil IS Dead

****

He must be; because evidently, he doesn't bother tampering with the words of God anymore.

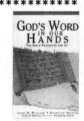

Look what prominent Christian teachers are saying ...

"Fundamental doctrines can be taught from any of these versions. **No doctrine of the Christian faith is really corrupted by the use of these translations.**[1]

Professor Daniel B. Wallace from Dallas Theological Seminary says:

"Nevertheless, I repeat: most textual critics for the past two hundred and fifty years would say that **no doctrine is affected by these changes.**"[2]

These scholars must believe that the devil has nothing to do with modern Bible versions that teach ...

Jesus is a begotten God— John 1:18 in the NASV.

Jesus only "grasped" equality with God— Phil. 2:6 in the ESV.

Jesus lied to his brothers— John 7:8–10 in the NASV.

Joseph is Jesus father—Luke 2:33 in the NIV.

Jesus is not omnipresent— John 3:13 in the NIV.

Jesus was a sinner liable to judgment— Matthew 5:22 in the NIV.

The deity of Christ is eliminated in 1 Timothy 3:16— See the NIV.

If you were the Devil, wouldn't you try to corrupt the Scripture of truth?

Available from

Learn more, get the book: WHICH BIBLE WOULD JESUS USE? The Bible Version Controversy Explained and Resolved By Jack McElroy www.JackMcElroy.com

1 J. B. Williams, General editor, *God's Word In Our Hands*, page XIV. 2 https://bible.org/article/why-i-do-not-think-king-james-bible-best-translation-available-today

Bible Version Hypocrisy

GOD'S WORD IN OUR HANDS
THE BIBLE PRESERVED FOR US

****

What Bob Jones University authors said:

"**When we use a faithful conservative translation** such as the [1] **King James Version**, [2] **New King James Version**, the [3] **New American Standard Bible**, [4] **or another version** of demonstrated accuracy *we can trust our Bible as the Word of God.* We can be confident that we have God's Word in our hands."[1]

What it means:

❶ They recommend 3 different Bibles with 2 very different Greek Texts. The 4th is "another" unknown Bible with an unknown text.

❷ THEY KNOW that all versions SAY and MEAN different things and that the two Greek texts are RADICALLY different.

❸ Yet they cleverly call all 4 different Bibles "our Bible," which means they're not referring to a particular book.

❹ They assert we can "trust our Bible" and refer to all these translations AS the Word of God."

"For they that are such serve not our Lord Jesus Christ, but their own belly; and by good words and fair speeches deceive the hearts of the simple."
Romans 16:18 KJB

Available from

Learn more, get the book: WHICH BIBLE WOULD JESUS USE? The Bible Version Controversy Explained and Resolved By Jack McElroy www.JackMcElroy.com

amazon
nook

1. J. B. Williams (Editor), R. Shaylor God's Word in Our Hands: The Bible Preserved for Us Ambassador-Emerald International P. 422.

Man Behind Almost All Modern Versions Claimed KJB Believers Don't Think

****

"Eugene A. Nida['s] <u>dynamic-equivalence</u> approach to Bible translation helped to shape **the Good News Bible**, the **Contemporary English Version, the New International Version**, and **the New Jerusalem Bible** … his theories and methods [have been spread] around the world."[1]

Eugene Nida
1914–2011

In a 2002 interview with *Christianity Today* Nida was asked: **"What is the impact of multiple translations?** He said: 'It makes people begin to think. **As long as all people had the King James Version, they didn't think.** It's terribly important to have different translations to get a good argument started.'"[2]

Author David W. Cloud reveals this about Nida:

1. "He believes the Scriptures were 'imperfect' and that God's revelation was not 'absolute truth,' even in the originals.
2. He says that the words of Scripture 'are in a sense nothing in and of themselves.
3. He says that Christ's blood was not an actual offering for sin but was merely a 'figure of the cost.'
4. That Christ's blood was merely symbolic of 'violent death' and that it was not a propitiatory offering to God for sin."[3]
5. "The accounts of angels and miracles are not necessarily to be interpreted literally."[4]
6. "Nida denies the substitutionary atonement of Jesus Christ."[5]

With a guy like this behind them, it's no wonder modern versions are a mess.

Available from

Learn more, get the book: WHICH BIBLE WOULD JESUS USE? The Bible Version Controversy Explained and Resolved By Jack McElroy www.JackMcElroy.com

CHICK
PUBLICATIONS

amazon

nook

WHICH
BIBLE
WOULD
JESUS USE
The Bible Version Controversy Explained and Resolved

JACK MCELROY

1. Philip C. Stine *Let The Words Be Written: The Lasting Influence Of Eugene A. Nida* See Amazon.com
2. Christianity Today October 7, 2002, Vol. 46, No. 11, Page 46 http://www.rrb3.com/bibles/spnbibl/nida_interview.htm

3. https://www.wayoflife.org/database/dynamic_equivalency.html; 4. David W Cloud, *The Modern Bible Version Hall of Shame* p. 274.; 5. Ibid.

They Say "No Doctrine Is Affected" By Word Changes in Modern Versions

****

Daniel B. Wallace is Professor of New Testament Studies at Dallas Theological Seminary and senior New Testament editor of the NET Bible:

"The question, then, is not whether modern translations have deleted portions of the Word of God, but rather whether either the KJV or modern translations have **altered** the Word of God. **I contend that the KJV has far more drastically altered the Scriptures than have modern translations.**

Daniel B. Wallace

"Nevertheless, I repeat: **most textual critics for the past two hundred and fifty years would say that no doctrine is affected by these changes.**"[1]

Isaiah 7:14 King James Bible 1611	Isaiah 7:14 Revised Standard Version 1952
Therefore the Lord himself shall give you a sign; Behold, **a virgin** shall conceive, and bear a son, and shall call his name Immanuel.	Therefore the Lord himself will give you a sign. Behold, **a young woman** shall conceive .... **New Jerusalem Bible (Catholic) 1985** The Lord will give you a sign in any case: It is this: **the young woman**… **NET Bible (1996–2008)** For this reason the sovereign master himself will give you a confirming sign. Look, **this young woman**…

What we're taught:

1. No doctrine is affected by textual changes in modern versions. And many say no doctrines are corrupted in "conservative" translations.
2. The King James Bible is "good translation" of a poor text.

Although this passage is a translational choice and NOT textual in nature …

Isn't the Virgin Birth doctrine negatively "affected" by these modern versions?

Available from

Learn more, get the book: WHICH BIBLE WOULD JESUS USE? The Bible Version Controversy Explained and Resolved By Jack McElroy
www.JackMcElroy.com

1. https://bible.org/article/why-i-do-not-think-king-james-bible-best-translation-available-today

Former Central Baptist Theological Seminary Professors' Fake News

****

"The beginning of the **modern movement** that asserts the essential inspiration and inerrancy of the King James version of the Bible in English **can certainly be traced** to the publication of a book in 1930. That book, *Our Authorized Bible Vindicated*, was written by Seventh Day Adventist missionary, educator and theologian Benjamin G. Wilkinson (1872–1968)."[1]

The real story is "King James Onlyism" has existed for over 200 years:

Jack P. Lewis author of *The English Bible From KJV To NIV,* said this about the KJB in 1981: "for more than two centuries ... the common man ... forgot it was a translation and came to think that it was the original Bible..."

David Daniell (1929–2016), Professor of English at University College, London, and Honorary Fellow of Hertford and St. Catherine's Colleges, Oxford, wrote: "From 1769, effectively, there grew the notion that the KJV was peculiarly, divinely, inspired."

Philip Schaff (1819–1893), president of the committee that translated the 1901 American Standard Version, wrote in 1891: "to the great mass of English readers King James's Version is virtually the inspired Word of God."

Richard Chenevix Trench (1807–1886), the famous philologist, wrote in 1858, "We must never leave out of sight that for a great multitude of readers the English Version is not the translation of an inspired Book, but is itself the inspired book..."

Alistair E. McGrath (b. 1953), Oxford Professor of Historical Theology, writes of the Authorized Version in 2002: "perhaps the greatest tribute to its success lies in the simple fact that for nearly two centuries, most of its readers were unaware that they were actually reading a translation."

How does something believed continuously for over 200 years become a "modern movement" in 1930?

Available from

Learn more, get the book: WHICH BIBLE WOULD JESUS USE? The Bible Version Controversy Explained and Resolved By Jack McElroy www.JackMcElroy.com

CHICK
PUBLICATIONS

amazon

---

1. Beacham and Bauder, *One Bible Only? Examining Exclusive Claims for the King James Bible,* P.44.

Christian Apologists: God Preserved Error— Not Truth

****

King James Bible 2 Kings 8:26	New International Version 2 Kings 8:26
Two and twenty [22] years old *was* Ahaziah when he began to reign…	Ahaziah was **twenty-two [22]** years old when he became king…

King James Bible 2 Chronicles 22:2	New International Version 2 Chr. 22:2
Forty and two [42] years old *was* Ahaziah when he began to reign…	Ahaziah was **twenty-two [22]** years old when he became king…

Everybody knows that 22 years old and 42 years old ARE the Hebrew readings.

Even the NIV Study Bible footnote (p. 640) actually admits that it:
  "The Hebrew reading of '42' would make Ahaziah older than his father…"

Finding a "**Bible Difficulty**" where none exists, famous Christian apologists Gleason Archer and Norman Geisler blame it on a "copyist error."[1]

So, what's the NIV solution?

They CHANGE THE TEXT to match their unbelief in God's preserved words and make it say what it absolutely DOES NOT.

<u>Here's the answer from a Bible believing perspective</u> …
Ahaziah, king of Judah, was 42 years old *politically*, **in the Kingdom of Omri and Ahab**, wicked kings of Israel, his maternal family, even though only 22 years old biologically. The key the experts missed is that the Bible also counts years from political events.
(For a full explanation, see WHICH BIBLE WOULD JESUS USE? Pp. 279–285.)

<u>Conclusion</u> Even though they have no problem changing "the original Hebrew" because they don't believe it …

You can trust every word of your King James Bible.

Available from

Learn more, get the book: WHICH BIBLE WOULD JESUS USE? The Bible Version Controversy Explained and Resolved By Jack McElroy
www.jackmcelroy.com

1 The Big Book of Bible Difficulties Howe and Geisler P. 194.

Prominent Fundamentalist Professor Says Souls Are Misled by KJB Only Advocates

****

Dr. Kevin T. Bauder, Research Professor of Systematic Theology at Central Baptist Theological Seminary of Minneapolis, MN said ...

"The critical Greek texts ... <u>are</u> in fact the Word of God. When King James only advocates make the rejection of certain Bible texts or versions a test of orthodoxy, they have gone too far. Their position on these matters ought to be opposed for the sake of the Bible itself. The errors of their view need to be exposed for the sake of souls who are being misled by them.

Can we hold up an <u>imperfect</u> manuscript copy, an <u>imperfectly</u> edited text, or an <u>imperfectly</u> translated version, and rightly say, 'This is the Word of God'? <u>The authors</u> ... <u>will insist that we can</u>."[1]

Anyone who's ever been to a multiple version Bible study knows that passages from different versions sometimes **SAY** and **MEAN** different things **and thus can't all be "the word of God."**

Dr. Bauder's concern for souls is laudable. But what of the soul of his student when he realizes that his Bible teacher **does** **not** **really** **believe** that **the** **book** he calls the "Bible" actually contains all of God's words and only God's words, without error?

Available from

Learn more, get the book: WHICH BIBLE WOULD JESUS USE? The Bible Version Controversy Explained and Resolved By Jack McElroy
www.JackMcElroy.com

CHICK
PUBLICATIONS

amazon

nook

1. Beacham and Bauder, *One Bible Only? Examining Exclusive Claims for the King James Bible*, 2001, pp. 19-21.

Clever Academic Gets
Beat at His Own Game

****

B.B. Warfield (1851–1921) was professor of theology at Princeton Seminary and is still admired by Fundamentalists. He wanted to defend his position of a verbally inspired Bible yet still hang out with textual and higher critics who believed the Bible contained errors and myths.

His Game: He knew that error in Scripture could **only be PROVED** if we had the original texts—which we don't. So, he popularized the theory that **ONLY** the original autographs were inspired. He wrote:

> **"We do not assert that the common text, but only that the original autographic text was inspired.** No 'error' can be asserted, therefore, which cannot be proved to have been aboriginal in the text."[1]

When someone found a supposed error in the Bible, he got to say: "But that's not what it said in the original autographs"—which he conveniently didn't have. **Cool, he wins the argument. Sort of...**

> This is the view of almost all evangelical and fundamental colleges and seminaries today. BUT...

This was an innovation. Since 1643 Presbyterian and Reformed orthodoxy as outlined in the ***Westminster Confession*** held that **both the originals and copies** were and are infallible and inspired.

His novel theory jettisoned the Bible doctrine of Preservation and made the words of your Saviour of none effect...

Heaven and earth shall pass away, but **my words shall not pass away.** Matthew 24:35
Heaven and earth shall pass away, but **my words shall not pass away.** Mark 13:31
Heaven and earth shall pass away, but **my words shall not pass away.** Luke 21:33

Warfield thought your Savior couldn't deliver on his promises and dropped the ball in the end zone. He didn't.

You can find all of his preserved, inerrant words in the King James Bible.

1. *Presbyterian Review* of 1881

The New Testament has Survived in "A Form That Is 99.5 % Pure"

****

So say authors Geisler and Nix in their book *A General Introduction to the Bible*.[1]

That means 0.5% of Dr. Geisler's New Testament is NOT PURE.

Dr. Norman Geisler

Rat Poison is 99.9% pure.

That means the rats eat only 0.1% toxic ingredients and die.

In contrast to this scholarly nonsense, our Lord said this of his word ...

> Thy word *is* very pure: therefore thy servant loveth it. Psalms 119:140.

Dr. Geisler's problem? He's rejected the pure words of God as they've appeared in the King James Bible for over 400 years

Available from

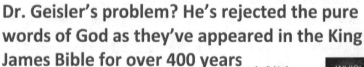

Learn more, get the book: WHICH BIBLE WOULD JESUS USE? The Bible Version Controversy Explained and Resolved By Jack McElroy
www.JackMcElroy.com

1. Geisler and Nix, *A General Introduction to the Bible*, 1968, Chicago Moody Press, p. 367.

"The King James Version (1611) ... died of 'old age,' including (1) outdated language, (2) an outdated text, (3) an outdated knowledge of the languages by the translators."[1]

****

Above are the words of Professor **Norman Geisler**, B.A, M.A., Th.B., and Ph.D, author or co-author of 70 books and hundreds of articles...

But according to a 2014 article from *Christianity Today Online*...

Dr. Norman Geisler

"When Americans reach for their Bibles, **more than half of them pick up a King James Version (KJV)**, according to a new study advised by respected historian Mark Noll.

The **55** percent <u>**who read**</u> the **KJV** easily outnumber the **19** percent who read the New International Version (**NIV**). And the percentages drop into the **single digits** for competitors..."[2]

The score is 55 to 19—A Blowout. They can say the King James Bible is dead all they want.

It still <u>sits atop the pile</u> DESPITE all its detractors.

Available from

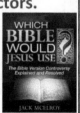
---

1 Norman Geisler, Bible Translations: Which Ones Are Best? Complete PowerPoint Library CD © 2008.
2 The Most Popular and Fastest Growing Bible Translation Isn't What You Think It Is http://tinyurl.com/n7nc3db

Prominent Scholar, Author, and Professor Fails to Do Homework

****

Dr. James D. Price was Professor of Hebrew and Old Testament (1972—2005) at Temple Baptist Seminary in Chattanooga, TN. In the introduction to his book, *King James Onlyism: A New Sect,* page 1, Dr. Price says:

"The King James only doctrine <u>is a new idea</u>. Growing up as I did in the 1930s and 40s, I have witnessed firsthand the development of **a new doctrine** among some fundamental churches—a doctrine that has come to be known as King James Onlyism.

"<u>This new doctrine</u> declares that the King James Version of the Bible is the providentially preserved Word of God, and is actually (or essentially) the only and final authority in all matters of faith and practice for the English-speaking world today.

"The idea that the King James version was the only one should use <u>was unheard of</u>. Everyone in conservative Christian circles understood that the King James Version was one of many translations of the Hebrew and Greek texts of the Bible and that **the final authority for doctrine, faith, and practice always has been the original Hebrew** words written by Moses and the Prophets **and the original Greek** words written by the apostles."

Here's a bit of history he must have missed ...

In the "Articles of Faith of the Barren River Association," a Baptist association of churches in Kentucky, **written in 1830**, we read this:

> "We believe that the scriptures of the Old and New Testaments, **as translated by the authority of King James, to be the words of God**, and is the only true rule of faith and practice."[1]

Looks like the *"New Sect"* is at least over 185 years old. If you're the teacher...

Do you give him a passing grade?

Available from

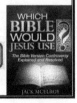

Learn more, get the book: WHICH BIBLE WOULD JESUS USE? The Bible Version Controversy Explained and Resolved By Jack McElroy
www.JackMcElroy.com

1. http://www.learnthebible.org/early-king-james-only-believers.html

Author James White Says YOU Need Correction

****

On page 19 *The King James Only Controversy: Can You Trust Modern Translations?*, Dr. White says:

> "Since this book made its appearance in 1995 … [t]here is a wider range of 'targets' for them [KJV only advocates] to shoot at now. Major new conservative translations, most notably the … ESV and the HCSB … adding to the lists of 'perversions' KJV Only advocates can produce.

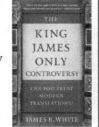

> "So the need remain strong for this work, not only as a corrective to the ongoing (if dwindling) KJV Only movement …"

Evidently, Dr. White wrote his book to:

(1) **correct** King James Bible believers' belief that God has preserved his words in a book and

(2) **debunk** their observation that modern versions really are perversions.

But hey …

If there weren't so many conflicting perversions, there wouldn't be so many "easy targets."

Available from

Will You Believe Your Saviour or James White?

****

Well–known author Dr. James R. White says you can't be 100% certain as to which Bible words are God's and which are not because he can't find a **scriptural reason** to do so.

"Are we not in reality saying, 'I *must* have certainty, therefore, **without any factual or logical** or even *scriptural* reason for doing so, I will invest the KJV translators with ultimate authority'? This truly is what KJV Only advocates are doing when they close their eyes to the historical realities regarding the biblical text.[1]

I call this the '**argument** for **certainty**.' This is the glue that holds the KJV Onlyism together…"[2]

But your Savior HAS promised you certainty …

Have not I written to thee excellent things in counsels and knowledge, **That I might make thee know the certainty of the words of truth**; that thou mightest answer **the words of truth** to them that send unto thee? Proverbs 22:20–21 KJB

The words of the LORD *are* pure words: *as* silver tried in a furnace of earth, purified seven times. Thou shalt keep them, O LORD, **thou shalt preserve them** from this generation for ever. Psalm 12:6–7 KJB

Dr. White is entitled to his opinion… even if it's wrong.

Available from

Learn more, get the book: WHICH BIBLE WOULD
JESUS USE? The Bible Version Controversy
Explained and Resolved By Jack McElroy
www.JackMcElroy.com

amazon
nook

1. *The King James Only Controversy: Can You Trust Modern Translations?*, p.134 2. Ibid. pp. 131–132.

Ever Tremble at the "Original Autographs"?

****

The Scripture Says:

For all those things hath mine hand made, and all those things have been, saith the LORD: **but to this man will I look,** even to him that is poor and of a contrite spirit, and <u>trembleth</u> <u>at</u> <u>my</u> <u>word</u>. Isaiah 66:2 KJB

The Lord's PURE words exist today because he PROMISED to PRESERVE them in Psalm 12: 6–7.

However, influential fundamentalist, Baptist evangelist and Pastor Dr. John R. Rice (1895–1980) said:

"**Inspiration is claimed for original autographs, not for translation or copying.** When we say that the Bible is inspired, we do not refer to the translations or copies but to the original autographs, written down under God's direction.... **But we do not claim for any copy or any translation the absolute, divine perfection that was in the original autographs. Inspiration refers to the original autographs.**"[1]

Dr. John R. Rice

According to Dr. Rice, any amount of trembling you do will be before an <u>uninspired</u>, <u>imperfect</u>, English <u>translation</u> of a <u>fallible</u> <u>copy</u> of a <u>copy</u> of original manuscripts that no longer exist.

Why would anybody <u>tremble</u> at such a Bible?

Available from

amazon
nook

Learn more, get the book: WHICH BIBLE WOULD JESUS USE? The Bible Version Controversy Explained and Resolved By Jack McElroy www.JackMcElroy.com

1.   Dr. John R. Rice, *Our God-Breathed Book, the Bible*, 1969, pp. 68-69.

Which "Tool" Do Bible Teachers Use MOST to Correct the Words of The Living God?

****

A. Rabbinic Commentaries

B. Greek and Hebrew Word Studies

C. The Septuagint (LXX)

D. The Dead Sea Scrolls

E. The Targums

F. Strong's Concordance

G. Hebrew-English Dictionaries

H. Greek-English Lexicons

I. Greek and Hebrew texts from Metzger, Scrivener, Berry, Ginsberg, and Green

J. Other Greek and Hebrew Study Tools and Interlinears

IF you guessed all of the above, you'd be wrong (although they're all used). Actually, the tool most often used by correctors of God's words is...

Their own personal preferences.

At the end of the day, they're certain of nothing more than **THEIR OWN VERSION** of what they THINK God said, which they create...**on the fly.**

In contrast to this nonsense, there's a 400-year-old, multibillion copy book called the King James Bible that contains all of God's words and only God's words.

How do you think the Lord feels when a man's words are substituted for his words?

Available from

Learn more, get the book: WHICH BIBLE WOULD JESUS USE? The Bible Version Controversy Explained and Resolved By Jack McElroy www.JackMcElroy.com

CHICK PUBLICATIONS

amazon

nook

What's the Bible We're Taught to Believe in That Nobody's Ever Seen or Read?

QUIZ

****

Here are your hints:

❶ It's the **official Bible** of most evangelical and fundamental churches.

❷ It's appealed to as **the final authority** in the statements of faith in many churches, schools, & seminaries.

❸ It **never existed** once in the history of the world.

❹ It **never** had a cover or binding.

❺ It's **not for sale** … at any price.

❻ It's **the only one that's inspired.**

❼ It supposedly **contains all of God's words without error.**

❽ It's **now lost** but attempts are being made to reconstruct it— even though no one knows for sure **exactly** what it says.

❾ It's **boldly and loudly defended** as the complete, verbally inspired "Word of God."

Give up? The identity of this mysterious Bible is …
"The Bible" made up of the original autographs.

You need the truth—a real Bible—A Book that's 100% error-free Scripture. Not a theoretical construct proposed by priestly academics who don't agree with each other on what should be in it.

The Lord has provided a book for you. It's brought forth good fruit for over 400 years— the King James Bible.

Available from

CHICK PUBLICATIONS
amazon
nook

WHICH **BIBLE WOULD** JESUS USE
The Bible Version Controversy Explained and Resolved
JACK McELROY

Learn more, get the book: WHICH BIBLE WOULD JESUS USE? The Bible Version Controversy Explained and Resolved By Jack McElroy www.JackMcElroy.com

The Shekinah Deception

****

Christians are taught to equate Shekinah to the presence of God's Spirit of the without ANY Biblical evidence.

Turns out that Shekinah is really a Canaanite goddess... From *Encyclopedia Mythica*:

> "**While the Bible does not mention the name Shekhina,** <u>she</u> **is nevertheless bound to extremely old traditions, and closely relates to the ancient goddesses. Particularly significant is the Canaanite goddess Ashera** who, at the beginning of the Israelites' settlement in the land of Canaan, was often referred to as Yahweh's Consort.
>
> The manifestation of a loving, maternal entity, **ready to defend her people <u>even from God Himself</u>**, brings a feeling of comfort that a paternal, invisible entity like Yahweh cannot bestow upon His worshipers."[1]

Shekinah: Another example of unbiblical, pagan nonsense introduced to Christians by duped Christian teachers.

Jack McElroy is a Born-Again Christian, businessman and entrepreneur with over 40 years of experience in various business disciplines. He is author of three books including *WHICH BIBLE WOULD JESUS USE? The Bible Version Controversy Explained and Resolved.* He is co-author of *Can You Trust Just One Bible* with David W. Daniels of Chick Publications. www.JackMcElroy.com

1. https://pantheon.org/articles/s/shekhina.html

Publishers Risk God's Wrath With Fake Maps

****

They do it in spite of the truth:
"And the children of Israel went into The midst of the sea upon the dry *ground*: and **the waters *were* a wall** unto them on their right hand, and on their left." Exodus 14:22KJB

Major Bible publishers today offer exodus from Egypt maps that look like this. ⎯⎯⎯⎯⎯➤

Notice that the children of Israel NEVER ONCE cross the Red Sea.

No Wall of Water ... No Miracle

The Zondervan KJV Study Bible
© 2002 by Zondervan

Their maps make your Lord out to be a liar.

Would you trade places with them on judgment day?

Learn more, get the book: WHICH BIBLE WOULD
JESUS USE? The Bible Version Controversy
Explained and Resolved by Jack McElroy
www.JackMcElroy.com

Available from

CHICK
PUBLICATIONS

amazon
nook

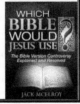

Illustration: http://www.freebibleimages.org/illustrations/moody-moses-red-sea/, from the1955 Moody Bible Institute filmstrip series.

Sometimes KJB Believers Feel Like Kevin in Home Alone

****

"You're such a disease."
"You're completely helpless."
"You're what the French call les incompétents."
"Look what you did, you little jerk!"
"I'm going to feed you to my tarantula."

And sometimes they're even told to get their no-good keister off the property.
To be fair, sometimes they can be pretty abrasive as well.

But none of this is surprising. Folks get very emotional when it comes to core beliefs. What's a King James Bible believer's core belief?

They've examined the evidence and come to the conclusion that they hold in their hands the true words of the living God without error. So in spite of all the insults...

They'll NEVER quit believing that their Lord has given them a BOOK containing all of his holy words of truth.

Available from

CHICK
PUBLICATIONS

amazon

nook

WHICH
BIBLE
WOULD
JESUS USE
The Bible Version Controversy Explained and Resolved
JACK MCELROY

Learn more, get the book: WHICH BIBLE WOULD JESUS USE? The Bible Version Controversy Explained and Resolved By Jack McElroy
www.JackMcElroy.com

Fair use images of movie posters: https://en.wikipedia.org/wiki/File:Home_alone_poster.jpg#filelinks

How the Grinch Stole the New Testament

****

Fenton John Anthony Hort (1828–1892) was a theologian and editor, with Brooke Westcott, of a critical edition of *The New Testament in the Original Greek*.

He made it his life's work to overthrow the Greek New Testament (Textus Receptus) underlying the KJB and all Reformation-era Bibles.

And Hort is the Grinch that stole the New Testament.

But how did he do it? How could he get the church to abandon the text believed since the church's foundation to be the words of the living God?

The more the Hort thought on the vile Textus;
    The more he purposed to destroy that Receptus.
"But how shall it be and what shall I do to deceive those foolish and ignorant Whos?"
    But you know, that old Hort was so smart and so slick. He thought up a lie, and he thought it up quick!
    "Ahh!" said the Hort, "I know what I'll do;
I'll fashion a fable their leaders think true."
    So, he spun up a story about a recension He hoped would stop any and all Who dissension.
And their leaders gave 'way their heritage without proof; Based on a fairy tale, nothing more than a spoof.

Have You Seen this Baby's Bible?

****

"A lot of people are like 'aren't you too young translate the Bible' and you know...

<u>A</u>, Don't worry about it, I just look young, I mean you don't know how old I am,

<u>and B</u>, I use the *E*Text Critic Bible* so, check it. Click.

I just chose a reading for 1 Timothy 3:15. You just saw me choose a "reading" for 1 Timothy 3:15!

With the *E*Text Critic Bible,* all I have to do is choose the reading I like best for each verse from an assortment they provide for me in the footnotes at the bottom of the page.

No big deal. If I can do it, you can do it!"

Sound silly? Not really. That's sort of how modern versions of the Bible are assembled and that's why there'll never be an end of "new" Bibles.

But there is a Bible without the various "corrupt" readings found in the Critical Text underlying most modern versions—the King James Bible.

Available from

Learn more, get the book: WHICH BIBLE WOULD JESUS
USE? The Bible Version Controversy Explained and
Resolved by Jack McElroy www.JackMcElroy.com

Image: The E*TRADE baby was used in advertising by E*TRADE, https://us.etrade.com/what-we-offer/our-accounts/?sr_id=BR

Who's a Real Heretic?

****

Who's a heretic? Some say Calvinists, others say Arminians, or Dispensationalists or non-Dispensationalists, or Preterists or my favorite, King James Onlysts. **I don't think any of them are heretics.**

In my view, <u>Dr. Robert Bratcher</u> (1920–2010) chief translator of The *Good News Bible* a.k.a. *Today's English Version*, is a heretic when it comes to his view of the Scripture. He was a pastor, chaplain, missionary, professor, Bible translator, **probably <u>a</u> <u>nice</u> <u>guy</u>, and <u>a</u> <u>real</u> <u>heretic</u>.**

Over 100 million copies distributed

Here are some of the statements he has made:

"**If we build our faith wholly on the Bible, then we are building our faith on shifting sand.** We must follow the facts or there is nothing to believe. We cannot literally follow Jesus, only go in his direction'."

"**Only willful ignorance or intellectual dishonesty can account for the claim that the Bible is inerrant and infallible.** To invest the Bible with the qualities of inerrancy and infallibility is to idolatrize it, to transform it into a false god."

"...to affirm that the Bible is the Word of God **implies** that the words of the Bible are the words of God. **Such simplistic and absolute terms divest the Bible altogether of its humanity and remove it from the relativism of the historical process.**"

"**No one seriously claims all the words of the Bible are the very words of God.** If someone does so it is only because that person is not willing thoroughly to explore its implications."

Page 1

"The Word of God is not words; it is a human being, a human life ... Quoting what the Bible says in the context of its history and culture is not necessarily relevant or helpful—and may be a hindrance in trying to meet and solve the problems we face."

"We are not bound by the letter of Scripture, but by the spirit. Even words spoken by Jesus ... do not necessarily wield compelling authority over us today. The focus of scriptural authority is not the words themselves. It is Jesus Christ as the Word of God who is the authority for us to be and to do."

"As a biblical scholar, I view with dismay the misuse of scriptures by fundamentalists; as ... Christians we listen with alarm to the simpleminded diagnoses and the simplistic panaceas proposed with smug self-assurance by Moral Majority people intent on curing the evils of this age."

"Jesus Christ would not enjoy omniscience. That is an attribute of God. ... **Jesus did not claim He and the Father to be one—which would be absurd.**" [1]

You don't suppose some of his theology seeped into his translation, do you?

There are more than 100 million—built by a Bible heretic—Good News Bibles (Today's English Version, TEV) out there...

Brethren, is there not a cause?

Learn more, get the book: WHICH BIBLE WOULD JESUS USE? The Bible Version Controversy Explained and Resolved By Jack McElroy www.JackMcElroy.com

Available from

CHICK PUBLICATIONS

amazon

nook

WHICH BIBLE WOULD JESUS USE

The Bible Version Controversy Explained and Resolved

JACK MCELROY

1. http://letusreason.thoughts.com/posts/criticisms-by-trinitarians-of-the-tev-gnb

Page 2

World's Most Dangerous Bible: Invisible, Yet Found Everywhere

****

<u>Here are the details:</u>

① **It's a do-it-yourself type Bible** that's created "on-the-fly" by teachers and pastors who "correct" the text of the Bible.

② **It's a totally customizable.** They can choose words to make the Bible fit their message.

③ **It's preference based.** Words from the true text are substituted with words from readings they prefer from a critical apparatus, commentaries, lexicons, word studies, concordances, the Septuagint, Dead Sea Scrolls, etc.

<u>Where does one learn to create such a Bible?</u>

Bible College and seminary, of course.

① **They take biblical languages like Hebrew and Greek.**

② **They get to try their hand at translating those languages into English** —which teaches them to undermine the text.

said, See, *here is* water; what doth hinder me to be baptized?

37 And Philip said, If thou believest with all thine heart, thou mayest. And he answered and said, I believe that Jesus Christ is the Son of God.

38 And he commanded th Not ariot to and they went d *original:* o Philip and the *omit* h¹; and

<u>Benefits to the teacher:</u>

① He has the ability to correct any Greek, Hebrew, English or any other language Bible to make it say whatever they need it to say at the time.

② He's beyond correction since it doesn't exist in print. It makes him look like a star.

③ He gains notoriety as an outstanding teacher of "the word."

④ He becomes the "go to guy" and final authority as to what the original words of God are.

<u>Why is it so dangerous?</u>

① Because the practitioner becomes the creator of his own "Holy Bible."

Page 1

Bible Version Secrets Exposed

② He now has greater authority than the most Holy Book because he chooses its contents.

Parents pay tens of thousands of dollars to send their sons off to school only to learn how to correct the words of the living God.

How sad ...

Here's what Mark Minnick, pastor of Mount Calvary Baptist Church, Greenville, SC, said he does when he sees **two different readings of the same text** ...

"I may be investigating a word only to discover that there is some question about whether **it was actually part of the original text as God inspired it**... since the difference **would alter** what I preached from this text, I would classify the variation as significant (S). What then does a conscientious expositor do with the variant when he preaches?

I truthfully acknowledge the variant. I point out that both readings teach truth that is found elsewhere in Scripture. And then I give my sermonic emphasis **to either one or both of the truths**...

Lest this last practice ... should sound too subjective or arbitrary, we must acknowledge that most preachers make this same kind of choice anyway when they restrict themselves and their people to one version over another."[1]

At the end of the day, Pastor Minnick is the final authority on what God said—NOT ANY BIBLE (IN ANY LANGUAGE) ON EARTH.

How do you think the Lord feels when a man's words are substituted for his words?

Learn more, get the book: WHICH BIBLE WOULD JESUS USE? The Bible Version Controversy Explained and Resolved By Jack McElroy
www.JackMcElroy.com

CHICK
PUBLICATIONS

amazon
nook

WHICH
BIBLE
WOULD
JESUS USE
The Bible Version Controversy
Explained and Resolved

JACK MCELROY

1. God's Word in Our Hands: The Bible Preserved for Us pp. 243, 246.

440

The #1 Reason for the Bible Version Controversy...

****

The Differences Matter–They Matter A Lot.

King **James Onlyists believe** that the differences in Bible versions DO MATTER **because they undermine the integrity and truthfulness of their Lord and Saviour Jesus Christ.**

❷ They believe that the introduction of competing and conflicting multiple versions has produced disbelief in any Bible (meaning book) and confusion in the church because of the obvious errors of fact, history, geography and science (and more) observed and documented in modern versions.

❸ They've been taught that the reliability of the Bible exists ONLY in the "message" and not the actual words. But they're not buying it.

❹ They believe the King James Bible fulfills their Saviour's promise to preserve his words given in **Psalms 12:6–7**:

> The words of the LORD *are* pure words: *as* silver tried in a furnace of earth, purified seven times. Thou shalt keep them, O LORD, thou shalt preserve them from this generation for ever.

Because of this belief, they're sometimes called "divisive" and "cultists."

****

Dr. Daniel B. Wallace doesn't think the differences matter. He's taught Greek and New Testament courses at Dallas Theological Seminary on a graduate school level since 1979 and authored nine books. He is the senior New Testament editor of the NET Bible, and he's executive director for the Center for the Study of New Testament Manuscripts. He says …

Daniel B. Wallace

> "The question, then, is not whether modern translations have deleted portions of the Word of God, but rather whether either the KJV or modern translations have **altered the Word of God**. I contend that the KJV has far more drastically altered the Scriptures than have modern translations. Nevertheless, **I repeat: most textual critics for the past two hundred and fifty years would say that <u>no doctrine is affected</u> by these changes."**[1]

Bart **EHRMAN**

Dr. Bart Ehrman is the author of more than twenty books, including five *New York Times* bestsellers. He is a New Testament scholar and currently Professor of Religious Studies at the University of North Carolina at Chapel Hill. Doctor Ehrman once debated author James White.

Here is a quote from the debate [2]

1. Daniel B. Wallace, "Why I Do Not Think the King James Bible Is the Best Translation Available Today," Bible.org, accessed 1/1/16 http://tinyurl.com/nryi7bx

Bible Version Secrets Exposed

"The differences in these manuscripts do matter.

It does matter whether the Gospel of John calls Jesus, the unique God.... If Jesus is the unique God, well, that's a very high statement that you find nowhere else in the bible. Did he say it or not?
It depends on which manuscript you read.

Is the doctrine of the trinity explicitly talked about in the bible? **It seems to me that should matter**. It depends which manuscripts you read.

When Jesus is going to his death in the Gospel of Luke, he did become so distressed that he began to sweat drops as if of blood? It's the passage that we get the term sweating blood from.
It depends which manuscript you read, **and it matters a lot** to understanding Luke's gospel whether Jesus went through that experience or not.

Did the voice at Jesus' baptism in Luke's gospel say that on that day of his baptism is when God adopted him to be his son? You are my son, today I have begotten you.
Depends which manuscript you read **and it matters a lot**.

I understand the arguments of people like James [White] and Dan Wallace, but sometimes they don't make sense to me even though I intellectually understand them.

Dan Wallace, whom he [White] keeps quoting, insists that in fact differences don't matter in the manuscripts. If the differences don't matter, why is it that he is undertaking a major project dealing with Greek manuscripts, a project that is going to cost hundreds of thousands of dollars? If the differences don't matter, what does he tell these people he's trying to raise money from? We'd like you to donate $50,000 to our cause because the differences don't matter. **Of course they matter...**"

Jack McElroy

Jack McElroy is a Born Again Christian, businessman, and entrepreneur. He is author of three books including *WHICH BIBLE WOULD JESUS USE? The Bible Version Controversy Explained and Resolved* and co-author of *Can You Trust Just One Bible*.

"Everybody who's ever attended a Bible study where multiple versions of the Bible are used knows all versions **SAY and MEAN** different things. Even a cursory investigation of the facts leads one to inescapable conclusion that unlike what most Christian leaders teach, the differences **DO affect doctrine**."

"The differences matter—of course they matter— they matter a lot. If they didn't there wouldn't be a Bible version controversy in the first place."

Available from

Learn more, get the book: WHICH BIBLE WOULD JESUS USE? The Bible Version Controversy Explained and Resolved By Jack McElroy www.jackmcelroy.com

CHICK
PUBLICATIONS
amazon
nook

WHICH BIBLE WOULD JESUS USE?

2. https://www.youtube.com/watch?v=moHlnA9fAsI Ehrman-White debate. About 4 minutes into Ehrman's final remarks.

Did the King James Translators Drop a Routine Fly Ball on Revelation 16:5?

****

King James Bible Revelation 16:5	English Standard Version Rev. 16:5
And I heard the angel of the waters say, Thou art righteous, O Lord, which art, and wast, **and shalt be**, because thou hast judged thus.	And I heard the angel in charge of the waters say, "Just are you, **O Holy One**, who is and who was, for you brought these judgments."

Author James White says they did.

"I would like to provide an expanded discussion of a textual error in the King James Version for those who demand a single example of 'error in the KJV!'... For the KJV only advocate, there is simply no way out of this problem."...the reading was "created out of the mind of Theodore Beza, one unknown to the ancient church, unknown to all Christians until the end of the sixteenth century" ... **"quite simply, before Beza, no Christian had ever read the text the way the KJV has it today."[1]**

But what do you say?
You're the umpire; here's what happened on the play:

❶ Dr. White is right; there is currently no known Greek NT manuscript support for the reading **"and shalt be,"** and it doesn't appear in a printed Greek New Testament until Beza's 1598 edition. **BUT...**

❷ There are only 4 Greek manuscripts of Revelation 16:5 dated before the 10th century but the 3 earliest witnesses of Revelation 16:5 don't even agree with each other.

❸ Some scholars [Robert B. Y. Scott (1899 –1987) and Charles C. Torrey (1863–1956)] believed the Book of Revelation was originally penned in Hebrew and only later translated into Greek.

❹ **If it's true** that the reading "shall be" was **"unknown to the ancient church, unknown to all Christians,"** then how come it appears in a Latin commentary on the Book of Revelation by Spanish theologian Beatus of Liebana in <u>AD 786</u> which preserved the work of the Donatist writer Tyconius, written around <u>AD 380</u>?

1 *The King James Only Controversy, Can You Trust Modern Translations?* James R. White, pp. 236-241.   Page 1

Bible Version Secrets Exposed

❺ If the original was written in Hebrew and then translated into Greek and Latin, then the original reading has just as much chance of showing up in Latin manuscripts as Greek.

❻ **There are an estimated 10,000 Latin manuscripts in existence. But no one's got the money, time, or inclination to dope out their contents.**

❼ Early 20th century textual critic Herman Hoskier cited the Ethiopian version as containing the phrase "shall be."

How can you come to any conclusion until you've seen all the evidence?

The Lord can reveal as much manuscript evidence as he wants. **But He has promised to preserve his words. His promises never fail.** (See Psa. 12:6–7).

The King James translators not only had all seven earlier English Bibles and all the editions of the Greek New Testament sitting on their table but also had access to some manuscripts no longer available today.

Nobody knows what evidence they had when they made the decision to go with the "shall be" reading.

The King James translators made a CHOICE. They chose to go with Beza's 1589 reading. James White calls their CHOICE "an error." **But a CHOICE based on evidence isn't an error—it's a CHOICE.**

Did the CHOICE the translators made slip by the Lord?

If it's an error and **NOT** the original reading, then is the Lord the village idiot by allowing a bogus reading (even of only 2 words) to be reproduced literally billions of times in King James Bibles over the years?

He could've easily moved the King James translators to stick with the old reading, but He didn't.

Instead of rolling on the floor laughing and yelling "gotcha" because he thinks he found an "error" in the King James Bible, maybe Dr. White should try to figure out WHY the Lord and the translators **PURPOSELY** placed a reading with little Greek manuscript support in the Bible **when they didn't have to.**

And besides ... Who's the official scorer, James White or the Lord?

Multi Version Confusion

Introduction

****

"Any conservative translation is good."

That's what some conservative teachers opine.

Nice-sounding, non-divisive words, aren't they?

But when you realize that many Bible versions say different things in the same location and even opposite things from one another, the whole construct collapses.

Where are God's words? . . . Can't get there from here.

Here's What Happens When You Don't Have One Standard Bible

****

	"The desert owl and the screech owl will roost …"
NIV, NLT **Zeph. 2:14**	The NIV, NLT report **two owls**.
	"the owl and the hedgehog shall lodge…"
ESV **Zeph. 2:14**	The ESV reports an **owl** and a **hedgehog**.
	"Both the pelican and the hedgehog Will lodge …"
NASB **Zeph. 2:14**	The NASB reports a **pelican** and a **hedgehog**. No owls at all.

It's nonsense like this that makes the Scripture look about as holy as a fantasy novel.

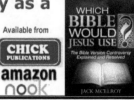

They Say Many Translations Give Us Insight into God's Word

****

Numbers 4:10 in the King James Bible says …
"And they shall put it and all the vessels thereof within a covering of **badgers' skins**, and shall put it upon a bar."
Here's Numbers 4:10 in various versions of the Bible…

World English Bible © 1997	They shall put it and all its vessels within a covering of **sealskin**	
NASB © 1995	in a covering of **porpoise skin**	
ESV © 2001	in a covering of **goatskin**	
NIV © 1973– 1984	in a covering of hides of **sea cows**	
NIV © 2011	in a covering of the **durable leather**	

1. The **same** Hebrew word is translated **five (5) different** ways.
2. **Only one** of these readings is true. Only one can be true.
3. **Choices** translators make sometimes affect **truth & doctrine**.

Just ignore the scholarly nonsense & trust the Bible the Lord's been blessing for over 400 years.

Available from

CHICK PUBLICATIONS

amazon

nook

Learn more, get the book: WHICH BIBLE WOULD JESUS USE? The Bible Version Controversy Explained and Resolved By Jack McElroy www.JackMcElroy.com

They Tell Us to Use Many Versions to Understand the Deeper Things of God ...

****

Numbers 11:12

NLT	Did I give birth to them? Did I bring them into the world? Why did you tell me to carry them in my arms like a **mother** carries a nursing baby? ...	**mother**
ESV	Did I conceive all this people? Did I give them birth, that you should say to me, 'Carry them in your bosom, as a **nurse** carries a nursing child,' ...	**nurse**
NKJV	Did I conceive all these people? Did I beget them, that You should say to me, 'Carry them in your bosom, as a **guardian** carries a nursing child,' ...	guardian
HCSB	Did I conceive all these people? Did I give them birth so You should tell me, 'Carry them at your breast, as a **nursing woman** carries a baby ...	**Nursing woman**
NET Bible	Did I conceive this entire people? Did I give birth to them, that you should say to me, 'Carry them in your arms, as a **foster father** bears a nursing child ...	foster father

And they have the nerve to call King James Bible believers crazy?

Available from

Learn more, get the book: WHICH BIBLE WOULD
JESUS USE? The Bible Version Controversy
Explained and Resolved By Jack McElroy
www.JackMcElroy.com

CHICK
PUBLICATIONS

amazon
nook

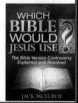

WHICH
BIBLE
WOULD
JESUS USE?
The Bible Version Controversy
Explained and Resolved

JACK MCELROY

How the ESV and NASB Embarrass Your Lord

****

They tell us the NASB and ESV are "highly accurate" and true to the "original" Bibles.

The "Bible" is supposed to contain God's holy words ... But look how they make the Lord contradict himself:

Eccl. 8:10	What does the Bible say happens to the wicked after death?
ESV	Then I saw the wicked buried. They ... **were praised**
NASB	So then, I have seen the wicked buried ... **they are soon forgotten**

Mat. 18:22	How many times did Jesus say you should forgive your brother?
ESV	Jesus said to him, "I do not say to you seven times, but **seventy-seven** times." [77]
NASB	Jesus said to him, "I do not say to you, up to seven times, but up to **seventy** times seven." [490]

2 Sam. 15:7	How long did Absalom wait to talk to King David?
ESV	And at the end of **four years** Absalom said to the king ... [4]
NASB	Now it came about at the end of **forty years** that Absalom [40]

Luke 10:1	How many did Jesus appoint in Luke 10?
ESV	After this the Lord appointed **seventy-two** others ... [72]
NASB	Now after this the Lord appointed **seventy** others ... [70]

Multiple versions aren't a blessing. They're confusion to God's children.

Available from

Learn more, get the book: WHICH BIBLE WOULD
JESUS USE? The Bible Version Controversy
Explained and Resolved By Jack McElroy
www.JackMcElroy.com

amazon
nook

The Devil Wins

* *

English Standard Version Hosea 11:12	New American Standard Bible Hos. 11:12
Ephraim has surrounded me with lies, and the house of Israel with deceit, **but Judah still <u>walks with God</u> and is <u>faithful</u>** to the Holy One.	Ephraim surrounds Me with lies And the house of Israel with deceit; **Judah is also <u>unruly against</u> God,** Even against the Holy One who is faithful....

Two "conservative translations" that say the exact opposite things; And YET...

Our professional, "go-to" Christian leaders and their students say:

BOTH versions are God's word.

BOTH are closest to the "original autographs."

BOTH are "highly accurate."

BOTH were translated by "godly", competent scholars.

BOTH are to be preferred over the antiquated King James Bible.

And the truth is ...

The Devil wins by deceiving men of high degree who are willingly ignorant.

Available from

WHICH **BIBLE** WOULD **JESUS USE**
The Bible Version Controversy Explained and Resolved

JACK MCELROY

Learn more, get the book: WHICH BIBLE WOULD JESUS USE? The Bible Version Controversy Explained and Resolved By Jack McElroy www.JackMcElroy.com

The Multi-Version Corruption of Psalm 116:15

****

King James Bible	**Precious** in the sight of the LORD is the death of his **saints.**	Praise the Lord for his comfort!

This verse has been a great comfort for tens of thousands upon the death of a believing loved one.
You'd think this would be a no-brainer. Perish the thought.
Look what they do to it ...

Contemporary English Version	**You are deeply concerned** when one of your loyal people **faces death.**	"Deeply concerned?" Didn't know God could be triggered.
Good News Translation	How **painful it is to the LORD** when one of his people dies!	"Painful?" To the Lord? Really?

And the winner is ....

NET Bible	The LORD **values the lives** of his **faithful followers.**	No saints, no death, nothing precious.

And we're supposed to believe all versions basically say the same thing?

They Tell Us to Consult Many Translations to Properly Study the Bible

****

Take the Sun Dial of Ahaz Quiz and see if you can tell what the Lord actually said. Did the ... (1) Sun or (2) Sunlight or (3) Sun's Shadow turn back on ... the (1) Sun Dial or the (2) Dial or the (3) Stairway of Ahaz?

King James Bible Isaiah 38:8	Behold, I will bring again the shadow of the degrees, which is gone down in the **sun dial** of Ahaz, ten degrees backward. **So the sun returned** ten degrees, by which degrees it was gone down.
English Standard Version Isaiah 38:8	Behold, I will make the shadow cast by the declining sun on the **dial** of Ahaz turn back ten steps. So the **sun** turned back on the dial the ten steps by which it had declined.
New International Version Isaiah 38:8	"I will make the shadow cast by the sun go back the ten steps it has gone down on the **stairway** of Ahaz." **So the sunlight** went back the ten steps it had gone down.
New American Standard Bible Isaiah 38:8	"Behold, I will cause the shadow on the **stairway**, which has gone down with the sun on the stairway of Ahaz, to go back ten steps," So the **sun's shadow** went back ten steps on the stairway on which it had gone down.

Maybe you're better off believing just one Bible to determine what the Lord said.

Available from

Learn more, get the book: WHICH BIBLE WOULD JESUS
USE? The Bible Version Controversy Explained and
Resolved By Jack McElroy www.JackMcElroy.com

amazon
nook

What is ACT Onlyism?

****

<u>ACT Onlyism</u> **"Any Conservative Translation" Onlyism** is taught in "conservative" colleges seminaries and pulpits across the country.

Students are taught to BELIEVE that God's pure words are found in **ANY Conservative Translation** like the ESV, NASB, NKJV, KJV, and HCSB. **But NOT** the NIV, NLT, The Message, etc., because they're somehow lesser translations.

<u>Sounds spiritual</u>. But ACT Onlyists DON'T have ONE Bible they actually believe. They "use" multiple versions and don't hesitate to correct the one they "used" 2 minutes ago. Thereby mocking God's word because of:

❶ **Missing or added verses** (both violate Deut. 4:2 and Rev. 22:18):

NASB has Mat. 12:47	**ESV doesn't**
NASB has Mat. 23:14	**ESV doesn't**
NASB has John 5:4	**ESV doesn't**

❷ **Material differences** (even opposites):

KJB <u>not</u> increased the joy	NKJV ___ increased the joy	Isaiah. 9:3
ESV ...Judah still walks with God	NASB Judah is also unruly against God	Hos. 11:12

What happens to the wicked after death? Eccl. 8:10	
NASB says they're **forgotten**	**ESV** says they're **praised**

ACT Onlyism—more scholarly nonsense brought to you by smart kids who should know better.

Available from

Learn more, get the book: WHICH BIBLE WOULD JESUS USE? The Bible Version Controversy Explained and Resolved By Jack McElroy www.JackMcElroy.com

Which Expert Should We Believe?

* *

Matthew 23:14	Matthew 23:14
New American Standard Version	English Standard Version
Woe to you, scribes and Pharisees, hypocrites, because you devour widows' houses, and for a pretense you make long prayers; therefore you will receive greater	**Verse purposely omitted**

"**The New American Standard Bible** has set the standard for faithful Bible translations for a generation. It is the favorite of so many who love the Bible and look for accuracy and clarity in translation."[1]

"My aim tonight is to help you be persuaded that exposing millions of people … to **the ESV** would undo the dominance of the NIV and put in its place a **more literal**, and yet a beautifully readable, memorizable Bible—**the English Standard Version**"[2]

Dr. R. Albert Mohler, Jr., president
So. Baptist Theological Seminary

John Piper, Pastor for Preaching and Vision at
Bethlehem Baptist Church in Minn., MN

Two Experts recommend two <u>conflicting</u> Bibles.

Why not just believe the Bible that's been reproduced billions of times and has a 400-year history of blessing by your Saviour?

Learn more, get the book: WHICH BIBLE WOULD JESUS USE? The Bible Version Controversy Explained and Resolved By Jack McElroy
www.JackMcElroy.com

Available from

CHICK
PUBLICATIONS

amazon
nook

1.http://www.lockman.org/nasb/endorsements.php; 2 http://www.desiringgod.org/resource-library/articles/goodenglish-with-minimal-translation-why-bethlehem-uses-the-esv

IS YOUR GOD
SCHIZOPHRENIC?

****

If your God recommends multiple versions of the Bible then he's got to be "loco in the coco." Here's why...

The NASB has Matthew 12:47.
The ESV doesn't.

> They both can't be the word of God
> unless your God is a schizophrenic.

How about ...

John 5:4?	The NASB has it; The ESV doesn't.
James 1:7?	The NASB and ESV have it; The RSV doesn't.
Matthew 21:44, Luke 24:12, and Luke 24:40?	The HCSB, NASB, and the ESV has them; The RSV doesn't.

The "go-to" folks in New Testament Textual Criticism tell us that there are at least **31** and possibly as many as **39** complete verses that shouldn't be in the Bible.[1]

**Multiple, conflicting Bible versions are NOT a blessing.
They cause doubt about what God actually said.
They're an embarrassment to
Christianity and an insult to God.**

Available from

CHICK
PUBLICATIONS

amazon
nook

WHICH
BIBLE
WOULD
JESUS USE
The Bible Version Controversy Explained and Resolved
JACK MCELROY

Learn more, get the book: WHICH BIBLE WOULD JESUS USE? The Bible Version Controversy Explained and Resolved by Jack McElroy www.JackMcElroy.com

1. Jack McElroy, WHICH BIBLE WOULD JESUS USE?, See Chapter 19.

ESV Strikes Matthew 12:47 From "The Bible" ... or Does it?

****

New American Standard Bible Mt. 12:47	English Standard Version Mt. 12:47
Someone said to Him, "Behold, Your mother and Your brothers are standing outside seeking to speak to You."	___ __ __ ___ ___ ___ ___ ___ ___ __ ___ ___ ___ ___ __ ___ __

They feed us this nonsense:
"When we use a faithful conservative translation such as the King James Version, New King James Version, the New American Standard Bible, or another version of demonstrated accuracy *we can trust our Bible as the Word of God*. We can be confident that we have God's Word in our hands."[1]

1 The God of the NASB speaks in Matthew 12:47.
The God of the ESV? He's a mute. Or he's gone into the witness protection program.

2 Either the "conservative" NASB translation **ADDED TO** "God's word," or the "conservative" ESV **TOOK AWAY FROM** "God's word".

Which is it?... Is Matthew 12:47 Scripture or not?

3 These "conservative" translations make your God look incompetent.

And they want us to shut up and <u>make</u> <u>believe</u> there's no difference in "translations" and words don't matter? Who's kidding who?

No spiritual battle to see here folks, move along.

Available from

Learn more, get the book: WHICH BIBLE WOULD JESUS USE? The Bible Version Controversy Explained and Resolved By Jack McElroy www.JackMcElroy.com

[1]Williams (Editor), Shaylor, *God's Word in Our Hands: The Bible Preserved for Us* Ambassador, Emerald Intl., Greenville, SC, P. 422.

Which God Said What?

✴✴✴✴✴✴✴✴✴✴✴✴✴✴✴✴✴✴✴✴✴✴✴✴✴✴✴✴

New American Standard Bible Acts 24:7	English Standard Version Acts 24:7
But Lysias the commander came along, and with much violence took him out of our hands,	___ ____ __ _____ ___ ____ ___ __ ___ ___ ___ __ _ ___ ____

They tell us "the Bible" presents the very words of "**the**" living God.

They tell us that in order to know "**God**" better we should consult a variety of translations.

They swear to us that the NASB and the ESV are **BOTH** very reliable and true to the originals. But …

- **The God of the NASB** insists Acts 24:7 is in his Bible.
- **The God of the ESV** insists it's not.

Obviously, one God is lying; but which one?

Sadly, they don't know.

Make no mistake. ANY CHRISTIAN LEADER who recommends two or more conflicting Bibles is (by definition) recommending TWO conflicting Gods despite what he professes.

Who Killed Goliath in Your Bible?

****

New International Version 2 Sam. 21:19	English Standard Bible 2 Sam. 21:19
In another battle with the Philistines at Gob, **Elhanan** son of Jair the Bethlehemite	And there was again war with the Philistines at Gob, and **Elhanan** the son of Jaare-oregim the Bethlehemite
killed <u>the **brother** of</u> Goliath the Gittite, who had a spear with a shaft like a weaver's rod.	struck down ___ _____ __ **Goliath** the Gittite, the shaft of whose spear was like a weaver's beam.

It used to be David. But now, <u>the ESV says it was Elhanan</u>.

> Both versions claim to be "holy," but clearly, one is in error.

The footnotes in both the NIV & ESV say that according to 1 Chron. 20:5 Elhanan killed Lahmi **the brother of** Goliath. **The ESV even says 1 Chronicles 20:5 "may preserve the original reading."**

If "the original reading" is TRUE that Elhanan killed Goliath's brother, then why didn't the ESV say that? The NIV did. **Does God want errors in his Bible?**

Multiple conflicting Bible versions are NOT a blessing. They cause doubt about what God actually said. They're an embarrassment to Christianity and an insult to God.

Available from

Learn more, get the book: WHICH BIBLE WOULD JESUS USE? The Bible Version Controversy Explained and Resolved By Jack McElroy www.JackMcElroy.com

amazon

Did the NIV "Add To" or Did the NASB "Take Away From" Psalm 145:13?

****

New International Version	New American Standard Bible
Your kingdom is an everlasting kingdom, and your dominion endures through all generations. The LORD is trustworthy in all he promises and faithful in all he does.	Your kingdom is an everlasting kingdom, And Your dominion endures throughout all generations. ___ ___ ___ ___ ___ ___ ___ ___ ___ ___ ___ ___ ___ ___ ___ ___

Here's the <u>same</u> <u>verse</u> from two modern versions. Either (1) someone added to the word of God, (2) someone took away from it, or (3) the Professional Christians who assemble these versions don't really know what God really said.

Which of the above verses is what God said? With all the talk about accuracy, you'd think they would've figured this one out by now. **But obviously they haven't.**

Unless you believe just one Bible, you can never be sure of what your Lord actually said because they say and mean different things.

What did the Lord really say? Trust the Bible that's been printing the truth for over 400 years in billions of copies. You will find the right answer in the King James Bible.

Learn more, get the book: WHICH BIBLE WOULD JESUS USE? The Bible Version Controversy Explained and Resolved By Jack McElroy
www.JackMcElroy.com

Available from

CHICK PUBLICATIONS

amazon

nook

WHICH BIBLE WOULD JESUS USE
The Bible Version Controversy Explained and Resolved
JACK MCELROY

Should AWANA Be Ashamed?
****

❶ "**Awana** [Approved **W**orkmen **A**re **N**ot **A**shamed] is a global, nonprofit ministry with fully integrated evangelism and long-term discipleship programs for ages 2 to 18."[1]

❷ **They offer curriculum in four Bible translations:**[2]
- The 1984 New International Version
- King James
- New King James
- English Standard Version

❸ **They recently added the ESV because:**
"The English Standard Version (ESV) gives churches another **trusted** translation of God's Word for Cubbies (preschool) through Journey (high school)."[3]

❹ The approved workmen at AWANA should have done their homework before giving children **COMPETING and some error-filled Bibles**. For example:

• The ESV has **known errors** (admitted by experts) inserted into the text in Matthew 1:7, 8, & 10.

• The NIV and ESV have **a known geography error** (admitted by experts) inserted into the text in Luke 4:44.

• The NIV and ESV have **a known error** (admitted by experts) inserted into the text in Mark 1:2.

• The New King James Version (NKJV) **undermines the historical integrity** of God's established words in English.

Kids DO matter. Why confuse them with conflicting authorities?

Available from

Learn more, get the book: WHICH BIBLE WOULD JESUS USE? The Bible Version Controversy Explained and Resolved By Jack McElroy
www.jackmcelroy.com

CHICK PUBLICATIONS

amazon

nook

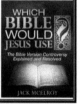

[1] https://www.awana.org/about/history;   [2] http://store.awana.org//esv/esv.default.pg.html/   [3] http://store.awana.org//esv/esv.default.pg.html/

Does Your God Make Meaningless Promises?

****

That depends on the character of your God ...

Most fundamental and evangelical pastors and teachers believe (as do KJB believers) that God promised to preserve his words.

But ...
They believe he preserved them **in a big pile of competing original language manuscripts, ancient versions and various printed texts.**

Do we have the Word of God today?

And ...
Some teach that ANY conservative translation (ESV, NIV, NASB, HCSB, NKJV, KJV and others) is good to read and study—**even though sometimes they say and mean different things; contradicting each other and even themselves.**

They want us to believe that God is a "<u>God</u> <u>of</u> <u>Many</u> <u>Versions</u>."

And Worse ...
They teach us that there is <u>NO</u> <u>BOOK</u> on the face of the earth in **ANY** language that contains **ALL** of God's words and **ONLY** God's words **without error.**

Which Means ...
Their <u>God</u> <u>of</u> <u>Many</u> <u>Versions</u> "fulfilled" his promise by leaving you bookless and confused. **His promise is therefore meaningless and faith in such a God is vain. But ...**

The God who gave us the King James Bible fulfilled his promise in a tangible and meaningful way; he gave us a BOOK.

Available from

WHICH **BIBLE** WOULD JESUS USE

Learn more, get the book: WHICH BIBLE WOULD JESUS USE? The Bible Version Controversy Explained and Resolved By Jack McElroy www.JackMcElroy.com

CHICK PUBLICATIONS
amazon
nook

Which Edition Question and Where Was the Bible Before 1611?

Introduction

****

This question is asked constantly. Sometimes derisively and sometimes sincerely.

It's answered in a number of different ways in this section.

The bottom line is that after the invention of the printing press about 1450, it was God's responsibility to get all of his words that were previously handwritten and located in various manuscripts into print.

Only God knew the location of all his words before the printing press arrived on the scene and after the original autographs had disappeared.

One thing's for sure, it was the Bibles printed during the Reformation era that changed the world.

If God had anything to do with getting his words into print, then it is the Bibles printed during this era that you should look at.

All modern English versions have their genesis in the 1881, 1885 Revised Version (except the New King James).

If God actually cares about his words enough to inspire them in the first place, then it only makes sense that he'd publish his true text early on and not wait until the late 19th century to finally feed it to his own children.

The concept of him waiting till then or even the mid to late 20th century to produce more accurate versions is nonsense.

Where Was the English Bible Before 1611?
****

The easy answer is that the Bible in English was a work in progress.

The final expression of God's inerrant words in the English language is in the Authorized Version 1st published in 1611. **Until that time this final expression didn't exist as a finished product, rather it existed in component parts–i.e., words.**

Many of the words were from the previous English Bibles that had been harvested since the year 1525 when William Tyndale's published the first printed edition of the NT in English.

Lest someone object to this observation, consider the fact that even the Scripture itself didn't come in one delivery. It came over a period of about 1,500 years with somewhere in the vicinity of 40 authors.

The King James translators started construction with The Bishops Bible as a base and incorporated other biblical building material. Previously published English Bibles delivered to the job site included Tyndale, Matthews, Coverdale, Great, Taverner's, Geneva, and Bishops.

These **previous English Bibles are part of the form and substance that provided the English building material (words) for The Authorized Version.** But they didn't limit themselves to these: they also used Greek and Hebrew editions as well as many foreign language versions.

Like the translators said in the preface:

> Truly, (good Christian reader) we never thought from the beginning that we should need to make a new Translation, ... but to make ... **out of many good ones, <u>one principal good one</u>,** not justly to be excepted against; that hath been our endeavour, that our mark.

It's been the ONE good one for over 400 years. And it still is.

Available from

Learn more, get the book: WHICH BIBLE WOULD JESUS USE? The Bible Version Controversy Explained and Resolved By Jack McElroy www.JackMcElroy.com

They arrogantly ask you...
"Where Was the Bible Before 1611?"

****

"Actually a better question for today is, 'Where was the Bible **AFTER the invention of the printing press?'**

How can a 17th-century translation be "The Bible?" How can the Lord pick only one Bible?

And why should one language have priority over another? Does this make any sense? Sure it does.

As we have already seen, **'The Bible' has to be one book—not two testaments in two different languages.** Or worse, only exist as the mythical "Original Bible."

Second, there has to be a standard—a 'go-to' book you can trust— a book that contains all of God's words and only God's words.

In the Song of Solomon we are reintroduced to the biblical concept of Chiefest.

In Song of Solomon 5:10, the woman refers to her beloved as "the chiefest among ten thousand." The marginal note in the 1611 King James Bible says: **"the chiefest. Heb. a standard bearer."**

When it comes to Bibles produced after the invention of the printing press, the King James Bible is by any and all accounts **'the chiefest among ten thousand.'**

Not only of the previous translations but also of any pretender to the position of "chiefest" from any modern version.

Its 400-year, billions of copies history proves it to be the Lord's 'standard bearer.'

The King James Bible is preferred above all others because an excellent spirit is in it and forasmuch as it is faithful, neither is there any error or fault found in it."[1]

1. From Chapter 9 of WHICH BIBLE WOULD JESUS USE?

They ask …

"Why did it take God Over 1,600 Years to Keep His Promise to Preserve His Word if it is Preserved in Elizabethan English?"

****

It didn't. God's true words were always available—exactly where the experts **STILL THINK** they are … in manuscripts, ancient versions, lectionaries, and patristic quotations.

All changed **AFTER** the invention of printing (circa 1450) when God's task was to get his words **INTO PRINT** and contained **IN A BOOK** …

What the questioner did not know to ask is this...

"Where did God place his true and pure words in English where I can find them today?"

The answer? Right where any critical thinking person would expect to find them—**in a BOOK**—so his own children can read and hide them in their hearts.

Which book is easy …

It's obvious; God has placed his **understandable, pure, and holy words** in the King James Bible.

And he proved it by making it the best-selling, most published, most read, most memorized, most believed, most trusted Bible in the history of mankind.

Learn more, get the book: WHICH BIBLE WOULD JESUS USE? The Bible Version Controversy Explained and Resolved By Jack McElroy www.JackMcElroy.com

Available from

466

They Say …

"Apparently, God Expects Every Christian To Know 17th-Century English in Order to Read His Word."

****

This objection is constantly leveled at **King James Bible believers** by the same folks who extol the value of "the original Greek" (which they don't have). How ironic …

Riddle me this; if some KJB English words are so hard to understand that we shouldn't bother to learn them and just "upgrade" to a modern version, then why do preachers bombard us with Koine Greek's tricky vocabulary, complicated grammatical rules, and terms like *optative mood* and *second aorist middle tense*? And let's not forget syntax and word order.

Is that supposed to be easier? Available from

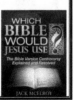

Learn more, get the book: WHICH BIBLE WOULD JESUS USE? The Bible Version Controversy Explained and Resolved By Jack McElroy www.JackMcElroy.com

They Mockingly Ask You... "Which Edition of the King James Bible Do You Use?"

****

No matter which edition of the King James Bible you choose ...

1. **None present Jesus a liar** like the NIV, NASB, ESV, and HCSB do in John 7:8–10 by eliminating the word "yet" from the narrative.
2. **None present Jesus as a sinner** like the NIV does by saying he got angry without a cause in Matthew 5:22 and Mark 3:5.
3. **None say Elhanan killed Goliath** (instead of David) like the NASB, ESV, and HCSB say in 2 Samuel 21:19.
4. **None say Jesus was "indignant"** (instead of compassionate) at the leper looking to get healed like the NIV says in Mark 1:41.
5. **None call Jesus a begotten God** (instead of begotten son) like the NASB does in John 1:18.
6. **None contain known errors** purposefully inserted into the text like the ESV does in Matthew 1:7, 8, and 10.
7. **None eliminate 16 entire verses** like the Greek text underlying the NIV, NASB, ESV, and HCSB do.
8. **None eliminate the proof text for the** Godhead made up of three that are one. i.e. **"three ARE one,"** commonly known as "The Trinity" like the NIV, ESV, NASB, and HCSB do in 1 John 5:7–8.
9. **None eliminate the proof text for the Incarnation explicitly stating that God became a man** like the NIV, ESV, and NASB do in 1 Timothy 3:16.
10. **None** have their **underlying original language source text revised** over time like the NASB and NIV.

They miss the fact that you actually HAVE a BIBLE you believe in instead of long-lost manuscripts that no one has.

Available from

Learn more, get the book: WHICH BIBLE WOULD JESUS USE? The Bible Version Controversy Explained and Resolved By Jack McElroy www.JackMcElroy.com

CHICK PUBLICATIONS

amazon
nook

WHICH BIBLE WOULD JESUS USE
The Bible Version Controversy Explained and Resolved
JACK MCELROY

The Answer to the "Gotcha" Question King James Bible Believers Are Constantly Asked

★★★

They smugly ask you...

"There have been thousands of changes in the King James Bible since 1611 so ...
Which revision do you believe; 1629, 1638, 1762 or 1769?"

Unlike most modern versions, there have been many editions of the KJB but no revisions of its underlying Greek and Hebrew texts.

Here's what the **American Bible Society** said this about **"revisions"** of the King James Bible English text ...

"The English Bible, as left by the translators (of 1611), has come down to us **unaltered in respect to its text** ... With the exception of typographical errors and changes required by the progress of orthography in the English language, **the text** of our present Bibles **remains unchanged, and without variation** from the original copy as left by the translators."[1]

𝔚𝔥𝔞𝔱'𝔰 𝔱𝔥𝔢 𝔫𝔢𝔵𝔱 ℚ𝔲𝔢𝔰𝔱𝔦𝔬𝔫𝔫𝔢?

Available from

Learn more, get the book: WHICH BIBLE WOULD
JESUS USE? The Bible Version Controversy Explained
and Resolved By Jack McElroy www.JackMcElroy.com

amazon
nook

1. Committee on Versions to the Board of Managers, American Bible Society, 1852.

They Ask ...

"Which KJB Do You Use, The 1769 or the 1611?"

****

 University of Chicago theologian and Greek NT scholar Edgar Goodspeed (1871–1962) said: "**The 1769 edition probably differs from the 1611 in 75,000 details**."

And he could be right. **Lots of well-meaning folks are handed that number and get nervous**. They think "how could the King James Bible be the perfect word of God when there were over 75,000 changes?"

The question is usually and insincerely asked to get you to doubt the words in the world's best-selling Bible with a 400-year history of spectacular results.

But the "75,000 details" is just a boogie man statistic used to undercut the King James Bible and sway your opinion.

O ver 99% of the differences (my estimate) are spelling updates. The rest are printing error corrections, grammar/orthographic updates and some translation tweaks. The differences don't mean any edition was wrong or flawed.[1] **They are simply different ways of presenting the same original language text.**

The folks who sincerely ask this question are confusing pure and perfect with identical. Printing errors notwithstanding ...

Anybody using a KJB today is using an edition of the Authorized Version of 1611 containing the pure words of God.

Available from

Learn more, get the book: WHICH BIBLE WOULD JESUS
USE? The Bible Version Controversy Explained and
Resolved By Jack McElroy www.JackMcElroy.com

CHICK
PUBLICATIONS
amazon
nook

WHICH
BIBLE
WOULD
JESUS USE
The Bible Version Controversy
Explained and Resolved
JACK McELROY

1 For a detailed analysis with examples, see Chapter 11 of WHICH BIBLE WOULD JESUS USE?

The Real Reason for the Fake Question

Hello
my name is

HYPOCRITE

✶✶

Asking the "Which edition of the King James Bible do you believe?" question is an excellent control technique meant to suppress discussion.

Ridicule works too.

<u>Both are frequently used</u> at most Christian colleges, Bible institutes, and seminaries to pressure students into uncritical acceptance of the politically correct position of *Original Autograph* Onlyism.

Teachers will say the King James Bible is "a reliable translation" and at the same time go out of their way to point out their "pet" list of errors and teach you that the KJB text is defective.

But some students see the duplicity and hypocrisy in that, challenging teachers and pastors: "How can you recommend the King James Bible as 'reliable' when it's so different from other versions? After all, it's got 16 entire verses extra. That's a pretty big difference, isn't it?"

That's when the trouble begins.

No wonder *Original Autograph* Onlyists get flack. It happens in churches all the time. Unfortunately, the discussion turns contentious because of the fundamental belief in the authority of "the Scriptures" and because the truthfulness of God is at stake.

Some believers didn't grow up in Christian homes nor did they go to a Christian college. **It's not their parent's religion; it's their own.**

They left off their sins and trusted in Christ <u>based on the words of a book</u>, not based on a backpack full of uncertain words and phrases.

Available from

WHICH
BIBLE
WOULD
JESUS USE

CHICK
PUBLICATIONS

Learn more, get the book: WHICH BIBLE WOULD JESUS USE? The Bible Version Controversy Explained and Resolved By Jack McElroy www.JackMcElroy.com

Why the Lord Isn't Ashamed of ANY Edition of the King James Bible

****

He has used and blessed them all over the past 400 years even with printing errors; spelling, grammar and orthographic differences; and translation tweaks.

The Lord wouldn't be ashamed to bring ANY historic edition of the King James Bible to your church with him, <u>including an original 1611 edition</u> (tens of thousands of reprints have been sold) **because:**

❶ **It's the original standard issue publishers need to compare their work to.**

Plus, he <u>could</u> teach on …

❷ **The Apocrypha;** although not inspired, it provides background information on the Old and New Testaments (like today's study Bibles) and wouldn't have been originally included if it didn't have some value.

❸ **The significance of the original spelling and punctuation.**

❹ **The variations in the translation** (i.e., he/she and his/her).

❺ **The translational and grammatical nuances** that exist in later printings that evangelical and fundamentalist academics have been using for over 100 years **to undermine the authority of the book.**

❻ **The question of English capitalization** of the word *Spirit/spirit*.

He'd NEVER bring in a modern version because he won't accept material error (i.e., errors of fact, history, geography, Science, & doctrine) in his holy book.

Available from

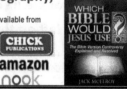

Learn more, get the book: WHICH BIBLE WOULD JESUS USE? The Bible Version Controversy Explained and Resolved By Jack McElroy www.JackMcElroy.com

The Truth About the Differences Between the 1611 and 1769 KJB Editions

★★★

<u>I've spent countless hours</u> (easily over 100) examining the differences between the 1611 and its subsequent editions. I compiled 102 pages of notes before writing my (~70,000 word) book.

Jack McElroy

<u>I've read and examined</u> the differences as presented in works by Prebendary F.H.A. Scrivener, Dr. James Price, and authors David Norton, Matthew Verschuur, and others.

<u>I did this</u> not only to settle my own beliefs but to be able to argue effectively for them also. A full explanation with examples is found in Chapters 11 and 12 of *WHICH BIBLE WOULD JESUS USE?*

The facts are these:

❶ There were printing errors in the first edition and some subsequent editions.

❷ Spelling and grammar were modernized in various editions including Dr. Thomas Paris's 1762 Cambridge Edition, as well as Dr. Benjamin Blayney's Oxford University editions in 1769. According to scholar and author David Norton, **the text was all but "fossilized" by 1769:**

> We must be absolutely clear what it really is: a text that all but fossilized in the 1760s. The modern KJB is a mutated version of a 17th-century text with partially modernized spelling, punctuation and presentation.[1]

❸ The translation was tweaked in **non-material ways** (on the whole to make it even more literal) up to 1638 by a couple of the original translators. Various publishers have produced editions reflecting a combination of these types of updates/tweaks over the centuries as well.

1. David Norton, *A Textual History of the King James Bible* (Cambridge, England: Cambridge University Press, 2005), 126.

Page 1

❹ The first printing of 1611 was many times referred to as the model. It's been reproduced in three successive centuries.

❺ There was never any revision of the underlying original language texts. The true revision took place in 1881/1885, which is why they appropriately titled it the **English Revised Version** (**ERV** or **RV**).

But aren't these changes to the text?

Although the presentation of the English translation has been slightly modified, the underlying original language texts remain unchanged.

The original committee that selected the textual readings and did the translation **disbanded** in 1610. Their work was completed. **The original language texts didn't change after that because there was no one appointed to do it.**

All of the changes have to do with the **presentation** of the **texts** in English.

After a thorough examination of various editions of the King James Bible, here's what the Committee on Versions said to the Board of Managers of the American Bible Society in 1852:

AMERICAN BIBLE SOCIETY

> The English Bible, as left by the translators [of 1611], has come down to us **unaltered in** respect to **its text** ... With the exception of typographical errors and changes required by the progress of orthography in the English language, **the text of our present Bibles remains unchanged, and without variation from the original copy as left by the translators.**[2]

2. American Bible Society. Committee on Versions, *Adopted, May 1,1851.* Cornell University Library Digital Collections (Ithaca, NY: Cornell University Library, 1851), 7. Page 2

What About the Differences Between King James Bibles Printed by the Oxford and Cambridge University Presses?

****

Every critic of the KJB knows the following places where Bibles printed by Oxford University Press and Cambridge University Press contain slightly different readings.

These are the four big examples presented over and over again in online forums as a reason for you to ditch the King James Bible.

Reference	1611 First Edition King James Bible	Cambridge	Oxford
Joshua 19:2	And they had in their inheritance Beer-sheba, **or** Sheba, and Moladah,	or	**and**
2 Chron. 33:19	His prayer also, and how God was in-treated of him, and all his **sinne**, and his trespasse,...	sin	sins
Jeremiah 34:16	But yee turned and polluted my Name, and caused euery man his seruant, and euery man his handmaide, whome **yee** had set at libertie at their pleasure,...	ye	he
Nahum 3:16	Thou hast multiplied thy merchants aboue the starres of heauen; the cankerworme spoileth & **flieth** away.	**flieth**	**fleeth**

The Joshua 19:2 explanation is lengthy[1] but here are the answers to the other references as presented in *WHICH BIBLE WOULD JESUS USE? The Bible Version Controversy Explained and Resolved* ...

1. See, *WHICH BIBLE WOULD JESUS USE?*, pp. 206–207.

Page 1

475

"2 Chronicles 33:19: Sinne can be singular or plural**. Hymn writer Robert Lowry understood that.

"What can wash away my **sin**? Nothing but the blood of Jesus."

Whose sins are singular? Both are accurate renderings of the original Hebrew in English.

Jeremiah 34.16: Dr. Peter S. Ruckman explains this one: "**BOTH variants in the AV (Jer. 34:16) were correct grammatically**, if one deals with the English text or the Hebrew text. They ("ye" in the Cambridge) were being addressed as a group (plural, Jer. 34:13; as in Deut. 29), but the address was aimed at individual men ("**he**" in the Oxford edition), within the group. Either word would have been absolutely correct according to that great critic of critics, the word of God (Heb. 4:12–13)..."[2]

Nahum 3:16: **flee:** verb
1. To run away, as from danger or pursuers; take flight. [**fleeth** away]
2. To move swiftly; fly; speed. [**flieth** away]
Both words carry the same meaning. [3]

Literally thousands of KJB editions have been printed, reset, and reprinted by hundreds of different print shops. **Like the excellent systems engineer that he is, the Lord built redundancy into the King James brand.** He provided more than one means to preserve his words in the various printings of the book ...

If you don't like the way the text has been presented in any edition of the King James Bible, you should dump the book. Find a better one.

2.   See, *WHICH BIBLE WOULD JESUS USE?*, p. 209., .3. Ibid. p. 209.

Page 2

How to Finally Answer Their KJV ONLY "Trick Question"

Intended to destroy your faith in the King James Bible, here's how to turn the tables on them...

****

Adapted from Chapter 12 of Which Bible Would Jesus Use? The Bible Version Controversy Explained and Resolved by Jack McElroy

They ask...

The trick question ...

"Which revision of the King James Bible is inspired, the 1611 or the 1769 edition?"

Jack McElroy
www.jackmcelroy.com

They pose this question to try and trick you into buying into their argument for rejecting the King James authority based on the "changes" that appeared in various editions.

There are revisions and revisions— don't buy the head fake.

When it comes to the King James Bible, there are two kinds of "revisions" you need to know about. One is used to "game you" and the other is a legitimate revision of the underlying text that makes the Bible say and mean different things.

Bible Version Secrets Exposed

The *Oxford English Dictionary* (*OED*) is said to be the accepted authority on the evolution of the English language.

According to Oxforddictionaries.com, the primary definition of *revise* is to: **"reconsider and alter (something) in the light of further evidence."**

A second meaning, one that critics of the King James Bible treat as though it means the primary definition above, is "to review; to re-examine; to look over with care for correction; as, to revise a writing; to revise a proof sheet."

Chapters 10–12 in *Which Bible Would Jesus Use?* have detailed and answered the most difficult "revision" instances in all the editions of the King James Bible.

Look around the Web and prove it for yourself. The instances you have just read are repeated over and over again in forums, blog posts, and articles. When someone feeds you the "which revision" argument, keep this in mind:

If you held the copyright to the King James Bible and all you did was correct printing errors, update spelling and grammar, and make some very minor tweaks in the presentation of the English translation, could you in good conscience slap "revised edition" on the cover and charge an extra $20 when you didn't change the underlying text one bit?

And besides, there absolutely was …

A real "revision" of the King James Bible.

It was published in 1885 and was appropriately called The English Revised Version (ERV).

---

1 Oxford Dictionaries, s.v. "revise," https://en.oxforddictionaries.com/definition/revise.

2 Webster's Dictionary (1828), s.v. "revise," http://webstersdictionary1828.com/Dictionary/revise

A Few Other Memes and About the Author

Introduction

****

This section will give you some insight into:

- Why I am a Bible libertarian and not a Bible fascist
- Why I don't recommend any modern version of the Bible
- How I determined that the KJB is the true English Bible
- Six reasons why I am King James only
- Why I am called divisive
- And some other commentary

Who Built Your Bible?

****

Building the Bible (meaning a physical book) is just as important as writing it in the first place. And so is making sure you get it without additions or subtractions. So is how it's translated.

It's the Lord's product and he's in charge of...
• **Creating it**—giving the words in the first place.
• **Constructing it**—assembling the component parts into books and assembling the books, letters, and other documents into A Book.
• **Copying it**—reproducing the text.
• **Carrying it**—translating the material into other languages.

The Lord is the owner of the words. The Holy Ghost is the General Contractor and overseer. He chooses the subcontractors that he will entrust the work to.

Every one of the Lord's words "are life," transcending all language barriers. Otherwise, you can't get life from his words as you read, memorize, or quote them to lost sinners hoping they'll get "life" by believing them.

All you have to do is find where he's displayed them.

I believe God has to provide his children with a book—a literal book; not a pile of variant textual readings that the experts are still searching for.

I believe that the Lord preserved his holy words through an assortment of manuscripts through the ages AND **he certainly has now gathered his words and placed them in one book after the invention of the printing press.**

Jack McElroy holding a KJB
"Great She Bible" AD 1611–1613

And I believe that that book should be easily recognizable by his children. Anything less doesn't fit the Lord's character.

His authentic words are in a book not scattered all over the place like we've been taught.

I'm a Bible Libertarian, Not a Bible Fascist

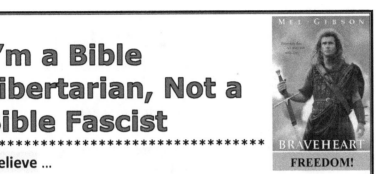

BRAVEHEART

I believe …   FREEDOM!

❶ **In freedom of choice and association,** a right fought for by men like the real William Wallace in Scotland (portrayed by Mel Gibson in Braveheart) and the Founding Fathers of the United States.

❷ **That everyone has the right to use and believe whichever Bible version they want,** no matter how error-riddled it may be.

❸ **That no one should be "forced" to believe ANY Bible** if they don't want to.

❹ **That people can be saved apart from the King James Bible.** The Lord uses various means to reach people including different Bible versions, tracts, personal testimonies, and more.

❺ **That "the Bible" is a book** and in English, it's **the 1611 Authorized Version**— commonly known as the King James Bible.

I simply make the case for the King James Bible based on my own research. If some are unconvinced, I harbor no ill will.
I wish them well and hope you will too.

Jack McElroy

Learn more, get the book: WHICH BIBLE WOULD JESUS USE? The Bible Version Controversy Explained and Resolved
By Jack McElroy www.JackMcElroy.com

Available from

CHICK PUBLICATIONS
amazon
nook

WHICH **BIBLE WOULD JESUS USE**
The Bible Version Controversy Explained and Resolved
JACK MCELROY

4 Reasons WHY I Don't Recommend ANY Modern Bible Version

****

<u>I'm a Bible libertarian</u>. I believe in freedom of thought, choice and association. I believe everybody is free to use **ANY Bible they want** no matter how error-riddled it is.

<u>My PRESUPPOSITION is that the Lord HAS provided a book that IS the Bible</u>. That book is the King James Bible. I fleshed out the reasons WHY in my book *WHICH BIBLE WOULD JESUS USE?*

<u>My purpose</u> in presenting my research is to show and comment on the differences, how they affect doctrine, and WHY there can only be one authoritative Bible per language because they all say and mean different things.

Top 4 Reasons Why

1. <u>I've documented</u> scores of errors of fact, history, geography, science, Doctrine, etc., found in modern versions because most are based on a faulty, erroneous and convoluted text. As a result ...
   Their "holy" Bibles are full of holes.
2. <u>I've documented</u> internal, cross-reference, and other contradictions in modern versions. I'm not a language technician (i.e., translator), but I can read and think.
3. <u>Like the manuscripts they're based on</u>, modern versions disagree with each other even to the point of not including the same verses.
4. <u>I do not believe the "history of the text" model presented by modern textual critics</u>. Plus, I believe modern textual criticism is subjective and sometimes arbitrary and capricious. It's a science; falsely so-called.

Available from

Learn more, get the book: WHICH BIBLE WOULD JESUS USE? The Bible Version Controversy Explained and Resolved By Jack McElroy www.JackMcElroy.com

CHICK
PUBLICATIONS
amazon
nook

Jack McElroy

HOW I Determined That the KJB IS the True English Bible and WHY Others Don't Agree

****

I arrived at my conclusion because of two things:

1. My presupposition that there has to be a book. It makes no sense to me that the Lord would leave his own children uncertain as to which words are his and which are imposters'.

In short, he had to reveal to us **the true text after the invention of printing** and clear up all the variant readings that exist in the manuscripts **by publishing A BOOK containing his PURE WORD.**

2. The identity of the book can easily be determined by deductive reasoning.

I assumed that the Lord Jesus Christ is behind the 400+ year success of the best-selling, most published, most read, most memorized, most believed, most trusted Bible in the history of mankind.

<u>Why others don't agree with me</u>.
IF they start with the presupposition that
1. Only the original autographs are inspired and inerrant and
2. All of God's authentic and infallible words cannot be found in any book or any language on the face of the earth, then ...

Our beliefs are mutually exclusive.

Available from

Learn more, get the book: WHICH BIBLE WOULD JESUS USE? The Bible Version Controversy Explained and Resolved By Jack McElroy www.jackmcelroy.com

Jack McElroy

Illustration: Mrs. Paul (Kay) Friederichsen "pure" added, *God's Way Made Easy*, p. 140.

483

6 Reasons Why I am King James Only

****

A short explanation for friends and loved ones...

❶ <u>I've learned</u> that all Bible versions say and mean different things.

❷ <u>I've learned</u> that the differences in Bibles are more than "skin deep." They affect meaning AND doctrine.

❸ <u>I've learned</u> that sometimes they say opposite things; conflicting with each other and containing errors of fact, history, and geography. **So I know there's something very wrong.**

❹ <u>I believe</u> that the Bible should not contain any errors in it because **it's only fitting for our Lord Jesus Christ to have a holy book that's inerrant.**

❺ <u>I believe</u> there **has to be just one book** that has all the right facts, numbers, history ,and geography in it so there is no confusion for God's children.

❻ <u>I believe</u> the King James Bible is the only pure English Bible because of its glorious 400-year history and billion copy+ reproductions.

I read it, believe it, and hide its words in my heart because I believe it contains the words of our living God without error, addition, or subtraction.

Learn more, get the book: WHICH BIBLE WOULD JESUS USE? The Bible Version Controversy Explained and Resolved By Jack McElroy
www.JackMcElroy.com

Available from

CHICK PUBLICATIONS

amazon
nook

Why I'm Called "Divisive" Because of My Stand on the KJB

Truth ALWAYS causes division. And contrary to popular belief, the Lord Jesus Christ said he came to divide NOT unite:

> Suppose ye that I am come to give peace on earth? I tell you, Nay; but rather division: Luke 12:51 KJB

And his book is like him.

Here's my core belief. It appears in the book *WHICH BIBLE WOULD JESUS USE? The Bible Version Controversy Explained and Resolved, pp. 7–8 ...*

"Deductive reasoning tells me that **there has to be a book—one book**...And it shouldn't be hard to find, either.

As a matter fact, God's book should be dripping with authority and should be obvious to any child of God. If it's the Lord's book, it should be a bestseller because of his blessing. Like him, it should have loving friends and fierce enemies.

- Like him, **it will both unite and divide men.**
- Like him, it should have the **power to change men's lives**.
- Like the Lord, who spoke with authority, even so his Bible should speak with authority. 'The officers answered, Never man spake like this man' (John 7:46). **Even so should his book speak like no other.**
- Like him, **it should be pure**—containing all of God's words and not adulterated with men's words.
- Like him, **it should have a name above all others.**
- And like the Lord, unto whom all power in heaven and earth is given, **it should be a powerful book. <u>I have such a book</u>.**"

Jack McElroy

Available from

Learn more, get the book: WHICH BIBLE WOULD JESUS USE? The Bible Version Controversy Explained and Resolved By Jack McElroy www.JackMcElroy.com

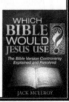

How Dr. James White & Jack McElroy Are Alike

****

Both are apologists (a person who offers an argument in defense of something controversial) and both are salesmen. BUT here is how they differ on the Bible version controversy ...

Dr. White is <u>pitching</u> a <u>position</u>. McElroy is <u>promoting</u> a <u>product</u>.

<u>Dr. White's position</u> is that it's impossible for ANY Christian to know WITH CERTAINTY all of God's words. **White sells <u>uncertainty</u>.**

"The desire for *absolute* certainty ... plainly lies behind ... KJV Only materials. It is argued that unless we embrace the KJV as our final authority, we have no final authority at all and, hence, all is subjectivity and uncertainty."[1]

"... KJV Onlyism... is by its nature anti-intellectual, anti-scholarship, and anti-freedom."[2]

<u>Jack McElroy's product</u> is a BOOK; The King James Bible. **McElroy sells biblical <u>certainty</u>.**

"Although the Lord preserved his holy words through an assortment of manuscripts through the ages, he has certainly gathered **ALL of his words and ONLY his words and placed them in ONE BOOK** after the invention of the printing press.

Anything less doesn't fit the Lord's character. Anything less means textual critics care more about his words than he does.

And I believe that that book should be **easily** recognizable by his children. And it is ...

His words are CERTAINLY found **in a Book** that's 100% error-free Scripture. They're in the world's best-selling, most published, most read, most memorized, most believed, most trusted Bible in the history of mankind; The King James Bible.

Have not I written to thee excellent things in counsels and knowledge, That I might make thee know the certainty of the words of truth; that thou mightest answer the words of truth to them that send unto thee? Prov. 22:20–21

Available from

Learn more, get the book: WHICH BIBLE WOULD JESUS USE? The Bible Version Controversy Explained and Resolved By Jack McElroy www.JackMcElroy.com

amazon

nook

1. *The King James Only Controversy Can You Trust The Modern Translations?*, Pgs. 130–134 ©1995, 2009 2. Ibid. James R. White ©1995 p. 151.

Are You a Calvinist, Arminian, or Biblicist?

****

A **"Biblicist"** is someone who claims to interpret the Bible literally. The Calvinist/Arminian controversy is interesting but can be contentious especially since most on either side claim to be Biblicists. But then, there's ...

The problem:
Most who claim to be "Biblicists" **CAN'T OR WON'T** show you the authoritative, inerrant Bible (i.e., the book) they BELIEVE in.

They profess a belief in a book they don't possess.

The Solution: Until they first agree on **WHICH BIBLE IS** the final authority on WHAT God actually **SAYS**, they're wasting time arguing theology.

O nly AFTER all parties agree on WHICH BIBLE contains God's inspired, inerrant words can you finally have a meaningful discussion on WHAT the Scripture of truth MEANS.

Available from

Learn more, get the book: WHICH BIBLE WOULD
JESUS USE? The Bible Version Controversy
Explained and Resolved By Jack McElroy
www.JackMcElroy.com

CHICK
PUBLICATIONS

amazon
nook

487

Have You Been "Red Pilled" Yet?

★★

Popularized by the 1999 film *The Matrix*, the pills are a metaphor representing the power of choice:

The red pill represents an uncertain future—BUT **FREEDOM** from the enslaving control of the machine-generated dream world and allowing escape into the real world.

The blue pill represented **a beautiful prison**—leading back to ignorance, living in confined comfort without want or fear within simulated reality of the Matrix.

I got "red pilled" when I got saved in October 1978.
What I discovered thereafter were these worldwide conspiracies ...

❶ **The world's biggest conspiracy is that eternal life can be EARNED.**
Taught by all religions & believed by billions, the Bible taught me the truth.

❷ **The second biggest conspiracy is evolution.** Taught by "experts" & believed by billions, this nonsense is debunked by the Scripture.

Once you take the "Red Pill" of TRUTH, all other conspiracies like the New World Order, The Fed, false flags, the JFK assassination, 9/11, the fake moon landings, and even the Bible version controversy are mere child's play.

Jack McElroy is a Born-Again Christian, businessman and entrepreneur with over 45 years of experience in various business disciplines. He is author of three books including *WHICH BIBLE WOULD JESUS USE? The Bible Version Controversy Explained and Resolved.* www.JackMcElroy.com

Pills: By W. Carter [CC BY-SA 4.0 (https://creativecommons.org/licenses/by-sa/4.0)], from Wikimedia Commons

Why I Unashamedly Promote My Books

****

A few folks have expressed their concern that I promote the work I do, which includes my writings about Bible versions. Here's why I do it.

Anybody who's ever attended a Bible study where multiple versions are used already knows that the versions say and mean different things— which, affects Bible doctrine. **If it didn't, then there never would be a "King James only controversy" to begin with.**

I have a cause, and a purpose.

The Cause is to promote the pure words of God as they appear on the pages of the King James Bible.

The Purpose is to provide valuable information to folks who actually believe that the Lord HAS indeed fulfilled his promise to preserve his holy words unto all generations. My purpose is to supply those "on the fence" with information that will help them in their quest for the truth. I have absolutely no desire to try and convince somebody entrenched on the other side of the fence. It's not worth my time or theirs.

****

The Lord's words to this generation of English-speaking people are found in the King James Bible. All other Bible versions are nothing more than that—versions, and incorrect and lousy ones at that—which, by the way, I prove in my book.

This is a self-funding business and ministry.

I don't ask for donations. I work to provide valuable information that took me a great time, effort, and expense to assemble. I sell my work and try to offer more value than what people pay for.

The most expensive asset we have is our time. The older I get, the more valuable it becomes because I'm quickly running out of it.

I have no problem with the concept of getting paid for value. **Anybody who has a job should be doing the same thing. Also, the Lord Jesus said ...**

"the labourer is worthy of his hire ..." Luke 10:7 KJB

I have yet to hear of someone who complains about how I do business show up at work on Monday morning and volunteer their services to their employer—for free. Somehow their argument goes in only one direction.

Learn more, get the book: WHICH BIBLE WOULD
JESUS USE? The Bible Version Controversy
Explained and Resolved By Jack McElroy
www.JackMcElroy.com

Available from

amazon
nook

Shock Claim:
God Forgets

****

❶ **Through the grace of our Lord Jesus Christ, we discover...**

As far as the east is from the west,
so **far hath he removed our transgressions from us.** Ps. 103:12

Christ takes away our cup of sin — then invites us to His BANQUET!

❷ **Plus, your Lord says there are some things he forgets ...**

I, *even* I, *am* he that blotteth out **thy transgressions** for mine own sake, and **will not remember thy sins.** Isaiah 43:25 KJB

For I will be merciful to their unrighteousness, **and their sins and their iniquities will I remember no more.** Heb. 8:12

Behold, for peace I had great bitterness: but thou hast in love to my soul *delivered it* from the pit of corruption: **for thou hast cast all my sins behind thy back.** Isaiah 38:17

He will turn again, he will have compassion upon us; he will subdue our iniquities; **and thou wilt cast all their sins into the depths of the sea.** Mic. 7:19

Our God "knoweth all things"
EXCEPT those he chooses to forget!

Jack McElroy is a Born-Again Christian, businessman and entrepreneur with over 45 years of experience in various business disciplines. He is author of three books including *WHICH BIBLE WOULD JESUS USE? The Bible Version Controversy Explained and Resolved.* www.JackMcElroy.com

Jack McElroy

Illustration: Mrs. Paul (Kay) Friederichsen, *God's Truth Made Simple* p. 86.

The 21 Best
"Back Against the Wall" Verses

****

Like you dear reader, I've faced difficulties during my life as a Christian. These verses were (and are) a great help to me and I hope they'll comfort you too …

1. Call unto me, and I will answer thee, and shew thee great and mighty things, which thou knowest not. *Jeremiah 33:3*
2. When a man's ways please the LORD, he maketh even his enemies to be at peace with him. *Proverbs 16:7*
3. Many seek the ruler's favour; but every man's judgment cometh from the LORD. *Proverbs 29:26*
4. A man's heart deviseth his way: but the LORD directeth his steps. *Proverbs 16:9*
5. O LORD, I know that the way of man is not in himself: it is not in man that walketh to direct his steps. *Jeremiah 10:23*
6. For promotion cometh neither from the east, nor from the west, nor from the south. But God is the judge: he putteth down one, and setteth up another. *Psalm 75:6-7*
7. Except the LORD build the house, they labour in vain that build it: except the LORD keep the city, the watchman waketh but in vain. *Psalm 127:1*
8. Man's goings are of the LORD; how can a man then understand his own way? *Proverbs 20:24*
9. The king's heart is in the hand of the LORD, as the rivers of water: he turneth it whithersoever he will. *Proverbs 21:1*
10. Put not your trust in princes, nor in the son of man, in whom there is no help. *Psalm 146:3*
11. The steps of a good man are ordered by the LORD: and he delighteth in his way. *Psalm 37:23.*
12. For now thou numberest my steps: dost thou not watch over my sin? *Job 14:16*
13. Doth not he see my ways, and count all my steps? *Job 31:4*
14. Thou hast enlarged my steps under me, that my feet did not slip. *Psalm 18:36*
15. The LORD lifteth up the meek: he casteth the wicked down to the ground. *Psalm 147:6*
16. God hath spoken once; twice have I heard this; that power belongeth unto God. *Psalm 62:11*
17. There are many devices in a man's heart; nevertheless the counsel of the LORD, that shall stand. *Proverbs 19:21*
18. Commit thy works unto the LORD, and thy thoughts shall be established. *Proverb16:3*
19. Commit thy way unto the LORD; trust also in him; and he shall bring it to pass. *Psalm 37:5*
20. All that the Father giveth me shall come to me; and him that cometh to me I will in no wise cast out. *John 6:37*
21. Let your conversation be without covetousness; and be content with such things as ye have: for he hath said, I will never leave thee, nor forsake thee. *Heb. 13:5*

Jack McElroy

Jack McElroy is a Born Again Christian, author, businessman and entrepreneur with over 40 years of experience in various business disciplines.
www.JackMcElroy.com

"I'm Forty, I'm not Married, I Don't Fly Jets, and I Don't Have a Dog? I Grow Up to Be a Loser."

Rusty in Disney's *The Kid*

What do you think about Thomas Edison's comments?

Here's what the Lord said...	Here's what Edison said...
All scripture is given by inspiration of God... 2Timothy 3:16	"All Bibles are man-made." http://www.notable-quotes.com/e/edison_thomas.html
Jesus said: And thou, Capernaum, which art exalted to **heaven**, shalt be thrust down to **hell**. Luke 10:15	"I have never seen the slightest scientific proof of the <u>religious theories</u> of heaven and hell, of future life for individuals, or of a personal God." Thomas Alva Edison, Columbian Magazine
Now **faith is** the **substance** of things hoped for, the **evidence** of things not seen. Hebrews 11:1 And this is **the record**, that God hath given to us eternal life, and this life is in his Son. 1 John 5:11	"For faith, as well intentioned as it may be, must be built on facts, not fiction— **faith in fiction is a damnable false hope.**"
Jesus said: For what shall it profit a man, if he shall gain the whole world, and lose **his own soul**? Mark 8:36 And many of them that sleep in the dust of the earth shall awake, **some to everlasting life**, and **some to shame and everlasting contempt**. Dan 12:2	"**I cannot believe in the immortality of the soul**... No, all this talk of an existence beyond the grave is wrong." Thomas Edison, quoted in *2000 Years of Disbelief, Famous People with the Courage to Doubt,* by James A. Haught, Prometheus Books, 1996
Jesus said: Sanctify them through thy truth: **thy word is truth**. John 17:17	"So far as religion of the day is concerned, **it is a damned fake...** **Religion is all bunk.**" http://atheism.about.com/library/quotes/bl_q_TAEdison.htm

Did Edison grow up to be a loser?

Jack McElroy is a Born-Again Christian, author, businessman and entrepreneur with over 40 years of experience in various business disciplines www.JackMcElroy.com

Jack McElroy

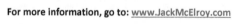

Jack McElroy

The Man Behind the Memes II

****

Charitable Cause

I heartily support the work of **Peoples Baptist Ministries to India and Beyond** and Dr. G.S. Nair. Here are a few reasons why…

I've known the founder, Dr. G.S. Nair since 1982. He has stayed in our home many times over the past 35 years. I've traveled  with him to supporting churches in the United States. But more importantly, I have visited him and seen the ministry in India firsthand. I know his work.

He's not just a "church planter," but he has created a system to produce "church-planting pastors" who have **planted over 4,000 churches** since 1976.

He's not just a "pastor– teacher," he's an educator who develops "pastor teachers" He's established 4 Bible colleges, a seminary, and 21 extension schools with a total enrollment of over 1,400 students.

He's not just a soul winner, but he's a soul-winning leader who teaches others how to win souls (**over 400,000 saved and now members of local churches**). These are souls saved through the ministry, not folks who've transferred their membership from other churches.

He's not just a "humanitarian," but he's a "biblical humanitarian leader" who has created a charitable organization that actually does and says everything we say we believe in. For example, he's established 25 orphanages providing homes for 490 children.

I was so impressed that wrote a book about the ministry. Avail. Amazon.

The mission also oversees seven private schools with 1,800 students, two vocational training centers for women, an assisted living home, a ministry to lepers, a ladies' home (mostly for widows, and a home for 25 abused girls.

For more information, go to: www.gsnair.org

Jack McElroy

The Man Behind
The Memes III

****

Entrepreneurial Summary

Jack McElroy has been the President of **McElroy Electronics Corporation** for over 40 years. The firm manufactures and distributes components for the transformer industry. He introduced a number of manufacturing innovations, improvements, and expansion opportunities and established McElroy Electronics' Wireless Division.

McElroy
Electronics Corporation

In 1987, he co-founded and was President of **Dutchess County Cellular Telephone Corporation** in Poughkeepsie, NY. Dutchess offered cellular service to the market under the Cellular One brand.

In 1998, he co-founded and was Chief Manager of **Minneapolis Cellular Telephone Company LLC** in Minneapolis, MN. MCTC offered cellular service to the unserved portion of the Minneapolis–St. Paul market.

McElroy's wireless entrepreneurial activities forced a showdown with the Federal Communications Commission. After seven years of prolonged litigation, McElroy defeated the FCC—twice. McElroy's cases were heard and decided by the U.S. Court of Appeals, D.C. Circuit:

McElroy Electronics Corp. v. FCC, 301 U.S.App.D.C. 81, 990 F.2d 1351 (1993), https://tinyurl.com/vyxqrf4x

McElroy Electronics Corp. v. FCC, 318 U.S.App.D.C. 174, 86 F.3d 248 (1996), http://tinyurl.com/o8qz9zz

McElroy successfully negotiated deals with these telecoms:

- Telephone and Data Systems
- United States Cellular Corporation
- NYNEX Mobile (now owned by Verizon Wireless)
- Bell Atlantic Mobile (now owned by Verizon Wireless)
- AirTouch Communications (now owned by Verizon Wireless)
- Hickory Tech Corporation
- Alltel Wireless Communications
- AT&T Wireless Services

McElroy
Rare Bible Page Collections

In 1991, he co-founded and is President of **McElroy Rare Bible Page Collections**. The firm marketed original leaves of a First Edition King James Bible printed in 1611, and original leaves of Robert Estienne's 1550 Edition of the Textus Receptus Greek NT.

McElroy Publishing

In 1992, he co-founded **McElroy Publishing** focusing on how-to educational books and critical thinking exposés of current biblical and life issues.

He holds a BS degree in Industrial Management from Lowell Technological Institute (now UMass Lowell). He and his wife, Susan, have been married for over 40 years. They have 4 children and 4 grandchildren.

For more information, go to: www.JackMcElroy.com

Jack McElroy

The Man Behind the Memes IV

****

Jack McElroy explains the WHY behind his works:

"I'm 68 years old. Every day I think about how I'm running out of time. It makes me focus on what's meaningful. More importantly, it makes me want to accomplish all I can for the Lord.

I'm reminded of a poem I learned a long time ago titled *Only One Life, 'Twill Soon Be Past* written by famous British cricketer C.T. Studd (1860–1931), who gave up fame and fortune to become a missionary to China. The final stanza reads:

Only one life, yes only one,
Now let me say, "Thy will be done";
And when at last I'll hear the call,
I know I'll say "twas worth it all";
Only one life, 'twill soon be past,
Only what's done for Christ will last.

C.T. Studd

The older I get, the more I realize how true and appropriate that poem is.

Some time ago, I read a Bible verse that said that King David (who killed Goliath) "died in a good old age having served his generation." I thought, What a great thing that after you've died somebody says that you "served your generation."

My core values encompass two areas: pleasing the Lord and serving my generation.

Pleasing the Lord

I try to please the Lord who sought me and bought me because that's why he made me. Consider Revelation 4:11:

Thou art worthy, O Lord, to receive glory and honour
and power: for thou hast created all things, and
for thy pleasure they are and were created.

The Scripture says God created all things for HIS pleasure. So, if you can put a smile on the Lord's face at the end of the day, it's a pretty fulfilling thing to do.

Serving my generation

My mission is to relay what I've discovered about Truth, Life and Death. All the books I've written and am working on deal with these important topics.

(1) **Truth:** The Lord Jesus Christ said "Thy Word is truth." So, I've written books about the Bible, which is the word of God and source of all truth.

(2) **Life and Death:** I wrote a book detailing the truth about what happens after death titled *How I Lost My Fear of Death and How You Can Too*.

(3) **Evangelism and Missions:** Jesus Christ came to save sinners and like Paul said "of whom I am chief. Me too. That's why I wrote a couple of books on missionaries."

For more information, go to: www.JackMcElroy.com

Recommended Resources

Jack McElroy Facebook:

- https://www.facebook.com/jack.mcelroy1?fref=gs&dti=5
  14650685228377&hc_location=group_dialog

Websites: There are many sites that list differences between the KJB and other versions but the following websites have detailed answers to the variations:

- Will Kinney's website:
  https://brandplucked.webs.com/kjbarticles.htm
- Dr. Ken Matto
  website:www.scionofzion.com/kjcomparisons.html
- http://www.kjvtoday.com/
- https://mundall.com/erik/NIV-KJV.htm Note: Eric Mundall is a Seventh-day Adventist

These books provide detailed examinations and explanations of verse and translation differences:

- *Look What's Missing!*, David W. Daniels
- *Answers to Your Bible Version Questions* David W. Daniels
- *The Modern Version Incursion* Dr. Ken Matto:
- *Fitly Spoken: Exploring the Language of the King James Bible*, David Jackson—2 Volumes
- *New Age Bible Versions* G.A. Riplinger
- *New Testament Text and Translation Commentary* by textual critic Philip W. Comfort.
  This language engineer to assembled all the important New Testament variant readings (over 1,400) that affect meaning and have impacted major English translations. He spells out the arguments IN PLAIN ENGLISH for the readings in modern versions. Once you know their reasoning, you can refute their conclusions.

Instructional Videos:

Jack McElroy's YouTube There are interviews with David W. Daniels from Chick Publications and Bible Version researcher, Will Kinney.

https://tinyurl.com/y3rt7jhv

Scripture Index

Bible Version Secrets Exposed

7:11	49
8:6	187
9:17	130
10:4–5	131
12:5–7	50,329
12:6–7	324,329, 325,330, 343,349, 384, 401,407, 428, 429,441,
14:1	212
18:30	330
18:32	330
18:36	492
19:7	51
19:8	330
22:16	309
33:11	407
37:5	492
37:23	492
51:5	52
58:7	113
62:9	382
62:11	492
69:28	399
75:6-7	492
78:36	275
83:18	261
90:2	142
93:4	113
103:12	123,491
116:15	301,451
118:23	334
119:140	330,349, 424
127:1	492

138:2	53,54
139:15	47
145:13	459
146:3	492
147:6	492
Proverbs	
1:32	212
2:6	317
3:6	55
4:7	317
6:6	56
7:27	58
11:16	213
11:30	57,266,289
16:3	290,291,492
16:7	492
16:9	492
17:8	132
18:8	214
18:16	132
18:17	33
18:24	133
19:6	132
19:18	134
19:21	492
20:1	59
20:24	492
21:1	492
21:14	132
22:20-21	428,487
22:21	60,349
23:33	310
23:13–14	135
24:21	112
25:23	215
28:12	113
29:26	492
30:28	136
30:5–6	330
Ecclesiastes	
1:6	215
3:11	216

8:10	137,449, 453
12:12	100
Song of Solomon	
1:13	113
2:12	113
5:10	465
7:5	113
Isaiah	
7:14	297,302, 303,419
8:1-4	302
9:3	217,453
12:2	261
14:12	109
20:3	113
23:3	139
26:3	316
26:4	261
27:9	113
30:17	113
34:16	399
38:8	61,276,452
38:17	491
40:3	152
43:25	491
53:11	62
57:4	113
57:15	216
59:13	113
66:2	429
Jeremiah	
10:5	277
10:23	492
17:9	308
17:13	211
23:30	111,382
27:2	218
29:11	138
32:12	399
33:3	492
34:13	476
34:16	475-6
Ezekiel	
27:12	139

Scripture Index

501

Scripture Index

CPSIA information can be obtained
at www.ICGtesting.com
Printed in the USA
FSHW021508270120

9 780962 219177